AF270522

LAW in the ERA of AI

BJARNE P. TELLMANN

LAW *in the* ERA *of* AI

CLIENTS, FIRMS, and the **FUTURE** of the Legal Industry

WILEY

This edition first published 2026

© 2026 John Wiley & Sons, Ltd

All rights reserved, including rights for text and data mining and training of artificial intelligence technologies or similar technologies. No part of this publication may be reproduced, stored in a retrieval system, or transmitted in any form or by any means, electronic, mechanical, photocopying, recording, or otherwise, except as permitted by law, without the prior written permission of the publisher. Advice on how to obtain permission to reuse material from this title is available at http://www.wiley.com/go/permissions.

The right of Bjarne P. Tellmann to be identified as the author of this work has been asserted by him in accordance with law.

This publication is sold on the understanding that the publisher and the author are not engaged in rendering legal, accounting, or other professional services. If professional advice or other expert assistance is required, the services of a competent professional should be sought.

Registered Offices:

John Wiley & Sons, Inc., 111 River Street, Hoboken, NJ 07030, USA

John Wiley & Sons Ltd, New Era House, 8 Oldlands Way, Bognor Regis, West Sussex, PO22 9NQ, UK

For details of our global editorial offices, customer services, and more information about Wiley products visit us at www.wiley.com.

The manufacturer's authorized representative according to the EU General Product Safety Regulation is Wiley-VCH GmbH, Boschstr. 12, 69469 Weinheim, Germany, e-mail: Product_Safety@wiley.com.

Wiley also publishes its books in a variety of electronic formats and by print-on-demand. Some content that appears in standard print versions of this book may not be available in other formats.

Trademarks: Wiley and the Wiley logo are trademarks or registered trademarks of John Wiley & Sons, Inc. and/or its affiliates in the United States and other countries and may not be used without written permission. All other trademarks are the property of their respective owners. John Wiley & Sons, Inc. is not associated with any product or vendor mentioned in this book.

Limit of Liability/Disclaimer of Warranty:

While the publisher and the authors have used their best efforts in preparing this work, including a review of the content of the work, neither the publisher nor the authors make any representations or warranties with respect to the accuracy or completeness of the contents of this work and specifically disclaim all warranties, including without limitation any implied warranties of merchantability or fitness for a particular purpose. Certain AI systems have been used in the creation of this work. No warranty may be created or extended by sales representatives, written sales materials or promotional statements for this work. The fact that an organization, website, or product is referred to in this work as a citation and/or potential source of further information does not mean that the publisher and authors endorse the information or services the organization, website, or product may provide or recommendations it may make. This work is sold with the understanding that the publisher is not engaged in rendering professional services. The advice and strategies contained herein may not be suitable for your situation. You should consult with a specialist where appropriate. Further, readers should be aware that websites listed in this work may have changed or disappeared between when this work was written and when it is read. Neither the publisher nor authors shall be liable for any loss of profit or any other commercial damages, including but not limited to special, incidental, consequential, or other damages.

Library of Congress Cataloging-in-Publication Data has been applied for:

Hardback ISBN: 9781394375714
ePDF ISBN: 9781394375721
ePub ISBN: 9781394375738

Cover Design: Jon Boylan
Cover Image: © icedmocha/stock.adobe.com
Author Photo: Courtesy of Bjarne Philip Tellmann

Set in Bembo Std 11/14.5 by Lumina Datamatics

SKY10156141_050726

For Alessandra, Mia, and Liv.

You make sense of what I do.

Contents

Foreword   *ix*
Acknowledgements   *xi*
About the Author   *xv*

Introduction   1

**PART I   How Corporations and Their Legal
Departments Co-Evolve**   **9**

Chapter 1   The General Counsel's Evolving Needs   13

Chapter 2   GC 1.0: Early Modern Globalisation (1945–1989)   23

Chapter 3   GC 2.0: Classic Globalisation (1989–2007)   33

Chapter 4   GC 3.0: The Fourth Industrial Revolution (2007–2022)   47

PART II   The AI Era   **61**

Chapter 5   GC 4.0—The AI Impact   63

Chapter 6   GC 4.0—The AI Factory   79

Chapter 7   GC 4.0—The AI Era Legal Department   91

PART III The Impact   **113**

Chapter 8   The Traditional Law Firm Model   115

Chapter 9   Nothing Changes—Until It Suddenly Does   131

Chapter 10 Alternative Legal Service Providers   151

PART IV What Might Emerge?   **165**

Chapter 11 New Law Firm Models   169

Chapter 12 The Hybrid   189

Chapter 13 Platforms   201

Chapter 14 What Can Law Firms Do?   215

Chapter 15 The Future of Legal Education   235

Conclusion   *251*
Chapter Notes   *255*
Index   *327*

Foreword

When there is a breakthrough in medical science, people seldom discuss what this will mean for doctors. Their focus, rather, is on patients. In contrast, when news emerges of technological developments that relate to the law, lawyers tend to ask what it means for them. This remarkable book is a strong antidote to that flawed line of thinking—it transports us to a future in which clients rightly take centre stage.

This is a world also in which AI is revolutionising the professions and those they advise.

Even now, scarcely a day goes by without our learning of some new and staggering advance in AI. At this time of great flux, the central message of the book is that AI and clients together will transform the legal industry.

This message will be challenging for some lawyers and exciting for others: challenging because the traditional model of legal service is under siege; and exciting in that all manner of new opportunities are arising to meet legal clients' needs in new ways.

The book is a work of both theory and practice, which reflects the author's background as a seasoned general counsel with a longstanding fascination with the broader forces that are driving change in society. His command of the relevant literature is evident on every page and he skilfully blends this insight with the details and demands of everyday legal practice.

The book charts the evolution of the role of general counsel, placing the in-house legal department in its broader social and economic context, while also explaining the ongoing shift in its remit. Major firms too are placed under the microscope. Their successful past is dissected and analysed, and new business and operating models are clearly laid out for the reader.

The author also gives extended consideration to the impact of AI on legal education and professional development. The classical models of law schools and law firms are exposed as unfit for the preparation of the next generation of legal professionals. Instead, rooted once again in his knowledge of what clients want, he lays out the wide range of new skills that lawyers of tomorrow are likely to need.

The legal industry really does need this book and should be grateful to Bjarne Tellmann for writing it so clearly and informatively. It is, at once, an education and a wake-up call. I fully expect that *Law in the Era of AI* will be widely read, cited, and enjoyed. I wish the book and its author every success.

Professor Richard Susskind CBE KC (Hon)
President, Society for Computers and Law
Author, *Tomorrow's Lawyers* and *How to Think About AI*

Acknowledgements

This book grew out of countless conversations with too many people to name, over nearly a decade. I have long had both a professional and a personal interest in how technology is reshaping the legal profession, but it was Richard Susskind, a long-time friend and mentor, who first planted the seed that I should examine these shifts from the client's perspective. Without his encouragement, and the inspiration I have consistently drawn from his work, this project would never have taken flight.

It was Sean West who, following a late-night dinner in London and fresh from completing his brilliant book, *Unruly: Fighting Back when Politics, AI, and Law Upend the Rules of Business*, introduced me to my publisher, Wiley. My deep gratitude goes to the entire Wiley team, including Bill Falloon, Sherri-Anne Forde, Gemma Valler, Alice Hadaway, Sheryl Nelson, Sarah Lewis, and Jajneswar Chhotaray for their professionalism, for believing in this project, and for guiding it safely into harbour.

A book is always a collective effort. My thanks go to David Hornik, Michael A. Gerstenzang, Carla Swansburg, David Wakeling, Emma Jing, Bob Mignanelli, Jim Delkousis, James Knight, Maria Varsellona, Wei Ling Lim, Nassib Abou-Khalil, Konstantin Bark, Rich Sauer, Áine Lyons, and Greg Bennett, all of whom generously shared their time, insight, and expertise.

I am equally grateful to Memme Onwudiwe, Hal Marcus, Eric Derk, Daniel Gold, Dan Hendy, and Ryan J. Donmoyer for inviting me onto their podcasts; to Helena Samaha, Eric Staal, Andrea Erasmus, Lindsay Kelly, Jennifer Thomas, Alexandra Varla, and Chase Simmons for inviting me to speak at their events and conferences; and to Dan Reed, Prashant Dubey,

Raj Karia, Sven Riethmueller, and Joseph R. Tiano, Jr, for thoughtful conversations, all of which helped me to explore and refine many of the ideas that ultimately found their way into the book.

My particular thanks go to Angela Clist for her sharp and deeply constructive comments on the draft, and to Adam Chilton, Andrew Murray, David Kershaw, Michele DeStefano, and Nancy B. Rapoport for their impactful contributions to specific sections and ideas.

Anthea Roberts and Jon Henderson have been invaluable sources of inspiration on AI and innovation more broadly. I have learned so much from both of you during our conversations, and the energy and clarity I have drawn from those exchanges have been immeasurable. I remain profoundly in your debt.

I owe a great debt to those whose insight and generosity have shaped my thinking along the way. I am particularly grateful to David B. Wilkins for his mentorship and for inviting me to Harvard Law School in April 2025 to contribute to his seminar on AI and the law.

The ideas I encountered and the people I met during that visit, including Mitch Zuklie, Andrew Trahair, and a remarkable group of students, were both insightful and energising. I was also inspired by many others on that trip, a number of whom I have acknowledged elsewhere in these pages.

Special thanks as well to Jan W. Rivkin at Harvard Business School (HBS) for his steadfast mentorship and encouragement over many years, and to Derek C. M. van Bever, also at HBS, for his generous engagement and incisive insights on innovative disruption. I am also grateful to Marco Iansiti for the formative course he taught at HBS, where I was first introduced to the concept of the AI factory, and to him and Karim R. Lakhani for kindly allowing me to use one of their illustrations in this book.

There are many others who have contributed in various ways and who I cannot thank individually, but I am deeply grateful for their support, energy, and advice. You know who you are.

A note on the role of technology in the making of this book. Given its subject, I made deliberate use of AI tools such as *Open AI's ChatGPT-5* and *Perplexity* throughout the writing process. They helped me organise my ideas, surface potential research leads for further review, and refine the clarity of my prose. Every argument, narrative choice, and factual interpretation remains my own, and all sources identified through AI were independently verified.

My deepest gratitude goes to Mia Tellmann, Molly Regan, and Stuart Horwitz for their tireless, selfless, and exceptional support. Mia provided outstanding research assistance; many of the insights in this book originated in her work. Molly patiently listened to my halting attempts to describe visual ideas and transformed them into excellent design work that made key concepts come to life. Stuart offered brilliant developmental editing, courageously challenging me on what needed to go and how to refine, clarify, and sharpen what remained. I have learned a great deal from him about writing and am deeply grateful. This book would not have been what it is without your remarkable input and support. You made it far better than it would have otherwise been.

Finally, writing can be hard on families. My wife Alessandra and our daughters Mia and Liv put up with many intense days, late nights, and missed weekends and holidays as I wrote. Their love, patience, and support made this project possible.

About the Author

Bjarne P. Tellmann is CEO of FjordStream Advisors GmbH—a boutique consultancy focused on helping legal organisations navigate disruption—and a Senior Visiting Fellow at The London School of Economics.

He spent three decades in senior global legal roles, including as General Counsel of Haleon plc, a FTSE 20 company, and as Chief Legal Officer and General Counsel at Pearson plc, a FTSE 100 company. Earlier in his career, he held leadership positions across Europe, the United States, Asia, and the Middle East at Coca-Cola, Aramco, Kimberly-Clark, and the global law firms of Sullivan & Cromwell LLP and White & Case LLP.

A recognised thought leader on legal innovation, he teaches and publishes on leadership, disruption, and digital transformation. He is the author of *Building an Outstanding Legal Team: Battle-Tested Strategies from a General Counsel* and has published widely, including 'Don't Let the Digital Tail Wag the Transformation Dog: A Digital Transformation Roadmap for Corporate Counsel', co-authored with Michele DeStefano and Daniel Wu.

Bjarne is an alumnus of Harvard Business School, The University of Chicago, The London School of Economics, and Boston University. His professional honours include General Counsel of the Year at both the British Legal Awards and the Legal Era Global Achievers Awards, the Burton 'Legends in the Law' Award, the Chambers' GC Influencers Global 100 Award, and a Lifetime Achievement & Services Award from The Legal 500.

Introduction

When the winds of change blow, some people build walls and
others build windmills.

—Chinese proverb

History is replete with moments when technological innovation transforms
society and work. Artificial intelligence (AI) is one such moment. It, along
with other emerging technologies, is not just making the delivery of legal
services more efficient; it is fundamentally reshaping what legal work is,
how it is delivered, and who is best placed to deliver it.[1]

I have spent 30 years as a corporate lawyer, working across major law
firms and multinational corporations, including as General Counsel (GC)
of two large public companies. My career has stretched across Europe, Asia,
the United States, and the Middle East, in executive roles spanning multiple
industries. In that time, I have watched the legal profession evolve—from
the tentative adoption of email and document management systems to the
rise of sophisticated legal operations teams and the growth of alternative
legal service providers (ALSPs).[2] Yet, nothing in those decades compares
with the scale, speed, and impact of the transformation now underway.

This book examines how AI is reshaping competitive dynamics in the
legal industry and why clients will be the primary force driving that change.
It explores the implications for law firms, considers the new legal services
models that may emerge alongside or in place of the traditional law firm,
and outlines the strategies firms will need to adopt to position themselves
for success.

AI is not simply another innovative tool. It is what economists call a 'general purpose technology' (GPT)—a breakthrough with broad applications that can spark complementary innovations. It will touch every sector of the economy in the years to come.[3] Like earlier GPTs, such as steam power in the nineteenth century or electricity in the twentieth, AI will reshape entire industries, redefining how companies are structured, how they operate, and how they create value.

Over the coming decade, nearly every business will re-engineer its core processes and operating models around AI. As this transformation unfolds inside companies, legal departments will evolve in parallel, adapting their structures, service models, and technologies to align with the needs of AI-driven enterprises.

As in-house legal teams retool, they will increasingly harness AI as a core driver. AI will fundamentally change how legal departments operate and, in so doing, will redefine what clients require from outside counsel. Transformed clients will expect law firms to adapt in turn, delivering greater efficiency, innovation, and value, while integrating far more closely with the client's own operations.[4]

Work once sent to outside counsel is increasingly getting done in-house, at far lower cost. For higher-margin matters that remain externally sourced, clients will expect seamless integration with their technology-led models. To meet those expectations, law firms will need to operate at the speed of AI and deliver services tailored to the client's evolving context.

Given these dynamics, law firms could soon face a perfect storm of disruption. Negative inflection points (signals in the environment that indicate imminent change) are difficult for dominant industry players to spot.[5] Many law firms are currently enjoying record profits, underpinned by long-standing competitive advantages and high barriers to entry. But those very same advantages can mask early signs of disruption and make it difficult for law firms to adapt or innovate. This book examines how they might respond.

The forces that will transform the legal sector are already taking shape, and several potential new models are gradually emerging. We will explore some of these.

Finally, as the legal services landscape shifts, lawyers will require new skills and capabilities. We will ask how law schools and universities can ensure graduates are well-equipped to succeed.

The discussion is divided into four parts.

Part I focuses on the client. To understand why legal departments are poised to disrupt the traditional law firm model, we will trace the client-side evolution: how multinational companies (MNCs) and their legal departments have evolved in tandem, what they look like today, and where they are heading.

In-house legal teams have evolved in step with MNCs as they have adapted to shifting geopolitical, technological, and macroeconomic forces. As corporate priorities change, so do the structure and role of legal departments. Those shifts in turn reshape how outside counsel is instructed and how they must operate.

Against this backdrop, two headline challenges now define the modern GC, reshaping how GCs work and what they require from legal service providers. The first concerns risk. Traditional compliance-focused models have given way to more dynamic, enterprise-wide approaches, prompting GCs to demand deeper, more integrated risk analysis. The second is the perennial 'more-for-less' challenge—the expectation to deliver more work, faster, and with greater efficiency, at lower cost. Both dynamics are being accelerated and transformed by AI, and law firms will increasingly be expected to help clients meet these evolving needs.

Part II examines how MNCs and legal departments are again undergoing profound structural change. AI represents a fundamental fork in the road for business. Some experts, such as Kai-Fu Lee, predict its impact may exceed that of electricity.[6] Whether one accepts that view or not, AI will undoubtedly transform how companies operate.

MNCs are rapidly re-engineering their structures and core processes around AI. They are building integrated digital platforms that enable automation, data-driven decision-making, and rapid scaling.[7] To take advantage of AI, MNCs must change their operating models, organisational infrastructures, and the teams they employ.

As these reorganisations mature, AI will become fully embedded in decision workflows. Processes will be increasingly automated, AI will augment human judgement, and continuous-improvement feedback loops will accelerate innovation. Smaller, cross-functional teams will deploy new products and services at speed, leveraging modular data and AI capabilities.[8]

Technology remains a double-edged sword. It drives innovation but also amplifies risks, shortens corporate lifespans, and intensifies legal and compliance challenges.[9] Legal departments will be expected to keep pace, becoming leaner, more skilled, and increasingly autonomous, enabled by an AI-powered platform that supports a fast-moving business.[10]

These foundational shifts will have major implications for law firms. Clients will become more sophisticated, agile, and digitally fluent, taking advantage of a plethora of new providers and solutions. Technology will also give clients enhanced visibility, including real-time dashboards and predictive analytics, enhancing their bargaining power. AI-enabled in-house teams will handle ever more complex work internally, at greater speed and accuracy and at near-zero marginal cost (i.e., with almost no additional cost per unit of work once the systems are in place). One recent study estimates that up to 20% of legal services could become commoditised (i.e., standardised and driven by price rather than expertise) as AI improves. This could result in 80% fewer billable hours on average for such services, with price reductions of as much as 50%.[11] As work dynamics shift, clients will expect external firms to refine and integrate work that often originates inside the legal department, rather than provide advice entirely from scratch.

Increasingly, competitive advantage, for both legal departments and law firms, will lie in the seamless integration of people, processes, data, and technology, not merely in hiring the best lawyers.[12]

Part III considers the implications of these dynamics, including how the traditional law firm model is structurally misaligned with these evolving client needs, and why, despite growing pressure for change, many firms will struggle to adapt.

We will explore some of the features of the traditional model that are particularly problematic, including the billable hour, underpinned by a human-centric 'pyramid structure' in which a relatively broad base of associates supports a relatively small number of equity partners.[13]

This model has been highly lucrative for firms, many of whom are currently enjoying record or near-record profitability.[14] However, clients are unhappy. One recent study found that 100% of GCs experienced cost, quality, or operational issues that led them to regret a law firm engagement.[15] Furthermore, 89% of GCs no longer viewed law firms as fully effective in meeting their resourcing needs.[16]

This growing client dissatisfaction should be viewed against the backdrop of what Clayton Christensen has called 'the innovator's dilemma', that is, the challenges incumbent organisations face when trying to adapt to disruptive change.[17] Disruptive innovations often start by serving low-end or underserved segments but improve over time and eventually overtake incumbents.[18]

There are numerous structural impediments inherent to the partnership model that make it hard for law firms to change. Profit incentives cause partners to prioritise short-term gains over long-term investments. Access to external capital is limited. And, in many jurisdictions, regulatory and ethics rules restrict non-lawyers from owning or participating in fee-sharing arrangements with law firms, constraining innovation.[19] These challenges are often compounded by a profession that is deeply rooted in precedent and tradition and often reluctant to embrace innovation and new ways of working.

ALSPs will also face mounting pressures to adapt. As more work moves in-house, corporate legal departments will become their largest competitors, especially in high-volume, commoditised work. Successful ALSPs will stay ahead of their clients' evolving operating models and position themselves to add value within emerging technology ecosystems. Those that remain narrowly focused on transactional support and legacy tools, however, will not survive.

Part IV will consider what new models might emerge.

We will begin by examining how traditional law firms might adapt. Many assume that, as AI moves up the legal services value chain, the most viable response will be to retreat to the 'high tower', narrowing their focus to highly bespoke, partner-led advisory work in complex domains that AI is unlikely to disrupt in the near-term.

This could be a viable and lucrative path for a select group of premier firms.[20] But the model does not scale easily, and competition will be intense. Only a few firms possess the truly niche skills needed to succeed. Many overestimate how much of their work is truly unique and underestimate the degree to which this approach would still require organisational transformation.

To remain competitive, boutiques will need to evolve. Their profit engines must move away from traditional associate leverage structures towards partner-led and value-based ones, while their delivery engines must increasingly rely on technology, automation, and multidisciplinary teams to reduce execution costs. There are numerous ways to structure such a model. But even with strong profitability potential, boutiques will be difficult to scale.

Other law firms might adopt corporate structures that, in their fullest form, adopt equity-based ownership, significant external shareholders (e.g., private equity firms, institutional investors, or the public), a board of directors, and a truly empowered and CEO-led executive team.

Shifting to such a model can unlock the capital inflows needed for major technology investments, strategic acquisitions, and holistic transformation. Attracting such capital has historically been difficult for traditional partnerships due to their structural fragility and the fact that their enterprise value mostly depends on the future earnings of partners rather than hard assets, retained capital, or scalable infrastructure. As a result, ambitious initiatives, especially those involving technology, often fall short.

Other professional sectors, including investment banking, have made similar transitions to corporate form for comparable reasons. As former Goldman Sachs CEO Lloyd Blankfein noted, the 'need for permanent capital made it inevitable that we would go public'.[21] The same logic might increasingly apply to law firms.

Regulatory and ethical restrictions on non-lawyer ownership and profit-sharing remain formidable in many jurisdictions. Yet reforms in several markets, including the United Kingdom, Australia, and parts of the United States, now permit 'alternative business structures' (ABSs), which allow non-lawyers to hold ownership or management interests in law firms under specific conditions. These regimes create space for experimentation with corporate features without requiring firms to fully incorporate.

Early outcomes have been mixed in markets, such as the United Kingdom, where some law firms have publicly listed. But the broader trend is clear: external investment, whether through full corporate structures or ABS-enabled ownership models, may become an important pathway to greater competitiveness, innovation, and operational excellence. Private equity is already rapidly consolidating adjacent professional-services sectors, with roughly one-third of the top 30 US accounting firms having been acquired by financial buyers in the past four years.[22] It does not require much imagination to see how that playbook could expand to the legal sector.

Meanwhile, alternative models will continue to emerge alongside law firms. One approach, inspired by the 'Big Four' auditing firms (Deloitte, EY, PwC, and KPMG), is the rise of *hybrids*. These are integrated, multidisciplinary organisations that combine legal advisory services with a broad range of complimentary offerings under one roof. These may include risk analytics, legal operations consulting, alternative legal services, and legal-technology solutions. Such firms have the potential to scale efficiently while deepening client relationships by delivering a broader set of integrated solutions.

Several large law firms are already moving in this direction, constructing what might be termed *proto-hybrids*: organisations where adjacent capabilities are evolving but remain secondary to the core legal advisory function. The emergence of true hybrids may also come from continued expansion by the Big Four or by leading ALSPs pushing deeper into legal services.

Another emerging model is the *platform*: a technology-enabled and data-driven infrastructure that connects clients with an array of legal providers, including law firms, consultants, and ALSPs. Platforms typically begin by matching supply and demand but can evolve into intelligent orchestrators that route work, manage workflows, and monitor performance on behalf of clients. Over time, platforms could become strategic components of the legal department operating model, embedding directly into both client and law firm workflows and transforming how legal work is sourced, priced, managed, and evaluated.

We will explore how these models might evolve and the implications for clients, firms, ALSPs, and other legal industry players.

Regardless of which new models emerge, the core challenge for law firms remains the same: how to adapt despite structural and cultural barriers. The corporate world is full of cautionary tales of incumbents that failed to respond to disruption and paid a heavy price. Law firm leaders would do well to heed those lessons and act now.

One way forward is to launch small, low-risk experiments that do not threaten or undermine the core business. In Part IV, we will look at several case studies of firms that are doing this successfully.

Law schools, too, must evolve to equip future lawyers with the competencies required in an AI-powered legal environment, including business acumen, technological fluency, creativity, and interpersonal skills. Although many academics are actively exploring how to modernise legal education, universities also face constraints that make timely and meaningful reform challenging.

The legal profession stands on the cusp of profound transformation. For those who prepare, the AI era offers exciting opportunities. For those who hesitate, it may prove unforgiving.

How Corporations and Their Legal Departments Co-Evolve

The greatest danger in times of turbulence is not the turbulence; it is to act with yesterday's logic.

—Peter Drucker[1]

To understand why corporate legal departments are now positioned to disrupt the traditional law firm model with AI as a key accelerant, we must trace their own evolution. This requires us to consider how MNCs and the legal teams that serve them have developed, how they operate today, and where they are heading.

As corporations have reshaped themselves in response to successive waves of geopolitical, technological, and operational change, so too have their legal departments, with far-reaching consequences for law firms and other external providers. The fortunes of outside counsel and alternative suppliers have always been closely bound to those of their clients.

The Four Eras of the General Counsel

Since the end of World War II, GCs have navigated four distinct eras. While these are not formally recognised historical periods, their demarcation reflects the major geopolitical, macroeconomic, and technological shifts that reshaped MNCs and, by extension, the legal departments that serve them.

Throughout these periods, the twin dynamics of risk and efficiency have taken on increasing relevance, reshaping how legal departments work and what they need from their external providers.

GC 1.0 (1945–1989) emerged during early modern globalisation, which was characterised by relative geopolitical and macroeconomic stability and the rise of the modern MNC. Legal needs were localised and relatively simple. Professional business managers were born, and with them the modern law firm. In-house teams were small or non-existent, and law firms captured most work through 'one-stop-shop' models.

GC 2.0 (1989–2007) began with the fall of the Berlin Wall and culminated with the introduction of the iPhone. This was the golden age of modern globalisation. As operational, technological, and macroeconomic complexity increased, the needs of MNCs outgrew what the one-stop-shop model could cost-effectively and qualitatively provide. Legal departments expanded accordingly, becoming more powerful and influential, often at the expense of law firms, which moved upmarket into higher-value work.

GC 3.0 (2007–2022) coincided with the rise of the Internet, social media, and platform economies. It heralded the start of the Fourth Industrial Revolution (4IR). Following the First (mechanisation), Second (mass production), and Third (early computerisation) Industrial Revolutions, 4IR integrated digital, biological, and physical systems, transforming industrial processes, manufacturing, and engineering.[2] It fused the emergence of smart and connected machines with innovations in areas ranging from gene sequencing and nanotechnology to renewable energy.[3] It was the integration of these technologies across multiple domains, rather than any single innovation, that made 4IR impactful, accelerating the pace of change, reshaping global supply chains, and introducing a new era of volatility and opportunity.

Facing growing volatility and cost pressures, MNCs diverted resources towards technology, process improvement, and R&D. Legal departments, forced to do more with less, turned to technology and outsourcing.

GCs became CEOs of their departments, driving efficiency and procurement discipline. As law firms struggled to adapt, ALSPs emerged at the margins, capturing lower-level work that had previously gone to firms.

GC 4.0 (2022–present) was triggered by the introduction of generative AI, marked by the public release of OpenAI's *ChatGPT*.[4] With innumerable applications across the economy, AI has the potential to reshape entire industries. Legal is no exception and the shift is foundational. As noted in the Introduction, Parts II–IV will explore the GC 4.0 era, including how companies and legal departments are evolving in the face of AI, the impact that it is having on external providers, and the implications that it will have on the sector as a whole.

History is the lens through which we can anticipate what comes next. To understand where the legal sector is heading, we must first understand the story of how legal departments have evolved—because it is on the client side that the change which will profoundly impact the industry first emerged.

1 | The General Counsel's Evolving Needs

Get closer than ever to your customers. So close that you tell them what they need well before they realize it themselves.

—Steve Jobs[1]

Before exploring the evolving backdrop of change in the corporate and in-house environments and its implications, it is worth exploring two headline challenges that have come to define the modern in-house legal function. Both are reshaping not only how legal departments operate but also what they require from their legal service providers.

The first is a fundamental shift in how risk is perceived and managed. Over the past decade, corporate risk management has moved beyond traditional compliance-focused models to more dynamic, enterprise-wide approaches.

The second is what legal scholar and AI expert Richard Susskind has termed the 'more-for-less challenge': the mounting pressure on legal departments to deliver greater volumes of legal work, more efficiently, faster, and at reduced cost.[2]

Both of these challenges are being accelerated and transformed by AI. Legal departments are increasingly seeking outside partners who can support them with innovative, holistic solutions for these challenges.

Evolving Approaches to Risk

The way MNCs perceive and manage risk is evolving, and GCs have been placed at the centre of that shift. As their involvement in risk management expands, GCs can no longer afford to view legal risk in isolation. Instead, they must adopt a broader, more integrated view of risk that includes its operational, reputational, regulatory, and geopolitical dimensions. In turn, they expect their external partners, including law firms, to do the same.

To remain competitive, law firms must move beyond a narrow legal lens and help clients navigate an increasingly complex and convergent risk landscape. The boundaries between legal, financial, reputational, political, supply chain, and other risks are dissolving, creating multidimensional challenges that unfold with unprecedented speed and reach. In a world shaped by the Fourth Industrial Revolution, where technologies and their applications fuse across domains, GCs are expected to anticipate, mitigate, and solve risk holistically. Law firms that wish to remain trusted partners will need to do the same.[3]

The Many-hatted GC

The role of the GC has grown to become one of the most demanding and multi-faceted in the corporate environment.[4] Traditionally, GCs were seen as the company's top legal experts. That is still the case, but now that is just the baseline. In addition to acting as the chief lawyer, GCs are increasingly expected to act as business leaders who are involved in formulating strategy, managing risk, and spearheading the company's ethics and compliance efforts.[5]

To succeed, GCs must possess a blend of skills, ranging from legal expertise, business acumen, and technological fluency to skills in crisis and risk management, leadership, and diplomacy.[6] Consequently, they have taken on additional formal roles and responsibilities beyond the legal department, including compliance, enterprise risk, the company secretariat, regulatory affairs, public policy and communications, environmental, social and governance (ESG) functions, cyber and corporate security, and even human resources.[7]

Much of this expansion reflects a broader recognition that GCs are uniquely well-positioned among executive leaders to help organisations manage and navigate risk. Their 'T-shaped' profile, in which they combine deep cognitive, analytical, and technical legal expertise with broad multidisciplinary and social skills, enables them to operate smoothly across boundaries.[8] They are spiders in the corporate web, coordinating regularly on risk-related matters across a diverse array of functions.[9] In many companies, GCs are formally in charge of chairing executive risk committees and reporting on risk-related matters to the board on a regular basis. To succeed in this environment, GCs can no longer afford to view risk through a narrow legal lens alone.

The Evolution of Corporate Thinking on Risk

To understand what GCs now expect from external partners, it is necessary to understand how corporate thinking on risk has evolved. As the risk environment has grown more complex and volatile, MNCs are redefining how they approach risk management, and they expect external partners to evolve in this respect as well.

Enterprise Risk Management Enterprise risk management (ERM) marked the first major step in the evolution of modern corporate risk management. It introduced a systematic, holistic approach that cut across departmental silos and traditional risk boundaries, enabling organisations to assess both strategic and operational risks through consistent and structured processes.[10] Rather than treating risk as the responsibility of individual units, ERM adopted a top-down view that treated each business unit as a portfolio and analysed how risks across the organisation might interact, enabling the organisation to identify potential risk factors that might remain invisible within any single silo.[11]

Prior to ERM, companies typically managed risks in isolation, assigning responsibility for specific risks to individual departments.[12] By the early 2000s, however, ERM began gaining traction as firms sought more proactive methods to identify, anticipate, and respond to threats.[13] A significant milestone came in 2004, when the Committee of Sponsoring Organisations (COSO), which was originally formed in 1985 to address fraudulent financial reporting, introduced its *Enterprise Risk Management—Integrated Framework*, which quickly became widely adopted.[14] An updated version, released in 2017, reflected a more complex risk environment along with heightened expectations around board and executive accountability.

The COSO ERM Framework represented a major leap forward by helping to institutionalise more effective internal controls and bring coherence to risk oversight.[15]

However, by the 2020s, events such as the COVID-19 pandemic, accelerating climate change, and a cascade of geopolitical, societal, technological, financial, and other 'black swan' events,[16] exposed key limitations. Chief among them was an over-emphasis on process and reporting. As one study observed, ERM was increasingly seen by some executives 'as a way to describe or justify choices already made, or to placate senior management, boards, or oversight groups' rather than as a tool for making better real-time decisions.[17]

Critics also highlighted another flaw: ERM often focused too heavily on predicting inherently unpredictable events rather than building organisational resilience. As one expert put it, 'It serves an organization better to focus on the results and consequences of a black swan and develop a business continuity and recovery plan (BCP), as opposed to attempting to predict its occurrence. By understanding the potential impact and vulnerabilities of the organization to a black swan and utilizing this information to develop a BCP, an organization is better equipped to address a major risk event if it occurs'.[18]

In short, it was becoming clear that MNCs needed to shift focus—from trying to forecast every possible disruption, to strengthening their capacity to respond to the unexpected. Resilience and adaptability were emerging as the new cornerstones of effective risk management.[19]

Resilience   By the early 2020s, in response to the limitations of ERM, the concept of *organisational resilience* began to gain significant traction. Resilience is commonly defined as 'the ability of an organization to anticipate, prepare for, respond and adapt to incremental change and sudden disruptions in order to survive and prosper'.[20]

Unlike ERM, which focuses primarily on prevention, controls, and risk awareness, resilience takes a more forward-looking and adaptive stance. Resilient MNCs emphasise continuous improvement, adaptive innovation, and performance optimisation, positioning themselves not only to withstand unexpected shocks but to emerge stronger from them.

As Dana Maor, Michael Park, and Brooke Weddle have noted, this can have many benefits:

> At a micro level, they demonstrate better shareholder returns and are better than their peers at integrating new technologies, supporting customers, building partnerships, and attracting and retaining employees. At a macro level, they fuel investment in new business, strengthen GDP, enhance productivity, and enable the rapid movement and growth of talent and skills. These companies prioritize leadership development and thus are driven by adaptable leaders who can facilitate the kinds of behavioral adjustments and mindset shifts required to be resilient in the face of change.[21]

In essence, resilience shifted the organisational focus from control to capacity-building, enabling organisations to adapt to risk events in real time, rather than attempting to eliminate uncertainty altogether.

Antifragility Some organisations have gone even further, aiming to evolve beyond resilience to actively leverage risk as a competitive advantage. These organisations embody what risk expert Nicholas Nassim Taleb calls 'antifragility'.[22] As Taleb explains, 'Some things benefit from shocks; they thrive and grow when exposed to volatility, randomness, disorder, and stressors and love adventure, risk, and uncertainty'.[23]

Antifragile companies don't just endure stress—they grow stronger from it.[24] Where resilient firms seek to recover and maintain stability, antifragile ones leverage adversity as a catalyst to transform, innovate, and grow.[25]

Dragonfly Thinking: Non-binary, Integrated Risk Decisions As corporate approaches to risk evolve from siloed and reactive to holistic, proactive, and even opportunity-driven, the need for more sophisticated decision-making frameworks has also grown. This need is especially acute in today's complex and fast-moving geopolitical and macroeconomic landscape.

One such method is Dragonfly Thinking™ (DT), developed by Anthea Roberts and Miranda Forsyth.[26] Dragonflies are among the world's most efficient predators, catching up to 97% of their prey. With up to 30,000 lenses on each of their eyes, they can see nearly 360° around, giving them a holistic view of their environment.[27] That capability is a perfect metaphor for what is required in the contemporary risk environment, which requires a wide-angle, multi-faceted view of risk. DT therefore seeks to move beyond narrow or binary decision-making by integrating and synthesising multiple perspectives, including arguments, counter-arguments, and even counter-counter-arguments, to develop a more holistic understanding of an issue.[28]

Rather than developing choices based on simple 'either/or' variables, DT encourages synthesis. It reflects the principle that 'the integrated whole is more valuable than the sum of its parts'.[29] By weaving together diverse viewpoints, organisations can make more informed and adaptive decisions; an essential capability in an environment where uncertainty and ambiguity are the norm.

Legal Advice Alone Is No Longer Sufficient

Given this evolution in how MNCs are approaching risk and the leading role GCs play in managing it, they require and are increasingly demanding more than siloed legal input from their outside partners. Today's challenges are simply too diffuse, interconnected, and fast-moving to be effectively addressed by leveraging the perspective of one silo alone.

As a result, GCs are refining what they expect from external advisers. Legal expertise remains essential, but it's no longer sufficient. GCs prefer partners who can provide multidimensional insight and integrate operational, reputational, regulatory, geopolitical, and other considerations into their advice to support better-informed and more well-rounded decision-making.

Traditionally, law firms have offered one piece of the puzzle. To remain relevant, they will need to evolve and broaden their perspective so that they can better help clients navigate an increasingly complex enterprise risk landscape with integrated, strategic guidance. That requires ever-closer integration with clients.

More for Less

The second headline challenge reshaping in-house legal departments is the well-documented more-for-less dynamic, that is, the growing demand for legal services amid shrinking resources.[30] One recent survey found that 81% of legal departments lack sufficient staffing to operate effectively, while 87% of GCs were concerned about their ability to invest in the talent and resources they need.[31]

The long-term trend has been one of continuous belt-tightening, particularly for smaller legal departments.[32] Even where legal budgets have risen slightly in recent years, those increases are often modest, frequently lag behind inflation,[33] or are earmarked for specific projects, which leaves little flexibility for investing in other priorities.[34] The result is mounting pressure on legal departments to do more with less, without compromising compliance, risk oversight, or business alignment.

If GCs fail to deliver legal services more cost-effectively, they risk reaching a tipping point where the resources they have available to them are no longer sufficient to manage the portfolio of risk they are tasked with handling. In response, many are rethinking how legal work is delivered. They are reallocating a greater share of their budgets towards technology and diversifying their sourcing strategies by partnering with flexible legal talent platforms, virtual law firms, and ALSPs.[35]

To succeed in this expanded role, GCs must increasingly operate like miniature CEOs, balancing legal risk with the broader strategic, operational, or financial considerations of the departments they lead. In pursuing new efficiencies, however, GCs must remain mindful that innovation cannot come at the expense of their core duty, which is to act as the organisation's legal and ethical guardian.[36]

Demand Drivers

Where is the rising demand for legal services coming from? It is being fuelled by a convergence of powerful forces, including regulatory growth, geopolitical volatility, and the disruptive impact of emerging technologies.

Regulatory Growth   Regulation is increasing not only in volume, but also in complexity, enforcement intensity, and unpredictability, making compliance a constantly shifting target. Globally, the number of regulations across all areas rose by over 84% between 2016 and 2023.[37] But beyond volume, the real challenge lies in the intricacy of the rules themselves. As Yin Yin Lu has noted, 'Chapter 1 of Title 12 of the US Code of Federal Regulations is 1,114 pages long and contains more than 600,000 words. If you had a reading rate of 300 words per minute, it would take in excess of 33 hours to finish. And that's just chapter one. There are 18 chapters in title 12, and 50 titles in total'.[38]

This kind of regulatory expansion, often seen in areas like data protection, ESG, antitrust, and financial compliance, is straining legal and operational teams across many industries. Sectors such as financial services, healthcare, technology, energy, and transportation are grappling with rising compliance costs and heightened enforcement risks, especially when regulatory requirements differ or directly conflict across jurisdictions.[39]

Meanwhile, regulatory priorities are shifting across jurisdictions in increasingly unpredictable ways, reflecting a more multipolar environment. In the United States, enforcement has become more selective, with recent pauses and policy reviews signalling potential shifts in focus and scope. By contrast, the European Union continues to expand its regulatory agenda, including an intensified emphasis on AI, digital resilience, and the carbon transition, among other areas. Uncertainty is particularly acute in rapidly evolving areas such as AI, where regulations remain fragmented and in flux.

Amidst the cross-jurisdictional uncertainty and shifting priorities, compliance and regulatory executives are increasingly concerned about their organisation's ability to keep pace with the accelerating change. In one recent report, nearly half of regulatory affairs respondents admitted their organisation had missed at least one regulatory requirement. Non-compliance is no longer a narrow legal issue; it has become a core business risk.[40]

Geopolitical Instability and Disruptive Technologies At the same time, geopolitical instability and a rise in black swan events are driving urgent and highly unpredictable legal demands.[41] For decades, global business operated within a relatively stable post-war order. That foundation is now shifting and, in some places, unravelling, without a clear replacement.

GCs are confronting a continuous stream of novel legal challenges: tariff wars, resurgent nationalism, changing international sanctions, and the erosion of regulatory frameworks. The legal consequences of macro-level disruption are increasingly complex and time sensitive.

Recent black swan events—such as COVID-19, Brexit, Russia's invasion of Ukraine, and a spike in climate-related disasters—have only added to this strain. In-house legal teams must now manage surges in unforeseen, high-stakes legal work alongside their already demanding day-to-day responsibilities.

Technology and the 'Unruly Triangle' Further compounding the pressure is the disruptive force of emerging technologies—particularly the rapid evolution of AI and the pervasive influence of social media platforms.

These technologies often emerge from powerful companies operating in loosely regulated spaces, creating unpredictable risk vectors.

As risk expert Sean West notes, we are navigating an 'Unruly Triangle', that is, a convergence of geopolitics, law, and technology that is producing entirely new categories of risk.[42] As he observes, 'We are facing a lot of unknown unknowns as technology businesses are largely unconstrained and in a risk taking position. When millions of people start talking to AI without understanding the risks—as is already happening—it will be tremendously challenging to put in place safeguards that undo or limit harm'.[43]

The Implication for GCs

In this multidimensional risk landscape, GCs are expected not only to respond in real time, but also to anticipate and mitigate the effects of emerging threats, many of which are novel, cross-border, and interdisciplinary. The result is increasing strain on their strategic, legal, and operational capacities, and a growing need for external support that matches the complexity of the challenges they face.

Supply Constraints—Rising Expectations and Shrinking Resources

Paradoxically, just as demand for legal services is surging, many companies are simultaneously reducing the resources allocated to their legal departments. This budgetary squeeze reflects a confluence of economic, structural, and technological forces that are reshaping corporate priorities.

Macroeconomic pressures, such as inflation, rising interest rates, and slowing global growth, are prompting organisations to cut costs across support functions, including in-house legal, while doubling down on revenue-generating areas such as sales, marketing, and R&D. This shift is being accelerated by rapid advances in AI and automation, which are drawing investments towards digital transformation initiatives and away from more traditional internal operations.

Structural changes in the global economy are reinforcing this shift. The rise of platform-based business models, such as those exemplified by Amazon, Uber, and Airbnb, has redefined market competition.

These 'platform economies' thrive on *network effects*—feedback loops in which each additional user makes the platform more valuable for others. As buyers, sellers, and service providers converge on the same digital ecosystems, value compounds exponentially, creating *winner-takes-most* dynamics in which a few dominant players capture outsized value while smaller competitors survive only at the margins. The result has been growing concentration across many digital markets, where success reinforces itself through scale, data, and network advantages.[44] In this environment, speed, agility, and innovation are often prioritised over stability and internal capacity.

One striking indicator of this volatility is the declining average lifespan of major companies. In 1958, the average lifespan of an S&P 500 company was 61 years. By 2023, it had dropped to just 18 years—shorter by decades than the average working lifespan of many employees.[45] This reflects a business environment defined by constant disruption, where long-term internal investment can often take a back seat to short-term survival and market share.

In this context, legal departments are frequently viewed as cost centres, not strategic enablers. As a result, GCs face a growing paradox: they are being asked to deliver ever more sophisticated legal advice, oversee broader risk portfolios, and manage increased workloads, all while operating with fewer resources and tighter budgets. On difficult days, it can feel as though GCs are being asked to do more with less, until there's nothing left to cut.

How Did We Get Here?

How did these dynamics come to define the modern in-house legal experience?

To answer that, we must trace the parallel evolution of legal departments and MNCs. The two have grown in lockstep: as MNCs expanded, diversified, and digitised, legal teams continually adapted their structures, capabilities, and operating models to meet shifting demands.

This symbiotic relationship is essential to understanding not just how today's legal departments are structured, but where they're headed, and why their trajectory could disrupt the traditional law firm model.

As MNCs increasingly reorientate around AI, data, and digital-first operations, legal departments are under pressure to transform in kind. That transformation could serve as a catalyst for broader changes in how legal services are sourced, delivered, and valued.

And as those trends evolve, the twin dynamics of risk proliferation and the more-for-less conundrum will continue to accelerate a shift in what GCs require from their outside providers.

2 | GC 1.0: Early Modern Globalisation (1945–1989)

Compared to today, the 1950s and early 1960s were the land of legal simplicity.

—Carl D. Liggio, Sr[1]

The period of early modern globalisation, which lasted from the end of World War II (WWII) up to the fall of the Berlin Wall and which might be called GC 1.0, was one of relative geopolitical and macroeconomic stability. Within this environment, the legal needs of early MNCs were relatively simple and localised. Few companies required large or powerful internal legal departments, and the influence of the GC was minimal.

The Gilded Age—Forerunner of GC 1.0

The roots of the GC 1.0 legal department stretch back to the late nineteenth and early twentieth centuries. This period, sometimes referred to as the *Gilded Age,* was characterised by industrial expansion and economic concentration. Industrial magnates, such as Andrew Carnegie (steel), John D. Rockefeller (oil), and Cornelius Vanderbilt (railroads and shipping), built vast enterprises that defined early modern capitalism.

The lawyers of the Gilded Age were highly regarded figures, often serving as both business leaders and legal advisers.[2] Roughly 75% of large company CEOs at the time were trained lawyers; a figure that in later decades would decline to just 5%.[3] These lawyers were also among the highest paid executives, with salaries that reached as high as 65% of the CEO's pay, compared to just 30% by the 1970s.[4]

The elevated status of the Gilded Age lawyer reflected both their legal insights and their commercial usefulness. At a time when capital markets were still developing, lawyers sat on boards, were frequently groomed as future CEOs, and played a critical role in securing funding.[5] They personified what became known as 'trusted counsellors', helping form large enterprises, while also adding business value.[6]

Change on the Horizon

However, changes in the broader environment ushered in a shift in the relative fortunes of these lawyers. The Great Depression and the New Deal expanded the role of governmental regulation and reduced the power and influence of the trusts, dispersing economic power. As the post-war order emerged, power had shifted from trusts to newly emergent MNCs.

The New International System

The end of WWII marked the beginning of a period of global economic integration and an increase in trade and investment that lasted until the fall of the Berlin Wall in 1989. While the Cold War left the global economy divided, with trade sharply divided along the 'Iron Curtain',[7] exports of merchandise from non-communist countries rose by 290%, the most rapid period of growth seen in the twentieth century.[8]

This growth was fuelled by the emergence of a new US-led international economic order that grew out of a conference held at Bretton Woods, New Hampshire, where delegates from 44 nations met in July 1944 to set new rules for the post-WWII international monetary system.[9] The outcome of the conference, which became known as the 'Bretton Woods System', laid the foundations for economic expansion. By promoting currency stability and fixed exchange rates, Bretton Woods set out a pathway for economic growth, trade liberalisation, monetary alignment, and post-war reconstruction that lasted throughout the GC 1.0 era.[10]

The Bretton Woods System and Its Legacy

Bretton Woods resulted in the formation of a new international monetary system designed to promote growth and prevent the economic instability that had plagued the inter-war period.[11] US President Franklin D. Roosevelt and Secretary of State Cordell Hull, both firm believers in Wilsonian notions of free trade, pushed for the establishment of a liberal international economic order.[12]

Backed by US gold reserves, the US dollar became the world's reserve currency. Other national currencies became fixed to the US dollar, which was itself convertible to gold at a fixed rate of $35 per ounce.[13] The International Monetary Fund (IMF)[14] and the International Bank for Reconstruction and Development (IBRD, now part of the World Bank Group)[15] were established to stabilise global markets and support post-war reconstruction efforts.[16]

In 1971, US President Richard Nixon suspended dollar–gold convertibility following persistent balance-of-payment deficits, formally bringing the Bretton Woods System to an end.[17] The new policy, known as the 'Nixon Shock', ended the convertibility of the US dollar into gold and launched the modern era of floating exchange rates. The ensuing financial volatility and capital mobility encouraged an opening of global markets, fuelled foreign investment by MNCs, and stimulated greater cross-border economic interconnection.

However, elements of Bretton Woods endured through the end of the GC 1.0 period and beyond. The US dollar remained the world's premier reserve currency. And the IMF and World Bank continued to play their roles, alongside other multilateral institutions, including new ones, such as the G7 (1975) and the G20 (1999), that emerged to help support the international economic system.[18]

Perhaps most importantly, free trade continued to grow through a series of multilateral negotiations,[19] including numerous rounds of free-trade talks known as the General Agreement on Tariffs and Trade (GATT).[20] The establishment of other multilateral institutions, including the European Economic Community (EEC)[21] and other regional and technical agreements, further solidified the ascendency of free trade.[22]

MNCs Expand Internationally

For MNCs, the GC 1.0 environment created a significant expansion opportunity. In addition to Bretton Woods, several international cartels that had restricted innovation and competition during the 1930s were dismantled, restoring competition in numerous product markets between domestic producers and foreign firms.[23] Consequently, merchandise exports from non-communist countries more than doubled in the early post-war years, growing from $53 billion to $112.3 billion between 1948 and 1960.[24]

The United States Leads the Way   Much of the early expansion was fuelled by private US foreign direct investment (FDI).[25] Between 1950 and 1970, FDI by US companies grew by more than 600%, with FDI accounting for 65% of the total growth in US overseas assets during the 1960s.[26]

US MNCs had several structural advantages in these early years. While the war had weakened European firms economically and operationally, US MNCs emerged strengthened from the stable political and economic environment that had existed in the United States. Many had also maintained investments in Latin America and other parts of the Western Hemisphere untouched by war.[27] Some had even established footholds in the United Kingdom, which they could leverage after the war to enter other European markets, giving them a head start over their foreign rivals.[28]

US MNCs also had a clear technological lead. Innovations in transportation and communications, which were scaled or accelerated during the war, allowed US firms to more effectively manage their international operations. And for MNCs in the emerging high-tech industries, advances in semiconductors, transistors, and integrated circuits strengthened their lead even further.[29]

Coca-Cola Follows the Troops   Some US MNCs expanded while the war was still in progress by following the US Army. The Coca-Cola Company is a case in point. During the war, the company expanded its presence in Europe and Asia by accompanying American troops as they advanced, building bottling plants along the way to serve US troops.[30]

In 1942, shortly after the attack on Pearl Harbor, Robert Woodruff, Coca-Cola's President, issued an order at the request of General Dwight Eisenhower to 'see that every man in uniform gets a bottle of Coca-Cola for five cents, wherever he is and whatever it costs our company'.[31] Although this was positioned as a morale-boosting gesture, it was a business masterstroke. As Coca-Cola was distributed to the troops, the emotional resonance of the product deepened. Indeed, as one GI wrote in a letter to his brother from Italy in 1944:

Today was such a big day that I had to write and tell you about it. Everyone in the company got a Coca-Cola. That might not seem like much to you, but I wish you could see some of these guys who have been overseas for twenty months. They clutch their Coke to their chest, run to their tent and just look at it. No one has drunk theirs yet, for after you drink it, it's gone; so they don't know what to do.[32]

Initially, the company tried to supply the troops with products shipped from the United States. However, wartime transport and logistical priorities soon made this unworkable, prompting the company to build bottling plants in-theatre, following the US Army as it advanced.[33] This strategy was transformative, as it allowed the company to establish 64 new bottling plants during the war. This not only enabled it to serve 10 billion bottles of Coca-Cola to US troops, 'from the jungles of New Guinea to officers' clubs on the Riviera'.[34] It also almost doubled the number of countries where the company had plants, giving it a significant presence in these new markets as the war ended.[35]

Local and Flexible

After the war, many US firms initially attempted to follow in the footsteps of Coca-Cola and export domestically manufactured products to new European markets. However, as persistent dollar shortages in Europe made this a challenging strategy, many eventually established local manufacturing subsidiaries.[36] This trend grew strongly following the formation of the EEC in 1957, with MNCs increasing their investments in European subsidiaries by a factor of nearly 15 between 1950 and 1970.[37]

As they expanded, US MNCs often gave foreign subsidiaries considerable freedom. The prevailing business philosophy of the day favoured agile, multi-divisional structures that allowed subsidiaries to adapt quickly to local markets.[38] IBM was a notable pioneer of this approach. Anticipating the needs of a more interconnected world, it replaced its old patchwork of joint ventures, licensing arrangements, and distributorships with a flexible network of wholly owned, independently managed subsidiaries, long before European trade barriers came down.[39] When they did, IBM's deliberately decentralised approach to production and decision-making gave it an edge.[40]

European and Japanese Competitors Gradually Emerge

US MNC dominance didn't last. A sustained period of economic growth in Europe and Japan during the 1950s and 1960s created opportunities for local companies to compete more effectively.

During these years, Western European economies enjoyed a period of sustained economic growth, with average per capita GDP growing by more than 4% per year.[41] This afforded European MNCs the ability to meaningfully expand outside their home markets. Companies such as Royal Dutch Shell, British Petroleum, and BASF in the energy and chemicals sectors; Volkswagen, Fiat, and Rolls-Royce in automotive; Unilever, Nestlé, and L'Oreal in consumer goods; and Roche, Bayer, and Glaxo in pharmaceuticals, rose to prominence in the international arena.

In Japan, the combination of land and labour reforms and the economic stimulus caused by the Korean War spurred industrial growth and ushered in a long period of significant economic expansion.[42]

Initially, Japanese MNC investments were centred on expanding their domestic capacity. However, in the late 1960s, accommodative export policies and rising foreign demand drove companies including Sony and Panasonic in the electronics sector; Toyota and Honda in automobiles; and Mitsubishi and Hitachi in heavy industries, to expand internationally.[43]

During this period, FDI remained heavily focused on the United States, Canada, and Western Europe. Other markets would follow in later periods, but the prevailing trend towards nationalisation in many emerging markets during this period made expansion there less attractive.[44]

Throughout this period, MNCs continued to favour the decentralised, multi-divisional structures that US firms had pioneered. It became the dominant organisational model for large corporations across the developed world, despite the continued decline of tariff rates during the period.[45]

While theoretically, greater openness might have encouraged a return to centralised control, decentralisation proved to be better suited for managing an increasingly complex and interdependent environment.

The Professionalisation Wave

As modern corporations emerged out of the trusts and monopolies of the Gilded Age, so too did an increasingly professionalised corporate management class.[46] MBAs, especially those with marketing and finance backgrounds, became the stars of the new corporate world. The lawyers of the Gilded Age were increasingly seen as out of step with the new, metrics-driven approach to business.[47] As MBA-trained managers rose in status and power, power shifted from generalists to credentialed professionals. Trusted internal advisers were increasingly replaced by legal functionaries that focused on narrow, routine legal matters, while complex matters flowed to a rising class of elite law firm partners.[48]

Law Firms and Law Schools

Modern law firms and elite law schools, both of which had taken shape in the early decades of the twentieth century, also scaled dramatically in the early post-war years as part of the professionalisation wave. Elite law firms adopted the *Cravath System*, an organisational model first pioneered by Paul Cravath of Cravath, Swaine & Moore. Cravath's model professionalised the practice of law, centring around two core groups of professionals: partners and partnership-track associates. Bright, ambitious young lawyers were hired as associates and entered a rigorous probationary period, sometimes referred to as a 'tournament of lawyers', during which their long-term potential was assessed. At the end of this period, they would either be invited into the partnership or asked to leave the firm.[49] Promotion from within was a defining feature of the model, and lateral hiring from other firms was rare, reinforcing a culture of institutional loyalty, internal training, and cultural cohesion.[50]

Legal education professionalised and scaled in parallel with developments on the law-firm side of the equation. At Harvard Law School, Dean Christopher Columbus Langdell, and later his compatriots at Yale, Columbia, and other schools, established the notion that law was a rigorous professional science. They developed and implemented a standardised curriculum that leveraged a systematic method of teaching, featuring the study of appellate cases and use of the Socratic teaching method.[51]

As their influence on the profession rose, these elite law schools formed close alliances with emerging elite corporate law firms, feeding students into the firms.[52] This nexus was a 'win–win' for both the law schools and the law firms, reinforcing elite status on both sides. The law schools focused on teaching students how to think like lawyers, while the elite law firms were tasked with teaching them how to practice law.[53]

A Second Nexus

This new breed of law-firm lawyer was ideally suited to the emerging professional management class that now ran most MNCs. To them, elite law firms offered both the technical expertise they sought as well as the institutional legitimacy they preferred. Outside firms became their go-to choice for sophisticated legal advice, creating a second nexus between firms and MNCs. In return for loyalty and steady work, firms offered MNCs 'one-stop shops', bundling sophisticated corporate work with more commoditised services.[54]

As Eli Wald has observed, 'This expansion of legal services served the interests of both parties: the large law firms used the influx of work to support their tournament of lawyers' partner-to-associate ratios, to provide their associates with work, and to grow. The entity clients used their affiliation with the by then recognized elite of the legal profession—Big Law—to legitimize and establish the elite credentials of their newly professionalized management'.[55]

The losers in the emerging arrangement between elite schools, elite firms, and aspirational managers were the in-house lawyers. Once the trusted counsellors of titans, they were now increasingly marginalised and relegated to routine work as the centre of gravity shifted to the firms.

The GC 1.0 Legal Department

As MNCs grew within this stable but geographically localised environment, their legal needs remained correspondingly narrow and domestic.

A Back-office Function

GC 1.0, legal departments, if they existed at all, were small, highly centralised and internally focused. Many corporations did not maintain legal departments until well into the later years of GC 1.0. Even as late as the 1970s and 1980s, one-quarter of all Fortune 1000 companies had no in-house legal team at all. Those teams that did exist were small relative to today's standards. In smaller companies, in-house teams were a rarity.[56]

GC 1.0 legal departments focused primarily on routine, administrative matters, with material legal work outsourced to large outside law firms. This approach reflected the relatively uncomplicated legal environment that MNCs operated in. Transactional complexity was limited and the prevailing approach among business executives was that most matters could be addressed without the need for legal muscle or, if necessary, through firms. Common sense and good commercial judgement would suffice in most cases.[57]

Most legal work was domestic. As noted above, local subsidiaries were mostly autonomous, managing their own affairs and requiring little legal input from HQ. In this decentralised environment, a strategically embedded and influential legal function was not necessary.

In the United States (and other developed markets), the GC 1.0 legal and regulatory environment was, by modern standards, a simple environment.[58] Most major US corporations only had to engage with a small number of federal regulatory entities—mainly the Federal Trade Commission, the Department of Justice, the Internal Revenue Service, and the Securities and Exchange Commission, as compared to more than 80 agencies by the mid to late 1980s.[59]

Litigation played only a minor role during the GC 1.0 era. It was not until the late 1970s and 1980s that it began to expand significantly. In 1970, there were just 127,280 filings in US Federal District Courts; by 1989, that number had more than doubled to 279,288.[60] By the dawn of GC 2.0, litigation had evolved into a central tool of US social policy, wealth redistribution, and corporate strategy. But during GC 1.0, it remained largely peripheral.

Given this environment, the GC 1.0 legal department was not viewed as a strategic partner, and complex or high-value work was delegated to outside counsel.

The GC was not a key part of corporate leadership. GCs often hailed from the company's primary outside law firm. Often, they moved in-house because they had not managed to successfully secure their partnerships or because they were nearing retirement. Many of them maintained enduring ties to their former firms, prioritising 'air trafficking' legal work back to their former colleagues.[61]

Law Firms as Knowledge Gatekeepers

Technology also played a role in this dynamic, even if it was a more subtle one. Before LexisNexis emerged in the 1970s, statutes, regulations, and case law in the United States could only be accessed via large, resource-intensive law libraries.[62] Elite law firms were the only private entities that had sufficient resources to house such libraries. In-house teams, often lacking such resources, became dependent on external counsel for access to legal information. Elite firms therefore functioned as the de facto gatekeepers of legal knowledge, making them both advisors and monopolistic custodians of critical information.

Change in the Wind

The elevated status of the GC during the Gilded Age and its relative decline during the GC 1.0 era reflected the needs of MNCs and the contexts in which they operated. As the great trusts of the Gilded Age gave way to a more regulated and professionalised environment, marked by a relatively simple and stable legal environment, the influence of the in-house lawyer diminished, while the relative power of the law firm partner surged. The limits of technology and access to legal knowledge further reinforced this imbalance.

However, as globalisation accelerated and operational complexity increased, the winds of change began to blow again. The forces that would come to define the GC 2.0 era, which were beginning to take shape by the end of the period, would transform the role of the GC and restore the in-house team to a place of greater prominence.

3 | GC 2.0: Classic Globalisation (1989–2007)

Profitability without values is like fuel without an engine.

—Tony Hsieh[1]

The Acceleration of Globalisation

While MNCs extended their global footprint during the GC 1.0 era, the transition to GC 2.0 ushered in a far more intricate and fast-moving operating environment.

This period was marked by an acceleration of the trade liberalisation glimpsed in GC 1.0, but also by other transformative forces: the opening of Soviet bloc markets; China's meteoric rise as a manufacturing powerhouse; and the digital revolution, which dramatically increased the speed, volume, and complexity of cross-border trade.

Advances in logistics, technology, and communications radically globalised production networks in what became known as the 'Supply Chain Revolution', laying the groundwork for today's hyper-connected world.

These changes didn't merely add complexity to existing models; they reconfigured supply chains, capital flows, and the organisational architecture of global enterprise.

As in Chapter 2, we begin by surveying the macroeconomic and geopolitical dynamics that defined this period before turning to their cascading impact on legal departments. It was in this shifting landscape that the GC 2.0 function rebounded from its diminished GC 1.0 state, evolving into a more strategic, embedded, and globally attuned force.

The Expansion of Economic Liberalisation

The fall of the Berlin Wall in 1989 marked the end of the Cold War and unleashed a wave of economic liberalisation across the former Soviet bloc. The integration of these post-communist economies into the Western liberal order drove unprecedented growth: in the decade that followed, global trade expanded by 85% while FDI surged by an extraordinary 580%.[2] Between 1994 and 1999 alone, FDI inflows to post-communist countries rose by 404%, reaching $28 billion.[3]

The 'End of History'

The 1990s represented a pivotal inflection point in the arc of globalisation. With the collapse of the Soviet Union, vast swaths of previously closed economies were rapidly integrated into the liberal capitalist framework.

This shift was not merely economic; it was ideological. The prevailing sentiment of the time, captured by Francis Fukuyama's 'end of history' thesis, held that Western liberalism had triumphed and should shape the future world order.[4] Writing in 1989, Fukuyama argued that 'What we may be witnessing is not just the end of the Cold War … but the end of history as such: that is, the end point of mankind's ideological evolution and the universalization of Western liberal democracy as the final form of human government'.[5]

This optimism appeared justified for much of the GC 2.0 era. Trade barriers fell and multilateral institutions expanded their reach. The North American Free Trade Agreement (NAFTA, 1994), the World Trade Organization (WTO, 1995), and the European Union's 2004 enlargement reinforced belief in a borderless, rules-based order. The launch of the euro in 1999 and the abolition of internal border controls across the Schengen Zone in 1995 further deepened European integration, reinforcing the sense that

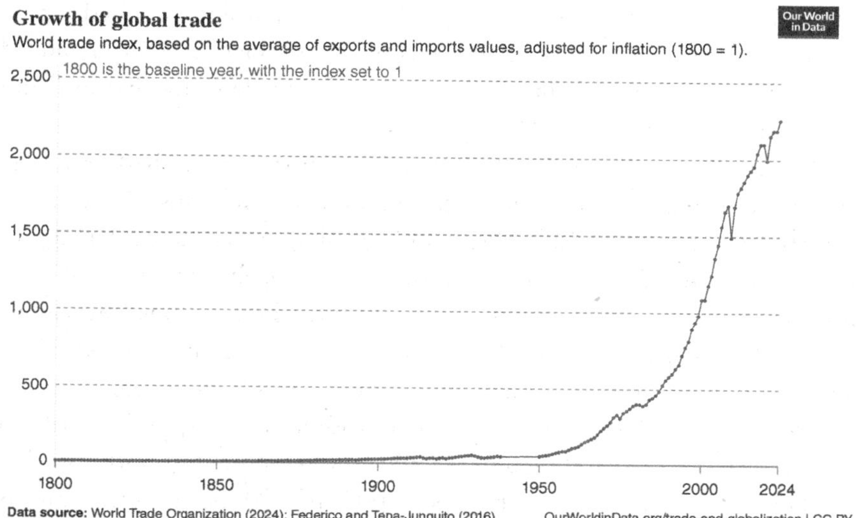

Figure 3.1   Growth of global trade 1800–2024.

Source: Our World in Data, 'Growth of Global Trade', 2024, https://ourworldindata.org/grapher/growth-of-global-trade.

liberalism and free trade had triumphed.[6] Even after 9/11, when national security concerns grew and the vulnerabilities of global interdependence became clearer, the pace of globalisation remained relentless (see Figure 3.1). By 2007, global trade reached a historic peak of 64.3% of world GDP, while FDI inflows topped $2.2 trillion, underscoring the resilience of the system.[7]

FDI and the Continued Rise of MNCs

Nowhere was this momentum more evident than in the explosion of FDI.[8] MNCs became central players in this system, not just as economic actors, but as architects of the new global order. These corporations were no longer bound by geography. They could move fluidly, seeking the most skilled workforce, the best research facilities, and the most favourable tax regimes.[9]

The World Trade Organization in 1995 and China's Accession

In 1995, the WTO replaced the GATT as the world's principal trade body, embedding a rules-based system anchored in five key trading principles: non-discrimination, negotiated liberalisation, transparency, promotion of fair competition, and development flexibility for emerging economies.[10]

Through these principles, the WTO systematically reduced trade barriers, curbed protectionist and discriminatory practices, and enhanced predictability and trust, which facilitated trade, fuelled globalisation, and unlocked new markets for MNCs.

China's accession to the WTO in 2001 was a watershed moment. WTO membership granted it most-favoured-nation status, shielding its exports from protectionist barriers and enabling access to 152 member markets. The Supply Chain Revolution allowed MNCs to unbundle and disperse their production processes globally, and China, with its vast labour pool and growing industrial base, became the linchpin of these value chains.[11] In turn, WTO membership allowed MNCs to tap into China's manufacturing potential with confidence, leading to an exponential rise in exports, as well as expanding global trade and investment opportunities.[12]

The results were dramatic. Between 2002 and 2007, China's net exports as a share of GDP more than tripled.[13] FDI inflows surged by 30% within a year of accession, fuelling job creation, technology transfer, and a shift towards high-tech manufacturing.[14] Foreign Invested Enterprises (FIEs) rapidly emerged as major players in China's export-driven economy, accounting for 45% of processed Chinese exports and generating approximately 11 million new jobs in China between 2001 and 2006.[15] By 2004, nearly 80% of FIE exports were in high-tech goods.[16] Chinese GDP growth soared (see Figure 3.2).

The Third Industrial Revolution

The Third Industrial Revolution (3IR), or the early computerisation revolution, marked a profound shift from the mechanical and analogue to the digital.

Emerging in the 1950s and reaching its zenith in the 1990s, 3IR followed two earlier waves of innovation. The First Industrial Revolution (1750–1840) ushered in mechanised production, centralised factories, and modern industrial capitalism. The Second Industrial Revolution (1860–1914) introduced standardisation and mass production, powered by a wave of advances such as the internal combustion engine, electricity and lighting, the telephone, radio, automobile, and airplane.[17]

The ripple effects of 3IR were transformative. It reshaped entire industries, ranging from education and healthcare to defence and finance,

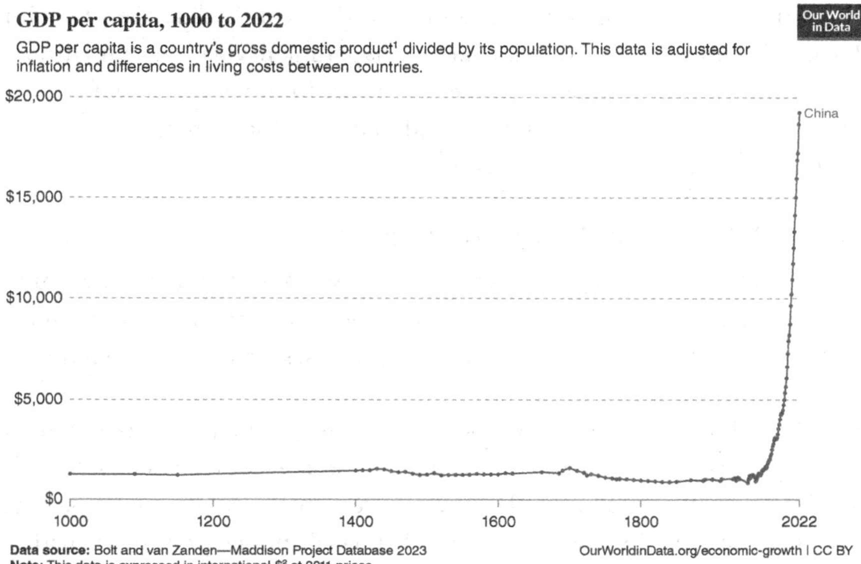

Figure 3.2　Chinese GDP growth.

Source: Our World in Data, 'GDP per Capita', Maddison Project Database, 2024, https://ourworldindata.org/grapher/gdp-per-capita-maddison-project-database?tab=chart&country=~CHN.

and fundamentally altered how institutions function, how decisions are made, and how leaders lead. This new era, foreshadowing the AI revolution to come, was defined by speed, complexity, interconnectivity, demanding new ways of thinking, organising, and governing.

At the heart of 3IR were two foundational innovations: microelectronics, the bedrock of modern computing, and the Internet, which connected everyone and everything. Together, they enabled breakthroughs from semiconductors to the World Wide Web, opening up new possibilities across commerce, communication, and mobility.[18]

The Internet: From Military Tool to Global Utility

Conceived in the 1960s by the US Department of Defence, the Internet began as a niche tool for academic and military use. Its transformation into a ubiquitous public utility gathered momentum in the 1990s, as computers became commonplace and software more intuitive.[19]

Critical to this shift was the launch of the World Wide Web by Tim Berners-Lee in 1990. The Web introduced hyperlink navigation, dramatically improving user accessibility. For the first time, Internet users could move easily between sites, driving widespread adoption for search, data sharing, email, and, increasingly, e-commerce.[20]

eBay and the Birth of Digital Marketplaces

By late 1994, the Web hosted 10,000 servers—2,000 of them commercial—and supported 10 million users.[21] That same year, 98 million consumers made a cumulative $60 billion in remote purchases, primarily through mail orders and TV shopping.[22]

The following year, eBay was born. It crystallised the Internet's potential to democratise commerce, empowering consumers to transact globally.[23] eBay's success illustrated how the Internet could connect disparate markets and communities. Its 'user-driven marketplace' model proved formative, shaping later platforms such as Amazon, Etsy, and Uber.[24]

The Rise of Platform Commerce

Amazon, founded in 1994, capitalised on the Internet's exponential growth which, by then, was expanding at 2,300% annually (see Figure 3.3).[25] Within months, it was shipping to all US states and more than 45 countries. By the end of its first year, it generated over $252 million in profits and was scaling rapidly.[26]

Key innovations followed. The 1-click purchase system simplified transactions, while two-day shipping redefined delivery standards. These developments recalibrated consumer expectations and reshaped the global retail landscape.[27]

As volumes and complexity grew, so too did concerns over security and trust. Secure and user-friendly payment platforms such as PayPal, together with innovations like Secure Sockets Layer (SSL) encryption, laid the groundwork for today's digital trust infrastructure.[28]

E-commerce Goes Mainstream

By the late 1990s, nearly every company was establishing an online presence. Websites became not only digital storefronts but also strategic engagement hubs. During this period, a wave of speculative exuberance

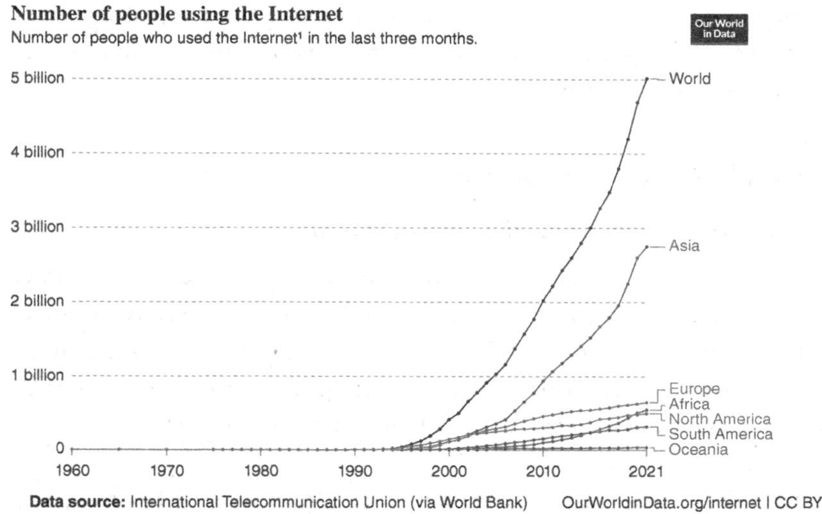

Figure 3.3 Internet usage 1960–2021.

Source: Our World in Data, 'Number of Internet Users', 2024, https://ourworldindata.org/grapher/number-of-internet-users.

powered US technology stock valuations to unprecedented heights. The Nasdaq index surged from under 1,000 points in 1995 to more than 5,000 by early 2000, before collapsing in what became known as the 'dot.com bust'. Between March 2000 and October 2002, the Nasdaq fell 77%, as many Internet start-ups went bankrupt. Even established technology leaders such as Cisco, Intel, and Oracle experienced stock price erosions of over 80%.[29]

Although the crash temporarily interrupted the ascent of e-commerce, its long-term effect was catalytic in that it weeded out speculative entrants. The companies that endured, such as Amazon and eBay, emerged well-positioned for long-term success, with durable customer bases, scalable operations, and proven business models that positioned them to define the next phase of digital commerce.[30]

The market correction had set the stage for a sustainable digital economy. During the 2000s, e-commerce and consumer adoption surged. What began as a retail phenomenon expanded rapidly to encompass banking, subscription-based media, and digital services, embedding itself into the routines of individuals and institutions worldwide.[31]

The Supply Chain Revolution

From Vertical Control to Global Distribution

The 1990s marked a profound transformation in how companies produced, distributed, and delivered goods and services. As China's awakening took hold and 3IR reshaped the global economy, many MNCs abandoned traditional 'vertically integrated' models (where they owned and controlled every stage of production) in favour of leaner, more distributed networks.

This shift was driven by a confluence of forces: lower labour costs in emerging markets, advances in logistics, and the rapid rise of the Internet. Together, these changes gave rise to a new era of complex, globally distributed supply chains that dynamically integrated production, distribution, and coordination across borders and time zones.[32]

Even as shocks like the dot.com collapse and major natural disasters such as the 1995 Kobe earthquake and later the 2004 Indian Ocean tsunami exposed the fragility of these networks, their momentum and economic logic proved irresistible. By the early 2000s, globally distributed supply chains had become the lifeblood of MNCs.

Technology as a Catalyst

A wave of new technologies underpinned this transformation. Real-time data analytics, RFID (radio frequency identification) tagging, barcode scanning, mobile platforms, e-commerce infrastructure, robotics, and automation all converged to redefine how goods were transported, monitored, and managed.[33]

These tools injected agility into supply chains that had once been rigid and linear. They enabled companies to improve forecasting, optimise delivery, and communicate seamlessly with suppliers and customers alike, generating richer insights into customer trends and operational risks.[34]

Although container terminals and shipping fleets also evolved to include larger vessels, more automated terminals, and improved quay and yard productivity, their essential technologies remained largely unchanged.[35]

The Humble Container as Hero

Perhaps no single innovation did more to enable global supply chains than the standardised shipping container. First introduced in the United States in the 1950s and adopted globally a decade later, containerisation revolutionised trade by allowing the seamless movement of goods across ships, trains, and trucks, bringing in the age of intermodal transport.[36]

By compressing delivery times and unlocking new efficiencies, containers facilitated the rise of global manufacturing hubs. In 1990, just under 29 million TEUs (20-foot equivalent units) of full containers were shipped globally. By 2002, that figure had nearly tripled to 78 million, excluding trans-shipment (containers transferred between vessels in transit to their final destination).[37] Between 2000 and 2005 alone, total container port throughput (the volume of containers handled by ports) grew from 236 million to nearly 400 million TEUs, representing an astonishing 11% annual growth rate.[38]

The container's impact went beyond logistics: it became a standardised unit of global commerce, which enhanced the power of complementary technologies, such as GPS tracking and automated logistics systems.[39] As James Hennessy has observed:

> By the 1980s, advances in personal computing allowed supply chain management to become a standalone operational function focussed on integrating and optimising the flow of products, information, and finances. Supply chain data standardisation and enterprise resource planning platforms further enabled end-to-end coordination. These innovations—supercharged by the arrival of the internet—helped unlock one of the most ensuring obstacles to globalized trade: rapid, efficient communication.[40]

Perhaps most critically, containerisation democratised access to global markets, reordering the geography of manufacturing in the process.[41] Remote producers, once excluded from global trade routes, could now plug into sophisticated freight systems through port hubs. Nowhere was this more apparent than in China, where coastal industrial zones rapidly gained an edge over landlocked competitors in the American Midwest and Western Europe.[42]

Governance in an Increasingly Complex Environment

As supply chains evolved into vast multinational webs, they became not only operational backbones but also strategic risks. Cross-border relationships, geopolitical volatility, and systemic risk all now had to be factored into corporate strategy in ways that were unimaginable in GC 1.0.

The legal implications of this were profound. The new supply chains required more active governance across numerous jurisdictions and markets, not only to manage efficiency but also to ensure operational resilience, regulatory compliance, and reputational integrity. Managing this complexity required first-rate governance, a holistic view of risk, and an enterprise-wide commitment to ethics.

The GC 2.0 Legal Department

The geopolitical, technological, and macroeconomic changes in GC 2.0 triggered a dramatic transformation in the quality, influence, and professional standing of GCs and in-house legal departments. Ben W. Heineman, Jr, General Electric's pioneering GC, has famously described this shift as the *'inside counsel revolution'*.[43] The days when GCs and their teams were relegated to back-office support roles disappeared. In this new era, GCs emerged as critical members of the C-suite and architects of corporate integrity in a globalised, high-velocity environment.[44]

From Back-office to Senior Leadership

By the end of the GC 2.0 period, 89% of GCs were reporting directly to the CEO.[45] Compensation soared once again, with many large-company GCs earning packages that equalled or even exceeded those offered by top-tier law firms.[46]

In-house teams also grew in scale and sophistication during this period, becoming magnets for top talent. Mid-level associates and junior partners were increasingly recruited from leading law firms, drawn by the opportunity to engage more broadly with business and secure better work–life balance.

Senior in-house roles, meanwhile, were increasingly filled by senior partners, reflecting the growing strategic prestige of corporate legal departments.[47]

By 2007, the legal departments of some US companies had more than 1,000 lawyers and annual budgets of over $600 million.[48] In-house practice had now become one of the fastest-growing segments of the profession.[49]

A Growing Risk Landscape

This transformation was driven in large part by the proliferation of legal, ethical, and operational risks associated with the changing environment. As MNCs deepened their presence in China and elsewhere, embraced distributed supply chains, and adjusted to the technological advances of 3IR, they encountered a heightened risk landscape, including enhanced regulatory scrutiny and complex geopolitical volatility. The rise of the Internet and social media raised the stakes, as corporate missteps now spiralled into global reputational crises within hours.

Scandals and a New Compliance Imperative

The early 2000s underscored these risks. Accounting scandals involving billions of dollars at Enron (2001), WorldCom (2002), and Tyco (2002) led to criminal prosecutions and the collapse of some corporate giants. In Europe, Siemens paid more than $1.6 billion in fines, penalties, and disgorgement of profits for a global bribery scheme, and the Italian dairy giant Parmalat collapsed under the weight of financial fraud. Scandals involving manipulated financial reports also impacted other leading European MNCs, including Royal Ahold and Vivendi Universal. Even Royal Dutch/Shell, one of the world's most financially conservative firms, admitted in 2004 to overstating its oil reserves by 24%, resulting in $151 million in fines.[50]

In each case, the theme was consistent: compliance systems had failed. Risks once seen as peripheral had moved to the core of the enterprise. The 2002 Sarbanes-Oxley Act (SOX) codified a new era of governance, imposing stringent financial disclosure rules and mandating internal controls and standards that aimed to improve financial transparency and reduce fraud risk, and new criminal offences were imposed.[51]

As these dynamics unfolded, MNCs were in the process of transforming organisationally, becoming larger, more matrixed (with reporting lines that spanned multiple regions, functions, and product groups), and more operationally diverse. With this scale came organisational complexity, leaving them increasingly exposed to the headwinds of this period.

A New Role for In-house Lawyers

This environment demanded a fundamental shift in how corporations used in-house legal teams. A fragmented, reactive approach to compliance and legal risk was no longer viable. To ensure a more preventative and appropriately pragmatic approach to emerging risks, organisational cultures had to evolve. In-house lawyers would now need to be deeply integrated into operational processes and business teams. Only legal professionals sitting from within the corporation and possessing a solid grasp of its business imperatives, risk appetites, and strategies could do this effectively. And as the wave of scandals had demonstrated to CEOs, this new breed of in-house lawyer would need to have the power to influence corporate decision-making.

In an era when organisations were rapidly growing and bureaucratising, business leaders could no longer rely primarily on the legal advice of independent outside law firms. By definition, outside counsel, who were external to the company, could not prevent problems from crystallising. They could only react once a problem already existed. Moreover, outside advisers would struggle to apply the appropriate level of commercial pragmatism in real time in an increasingly complex operating environment. Large companies were vastly more complex than they had been in earlier eras. By 2007, IBM employed nearly 400,000 people across more than 170 markets and Walmart's revenues were larger than the GDP of South Africa.[52] It became increasingly obvious that a handful of outside lawyers alone could not navigate this kind of complexity or manage its consequent risks.

As Eli Wald has noted:

> Corporate America's growing legal needs increasingly demanded early, proactive attention as a matter of right, rather than as a reactive matter of attorney–client relationships … Even as large law firms were transitioning to offer 24/7, around-the-clock hypercompetitive services, they were, by definition, reactive and could not handle the masses of information one needed to possess and master to effectively address the legal needs of their clients, seas of associates and their billable hours notwithstanding. This had to be done in-house.[53]

Consequently, as leading companies harmonised their policies globally, legal and compliance professionals became increasingly embedded into business teams and structures.[54]

In-house lawyers had transformed from the back-office technicians of GC 1.0 to frontline navigators in GC 2.0, helping business leaders operate with integrity in an unforgiving environment. This required a new breed of talent and skill. As Heinemann observed, the GC had become 'an important voice on performance, integrity, and risk, with a vital, distinct point of view and strong proactive role', while in-house counsel at all levels were meant to be 'partner-guardians' and 'lawyer-statesmen' who could help MNCs 'achieve high performance with high integrity'.[55]

As the influence and scope of responsibilities of the GCs grew, some of them even began replacing their legal-sounding 'General Counsel' title with a new one: 'Chief Legal Officer', intended to signify both the internal elevation of the role as a core member of the C-suite and a heightened public profile.[56]

By the close of the GC 2.0 era, the in-house function had grown in stature, size, and institutional sophistication. In-house roles became increasingly professionalised and specialised career tracks had emerged for in-house lawyers. The in-house legal team had become an essential and perfectly adapted component to the complex world MNCs now inhabited.

4 | GC 3.0: The Fourth Industrial Revolution (2007–2022)

The changes are so profound that, from the perspective of human history, there has never been a time of greater promise or potential peril.

—Klaus Schwab[1]

Convergence and Disruption

GC 3.0 was occasioned by the Fourth Industrial Revolution (4IR), a period defined by profound technological shifts that blurred the boundaries between the physical, digital, and biological worlds, disrupting whole industries in the process.[2]

The GC 3.0 era began in 2007, with the launch of the iPhone, and ended in 2022, with the arrival of Chat GPT. 'Moore's Law', the observation first made in 1965 by Intel's co-founder, Gordon Moore, that the number of

47

transistors on a microchip doubled roughly every two years with minimal cost increases, drove accelerating gains in computational efficiency.[3] Together with the broader advances of the 4IR, the rise of smartphones, 5G networks, and Cloud computing became possible.

A new generation of digital-first business models were also born, characterised by winner-takes-most dynamics. These dynamics produced a handful of dominant players, such as Facebook and Google, that captured outsized value.[4] These patterns became increasingly common across digital markets, where the underlying economics of software platforms enabled rapid scaling without proportional cost increases. As these networks expanded, their value grew, reinforcing market concentration and entrenching the advantages of early movers. In this environment, cross-border data flows surged, and intangible assets replaced physical ones as the main source of corporate value.

This period also saw increasing social, geopolitical, and macroeconomic turbulence. Fast-moving crises, including the Global Financial Crisis (GFC) and the COVID-19 pandemic, collided with slower-burning challenges like climate change. Together, these dynamics accelerated the pace of change, which increased volatility.

Consequently, the demands placed on GC 3.0 legal departments grew. All the dynamics of GC 2.0 remained, but now they had a new edge: companies needed more and better support, more quickly and cost-effectively. This more-for-less dynamic became a defining challenge, forcing GCs to evolve as business leaders. Strategy, procurement, technology, culture, and change management became new priorities.

Fortunately, the same technological forces that disrupted business also empowered GCs to develop better service delivery models and monitor outside suppliers more effectively. Legal operations teams emerged as key department players that helped GCs manage all this, and ALSPs became strategic suppliers.

The Broader Context of 4IR

Technology—Microchips and Exponential Growth

4IR ushered in a series of mutually reinforcing technological advances that set it apart in terms of both the speed at which breakthroughs occurred and the impact they had on business and society.

As World Economic Forum (WEF) Founder Klaus Schwab noted in 2015:

The speed of current breakthroughs has no historical precedent. When compared with previous industrial revolutions, the Fourth [Industrial Revolution] is evolving at an exponential rather than a linear pace. Moreover, it is disrupting almost every industry in every country. And the breadth and depth of these changes herald the transformation of entire systems of production, management, and governance.[5]

The exponential gains in microchip performance enabled by Moore's Law underpinned many of the dramatic advances in computing power and memory that defined the era.[6] By 2007, integrated circuits packed nearly 400 million times more switching elements than the first prototype developed in 1958.[7] By 2015, computing power had increased an astonishing one trillion-fold compared to 1956. Today, a typical smartphone delivers approximately 100,000 times more processing power, one million times more RAM, and seven million times more ROM than the computer that navigated the Apollo missions to the moon.[8]

The Watershed Year of 2007　　2007 marked the dawn of the GC 3.0 era because it was the year when gains in computing power reached a critical threshold, unleashing a wave of breakthrough technologies that reshaped how people connect, collaborate, and create. In that single year, the world seemed to pivot, as innovations converged and scaled at unprecedented speed:[9]

- Apple's iPhone launched, igniting the smartphone revolution.
- Google launched Android, an open platform that enabled smartphones to scale globally.
- Intel deployed non-silicon materials into its newest microchips, extending Moore's Law.
- Storage capacities surged, allowing Big Data to scale exponentially.
- The Internet surpassed 1 billion users worldwide.
- Facebook and Twitter scaled, ushering in the age of mass social media and micro-blogging.
- IBM began developing 'Watson', the first cognitive computer to integrate machine learning and AI.

- Amazon launched the Kindle, enabling consumers to download thousands of books instantly.
- Airbnb was founded and within a decade offered five million listings—more than the top five hotel chains combined.[10]
- The cost of DNA sequencing dropped sharply, driven by advances in computing and storage, which paved the way for personalised medicine at scale.

As Tom Friedman observed:

2007 surely constituted one of the greatest leaps forward in history. It suffused a new set of capabilities to connect, collaborate, and create throughout every aspect of life, commerce, and government. Suddenly there were so many more things that could be digitized, so much more storage to hold all that digital data, so many faster computers and so much more innovative software that could process that data for insights, and so many more organizations and people … who could access those insights, or contribute to them, anywhere in the world through their handheld computers—their smartphones.[11]

2007 was more than just a year of milestones. It marked an inflection point that began to redefine what was possible for individuals, organisations, and entire industries.

A World Transformed by Smartphones

At the heart of all this change was the explosive rise of the smartphone. In 2007, just 122 million smartphones were sold worldwide. By 2020, annual sales had increased to 1.6 billion.[12]

It is difficult to overstate the impact smartphones have had on society, the economy, and the corporate environment. They ushered in an 'always on' culture for both customers and employees that transformed how people shop, work, and play, placing user connectedness at the centre of modern life. Entertainment, marketing, and business rapidly restructured around a mobile, app-based society. By 2022, mobile commerce had become a $1.4 trillion industry, accounting for more than half of all e-commerce.[13]

Social media expanded with breathtaking speed off the back of smartphones. What started as a niche industry in 2007 had become deeply woven into the social fabric by the mid-2010s. In 2019, Facebook had 2.4 billion users, while Twitter and WhatsApp had 1 billion users each, and one in three people worldwide were active on social media platforms.[14] This seismic shift transformed how companies engaged customers, how people consumed news and information, and even how political opinions were shaped. Corporate news, both positive or negative, now travelled at the speed of Twitter, creating an urgent need to rapidly anticipate and shape narratives. Lawyers tasked with vetting these narratives needed to stay ahead of the curve as events unfolded.

Cloud Computing

Cloud computing scaled during the 2010s, becoming the primary engine that drove these digital shifts. The Cloud made it possible for computer services, including servers, storage, databases, networking, software, and analytics, to be flexibly delivered at scale and speed via the Internet.[15] Applications could be hosted by Cloud providers on powerful servers located in remote data centres, which allowed customers to access all the computing power they needed, whenever they needed it. The capital expense of buying and maintaining computer hardware was removed, enabling companies to move to a 'pay-as-you-go' model that dramatically lowered costs and entry barriers.[16]

This innovation generated enormous benefits across the value chain. Consumers benefited from near-instant access to applications and services, while companies could cost-effectively power everything from remote work and integrated customer engagement across physical, digital, and social channels to research, business systems, and back-office operations.

By 2010, large Cloud providers, including Amazon Web Services (AWS), Microsoft, and Google, were rapidly scaling, while open-source platforms, such as OpenStack, were driving broader adoption.[17] AWS, which initially targeted start-ups, positioned its services as a way to flexibly and cost-effectively launch new businesses. The ability to shift computing costs from capital expenditure (CapEx), which required heavy upfront investment in hardware, to operating expenditure (OpEx), based on flexible, usage-driven payments, was transformative for smaller companies. This *pay-as-you-go* model lowered barriers to entry, allowing businesses to scale their technology spending in line with growth.[18]

Macroeconomic Turbulence Meets Goldilocks

The GC 3.0 macroeconomic landscape was bookended by financial shocks. Yet, for much of its duration, it was defined by a long stretch of financial stability that enabled the rise of platform economies and digital-first business models.

The era began with the GFC (2007–2009), the most severe global economic shock in over 70 years.[19] In response, the US Federal Reserve cut interest rates to near zero and launched three rounds of quantitative easing, expanding its balance sheet by roughly $3.6 trillion.[20] Central banks in Europe and Asia followed suit with unprecedented interventions.

While the global recovery was uneven, these measures set the stage for the longest economic expansion in history.[21] The subsequent decade became known as the *Goldilocks* economy: neither too hot nor too cold, it combined low inflation, low interest rates, and steady growth.[22] Despite massive stimulus, subdued wage growth and cheap imports held down consumer prices, boosting corporate earnings and creating ideal conditions for investors.[23]

However, as Lawrence H. Summers observed, this period of apparent economic stability masked underlying structural imbalances. Persistently low interest rates and a global savings glut created an inflated sense of economic health. The world had entered an 'age of secular stagnation', in which advanced economies suffered 'from an imbalance resulting from an increasing propensity to save and a decreasing propensity to invest', with excess savings acting as a drag on demand, reducing growth and inflation.[24] Summers warned that much of the growth seen in markets such as the United States was being fuelled by 'dangerous levels of borrowing that translate excess savings into unsustainable levels of investment'.[25]

At the same time, tectonic geopolitical shifts were underway. The post-WWII political order was fraying. As Ian Bremmer and Nouriel Roubini wrote in *Foreign Affairs* in 2011:

> *We are now living in a G-Zero world, one in which no single country or bloc of countries has the political and economic leverage or the will to drive a truly international agenda. The result will be intensified conflict on the international stage over vitally important issues, such as international macroeconomic coordination, financial regulatory reform, trade policy, and climate change.*[26]

In this new era, multilateral institutions would weaken, transnational coordination would erode, and the management of global crises would become more fragmented and reactive.

From Global Flows to Digital Dominance

Traditional global flows of goods, services, and finance, which peaked in 2007 at roughly $30 trillion, or 53% of global GDP, flattened out over the following decade. In their place, digital flows surged. By 2016, cross-border data traffic had grown 45-fold since 2005 and was exerting a greater impact on global GDP than trade in goods.[27] Cheap Cloud services, low-cost debt, and expanding bandwidth ushered in a new era of globalisation defined less by container ships and more by packets of data transmitting information, ideas, and innovation at near-zero marginal cost.[28]

This shift opened new possibilities for companies of all sizes to operate across borders at scale. Digital platforms flourished by combining accessible global customer bases with highly effective, data-driven ways to reach them.[29] As McKinsey observed at the time, digital platforms were redefining globalisation by automating interactions and driving the marginal cost of adding new users nearly to zero.[30]

Platform Models and the Rise of Winner-takes-most Dynamics

Platform-based business models thrive on network effects, creating *winner-takes-most* dynamics that intensified competitive pressure across industries. These platforms derived value from digital ecosystems connecting buyers, sellers, and service providers: the more users they attracted, the more valuable they became.[31] As a result, value shifted decisively from tangible assets to intellectual property and data. By 2020, intangible assets accounted for 90% of the market value of the S&P 500, compared to 68% in 1995.[32]

The COVID-19 pandemic (2020–2022), known as the Great Lockdown, brought renewed economic hardship, triggering the worst recession since the Great Depression.[33] Yet it also radically accelerated digitisation, as billions of people confined to their homes shifted work, commerce, and social interaction online. Years of digital adoption were compressed into months, locking in and amplifying the trends that were already underway, including the rising dominance of platform economies.[34] Scale and flywheel effects (self-reinforcing loops where growth drives further growth) became even more decisive competitive advantages. In 2020, Apple became the first company to reach a $2 trillion valuation, and other platform companies saw their market dominance deepen.[35]

The Rise of Polycrises

Volatility in the GC 3.0 era was not confined to technological innovation, digital disruption, or winner-takes-most marketplaces. It was compounded by an unrelenting series of unpredictable events with outsized impacts that shook the foundations of the global order established in GC 1.0. These included the GFC (2007–2009), the Arab Spring (2011), Brexit (2016), the elections of Donald Trump as US President (2016 and 2024), the COVID-19 pandemic (2019–2022), and Russia's invasion of Ukraine (2022). Layered atop these were slow-burn crises: climate change, intensifying US and China tensions, and an ever-growing drumbeat of sophisticated cyber-attacks. And all of this seemed to be playing out in the G-Zero world that Bremmer and Roubini had warned of.

MNCs found themselves grappling with blurring industry boundaries, where companies like Amazon were sometimes both their biggest competitors and their biggest customers. Markets morphed in real time as the geopolitical landscape shifted, marked by rising nationalism and retreating globalisation. The intricate global supply chains painstakingly constructed in GC 2.0 were suddenly exposed as fragile, prompting companies to reprioritise resilience over efficiency and reconfigure their networks for a more volatile world.

Employees, too, were navigating new tensions in the post-COVID era, as debates around hybrid working collided with an increasingly shallow talent pool.[36] As the WEF warned:

Concurrent shocks, deeply interconnected risks and eroding resilience are giving rise to the risk of polycrises—where disparate crises interact such that the overall impact far exceeds the sum of each part. Eroding geopolitical cooperation will have ripple effects across the global risks landscape over the medium term, including contributing to a potential polycrisis of interrelated environmental, geopolitical and socioeconomic risks.[37]

Against this backdrop, and to survive in a risk-heavy environment, capital had to be redeployed to shore up technology investments and build resilient organisational structures. The total R&D expenditure of the world's top 2,500 firms surged from \$383 billion in 2007 to \$1.3 trillion in 2022.[38] To fund this, CFOs adopted *zero-based budgeting*—a discipline requiring each expense to be justified from scratch rather than carried forward from the prior year—and trimmed costs wherever possible. By 2020, 43% of CFOs surveyed by McKinsey were streamlining their budgeting processes to react faster, while 65% anticipated using rolling forecasts so that they could reallocate funds more dynamically.[39]

As companies restructured and adapted to a fast-changing environment, pressure began to build within the GC 3.0 legal department. In-house teams that had been somewhat shielded from the full force of corporate efficiency drives in the GC 2.0 era now found themselves under growing scrutiny to deliver more value with fewer resources. The pressure was on; every part of the enterprise was expected to contribute. GC 3.0 presented a clear mandate for both companies and legal departments to adapt continuously or risk irrelevance.

Legal Departments in the GC 3.0 World

The More-for-less Challenge

As a result of these dynamics, managing legal costs became an increasingly urgent priority for in-house legal teams. These pressures crystallised in the immediate aftermath of the GFC, which ushered in what David B. Wilkins and María J. Esteban have described as a 'global age of more-for-less'.[40]

The era's macroeconomic and geopolitical headwinds, coupled with the disruptive pace of technological change, triggered a sharp rise in demand for legal services. Legal departments, if anything, were more influential than they had been in GC 2.0. Yet, downward pressure on corporate budgets meant that, like HR, finance, and other support functions, they were expected to deliver first-rate services with the same or fewer resources than in the past. Flat or declining budgets became the norm: in 2015, the Association of Corporate Counsel reported that 65% of GCs anticipated little to no budget growth in the coming year.[41]

For many GCs this was new territory. The days of GC 2.0, when funding often accompanied an expanding global risk horizon, were over—and many teams struggled to adjust.[42] Success now depended on mastering the more-for-less dynamic.

As Mark Liggio observed:

No longer could corporations ignore the cost of legal services, even in the bet-your-life cases. The upward-spiraling cost of legal services required all to take notice of their impact on the bottom line. These costs forced management to reevaluate how services are to be provided and whether a Volkswagen might be as cost-effective as a Rolls Royce. It required management to start making risk/benefit analyses.[43]

At first, in the absence of robust spending data and metrics, legal departments experimented with a wide—and often arbitrary—range of cost-control measures: preferred-provider programmes, electronic billing systems, alternative fee arrangements, rate freezes, and stricter billing guidelines. By 2008, well over half of departments reported also applying more aggressive negotiation tactics with outside counsel.[44] Yet the impact of these early initiatives was mixed at best.

Over time, it became apparent that legal departments needed a more sophisticated and structured approach. As I wrote in 2017, they had to 'shelve the financial machete ... and learn to work with a scalpel, leveraging sophisticated procurement techniques that previously were only used by purchasing experts'. They also had to 'become far savvier consumers, stratifying needs across different types of providers, crunching numbers to identify opportunities, rolling out technologies and tools, and tirelessly improving transparency and strategic partnership principles'.[45]

Equally important became being able to communicate legal costs, risks, and benefits in ways that resonated with corporate leadership. Business colleagues spoke and thought in the language of numbers, charts, projections, and metrics. Increasingly, in-house lawyers did the same. To enable that metamorphosis, legal departments turned to a new breed: the legal operations professional. These new operatives possessed financial acumen, business understanding, and the ability to make a case through data.[46]

The Rise of Legal Operations

The legal operations profession emerged in direct response to the pressures reshaping corporate legal departments in GC 3.0. While its roots lie in risk management and cost control, legal operations came into their own during this period. Today, legal operations professionals bring expertise across a broad range of fields that include finance, marketing, data analytics, learning and development, project management, and technology adoption. They also play a critical role in helping lawyers manage risk and monitor compliance in an increasingly complex regulatory environment.[47]

In the pre-GC 3.0 era, legal operations managers (if they existed at all) were confined to a narrow set of tasks, such as outside counsel spend management and administrative support. But the GFC and the intensifying more-for-less challenge transformed legal operations from a back-office cost function into a strategic enabler of efficiency, technology adoption, and value creation.

Throughout the 2010s, legal operations functions assumed an ever-widening set of priorities: technology acquisition and implementation, data analytics, project management, and process improvement. Increasingly, legal operations became the 'engine room' of the department, generating the insights, methodologies, and best practice required to run a complex legal organisation at scale.[48]

As technology advanced and became strategically indispensable, legal operations evolved again—moving beyond support functions to focus on high-value priorities such as strategic planning, technology estate management, business forecasting, dashboard and key performance indicator (KPI) development, contract and document management, workflow optimisation, vendor and procurement strategy, and change management. The role matured from a largely administrative one into a critical enabler of leadership.

As Sterling Miller notes, 'From what was once a lower-level job, legal operations professionals often play a critical leadership role in the legal department, bridging the gap between legal and business teams through (i) metrics-driven decision-making, (ii) resource optimization, and (iii) innovation that empowers the legal department to act as a true business and strategic partner—and not just a cost center'.[49]

In 2007, legal departments devoted negligible resources to legal operations. By the early 2020s, however, dedicated budget lines for legal operations had become standard in large departments. By 2022, 61% of legal departments reported employing at least one legal operations professional, up from 21% in 2015.[50] The larger the company, the more prominent the function became.[51]

This expansion was mirrored in the growth of the Corporate Legal Operations Consortium (CLOC), the profession's leading industry association. What began in 2010 as an informal book club of seven people had, by its formal launch in 2016, grown to 579 members across 377 organisations. By 2022, CLOC had 4,238 members across 1,441 organisations in 57 countries.[52]

Legal operations became firmly embedded in the corporate legal landscape, having come of age during the 2010s. By 2021, legal technology expenditure already accounted for an average of 13% of legal department budgets, underscoring its growing strategic importance.[53]

The more complex and demanding the environment became, the more this expertise was needed. And as technology continues to evolve, with AI becoming an increasingly powerful driver of legal department efficiency, its role is set to expand further in the next decade.

Alternative Legal Service Providers

As legal operations professionals brought a new level of sophistication to how legal departments were managed, GCs began to take a fresh look at how they could drive efficiency along the entire legal service delivery chain. Legal work was deconstructed into discrete tasks and sub-tasks, from initial client intake to final delivery. Each element of this chain was assessed and allocated to the most efficient internal or external provider. Processes were streamlined, technologies deployed, and KPIs developed to provide visibility and drive accountability. Budget allocations between internal teams and external counsel were scrutinised more rigorously than before.

As these efforts delivered results—greater efficiency, deeper insights, and improved customer satisfaction—expectations rose. At the same time, advances in high-speed computing and low-cost Cloud storage enabled a new class of outside suppliers to emerge in the mid-2010s: the ALSP.

At first, ALSPs focused on providing GCs with cost-effective solutions for high-volume, repetitive legal tasks traditionally handled in-house, such as contract management.[54] But as needs grew and technology evolved, the scope of services offered and the types of ALSPs expanded, with the Big Four expanding into the space. ALSPs began to offer solutions all along the value chain, from consultancy, staffing solutions, and legal managed services, to software and technology tools.[55]

These new solutions enabled GCs to scale and refine their unbundling strategies (disaggregating legal work and allocating it to the most efficient mix of in-house teams, law firms, and alternative providers), fundamentally reimagining how legal services could be delivered.

The ALSP market scaled rapidly. Virtually non-existent in 2007, it grew to an $8 billion market by 2017 and reached $10.7 billion in 2019.[56] A growing amount of the work traditionally done in-house or by law firms began being done by ALSPs.[57] By 2021, 71% of corporate legal departments were engaging ALSPs as part of their service delivery models.[58] Law firms began employing ALSPs as well, not only to benefit from their specialised capabilities but also to respond to mounting client demands for greater efficiency and lower costs. By that same year, 79% of law firms surveyed reported using ALSPs in some capacity.[59]

Clearly, ALSPs had arrived and were poised to capture even greater market share as technology advanced.

Role Proliferation, Risk Convergence, and the Rise of the T-shaped GC

One additional development during GC 3.0 was the noticeable increase in the number of roles and responsibilities that GCs began to assume. They moved from the narrow technical legal focus of GC 1.0 to becoming experts in the many business dimensions needed to lead and manage large, complex functions. That required fluency across a range of new disciplines, including strategy, operations, technology, leadership, culture, and change management.[60]

During this period, many GCs also began to assume responsibility for a host of other verticals and capabilities well beyond the legal department. As noted in Chapter 1, these included heading up a diverse array of other areas within the company. GCs had to do all of this while not losing focus on their primary mandate: to be a first-rate professional legal adviser and guardian of the company's integrity and reputation.

The ability of GCs to integrate their legal expertise with these new duties reflected their 'T-shaped' nature. T-shaped professionals are able to combine deep cognitive, analytical and/or technical skills with a broader array of multidisciplinary and social skills, including collaboration across disciplines.

As Tim Brown has noted:

The vertical stroke of the T is a depth of skill that allows them to contribute to the creative process. That can be from any number of different fields: an industrial designer, an architect, a social scientist, a business specialist or a mechanical engineer. The horizontal stroke of the T is the disposition for collaboration across disciplines.[61]

GCs are inherently T-shaped in that, to succeed, they must possess both legal expertise and the ability to be enterprise-wide connectors. Lawyers touch almost every part of the company, in addition to supporting the board. Because they form a relatively small and cohesive group, they communicate effectively with each other through dense, highly effective networks.[62]

Executives increasingly saw value in giving T-shaped GCs these broader accountabilities in part because (as noted earlier in this book), corporate risk itself was morphing and converging. In a world where traditional risk verticals were blurring and resiliency and antifragility became the order of the day, T-shaped qualities became invaluable. As British author and journalist at the *Financial Times*, Gillian Tett noted in her 2015 book *The Silo Effect*, organising risk around verticals can cause institutional blindness because it limits information and restricts thinking.[63]

Broad connectors make good sense in this context.

Role Overload

But this evolution came at a cost. The GC 3.0 environment produced a job description of almost impossible complexity. GCs were now expected to be strong C-suite leaders, strategic business partners, guardians of ethical integrity, and outstanding legal advisers, all while overseeing multiple functions outside their core domain. Many moved beyond T-shaped to what some have called *comb-shaped*: leaders who combined deep legal expertise with multiple additional spikes of knowledge and responsibility.

Yet, as MNCs leaned into the volatile, interconnected environment of GC 3.0, there was no way around it. The GC role had to be constructed in this way—it simply couldn't be disaggregated without losing its effectiveness.[64]

PART II
The AI Era

Artificial intelligence and generative AI may be the most important technology of any lifetime.

—Marc Benioff, Co-founder, Chairman, and CEO of Salesforce[1]

GC 4.0 started with the launch of Chat GPT in 2022. The widespread corporate and consumer use of generative AI marked a milestone, redefining how humans interact with machines and how value is created.

As will be discussed in Chapter 5, the primary reason for AI's transformative impact is its general-purpose nature: it catalyses a broad range of complementary innovations that upend markets and transform economies.

AI is also changing the very nature of firms, including how they are structured, how they operate, and how they compete. Digital processes can scale in ways that are unimaginable in an analogue environment. As we saw in Chapters 3 and 4, digital businesses favour first-movers, creating winner-takes-most dynamics. The more a firm can harness digitisation, the more value it can create and capture.

In GC 4.0, the digital and analogue worlds are colliding and merging. In a real sense, every business is now a technology business.[2] The implications are profound. As ever more activities become digitised, the existential pressure on firms to digitally transform will increase. Interestingly, doing so doesn't require particularly sophisticated AI. Even so-called 'weak AI' (i.e., systems that are limited to performing pre-programmed tasks) can significantly improve competitiveness.[3]

For legal departments, the same pattern we saw in earlier eras holds. As MNCs adapt to a transformed operating environment, in-house legal teams evolve in tandem, reshaping the competitive dynamics of law firms and other external providers. In GC 4.0, these changes will impact everything from the composition of the workforce and the skills needed, to the organisational structures, service delivery models, and technologies that will be applied.

The exact contours of the GC 4.0 legal department are still emerging, but they will likely be characterised by a stable, technology-driven base, supporting a specialised, agile, and market-facing front. As these structures take hold, resources will gradually shift away from traditional law firms and towards technology and specialist expertise. These changes will accelerate with the rise of 'agentic AI' (autonomous, goal-driven systems that extend the capabilities of generative AI) and the continued disruptive power of Moore's Law, setting the stage for the transformations examined in the chapters that follow.[4]

As these changes take hold, they will redefine how law firms are perceived and used. The consequences of this, and the organisational and legal services models that might emerge in its wake, will be the subject of Parts III and IV.

5 | GC 4.0—The AI Impact

Even though they see a lot of disruption coming, many really smart, well-managed companies are underestimating the scale, scope, and speed of disruption.

—Andrew McAfee[1]

AI is massively transforming and disrupting our world. It is, perhaps, the most impactful technology in history. Sundar Pichai, CEO of Alphabet and Google, believes it will transform whole industries and nearly every aspect of human life.[2]

Before exploring how companies and legal departments are evolving in the face of AI, it is worth considering what AI is and why it is so impactful. As we will see, at the heart of its impact is the way that AI-centric operating models remove traditional constraints on scale, scope, and learning. This is what allows digital-first organisations to grow faster, adapt more rapidly, and capture more value relative to their analogue counterparts.[3] The more a company is designed to optimise for digitisation and AI, the more its operating model can absorb additional scale, expand its scope, and accelerate learning. And digital technologies allow these expansions to take place at near-zero marginal cost.[4]

These dynamics allow digital firms to capture more insights in the form of data. The more a company knows about its customers, the more effectively it can innovate, create personalised experiences, and deliver new sources of value. These improvements in turn generate more data and better insights, which drive the next round of innovation, creating a self-reinforcing flywheel of growth, learning, and value generation.[5]

Traditional organisations can also achieve these effects. However, in non-digital environments, there are limits to how far an organisation can grow before complexity, cost, and declining service levels set in and place a ceiling on further growth. By contrast, in digital systems, scale is self-reinforcing. Expansion tends to improve speed, efficiency, and quality, rather than erode them.

What Is AI?

We will explore these dynamics in greater depth below. But before doing so, it is helpful to unpack more carefully what 'AI' means. However, arriving at a clear and universally accepted definition is surprisingly difficult, perhaps partly because the technology is evolving so rapidly.

I Know It When I See It …

Surveying the landscape of possible definitions, one is almost tempted to adopt US Supreme Court Justice Potter Stewart's famous threshold test for obscenity: 'I know it when I see it'.[6]

The bottom line is that there is no consensus on what AI is and what it is not. A 2025 academic study that analysed 105 definitions from regulations, legislation, national strategies, and international agreements across 62 jurisdictions and institutions provides a case in point. It found widespread conceptual confusion: most definitions lacked a basic understanding of the technology; a quarter of the jurisdictional definitions were broad enough to classify a sundial as AI; and a third failed to define it at all.[7]

There is also tremendous disagreement among experts.[8] When 400 of them, across 48 countries and 131 different institutions, were asked to choose from a range of definitions, the most widely accepted one garnered just 56% of the vote.[9]

Arriving at a perfect and all-encompassing definition will likely remain out of reach for the foreseeable future. For the purposes of this book, Paul D. Weizel's definition (2025) provides a workable foundation:

Artificial intelligence refers to a computer program that uses machine learning techniques to accomplish complex goals that would normally require human-level intelligence.[10]

Weizel's definition might benefit from one caveat. As Richard Susskind recently noted, 'AI systems are increasingly *outperforming* humans and doing things which are *beyond* the capabilities of humans' (emphasis added).[11]

As for related terminology, we will adopt the following definitions from McKinsey:[12]

- **Machine Learning.** Algorithms that detect patterns in large datasets and learn to make predictions by processing data, rather than by receiving explicit programming instructions.
- **Deep Learning.** The use of neural networks, inspired by the ways neurons interact in the human brain, to ingest data and process it through multiple iterations that learn increasingly complex features of the data and make increasingly sophisticated predictions.
- **Generative AI.** A branch of deep learning that uses exceptionally large neural networks called large language models (with hundreds of billions of neurons) that can learn especially abstract patterns. Language models applied to interpret and create text, video, images, and data are known as Generative AI.

The Rise of Agentic AI

Agentic AI, which represents an additional stage in the evolution of AI, has the capacity to profoundly alter the practice of law.

Defining Agentic AI Agentic systems go beyond answering prompts. They set sub-goals, select tools, and execute multi-step actions in pursuit of defined objectives with minimal supervision.[13] Unlike earlier models, they can handle open-ended tasks, adapt dynamically to unforeseen conditions, and generate novel solutions in natural language. These are capabilities that edge into domains once reserved for human judgement.[14]

Agentic systems typically comprise multiple agents working together, with specialised agents handling different aspects of a task under the direction of an orchestration layer that ensures alignment with the overarching objective.[15] In Cloud computing terms, an agentic AI system resembles a workflow, while each intelligent agent functions as an autonomous actor within it.[16]

How Agentic Systems Work   IBM describes the concept as follows:

Agentic AI is an artificial intelligence system that can accomplish a specific goal with limited supervision. It consists of AI agents—machine learning models that mimic human decision-making to solve problems in real time. In a multiagent system, each agent performs a specific subtask required to reach the goal and their efforts are coordinated through AI orchestration.[17]

Anwesha Mukherjee and Justin Chang illustrate the distinction between generative and agentic approaches with a practical example:

To illustrate how this shift might impact consumers, consider the task of planning a trip to Vietnam. A conventional travel chatbot might answer specific questions about flight schedules or suggest popular tourist destinations. In stark contrast, an agentic AI travel assistant could autonomously construct a complete and personalized itinerary, including booking flights that align with the traveler's preferences and budget, reserving accommodations consistent with their past choices, scheduling tours to significant sites like the My Son Sanctuary, and even arranging dining reservations at restaurants known for authentic Vietnamese cuisine. Furthermore, this agent could proactively monitor weather forecasts to optimize outdoor activities, negotiate with local tour operators for better rates, and dynamically update the itinerary in response to real-time events, such as flight delays or local festivals.[18]

Application in Legal Practice   While still in its early stages, agentic AI has the potential to disrupt legal practice because of its ability to operate with contextual awareness and strategic reasoning. Early applications already include automating client intake forms, tracking hours, and summarising research, as well as more sophisticated tasks, such as drafting and reviewing documents, supporting case preparation, and conducting regulatory analysis.[19]

These systems are advancing rapidly, and hybrid workforces consisting of equal parts agents and humans working alongside each other may not be far off.[20]

Risks and Governance Challenges Given their capacity to operate autonomously, agentic systems introduce new risks. Organisations will need to apply appropriate governance and oversight mechanisms to guard against unintended actions, as well as conduct rigorous testing, verification, and auditability as these systems take on more complex and sensitive work.[21]

Why Is AI So Impactful?

As discussed in the Introduction, AI is what is known as a *general-purpose technology* (GPT). Most technologies are narrowly designed for specific tasks. A pencil sharpener sharpens pencils, but it won't impact much beyond that. GPTs, by contrast, drive systemic change. They reconfigure economies because they enable cascades of complementary technologies and innovations across a spectrum of industries.

Other GPTs include the steam engine, electricity, or the internal combustion engine. Each one unleashed waves of complementary innovations that in turn generated new possibilities, giving rise to entirely new industries.

As Erik Brynjolfsson and Andrew McAfee have observed:

The internal combustion engine ... gave rise to cars, trucks, airplanes, chain saws, and lawnmowers, along with big-box retailers, shopping centers, cross-docking warehouses, new supply chains, and, when you think about it, suburbs. Companies as diverse as Walmart, UPS, and Uber found ways to leverage the technology to create profitable new business models.[22]

GPTs have three defining features. Their *reach is pervasive*, impacting a range of industries, organisational levels, and business functions. They also *rapidly improve*, becoming more efficient, cost-effective, and capable as they scale. Finally, they catalyse *complementary innovations*, generating new business models and product categories.[23] All three of these can be seen in AI systems today. We will examine each in turn.

Pervasiveness

AI has rapidly become ubiquitous, at both consumer and industry levels, often in ways we barely notice.[24] For individuals, the most visible manifestations of AI are the algorithms that power search engines, email filters, and social media feeds, as well as those that run retail and entertainment platforms.[25]

Generative AI, in particular, is spreading across the consumer landscape at unprecedented speed. In the three years following its 2022 public rollout, for instance, ChatGPT soared from zero to 800 million users, hitting 365 billion annual searches in just two years versus the 11 it took for Google to reach that same level in 2009.[26]

In the corporate sphere, AI's penetration is even more evident. A 2024 study that reviewed over 200 sources noted that AI has 'a broad range of applications across multiple industries' and 'has become integral to numerous fields, revolutionizing industries and addressing pressing global challenges'.[27] From education to life sciences, to imaging, healthcare, autonomous mobility, recommendation engines, industrial monitoring, robotics, and manufacturing, the impact has been dramatic.[28]

AI's pervasiveness in the workplace is also profound. A 2023 survey involving 14,000 users across 14 countries found that more than half of all users were working with generative AI tools, with 71% reporting productivity gains. In some professions, such as programming, adoption was nearly universal, with 92% using it at work.[29] This trend looks set to continue: nearly two-thirds of business leaders believe generative AI will have a 'high' or 'extremely high' impact on their organisations.[30]

This momentum is reflected in corporate spending. Companies invested approximately $246 billion in AI technologies in 2024, including $44 billion in generative AI—more than double the levels in 2023. Generative AI adoption by companies surged from 55% in 2023 to 75% in 2024. And investment in AI is expected to grow at a compound annual growth rate (CAGR) of 32.8% between 2023 and 2028, with spending on generative AI alone to exceed $304 billion by 2028—a CAGR of over 74%.[31]

Rapid Improvement

AI technologies are also improving at a remarkable rate (see Figure 5.1). Some liken it to the 'Cambrian Explosion', an era about 530 million years ago when complex life forms evolved rapidly, except this time humans are driving the acceleration. As Storrs Hall has noted:

The combination of massive computational resources, advanced algorithms, and vast datasets creates conditions analogous to the rich primordial seas that spawned complex life … We are not merely witnesses to this transformation but active participants in it. Every interaction with AI systems, every training dataset we create, every architectural innovation we implement contributes to the evolutionary pressure that drives these systems toward greater complexity and capability.[32]

Generative AI has had a particularly rapid trajectory of improvement as compared to earlier AI systems.[33] In just a few months, OpenAI's GPT system went from outperforming approximately 10% of human test-takers on a version of the US bar exam to outperforming 90% of them.[34] In just three years, generative AI systems went from performing no better than random guesses on multi-subject reasoning tests, to outperforming expert humans, achieving scores on the 90th percentile across all subject areas.[35]

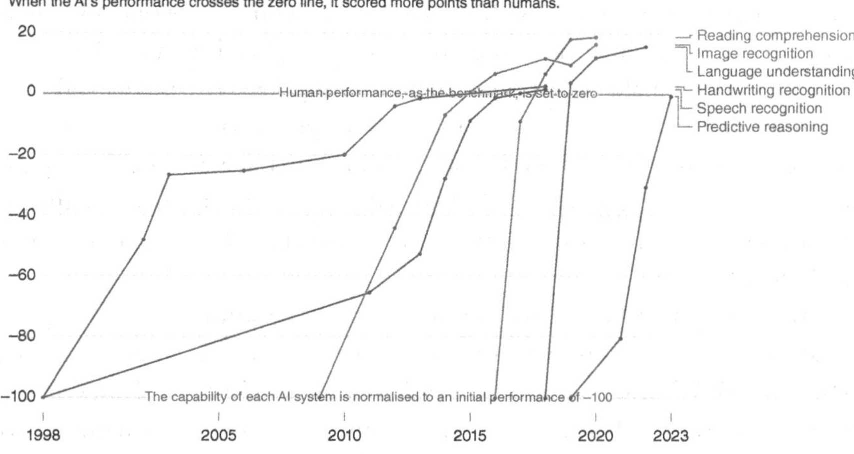

Figure 5.1   Rapid improvement of AI systems.

Source: Our World in Data, 'Test Scores of AI Capabilities Relative to Human Performance', 2024, https://ourworldindata.org/grapher/test-scores-ai-capabilities-relative-human-performance.

Looking ahead, AI will become exponentially more efficient, cost-effective, and capable, revolutionising numerous fields and significantly altering our lives in the process.[36] AI is becoming less of a tool and more an autonomous collaborator that will augment human intelligence, accelerate decision-making, and make nearly every corporate activity more predictive and less reactive.

AI's ability to autonomously refine and improve, without human input, will only accelerate this trajectory. As systems ingest ever larger datasets, their learning will compound, unlocking breakthroughs at an even greater pace.

In the coming decade, nearly every business will transform their core processes and operating models.[37] As corporations undergo deep structural and operational shifts to harness the power of AI, corporate legal departments will evolve alongside them, becoming more efficient, agile, and technology-enhanced. These shifts will profoundly change what GCs expect from their law firm and other partners.

Complementary Innovation

In addition to pervasiveness and rapid improvement, AI is catalysing waves of complementary innovations, that is, second and third-order inventions that emerge *around* a GPT, with effects that extend far beyond its initial applications.[38] Machine learning, deep learning, and natural language processing (a subfield of AI that enables computers to understand and communicate with human language) have given rise to automation, resource optimisation, and predictive decision-making across fields ranging from healthcare diagnostics and financial forecasting, to manufacturing and supply chains. And these advances are, in turn, unlocking other novel capabilities.[39]

AI is also improving R&D productivity. A Stanford study, leveraging company-level data from tens of thousands of firms across multiple sectors, found that R&D productivity has been getting costlier and slower across the US economy.[40] For example, the number of researchers required to double microchip density in 2020 was 18 times higher than in 1971. Qualitatively similar dynamics were found across many industries, ranging from biopharma to agriculture.[41]

AI can reverse this. A 2025 McKinsey study estimates that AI has the potential to speed up innovation cycles across sectors that account for 80%

of all large corporate R&D spending. In intellectual property (IP)-heavy industries, it could double the innovation rate, while in sectors that produce complex manufactured products, cycles could be accelerated by 20–80%. The size of the prize could be as high as $360 billion to $560 billion in annual incremental value from AI-accelerated innovation.[42]

In design, large language models (LLMs) and generative AI have increased the number of design candidates that companies can generate and evaluate, whether for three-dimensional store layouts, novel protein structures, or rocket-engine geometries.[43] AI-trained surrogate models called 'digital twins' can predict physical outcomes more efficiently than computationally intensive physics–based models, improving both the speed and scope of testing.

Beyond design, AI is transforming research by synthesising insights from large datasets, streamlining knowledge management, and collaborating with humans in ideation and concept development. In science, generative AI is identifying novel proteins and materials with desirable properties, paving the way for innovations that were previously unimaginable.[44]

Operating Models in the AI Era

AI-powered companies operate and compete in fundamentally different ways from traditional companies. Their core resource is data, which is continuously gathered, analysed, and acted on at scale by AI engines. Enterprise-wide data 'architectures' cut across and integrate virtually all operating processes. Human and organisational bottlenecks are removed from critical workflows, allowing algorithms and software to execute critical tasks autonomously. This allows humans to focus on designing, refining, and supervising the system while enabling the business to scale at a marginal cost that is close to zero.[45]

This model removes traditional constraints on scale, scope, and learning, allowing companies to grow faster, adapt more rapidly, and capture more value.

Disrupting Traditional Models

Companies generate value through their *business models* (which define how they capture and create value) and their *operating models* (which define how they deliver that value to customers). AI-driven companies have disrupted both, with perhaps the most interesting aspect for our purposes being how they change operating models and, in particular, the effects on scale, scope, and learning.

Business Models: Decoupling Creation and Capture   A business model articulates a company's strategy—how it creates value for customers and how it captures some of that value for itself. Traditionally, both have been largely centred on the customer.[46] To create value, firms traditionally provide products or services that address a customer's specific needs, while differentiating themselves by offering attractive features along dimensions such as cost, quality, or brand. In traditional firms, value is primarily captured through pricing strategies (premium prices, discounts, licences, etc.).

For instance, a budget airline creates value by solving a customer's transportation needs, differentiating itself from its competitors by offering 'value-for-money' in an economy-class setting, while an airline seeking to capture business travellers might offer a premium experience in a business-class setting.[47] Value is captured in both cases from customers via price points that align with each offering.

In digital companies, however, value creation and capture can be more flexibly recombined in various ways across different stakeholders. For example, Facebook might create value for its users but provide the product at no cost to them, capturing value instead from advertisers and other stakeholders in its ecosystem. While traditional companies certainly also innovate their business models, digital businesses can do so faster and at greater scale.[48]

Operating Models: Scale, Scope, and Learning   If the business model is the firm's blueprint for how to create and capture value, the operating model is its plan for translating that blueprint into operational reality by defining the organisational structures, processes, technologies, and other resources needed to deliver it.[49]

While operating models can be complex, their primary purpose is to allow firms to deliver value *at scale* (reaching as many customers as possible at the lowest cost), extend *scope* (offering an optimal range of products or services), and adapt to change through continuous *learning* (essential in a rapidly changing world).[50]

These three levers have driven corporate success long before the AI era. Indeed, large corporations emerged in the wake of the transportation and production advances of the Industrial Revolution precisely to exploit the resulting economies of scale and scope.[51] Walmart has leveraged the power of scale, with its large store network and efficient supply chain, to achieve cost leadership and competitive pricing. General Electric's diversification into numerous industrial sectors with a wide range of products and services exemplified the power of scope. And Toyota's adoption of the *Kaizen* philosophy of continuous improvement allowed it to set benchmarks for efficiency and quality.[52]

The Limits of the Analogue Operating Model

Despite their demonstrated successes, there are limits to how far traditional operating models can expand before complexity sets in. As we saw in Chapter 2, the pre-digital MNCs of GC 1.0 developed hierarchical and siloed operating models to manage this complexity. As they expanded geographically and broadened their scopes, their operating models evolved. The multidivisional administrative model of the 1950s and 1960s granted substantial autonomy to each operating unit, while professionalised bureaucracies imposed corporate hierarchies along functional lines.[53] While perfectly evolved for their time, this pre-digital model now imposes a ceiling on growth.

As Iansiti and Lakhani have observed:

Think of the long lines in your favorite retail store when there are too many customers, or the confusion that emerges when a rapidly growing firm hires too many new employees, or the quality problems that plague a manufacturing plant when demands for capacity or product variety are increased. Ultimately, complexity becomes the downfall of traditional organizations, increasing operational costs and decreasing service levels.[54]

Beyond a certain point, diseconomies of scale set in, and size and complexity conspire with localised decision-making, isolated data, and technology pockets to prevent effective communication and coordination.[55]

Benefits of AI Models

In contrast, AI-centric models eliminate these constraints. In fact, the more digitised a firm becomes, the greater its potential for scale, scope, and learning (see Figure 5.2). For instance, Amazon's digital systems not only continue to scale and improve despite the size and complexity of the company, they actually improve the more consumers use them.[56]

Digital operating models minimise direct human involvement across critical product and service delivery workflows, where technology is often better placed to act efficiently and at scale. Instead, people are redeployed to roles where they add the most value, including architecting systems, setting objectives, and establishing governance and ethical guardrails.[57]

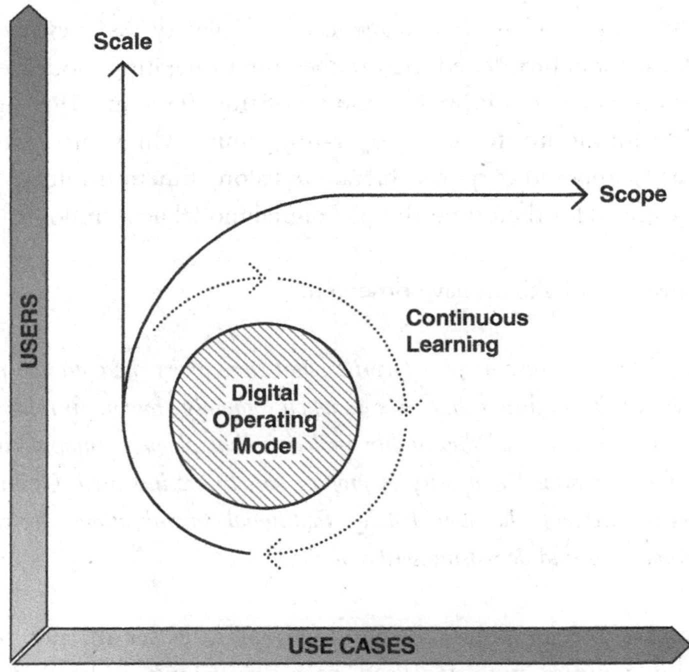

Figure 5.2   Scale, scope, and learning in digital operating models.

Source: Illustration by Logica Design.

Economies of Scale

By removing human and organisational bottlenecks, AI models can scale with minimal incremental cost.[58] In digital models, the incremental cost of serving one additional customer is negligible once the core infrastructure (including the technology stack, design, programming, and servers) is in place. Additionally, the more users a digital platform attracts, the more valuable it becomes, attracting ever more users, which in turn makes the model even more valuable, accelerating its growth further.

As Lauren Landry has noted, 'Etsy and eBay offer vastly more value to users if one million, instead of 100, sellers use their platforms. Uber and Lyft provide greater convenience and reliability to riders when more drivers join their platforms. When it comes to social media sites, users find the channels more interesting and varied as more people sign up'.[59]

These network effects, together with the near-limitless ability of digital systems to scale, give rise to a winner-takes-most dynamic for the largest business.[60]

Netflix SaaS (Software-as-a-Service) platforms, such as Netflix, are good examples of this scalability effect. The company's initial investments in content production and *streaming* technology were substantial. However, the platform now operates globally with minimal marginal cost. Adding millions of additional users requires no significant additional resources, which allows them to scale geographically almost without limit.[61]

Though the competition does seem to now be catching up with Netflix, this dynamic has been profoundly disruptive for traditional businesses which, by contrast, must add ever greater resources to manage increased volume and complexity.

Economies of Scope

AI models can also drive economies of scope well beyond what traditional companies can handle. Digital platforms are inherently modular: their core capabilities, including APIs and data layers, allow them to seamlessly and at limited cost connect dissimilar products, services, and stakeholders together.

Apple For example, Apple's digital ecosystem integrates hardware, software, and services, including devices, iCloud, Apple Music, and the

App Store, into an integrated whole. User data feeds customisation, recommendations, and other features that increase the system's overall value. This creates a flywheel effect: once customers enter the Apple ecosystem, they become more likely to use other Apple products and services, which boosts loyalty, retention, and network effects. Google, Microsoft, Amazon, and Meta exhibit similar dynamics.

Learning

Digital companies also learn and innovate faster than their traditional competitors. Whether it's generating customer insights from user data, identifying patterns in scientific research, or improving workflows, insights can be generated immediately and applied rapidly across their ecosystems at speed.

Tesla   Tesla provides a case in point. With over five million connected Tesla vehicles on the road, driving a collective 50 billion miles per year (more than 100,000 miles per minute), the company benefits from an enormous feedback loop.[62] Each car collects real-world data through eight cameras that provide 360° coverage. That data is transmitted back to Tesla, where a system of 48 neural networks converts two-dimensional images into three-dimensional spatial maps. The system ingests more than 1.5 petabytes of fleet data per training cycle, which it uses to improve autonomously.[63]

This approach powers Tesla's Full Self Driving (FSD) system. The end-to-end neural network is self-taught: it learns what objects are and how to respond to them based on actual human behaviour, enabling it to read social driving cues, navigate complex construction zones, and make judgements that would normally require thousands of lines of code to approximate poorly.[64]

Tesla also pushes updates back out via its Over-the-Air (OTA) delivery, providing upgrades and patches that benefit the fleet. Unlike traditional automakers, which require drivers to go to a dealer or service centre for upgrades, OTA wirelessly and seamlessly updates every vehicle in Tesla's fleet. These patches enhance safety, extend battery range, and add new features. OTA also allows the company to remotely diagnose and analyse vehicle performance, enabling owners to pre-emptively address issues. It can also personalise its updates, taking into account each vehicle's configuration and owner preferences.[65]

Since 2020, 37% of Tesla's recalls have been resolved through OTA updates, which is well above industry norms. While traditional recalls achieve an average compliance rate of 70%, with older vehicles falling below 50%, Tesla's approach ensures near-total coverage at minimal cost.[66]

Digital Eats Analogue for Breakfast

These dynamics make it very difficult for traditional companies to compete with digital models. Traditional firms lack the infrastructure to scale at low marginal cost and they are unable to seamlessly bundle dissimilar products and services.

Consider Netflix: in 2024 it had 14,000 employees who supported 302 million customers in over 190 countries around the globe (21,571 users per employee). By contrast, Comcast employed 182,000 people to serve just 32 million US accounts (160 customers per employee).[67]

The performance gap is real and growing. A recent McKinsey study found that companies with leading digital and AI capabilities outperformed digital laggards by two to six times on total shareholder returns (TSR) across more than 1,000 companies and multiple sectors.[68] The digital maturity gap between the top and bottom performers is not static; it widened by 60% between 2016–19 and 2020–22.[69]

Over time, this gap has a compounding effect on performance, and laggards fall ever further behind. By rewiring their organisations to put digital and AI at the core, digital leaders can rapidly identify weaknesses in their operating models, design effective digital solutions, and drive enterprise-wide adoption. That allows these companies to consistently identify value faster, pursue it more effectively, and capture a greater share of it—over and over again.[70] This flywheel effect will only increase as technology improves.

Consequently, an increasing number of companies are digitally transforming. In a 2024 survey of 1,000 senior executives across 20 industries and 59 countries, BCG found that the share of firms experimenting with AI grew from 47% in 2023 to 98% in 2024.[71]

How precisely companies are structuring themselves for the AI era and how that is impacting their legal departments is what we will turn to in the next two chapters.

6 | GC 4.0—The AI Factory

AI will change the way we work and run our businesses in the
same way that the introduction of the internet did.

—Richard Potter[1]

In Chapter 5 we saw how AI can impact competition because of digital
operating models, which scale, scope, and learn in ways that traditional
companies cannot. We also noted how the outperformance of AI operating
models has driven most traditional companies to begin their digital
transformations. In this chapter, we will look more closely at what that
transformation involves at the enterprise level.

The AI Factory

Digital companies are structured differently from traditional ones. Some
digital companies, such as Facebook or Google, sell information. Others, like
Amazon or eBay, also sell physical goods. Underneath their hoods, however,
digitally native companies all have a common operating architecture. It is
one that Harvard Business School professors Marco Iansiti and Karim R.
Lakhani have termed the 'AI factory' in their seminal work, *Competing in the*

Age of AI: Strategy and Leadership When Algorithms and Networks Run the World.[2] The AI factory is the model traditional companies must aspire to if they want to transform and compete in the AI era.

AI factories contain a self-reinforcing logic: data is collected and used to train algorithms. The algorithms identify patterns in the data, which they use to make 'predictions' (i.e., informed guesses) about future outcomes, such as sales performance. Those predictions are then tested in a controlled environment and the outcomes are fed back into the system. In this way, the algorithms learn from the tests and refine their predictions. The predictions get better over time as these activities are continuously conducted.[3] This constant dynamic of data-based predictions, testing, and refinement allows digital models to scale at an exponential rate and improve on a continuous basis.[4]

Over time, as the AI factory improves, a growing amount of the work that was previously done by humans can be delegated to AI systems.

As Iansiti and Lakhani have observed:

> *No human auctioneer gets involved in the millions of daily search-ad auctions at Google or Baidu. Dispatchers do not decide which car is chosen on DiDi, Grab, Lyft, or Uber. Sports retailers do not set daily prices on golf apparel at Amazon. Bankers do not approve every loan at Ant Financial. Instead, these processes are digitised and enabled by an AI factory that treats decision making as an industrial process.*[5]

As we will see in Chapter 7, a similar dynamic of increasing automation to unlock scale, scope, and learning advantages will also reshape legal departments and other support functions within AI-enabled companies.

How Are AI Factories Set Up?

AI factories have *data pipelines* that collect, sort, protect, and integrate incoming information so that it can be used by the factory's AI models.[6] For example, Amazon's data pipeline gathers enormous amounts of customer data, including browsing histories and purchasing patterns so that its models can predict customer preferences and create personalised recommendations.[7] Having a clean and well-organised data foundation is critical because the outputs of the AI factory will only be as good as the inputs it uses (i.e., the 'garbage in, garbage out' principle).[8]

Once the pipelines have organised the data, *algorithms* analyse them to generate predictions about various actions that the company might take to improve business outcomes.[9] The algorithms must be carefully selected and configured to fit the type of data being collected and the kinds of predictions the system is intended to generate.[10] Tesla's algorithms, for example, are designed to analyse inputs from its global vehicle fleet in order to improve safety and efficiency.[11]

Next, the AI factories' *experimentation platforms* run controlled experiments to test, iterate, and improve upon the predictions that the algorithms make.[12] These platforms basically enable an AI factory to validate the algorithm's predictions and make them as effective as possible.[13] Platform experiments might, for example, compare two versions of a webpage by showing users these versions at random and then using statistical analysis to conclude which one was most effective.[14]

Underlying all of this is foundational *software infrastructure* that connects users and makes the data pipeline, algorithms, and experimentation platforms work effectively. This software layer links everything together.[15] Without it, outputs would be sub-optimal. For example, insufficient infrastructure makes it hard to manage data processing at scale, resulting in inaccurate predictions.

This happened with Netflix. In its early years, the company had already developed powerful predictive algorithms. However, it lacked the software capacity to process large datasets at scale, resulting in poor user recommendations that negatively impacted customer experience. To address that challenge, Netflix invested significantly in Cloud-based infrastructure, which enabled it to more efficiently process data at scale. The result was a significant improvement in its recommendation accuracy, which enhanced user experience and boosted retention rates relative to competitors.[16]

The AI Factory Journey

Building an AI factory is an iterative effort. It takes both time and resources and requires a company to have the will to undertake substantial change. This is especially true in the later stages.

According to Iansiti and Lakhani, companies typically progress through four stages on their way to becoming AI factories (see Figure 6.1).

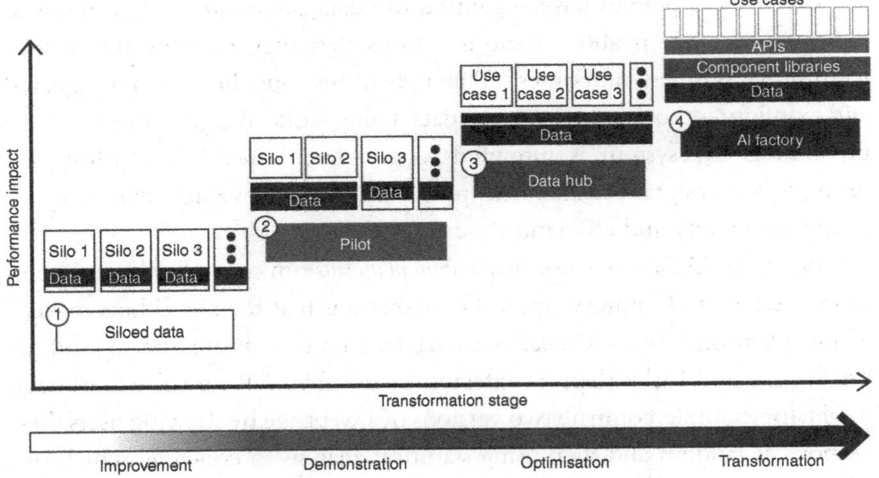

Figure 6.1   Four stages of digital operating model transformation.

Source: Marco Iansiti and Karim R. Lakhani, *Competing in the Age of AI: Strategy and Leadership When Algorithms and Networks Run the World,* Harvard Business Review Press, 2020.

Stage 1 is the starting point. This stage is emblematic of pre-digital MNCs. Data is fragmented and stored in isolated siloes inside autonomous or semi-autonomous corporate units. Often, these siloes have been haphazardly assembled, making it difficult and expensive to use the data for any enterprise-wide purpose. This problem can be compounded if, as is often the case, each unit uses highly customised and incompatible legacy IT systems.[17]

Stage 1 structures were well suited to GC 1.0 MNCs. In pre-digital environments, specialisation and autonomy drove productivity and innovation. But in the AI era, fragmented data architectures are anathema because they inhibit scale, scope, and learning, making it difficult to connect information across siloes or integrate it with broader datasets outside the company. They also make it nearly impossible to generate holistic customer insights that draw upon cross-enterprise information.[18] In an environment in which digitised competitors leverage holistic insights to outpace rivals, such inefficiency can be fatal, giving Stage 1 organisations a powerful incentive to change.

Stage 2 is the first step in the transformation journey. Companies usually 'dip a toe in the water' by launching a pilot project to combine and organise data from across several siloes into one repository. The pilot, which unlocks new applications and operational efficiencies, proves the value of analytics-based decision-making. The pilots, often carried out by consultants, are relatively easy to undertake as they involve low investment levels and little in the way of organisational change.[19]

Stage 3 is where the rubber meets the road. To reap organisation-wide benefits at greater scale, companies must expand beyond limited pilots and create larger 'data hubs' that aggregate and organise data from across many parts of the organisation. Achieving this can be expensive, as well as technically and organisationally complicated. It requires the company to restructure many existing processes and systems, which can disrupt operations.[20] MNCs often start their Stage 3 journey by setting up a hub for their data science and analytics teams. This hub can then be deployed in a 'hub-and-spoke' fashion across a large number of enterprise-wide applications, products, and business units.[21] Additional hubs can then gradually be built off the back of these initial efforts.

In **Stage 4**, the company has built an 'AI factory', a company-wide, AI-powered operating model, centred around a 'platform' (an integrated foundation of data, algorithms, and software). This model allows the company to bring together information from across the business, learn continuously, create new products and services, and improve how it operates. With these capabilities, the company can grow and scale far more efficiently, adding new users and services at minimal marginal cost.

Moreover, because platforms are designed to be modular, they can easily connect internal systems with outside networks, allowing the company to tap into ideas and value from partners and providers. As automation matures, humans spend less time on routine execution and more time focusing on higher-value work, such as designing, governing, and improving the platform, making it even more effective over time.[22]

Getting from Stage 3 to Stage 4 requires more organisational change and material levels of investment. In Stage 4, companies also must put in place more comprehensive policies and solid governance to ensure the system they are building is secure and run in accordance with legal and ethical requirements. An additional hurdle at this point is ensuring the trustworthiness of the underlying data. The GC 4.0 legal department has a large role to play in this transformation. However, the journey from Stage 3 to Stage 4 can be less challenging than the journey from Stage 2 to Stage 3 because, by Stage 3, the company has in place many of the foundations needed for Stage 4.[23]

AI Factories in the GC 4.0 Era

Iansiti and Lakhani introduced the concept of the AI factory in 2020. Many new variables have arisen in the years since that they were not able to take account of, including the COVID-19 pandemic, generative and agentic AI systems, and regulatory, geopolitical, and ethical developments.

However, none of these events have weakened the central logic of the AI factory model (i.e., that digital platforms remove constraints on scale, scope, and learning). However, as GC 4.0 MNCs build their AI factories they must consider and navigate a range of new expectations and demands, many of which were less mission critical than they were at the time Iansiti and Lakhani were writing. We will consider some of these in turn below.

COVID-19

While the COVID-19 pandemic was highly disruptive, it also validated the power of digital models for both digitally native and traditional companies. If anything, it made the need to transform from Stage 1 to Stage 4 even more urgent and compelling.

During the lockdowns, digital companies such as Zoom, Amazon, and Microsoft rapidly scaled and expanded their scopes.[24] But the crisis also showed how traditional firms were able to re-engineer their operating models and leverage digital platforms over relatively short timeframes. During the pandemic, traditional companies such as Target, Starbucks, Home Depot, and IKEA quickly developed 'hybrid' models that integrated digital platforms with legacy physical assets to generate new competitive moats.[25]

At first, companies with large physical stores and warehouse footprints seemed to be at a disadvantage given the costs and overheads they incurred. However, as they moved from Stages 1 or 2 to Stage 3, many legacy companies were able to transform their properties into fulfilment centres or 'final mile' delivery points for customers who purchased products online via newly refurbished digital storefronts. Each digital transaction and at-store delivery generated real-time localised data on market conditions, trends, and customer preferences. As they rapidly digitised, legacy companies fed this data into their new platforms, generating learnings that they leveraged to increase scale and scope and improve value chains, customer experience, and response times.

Many legacy companies consolidated and further developed these hybrid strategies long after the pandemic ended, giving them strong competitive moats versus digital-only companies.

Walmart   Walmart is a case in point. Founded in 1962, it is the world's largest company in both revenue terms ($680 billion in 2024) and employees (2.1 million), accounting for 10% of all US retail spending, excluding cars, and 25% of all grocery purchases.[26]

To compete with Amazon and other digital-native retailers during COVID-19, the company thoroughly re-engineered its operating model, building a digital and AI-enabled foundation, and replacing its fragmented IT systems with an integrated, Cloud-based architecture.[27]

Walmart adopted an 'omnichannel' strategy, integrating physical stores with a powerful and scalable e-commerce platform.[28] The strategy allows Walmart to play to its strengths as a brick-and-mortar retailer (over 10,500 stores globally, of which nearly 5,000 are in the United States, with 90% of Americans living within 16 km of one), while leveraging powerful digital platforms to capture and use customer data to scale, scope, and learn as if it were a digital native.[29]

One of the core elements of this strategy involved leveraging the company's 'click-and-collect' service, in which customers can browse and order online and pick their items up in Walmart's physical stores—or vice versa. Customers find this to be convenient as it allows them to receive their orders more quickly while also avoiding delivery fees. As its digital footprint has expanded, Walmart also began operating a digital third-party marketplace that now offers hundreds of millions of products. It earns a reported 12% commission on sales, and merchants who use the company's logistics network pay Walmart an additional 8% on such sales.[30]

The stores, which carry up to 120,000 items, now serve three functions: they are retail outlets for in-store purchases; they are fulfilment centres for the delivery of online purchases; and they are data hubs that generate powerful insights about Walmart's in-store and online customers.[31]

The data is fed into the company's Cloud-based machine learning platform, giving it real-time insights into local demand, in-store behaviour, and inventory movements.[32] Its platform allows it to run targeted campaigns and learn in real time, which in turn gives it the ability to better personalise the shopping experience and improve operational efficiency.[33] This physical–digital combination is hard for pure digital retailers to replicate at scale.[34] As fintech platform *AI Invest* has noted, 'Together, these tools form a "data flywheel": Walmart's 10,500 stores and 250 million weekly shoppers generate vast datasets, which refine AI models, which in turn enhance customer experience and operational efficiency, generating even more data'.[35]

The strategy has also yielded significant financial upsides. Walmart's online sales are growing at 20% a year, and its 2025 market capitalisation is $750 billion, up by 50% in just one year. Its price-to-earnings ratio exceeds Alphabet, Amazon, Apple, Meta, and Microsoft.[36] In February 2026, Walmart's market capitalisation crossed the $1 trillion threshold, making it the first traditional retailer to hit that milestone.[37] The strategy has also opened new revenue streams, including delivery subscription, which doubled in size between 2019 and 2024.[38]

Generative and Agentic AI

Generative and agentic AI applications had not yet emerged on a large scale when the AI factory was conceptualised. Far from impairing its logic, however, these new tools reinforced it.

Generative AI can create content, including software code and marketing designs, allowing AI factories to go beyond prediction-making and expanding the range of activities that AI factories can engage in.[39] This range will likely further increase as generative AI systems evolve.[40]

Agentic AI systems add to this new array of capabilities; they can actively pursue specific goals, learn from their environments, adapt to new information, and iteratively improve upon their own output.[41]

This speeds up learning and feedback loops by reducing the need for human oversight.[42] Walmart, for instance, uses agentic AI tools to carry out a broad array of tasks, ranging from real-time sales information and highly precise workflows to helping customers find products or create personalised experiences. Agents also help streamline supplier onboarding, automate advertising campaigns, and improve internal innovation efforts.[43]

The combination of generative and agentic systems reinforces the AI factory model even further because they complement each other. For instance, generative AI makes agentic AI systems more effective by adding natural language interfaces that ease communication with human users. Other AI technologies, such as predictive, vision, and conversational models, will likely further accelerate the efficacy of these tools in ways that benefit AI factories.[44]

Humans in the Loop

In the years since Iansiti and Lakhani wrote about the AI factory, the debate over how labour should be divided between humans and machines has grown substantially. Companies must factor this in to a greater extent today than was the case in 2020.

The debate began as a narrower discussion about 'humans in the loop' in the machine learning and AI system design contexts. However, as generative and agentic AI systems have emerged, the debate has broadened. Where should human oversight begin and end? Where should humans execute and where should they only supervise? What roles should people play in developing systems, setting objectives, or establishing legal, ethical, and governance frameworks?[45]

These questions become increasingly important as technology continues to improve. Regardless of where the touchpoints end up getting established, companies are under growing pressure to set controls and clear lines of accountability. Norms could, however, emerge that give MNCs widely recognised parameters that they can leverage as they digitise.

Regulatory, Geopolitical, and Ethical Dimensions

The AI regulatory landscape has expanded in recent years. Unfortunately, it is also unstable and uncoordinated, which makes it hard for companies to understand what the rules are, let alone comply with them.[46] While the landscape has broadly shifted from 'soft law' to more binding regimes, there is no consensus on standards, and rules in major markets keep shifting. Moreover, there is a lack of clear and consistent definitions.[47] As companies digitally transform, they need to monitor these areas and 'navigate the grey' in real time, imposing increased risks on the business and placing additional burdens on the legal and compliance teams.

Geopolitical tensions have also grown, and AI is now viewed in many countries as a strategic national asset. The United States, China, and the European Union have all imposed ever-greater restrictions on the export of data and technology, and cross-border AI investments are coming under growing scrutiny. This restricts how and where companies can collect, store, and deploy data, which can disrupt their learning loops and force them to maintain data siloes. This, too, is a rich new source of work for GC 4.0 legal teams.

Finally, ethical concerns have also intensified. Certain themes keep coming up, including *fairness and bias* (ensuring systems and datasets don't discriminate);[48] *transparency* (ensuring clarity on how models work, what data they use, and how outputs are generated); *privacy and security* (ensuring that personal and sensitive information is secure and not misused); *safety* (ensuring that systems are safe to use); and *environmental* (minimising energy and other resource usage and embedding sustainable practices).[49] Other concerns include the impact AI systems will have on employment, and minimising the impact they have on political and social polarisation, and income inequality.

Companies are under growing pressure to recognise that digital operating models are more than just technical constructs. To gain social licence—the implicit public trust and acceptance needed to operate responsibly—companies must take into account the social context of their AI systems, including the impact they can have on stakeholders, institutions, cultures, norms, and spaces.[50] All of this, too, is further 'grist in the mill' for the GC 4.0 legal team.

How Are Traditional MNCs Transforming?

For legacy companies, digital transformation is no longer optional in the GC 4.0 era, as failure to act now risks leaving them at a profound competitive disadvantage.[51] Virtually all MNCs are now transforming, with roughly 90% in various stages of the transformation journey.[52]

However, the level of structural and operational changes needed to achieve Stage 4 are significant. Success requires rethinking strategy, systems, synchronisation, and stewardship.[53] AI investments must be aligned with a coherent and enterprise-wide strategy, supported by modular, interoperable platforms and robust data ecosystems. Leaders must synchronise data and systems, redesign processes, reconfigure roles and teams, and prepare people for AI-enabled ways of working, all while ensuring that proper governance, including transparency and compliance, gets embedded into every initiative.[54]

These are heavy lifts, and many organisations remain in the foothills. One recent survey found that although every company is racing to adapt, many remain constrained by challenges across these imperatives, while only a few have achieved enterprise-wide AI integration.[55]

A complementary MIT survey placed companies on a four-stage continuum:

- 18% were AI future ready (Stage 4);
- 46% are developing AI ways of working (Stage 3);
- 23% are still building pilots and capabilities (Stage 2); and
- 13% are still experimenting and preparing (Stage 1).[56]

Since 2022, companies have continued to advance across this continuum, with a growing proportion moving into the higher stages of AI maturity.[57]

It is normal for transformational technologies to take time to embed at scale. It took approximately 30 years for electricity to become the dominant power source in American factories.[58] The Internet emerged in the 1970s, but it didn't disrupt business models until the 2000s.[59] While some claim AI is the most rapidly adopted technology in history, it will also take time for AI to embed itself in companies.[60] Infrastructure and processes are hard to change and some companies are only now coming to terms with the transformational challenges AI will require.

As Paul Hlivko observes:

Too many enterprises assume foundation models will deliver value out of the box. But without serious investment in the hard stuff—applications, integration, data infrastructure, workflow redesign and change management—AI remains a flashy prototype: impressive in demos, but ineffective at scale. Ironically, the companies that win will be the ones that make AI boring: seamlessly embedded, consistently reliable, and quietly transformative where the real work happens.[61]

However, the direction of travel is unmistakable. The gap between leaders and laggards is growing, but over time all companies will restructure around AI. Even in the most traditional industries, it is already transforming businesses.

John Deere

John Deere provides an illustrative case in point. John Deere, which was founded in 1837, is the world's largest agricultural equipment manufacturer. In 2019, it began rolling out a digital operating model that has transformed it from being a traditional equipment manufacturer into being a platform company that operates in equipment, data, and services.[62]

Equipment as a Platform Enabler At the heart of the company's digital strategy are intelligent machines. Its tractors and combines contain sophisticated technology stacks, including lidar, radar, and advanced camera systems, that enable them to perceive their environments, navigate terrain, and precisely execute real-time tasks.[63] As Lane Arthur, John Deere's Vice President of Data, Applications & Analytics, explains:

> *On combines, we have a camera that has a machine learning app. As the grain is going through the chute [during harvest], we're making rapid, real-time adjustments to the quality of that stream, and changing fan speed and other things so that we collect the most grain possible. That's the kind of technology that we've moved into over time. We're doing this on every one of our machines.[64]*

The machines (some of which are autonomous) act as 'sensors on wheels' that send geolocated data to the company's Operations Centre, where the information is processed by machine learning tools and regularly transmitted back to both the machines and the farmers. Insights pushed to machines help them improve on the ground, including weeding and spraying pesticides more effectively.[65] The company also transmits software upgrades 'over the air' directly to the machines.[66] Farmers get bespoke advice and insights from the Operations Centre via smartphone applications, helping them run their farms more efficiently.[67]

Through this digital transformation, John Deere has created a self-reinforcing data flywheel and a formidable moat. As of 2024, more than 500,000 machines were connected to the company's network, with a target of 1.5 million by 2026.[68]

By integrating hardware, software, and services, the company delivers tangible benefits to customers while also diversifying its business model, which now includes a recurring revenue stream based on software, data, and analytics.[69] John Deere's transformation shows how traditional companies can make the transition to embedding platforms at their core, reaping the benefits of an AI factory model.

The AI factory journey is not just profoundly changing the structure and operations of MNCs. It is also changing enabling functions, including legal departments, which is what we will now turn to.

7 | GC 4.0—The AI Era Legal Department

> To succeed in the AI era, legal departments must fundamentally redesign how they deliver legal services, calibrate risk, and drive impact for the businesses they serve.
>
> —Áine Lyons, VP & Deputy General Counsel:
> Global Legal Services & Strategy, Workday[1]

As we have seen, the AI era is profoundly reshaping how corporations are structured and operate. Consequently, business model innovation is the number one challenge for CEOs.[2] Boards are also getting involved, with investors pushing for more formalised AI oversight, with many expecting regular updates from the executive on digital transformation.[3]

As corporations digitise ever more corporate activities and processes, support functions are also modifying their structures and service-delivery models.[4] This is not just because CEOs and boards are pressuring them to do so. The main reason is that GC 3.0 era approaches cannot effectively deliver services in a GC 4.0 era environment.

If one function digitises while another does not, structural mismatches ensue. A GC 3.0 marketing team, for instance, might have produced two or three versions of a marketing plan for the legal department to review. In the GC 4.0 environment, that same team can generate dozens or even hundreds of variations of that plan. At the same time, the accelerated pace of business in the AI era has compressed turnaround expectations. Where the legal team might once have had weeks to review drafts, it may now only have days. A GC relying only on traditional human resources alone will quickly feel the squeeze of the more-for-less challenge. Costs and headcount will rise while output and quality decline.[5] In this new environment, it is simply not possible to keep pace without digital transformation, and those unable to evolve will be replaced by those who can.

Scale, Scope, and Learning

As we saw in Chapter 5, digital operating models allow firms to deliver value in three powerful ways: by achieving *scale* (reaching more customers at lower cost), extending *scope* (offering a wide range of products or services), and accelerating *learning* (continuously improving through data and feedback).

AI-enabled support functions, including legal departments, can also harness these same effects to transform how they operate. As in-house legal teams adapt to the digital transformations reshaping their companies, they too will begin to exhibit the scale, scope, and learning dynamics that define digital platforms. The sections that follow examine how these forces are reshaping the legal department's service delivery model.

Scale—Expanding Capacity Without Increasing Resources

Once workflows are digitised and AI-enabled, legal departments can handle significantly greater client and document volumes at dramatically lower cost. Scale in this context involves the ability to extend the department's capacity and reach without a corresponding increase in costs. When routine activities, such as document review, drafting, and analysis, get automated, human lawyers can be redeployed to higher-value work where judgement, strategic insight, and oversight are needed.

JP Morgan—COIN and Katana Lens JP Morgan Chase provides a case in point. To manage its growing volume of complex legal and financial contracts, the company developed an AI-enabled contract intelligence platform called *COIN* (short for contract intelligence) that extracts key clauses, interprets terms, spots risks, and standardises language.[6] The bank also launched *Katana Lens*, an AI-enabled risk management platform that draws from a centralised data lake containing more than 800 sources, ranging from trading positions and client onboarding data to sanctions checks.[7] Katana Lens analyses aggregated datasets, detects patterns and anomalies, and instantly highlights emerging risks for human review.[8]

The impact was transformative. COIN reduced contract review time from roughly 360,000 hours per year to mere seconds.[9] The platform processes over 12,000 commercial credit agreements *per second*, with an error rate of just 1%, saving the company $150 million in fraud losses in its first year alone.[10] Regulatory compliance and risk assessment have also improved.[11]

Beyond these immediate gains, COIN became a springboard for broader AI adoption across JP Morgan's legal and compliance functions, freeing the legal team to focus on higher-value tasks, including negotiation strategies and providing complex advisory work, rather than routine document tasks.[12]

Meanwhile, Katana Lens improved productivity by 25% even as the risk team's workload grew by 35%. This allowed the team to redeploy 150 full-time employees to frontline roles without adding headcount. Risk detection also improved significantly, resulting in 42% fewer risk-related losses and generating over $500 million in annual savings, while regulatory compliance strengthened through continuous monitoring of more than 600,000 new regulatory changes each year.[13]

Scope—Extending Reach Across the Enterprise

While scale in a digital model increases the legal department's capacity to handle more work with the same or fewer resources, the *scope* dynamic expands the range of problems it can tackle and the ways it can benefit the work being conducted across other functions. In AI-enabled organisations, data generated in one support function (e.g., the legal department) can often be reused or repurposed elsewhere in the company by another support function (e.g., the finance or HR teams), which multiplies the value of the data across the enterprise.

One example of this involves ESG data. Traditional ESG evaluations were manually generated and the data collected was difficult for other functions to access. AI-enabled ESG tools, by contrast, can aggregate data in ways that are accessible enterprise-wide. The data collected is broad-based and can include geopolitical and regulatory updates, industry trends, supplier reports, and audits, as well as social media posts, sensor data, and third-party assessments.[14]

This information is useful not only for the ESG team. Compliance and legal departments can use it to quickly detect or predict regulatory or governance risks, while the procurement functions can leverage it to make data-driven sourcing decisions or identify procurement-related violations.[15]

Honeywell presents another example of the benefit of extended scope. The company is integrating department-specific and previously siloed data from across its invoicing, customer, and contract management systems to generate greater efficiency. As Barbara Rogers, Honeywell's Vice President, Legal Operations, Strategy and Transformation explained, previously 'somebody would have to take a purchase order or an invoice and go back into the [contract management] system and see if they could figure out what contract it was related to'. Now, with streamlined terms and interconnected systems, contract negotiation and signing times have been cut by several days and are expected to fall by as much as five over time. Conservatively, these improvements could free between $10 and $50 million in working capital.[16]

Learning—Continuous Improvement Through Feedback Loops

AI-enabled support functions also benefit from continuous learning loops. As new information comes in, AI systems add it to what they already know, taking both new and old information into account and updating their settings to adapt to the new environment.[17]

Examples include financial market prediction tools, which retrain to remain accurate; fraud detection tools, which learn and adapt to changing fraud behaviours; and customer support chatbots, which learn and respond to changing customer needs or new product information.[18] The ESG systems discussed immediately above also learn continuously.[19] JP Morgan's COIN also continuously improves, training itself with new data and expanding its range of activities.[20]

Humans in the Loop

Much like AI factories, enabling functions are moving humans out of critical paths to leverage scale, scope, and learning benefits. In the marketing context, for example, many companies are fully automating certain types of decisions and taking humans out of the loop entirely. In repetitive, high-speed decisions, such as those needed for programmatic ad buying (i.e., where digital ads are displayed almost immediately to users), full autonomy is essential because numerous decisions, including matching users, bids, and content, must occur at great scale within milliseconds. Other cases, such as whether to continue with an advertising campaign or go with a specific commercial, may require hybrid decision-making or full human input.[21]

GC 4.0 legal departments are also evaluating where to keep humans in and out of the loop. In some cases, full autonomy can radically improve outcomes. Fully automated legal invoicing tools, for example, significantly outperform human experts across every metric: they are more accurate (up to 92% vs. 72%), faster (3.6 seconds vs. 194–316 seconds), and cheaper by a wide margin (99.97%).[22] In other cases, humans remain in the loop but are augmented by AI, generating significant performance gains. For example, by adopting hybrid approaches in the contract negotiation context, Iberdrola's legal department reduced negotiation and signing times by one-third.[23] Similarly, ASML's legal team increased task speeds by 15–20% by leveraging AI tools to support humans across a range of activities, from policy clarification and legal contracting to regulatory compliance and litigation assessment.[24]

The Changing Legal Department Landscape

The GC 3.0 legal department was a lighter, more multidisciplinary and cost-conscious version of GC 2.0. Teams of lawyers were organised into departments of *specialists* (legal or other experts who specialise in key areas of risk or activity, such as litigation, M&A, competition, compliance, etc.), *generalists* (who focus mainly on partnering with the business units), and *legal operations* (providing technology, process optimisation, vendor and budget management, and other organisation-wide solutions).[25] Technology, a growing part of the legal budget, was centred on core capabilities, such as contract and matter management, e-billing, e-discovery, and IP tools.[26]

GC 4.0 legal departments are evolving this model and adapting their service delivery approach as MNCs transform. And as in previous eras, these changes will have knock-on effects for law firms and other suppliers.

Central to the GC 4.0 model is technology, specifically AI. To scale, scope, and learn in tandem with the rest of the company, GC 4.0 legal departments are reconfiguring themselves and their operations around it. This shift also allows GCs and their teams to keep up with the two headline challenges discussed in Chapter 1: the evolution of risk and the more-for-less challenge.

The transformation to GC 4.0 models is already underway. By 2024, 95% of GCs reported their departments were engaging with generative AI, with 93% of them anticipating it would deliver value within 12 months.[27] Nearly 72% of legal operations professionals in that same year believed generative AI would become an essential part of the legal profession.[28]

Drawing on developments to date, we can tentatively sketch an outline of what GC 4.0 legal departments might look like in the near future.

GC 4.0 Organisational Architecture

As illustrated in Figure 7.1, the organisational architecture of the department is a layered pyramid. At the base is an expanded, multidisciplinary *legal operations team*. These professionals are accountable for selecting, integrating, and overseeing the technologies that make up the department's technology platform, in alignment with budgetary constraints and strategic objectives.

The *technology platform* is at the heart of the model. It is the engine that enables scale, scope, and learning, underpinning effective and rapid service delivery.

Above this foundation sits a team of *legal specialists*, organised around critical areas of risk and value. They draw on the platform's data, processes, and tools to provide deep expertise where and when it is most needed.

At the apex is an agile front end of market-facing *legal generalists*, embedded within fast-moving business teams. Supported by the specialists and

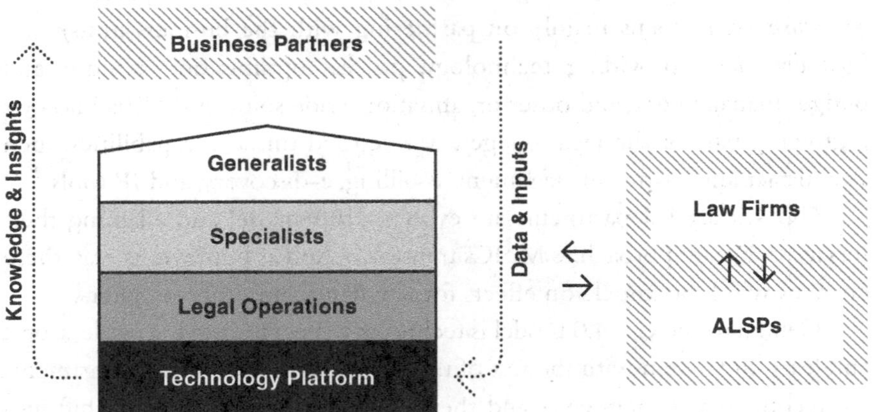

Figure 7.1   GC 4.0 legal department organisational architecture.
Source: Illustration by Logica Design.

empowered by the technology platform, they operate semi-autonomously, providing legal support to the business teams as they develop new use cases for the company's AI factory.

Legal Operations as the 'Engine Room'

The engine room of the GC 4.0 operating model is an expanded and more strategically orientated legal operations team. To deliver value in the GC 4.0 environment, this team will grow significantly in both scale and scope. This is already happening: 83% of legal operations professionals reported that they have benefitted from budget *increases* in the past year, with 81% expecting further increases to come.[29] Their responsibilities are also growing, and they are playing an increasingly strategic role.[30]

The GC 4.0 legal operations team comprises specialists across a range of disciplines, including strategy, technology, procurement, finance, process, design, training and development, analytics, and change management. This expansion is necessary to cover the team's growing mandate, which includes:

- Developing a technology strategy that dovetails with departmental objectives.
- Curating and structuring critical data.
- Identifying and overseeing emerging technologies.
- Designing service delivery models that embed technology into processes and capabilities.

The following tasks in particular are becoming increasingly critical components of the GC 4.0 legal operations team.

Technology Selection   Selecting the right legal technologies, already a complex endeavour, is set to get even more difficult. The legal technology market, which will reach $50 billion in value by 2027, is expanding rapidly, with generative AI accelerating this growth.[31] In an environment rife with hype, legal operations leaders cut through the noise and select relevant and effective tools that generate a sufficient return on investment. Tools must align with department strategy, be safe and easy to use, fit within budget, and address critical bottlenecks.

As expectations rise and budgets tighten, the focus will shift to making more deliberate and strategic investments that deliver measurable impact.[32]

Technology Integration   GC 4.0 legal operations teams are accountable for ensuring that legal technologies can seamlessly integrate across the department's technology stack and within the enterprise-wide estate. Integration simplifies operations, enhances collaboration, facilitates learning, and upskills individuals. Already a key task, this is likely to become ever more critical.[33]

Technology Adoption   Ensuring that new technology gets adopted by users is critical to strategic success. As PwC has observed, 'three quarters of digital transformations fail to generate returns that exceed the original investment, and of those that fail, 70% are due to a lack of user adoption and behavioural change'.[34] This is a major pain point today. A 2024 survey found that 58% of legal operations professionals struggled to implement new tools or resources because of a lack of leadership buy-in or team resistance. AI adoption governance is also surprisingly underdeveloped. Only 3% of AI tools currently being used by legal teams have been explicitly approved, and only 37% of organisations have policies in place for AI use. As the authors of the survey noted, 'These figures highlight a significant gap between the rapid advancement of AI technology and the governance structures needed to manage its use effectively and ethically. This disconnect exposes organizations to potential risks and liabilities, underscoring the urgent need for comprehensive AI policies and approval processes'.

Clearly, as technology becomes even more central to department strategy, GCs must empower legal operations teams with decision rights in this space and equip them with more change management expertise.

All of these expanded responsibilities come on top of the existing duties that legal operations currently carry out, suggesting continued growth for this important part of the GC 4.0 team.

Technology Platform

If legal operations is the 'engine room', the legal technology platform is the engine. In GC 4.0, it has evolved from being a stack of technologies to being an integrated system of capabilities.

Like the company's AI factory, the legal technology platform enables scale, scope, and learning. However, there are also significant differences between them. While the AI factory runs the company's overall business model and invents new use cases, the legal platform is function-specific and purpose-built to handle legal, governance, and risk matters.

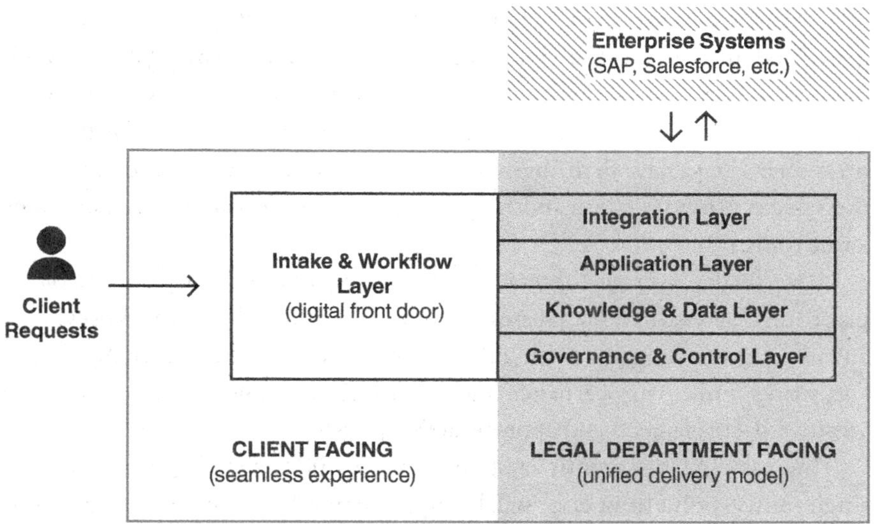

Figure 7.2   GC 4.0 legal department technology platform.

Source: Illustration by Logica Design.

All of the information that the department generates and manages is converted into structured data and insights that create a virtuous cycle of continuous learning and improved output at ever lower cost.

As can be seen in Figure 7.2, the legal platform consists of five layers: *intake and workflow; knowledge and data; application; integration;* and *governance and control.*

While some of these layers already existed or were being developed in GC 3.0, GC 4.0 will take them to a new level, and vastly improve them.[35]

Intake and Workflow   Intake and workflow act as the legal department's digital 'front door' for incoming requests. In GC 4.0, intake and workflow are consistently managed for every incoming request, reducing bottlenecks and increasing scale.

Clients access the intake layer either directly through a legal portal or via embedded workflows in other applications they might use more frequently. They use it to submit requests for legal or compliance work.

Each request is then scored for risk and complexity and routed appropriately. Simple and low-risk matters are directed to chatbots or other self-service options. Riskier or more complex matters are directed to a hybrid environment, where an AI-enabled preliminary response is generated and sent to the right human expert (e.g., a paralegal or lawyer, depending on the nature of the request) for validation. Complex or high-risk matters are routed to the best-placed human expert for internal or external (e.g., law firm) handling. In addition to routing and assigning, the system provides clients with updates, manages deadlines, and generates audit trails.

The intake layer also interacts with other parts of the legal technology platform. For example, it creates structured metadata[36] for the knowledge and data layer; connects with other applications via the integration layer; and works with the governance and control layer to ensure that personal or sensitive data is flagged and appropriately handled.

Increasingly, as agentic systems evolve and expand, the traditional single-entry-point front door will be supplemented with or replaced outright by a network of agents embedded across the company, each of which can steer work requiring legal input into the department. Incoming tasks will be received by intake agents that determine how to triage incoming requests, for example, trigger automated workflow or autonomous tools, or send to human in-house teams for further evaluation.

Knowledge and Data Layer The knowledge and data layer is the central repository where information gets collected, cleaned, standardised, and stored. This layer works off metadata that is organised in ways that allow the technology platform to conduct advanced searches, run analytics, and retrain models.

Raw data, that is unstructured information (e.g., contracts, regulatory updates, communications, and invoices) that is not usable until it has been cleaned, processed, and sorted by this layer, fuels outputs that constitute the department's institutional memory and best practices. These might include playbooks,[37] clause libraries, checklists, templates, and workflows. The knowledge and data layer continually uses new raw data to build new outputs or improve existing ones. The more data it has available, the better and more plentiful the outputs become.

Application Layer The application layer consists of all the user-facing tools and applications used by people, including self-service, contract and document management, e-billing, dashboards, drafting, and analytics tools.

Which applications get embedded here will vary, depending on the needs of the department. Some may be purpose built, but most will be purchased externally, with varying degrees of customisation. However, they are all modular and can be easily integrated within the technology stack. Many will also be compatible with enterprise systems commonly used by business partners, allowing them to be accessed from Salesforce, Microsoft, or other systems. Increasingly, AI agents act within and between these apps, making the department's work environment increasingly automated and autonomous.

Configuring the application layer requires significant thought and care by the legal operations team because the quality of the output from the platform as a whole is directly tied to the applications people can use.

Integration Layer The integration layer is a critical bridge that both integrates the department's technology stack into a coherent system and connects it with the broader enterprise architecture.

This layer enables data to move in many directions. Structured data is integrated across all legal technology platform layers. Data from other enterprise systems (e.g., HR or finance or procurement data) can be uploaded into the legal platform. Finally, legal and compliance data can be pushed from the legal platform into other enterprise systems to enhance insights across the business. For example, contractual data might enhance spend analytics by the procurement function or budget tracking by finance.

Governance and Control Layer The governance and control layer provides an oversight framework for the platform, ensuring data and tools are used ethically, securely, and in line with the company's and department's policies.

This layer contains numerous components. A data governance component ensures data quality, preventing GIGO issues and establishing clear ownership rights. A compliance component integrates regulatory requirements and company policies into workflows to ensure rules are automatically enforced and tracked. An AI component ensures oversight of AI tools and coordinates decision rights, bias checks, and where and how humans are kept in the loop. Finally, identity and access management components ensure security and privacy are maintained, while a performance component tracks KPIs, returns on investment, and other metrics.

AI Agents   Agentic AI builds upon these layers, moving the legal platform from being an automated system to being a semi-autonomous environment where intelligent digital workers handle complex, multi-step workflows, minimising human intervention across critical paths.[38] As we saw in Chapter 6, this facilitates scaling.

Specialists and Generalists

Above the legal operations and technology platform foundations sit the human professionals. *Legal specialists* are deep subject matter experts in areas that are of critical importance to the business. These may include experts in competition law, corporate and M&A, environmental and regulatory affairs, litigation, intellectual property, and so on. Specialists draw on the platform's data, processes, and tools to provide deep expertise as and when most needed.

A team of agile, front-end, market-facing *legal generalists* is embedded within fast-moving business teams. They are supported as needed by the specialists. However, in an increasingly fast-moving business environment, they are also able to draw upon the outputs from the legal technology platform to operate semi-autonomously, which enables them to provide more agile and upskilled legal support to the business teams in real time.

Hybrid Delivery Teams

Some large legal functions are introducing an additional layer between legal operations and specialists and generalists. This layer is a hybrid delivery group, combining multidisciplinary professionals with enabling technology. It operates as an internal ALSP, focusing on the scalable, repeatable delivery of legal services across the department. By centralising and industrialising this work, the model frees specialists, generalists, and legal operations teams to focus on strategic matters and deeper client partnership.

How Long Is the 'Long Term'?

It is not yet clear how long these adaptations will take to fully bear fruit. As American baseball legend Yogi Berra noted, 'it's tough to make predictions, especially about the future'.[39] However, as Richard Susskind has observed, most of the claims made about the impact of AI on the law greatly overestimate the likely short-term effect but understate how it will impact things over the long-term.[40] The rapidly evolving landscape of today suggests that 'the long-term' may not be too far off. Indeed, as William Gibson is alleged to have quipped, it may be that 'the future is already here—it's just not evenly distributed'.[41] And of course, legal departments will evolve in response to variables and developments yet to come, with each department changing in ways that are uniquely configured for the industrial and corporate contexts in which they operate.

With these caveats, what seems certain today is that broad-based and profound technology adoption centred around legal platforms will radically impact nearly every facet of the legal department.

Unilever—Designing a Scalable, AI-ready Legal Function

Unilever's legal department exemplifies how a large legal function across a multinational business can organise itself to operate with agility, scale, and business alignment in the AI era.

Over the past several years, Chief Legal Officer and Company Secretary, Maria Varsellona and her team have evolved the department's delivery model toward a modular, integrated design that optimises the deployment of legal expertise, while also leveraging technology and process excellence to scale work efficiently across the enterprise.

The department is structured around three interconnected pillars: *the Corporate Centre, the Business Group*, and *the Powerhouses*, supported by Legal Operations and an impressive technology platform. Together, these components form a cohesive operating system that combines depth, proximity, and scale, laying the foundations for AI-enabled service delivery.

Corporate Centre

The Corporate Centre comprises a team of specialist lawyers embedded across key locations globally. These lawyers support the company's most material domains, including litigation, corporate governance, M&A, competition law, data privacy, IP, employment, compliance, and supply chain including procurement. Their role is to leverage their expertise to help the business achieve its strategic priorities in accordance with enterprise-wide standards and consistent legal interpretation.

Business Group

The Business Group pillar consists of experienced, business-embedded lawyers who sit directly within Unilever's commercial organisations around the world. The structure mirrors the company's operating model. Lawyers in this pillar have strong commercial fluency and close proximity to decision-makers. Their role is to support business outcomes, applying legal judgement in context as strategic partners. Deep knowledge of the business environment is a central feature of this pillar.

Powerhouses

The Powerhouses form the department's scalable delivery engine. Based in multiple global hubs (including Mexico, Spain, and India), these teams support a wide range of legal activities across both the Corporate Centre and Business Groups, including litigation support, privacy and employment workflows, contracting, and compliance operations work.

Over time, the Powerhouses have evolved into a fully integrated extension of the legal organisation, with team members working closely with and across the organisation. A recent organisational shift moved reporting lines from a centralised management structure to direct reporting into the specialist teams they support. As Varsellona explains, 'Our Powerhouse teams … are responsible for a range of diverse legal tasks [that] … help us to increase efficiency and streamline our ways of working. If I were a young lawyer, I would love to work there'.[42]

Legal Operations

Legal Operations is increasingly focused on driving operational fluency and embedding continuous improvement and seamless integration across the organisation. The team supports three core areas:

- **Financial and performance management** to provide visibility into spend, value, demand patterns, and operational performance.
- **Technology enablement** which seeks to leverage enterprise solutions to optimise workflows, knowledge management, and automation.
- **Operations coordination** including providing programme and project management, process optimisation, and administrative support across the Powerhouse hubs to ensure consistent execution and continuous improvement.

Technology Platform

Unilever's legal department is supported by an evolving technology ecosystem, designed to increase productivity, enhance insight, and improve integration with enterprise systems. As Varsellona explains, 'A key enabler of our strategy is our digital transformation. For our legal team, AI allows us to drive this transformation while step-changing our operational effectiveness. It clearly reduces the amount of time we spend on repetitive tasks, allowing us to dedicate more time to strategic legal work'.

At the same time, Unilever's legal experts developed a robust framework for a responsible use of AI across the business, which is pivotal as the company prepares for the implementation of agentic AI solutions.

The department's technology platform increasingly includes AI-native tools, which reflect the team's view that AI is an opportunity. The legal team was an early adopter of AI-native tools, including Thomson Reuters' *CoCounsel* and Microsoft's *Copilot*.[43] The tools are used in the delivery centres and across the wider legal department.[44] Technology enhancements are saving people in the department an average of 30 minutes a day.[45]

Solid Foundation   Taken together, Unilever's technology platform has evolved into a coherent and increasingly sophisticated ecosystem that is integrating legal data, workflows, and insights across the team, supporting scalable and repeatable service delivery via the Powerhouses, and providing a solid foundation for AI-enabled legal work to scale across all three pillars of the department and across the enterprise in the years to come.

Key Learnings

- **Organise for depth, proximity, and scale.** A model consisting of lawyers covering a range of domain expertise and/or business partnering focus, underpinned by a technology platform, enables specialist depth, business-embedded influence, and scalable delivery.
- **Use scalable hubs to optimise legal service delivery.** Centralising key workflows in the Powerhouses allows the team to optimise work allocation across the organisation.

(continued)

> (*continued*)
>
> - **Position Legal Operations as an integration layer.** Legal Operations aligns finance, data, workflows, and platform strategy across the function.
> - **Invest in digital fluency, not just tools.** Capability-based adoption outperforms isolated use-case deployment.
> - **Build legal workflows on enterprise platforms.** Integrating legal data into enterprise systems enables scale.
> - **Prepare now for agentic AI.** The shift from automation to orchestration will reshape roles, workflows, and team structure.

Human Professionals

Humans may be organised in much the same way in GC 4.0 as they were in GC 3.0, with specialists, generalists, and legal operations forming the department's organisational backbone. However, how humans work, what areas of expertise they will need, and the skills they must employ will all shift.

As workflows become increasingly automated and autonomous, lawyers and other legal professionals must learn to work in hybrid environments, including being able to collaborate with and manage teams of AI agents. Domain knowledge will be augmented by ever more powerful technology that deepens the expertise of specialists and empowers non-specialists to act more rapidly on the frontlines across a growing range of subjects within which they are not experts.

New areas of subject matter expertise, particularly for specialists, will also emerge, including new capabilities in technology-related domains such as privacy and security, AI governance, regulation and model risk, data analytics, and prompt engineering.

As for skills, given the pace of change and the centrality of technology, human experts must become increasingly adaptable. They will need to be able to constantly learn so that they can rapidly adopt new tools and systems and supplement their existing knowledge base with critical new disciplines.

As technology becomes central to legal service delivery, specialists and generalists will also need to work more closely with experts across other domains in legal operations. The more rapidly they can acquire a working knowledge of these other disciplines, the better they will be at operating in this new reality.

Lawyers will also need to get comfortable operating in a world that is far more metrics-driven, with ever more accurate KPIs becoming the benchmarks of excellence. An understanding and awareness of how to track and measure that will be important.

Human-centric capabilities, including strategic thinking, communication, emotional intelligence, and creativity, will increase in importance as work duties shift, particularly as humans move away from critical paths and focus their efforts on strategic-level decision-making.

Taking all of this into account, the notion of a *T-shaped* lawyer, as discussed in Chapter 4, combining deep technical expertise in a specific discipline with broad multidisciplinary and social skills, will become ever more important in a world where creativity, adaptability, and collaboration are key to success.[46]

Workday: Building an 'AI-first' Legal Department

Workday's Legal, Compliance, and Corporate Affairs (LCCA) function exemplifies how forward-looking legal departments are evolving towards the GC 4.0 organisational architecture.[47]

Recognising the transformative impact AI will have on business and the economy, Workday has placed it at the core of its corporate strategy, aiming to become the intelligent digital 'front door' for the workplace.

LCCA is mirroring this enterprise ambition through a parallel transformation of its own by redesigning its operating model, systems, and talent to create an intelligent, data-driven legal ecosystem. The legal team is already in the vanguard: at a recent company-wide town hall, it was showcased for its AI-enabled transformation. As Greg Bennett, Director of Legal Operations, explains, 'we've been working hard to build a centralised, metrics-driven operating model underpinned by AI and emerging technology that draws from both legal and enterprise-wide data and systems'.

Technology Platform

At the base of its organisational architecture, LCCA is developing a sophisticated technology platform that unites workflows, analytics, and governance, and previously siloed systems such as document management, e-billing, and matter management, into a single, intelligent ecosystem of trusted content and knowledge.

Platform Layers

LCCA's platform encompasses the multiple layers characteristic of a GC 4.0 legal department, all underpinned by a rapidly evolving suite of agentic tools (see Figure 7.3).

Intake and Workflow: The 'Client Front Door'   The client front door acts as a dynamic triage layer between the business and LCCA, serving as both an intake mechanism and a collaboration hub. It 'orchestrates' incoming requests; triaging, tracking, and, where possible, resolving matters via self-service tools, while offering access to curated legal knowledge and workflows. In keeping with its agentic focus (see below), the traditional single-entry-point front door model is being replaced by a network of agents embedded across the enterprise, each of which serves as a gateway into the function, with other agents deciding whether requests get handled autonomously, get escalated to a human, or trigger automated workflows.

Knowledge, Data, Integration, and Governance: The 'Knowledge Intelligence Layer'   At the heart of LCCA's platform lies a sophisticated data layer that uses AI to classify and tag content on intake and contextualise

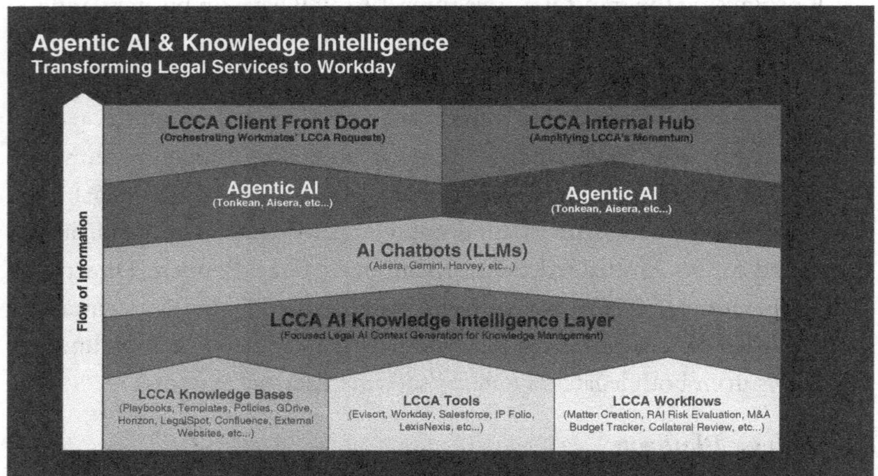

Figure 7.3   LCCA technology platform layers.

Source: This chart was provided to the author by Workday and is reproduced here with Workday's kind permission.

it on retrieval while also ensuring it can be universally accessed by all of the department's AI systems. As Bennett notes, 'the most impactful element for building and driving an effective AI-driven platform is the prevalence of content and data'.

LCCA has evolved its use of data so that it is no longer linear; as Bennett explains, LCCA data 'has become spherical, driving universal integration, and enabling the scale, scope, and learning of our combined AI models and specific AI agents alike. This has opened up huge opportunities, not just in Legal, but across the enterprise'.

This knowledge intelligence layer includes:

- A **managed content layer** that collects, standardises, and stores metadata by practice area, location, sensitivity, and purpose.
- A **uniform data layer (UDL)** that integrates and contextualises structured legal data (matters, contracts, spend, compliance, etc.), creating a single, validated source of truth accessible to both humans and AI agents.
- A **knowledge management governance layer** that ensures compliance with enterprise-wide AI policies and ethical standards, where Legal acts as both user and guardian of ethical and compliant deployment.

Applications: The 'AI and Human Consumption Layer' On top of this foundation sits the department's AI and human consumption layer, where applications and agentic systems leverage trusted content and data to deliver insights and automation. These include LCCA's 'everyday AI' tools (including Gemini, Slack AI, and Zoom AI), which enhance collaboration and efficiency; its *major projects*, which focus on more advanced systems (e.g., the agentic *companion personas* discussed below); and LCCA-specific *internal solutions*, including workflow, contract management, matter management, e-billing, and other tools.

Rather than treating AI as a special project, it has become an embedded behaviour at LCCA that extends its reach into complex, cross-functional workflows.

Among the department's most impactful deployments is Workday's *Evisort Contract Intelligence* tool, which they started to use in 2021 (Evisort was acquired by Workday in 2024). This AI-powered tool automatically ingests and analyses contract data, turning static documents into searchable data assets. It has:

- Saved over 45,000 hours per quarter in contract review and analysis.
- Centralised 100,000+ contracts into an intelligent repository.
- Reduced M&A diligence from weeks to hours, saving the company over $50,000 per transaction.

These outcomes illustrate how AI, data, and a learning-orientated culture can combine to deliver measurable value.

Agentic Support

One of the most distinguishing features of LCCA's digital strategy is its vision to implement and use next-generation autonomous, workflow-driven AI agents and digital assistants to move beyond static automation. These agents increasingly orchestrate actions within the department and enterprise-wide. They can interpret natural language, infer intent, and execute multi-step workflows across systems. Key characteristics include:

- **UDL integration.** Agents connect directly to curated, access-controlled datasets, forming a unified AI knowledge ecosystem.
- **Persona-based design.** Rather than siloed bots, LCCA is building persona-based 'super agents', including:
  - A **sales companion agent** embedded in Salesforce, which aggregates content from multiple teams (e.g., legal, product, and security) and provides live support for business partners.
  - A **legal companion agent** that automates low-risk requests and routes more complex tasks, as well as surfaces internal legal knowledge.
  - A **workmate agent** that answers recurring queries on governance and policy.

Together, these represent a shift from automation to true digital collaboration, with autonomous AI personas able to augment human expertise at scale.

Connecting into the Enterprise

To anchor its advances, LCCA is migrating its operational backbone to *Litify* on Salesforce, unifying matter, spend, and analytics data with Workday's commercial systems. This integration collapses siloes, standardises KPIs, and embeds legal insights directly into enterprise decision-making.

LCCA specifically chose Litify in part because it could be incorporated in this manner. As Bennett describes it, the system represents the department's 'main reactor', enabling data on the business of legal to be integrated with data on the business of the company.

Impact and Lessons

LCCA's transformation has delivered measurable results: tens of thousands of hours saved each quarter, faster cross-functional decision-making, and significant financial returns. More importantly, it marks a structural shift from a GC 3.0 legal function into a GC 4.0 one: digitally native, data-driven, and AI-enabled.

The team has achieved impressive results so far, but it is only getting started. Ultimately, the shift is cultural and strategic. As Áine Lyons, Senior Vice President & Deputy General Counsel: Global Legal Services & Strategy, notes, every Workday employee now has an AI development goal. 'It's a new way for legal departments to think about data. They are not usually tightly integrated into the enterprise. I think your CIO and your CTO need to become your partners. And what we're discovering is that the more integrated we become, the more impact we can deliver. This ultimately leads to more budget, traction, and support.'

Key Learnings

- **Platform thinking.** Unify legal technology into a single, data-driven ecosystem.
- **AI integration.** Embed AI throughout, not as a side project but as a core operational layer.
- **Agentic models.** Deploy intelligent agents to augment human expertise.

(continued)

> (*continued*)
>
> - **Enterprise connectivity.** Integrate legal data directly with enterprise systems for strategic impact.
> - **Governance and ethics.** Balance innovation with oversight through robust governance.

Law Firms, ALSPs, and Other External Providers

The GC 4.0 operational architecture will have profound implications for law firms, ALSPs, and other external providers.

We will explore this in greater detail in Part III. At this stage, what is worth noting is that the GC 4.0 legal team sits at the centre of an ever more powerful technology platform that is integrated within an AI factory corporate model. This new model reconfigures how legal services are sourced, both internally and externally.

Clients will no longer view outside vendors in isolation from these dynamics. Rather, they will increasingly see vendors as interoperable nodes that connect into the AI factory model. The value vendors bring in this environment will no longer depend solely on the services they can provide (e.g., legal expertise and judgement for law firms, scale and process expertise for ALSPs). While that will remain important, it will increasingly be supplemented by how well vendors can connect into client platforms and address the shifting needs of the GC 4.0 environment.

For vendors to succeed, they must not only be able to closely configure and integrate with their client's technology platforms; they must also be able to deeply understand the new environment their clients operate in. That includes appreciating and being able to deliver the kinds of services and solutions clients need in the AI era, including holistic risk mitigation and effective cost management.

To succeed in a world where work technology increasingly allows work to be unbundled and sourced to the most efficient provider, vendors must also understand where and how they bring value—and how that value should be priced in a GC 4.0 reality.

The Impact

AI is a technology with almost every use case imaginable.
—Mustafa Suleyman, CEO of Microsoft AI and Co-founder and
former Head of Applied AI at DeepMind[1]

As we saw in Part II, GC 4.0 represents a fundamental shift in how companies and their legal departments operate. The scale, scope, and learning advantages enabled by AI factories are driving an economy-wide digital transformation. By 2024, 94% of large organisations in the United States and the United Kingdom reported having a digital transformation strategy, with three-quarters of business leaders ranking investment in transformation, AI, and machine learning as critical priorities.[2]

This strategic intent is reflected in extraordinary levels of capital expenditure. In early 2026, Google's parent Alphabet, Amazon and Meta announced that collectively they intended to spend more than $660bn in AI-related investments in 2026 alone.[3] To put that into perspective, this was more than the entire European Union spent on defence in 2024.[4] Morgan Stanley projects $2.9 trillion in AI-related hardware and infrastructure investment between 2025 and 2028, while McKinsey estimates that global data centre spending alone will reach $7 trillion by 2030.[5]

So far, markets appear to be largely unfazed by the size of these investments. In 2025, Nvidia became the first company in the world to reach a $5 trillion market capitalisation, with Microsoft ($3.8 trillion),

Apple ($3.4 trillion), Amazon ($2.4 trillion), Alphabet ($2.4 trillion), and Meta ($1.9 trillion) not too far behind.[6]

This acceleration coincides with continuing exponential growth in computational capacity. If Moore's Law holds for another decade at its historical pace, the implications will be profound. AI is already encroaching on sophisticated legal work. In 2025, Goldman Sachs CEO David Solomon noted that AI can now draft 95% of an initial public offering prospectus within minutes—a task that previously took teams of bankers, lawyers, and accountants many weeks of hard work. 'The last 5% now matters', Solomon noted, 'because the rest is now a commodity'.[7]

As capabilities expand, in-house legal departments will gain access to specialist capabilities that rival those of law firms. GCs will rethink how they source and provide external legal services. The implications for firms are significant. Record profitability breeds complacency just as client dissatisfaction and technological disruption are eroding the foundations of the traditional model.

That model rests on a human-centred pyramid, where large cohorts of junior lawyers generate billable hours to sustain a small group of equity partners. Pricing remains largely tied to time spent rather than value delivered, though we are starting to see some signs of change. It is unclear how the traditional structure can endure when digitally transformed clients, capable of performing much of the work themselves, expect external partners to tightly integrate with their AI-driven delivery models.

This is a classic case of what Clayton Christensen described as the *innovator's dilemma*. Dominant incumbents often fail to adapt to disruptive technologies, investing instead in incremental improvements while new entrants redefine the basis of competition. While they typically offer inferior performance at first, these entrants improve over time and move up-market, eventually displacing the incumbents with a very different value proposition.[8] The legal industry is not immune to this dynamic.

Part III explores how these forces will impact law firms. It considers which are likely to adapt and survive, how alternative models might evolve alongside them, and what steps firms may take, within their structural constraints, to prepare for what lies ahead. Finally, it assesses what the implications of this disruption might be on ALSPs.

8 | The Traditional Law Firm Model

There may be nothing as vulnerable as entrenched success.
—Clayton M. Christensen, Dina Wang, and Derek van Bever[1]

For more than a century, law firms have played an outsized role in the economic and political system. They have been at the forefront as globalisation accelerated, advising MNCs and governments alike on the world's largest and most complex transactions, facilitating the opening of new markets and shaping the regulatory environment that underpinned the development of global supply chains. Law firms have elevated the quality of legal practice and the administration of justice, providing thought leadership on policy and regulation, while serving as talent magnets that have attracted and trained generations of the profession's best and brightest.

Throughout this period, the traditional law firm operating model has proven to be remarkably resilient. It has weathered macroeconomic shocks, geopolitical upheavals, regulatory changes, and shifting political winds. Firms have rapidly adapted. They expanded into emerging economies, developed alliance networks, and cultivated expertise in new practice areas. By maintaining a diverse portfolio of practices, with some (e.g., M&A, intellectual property, and real estate) that thrive in times of economic expansion and others (e.g., bankruptcy, restructuring, and labour and employment) that are counter-cyclical, firms have proven to be 'all-weather' businesses, able to prosper regardless of what economic winds are blowing.

But GC 4.0 presents a different type of challenge. AI-driven transformation will create a growing gap between what digitised clients need and what law firms can deliver under the traditional model.

The Traditional Law Firm Model

The origins of the traditional law firm model date back to the early 1900s, when Paul Cravath, a partner at the law firm of Cravath, Swaine & Moore, pioneered what became known as the 'Cravath System'. As discussed in Chapter 2, the model was ideally suited to the needs of the emerging professional class within GC 1.0 MNCs.

At the heart of the model is a leverage-dependent, pyramid-shaped organisational structure (see Figure 8.1). At the base of the pyramid are large numbers of salaried professionals, including paralegals, support staff, and junior and senior salaried lawyers (associates), as well as salaried partners (non-equity partners). There may also be a small number of 'of-counsel' lawyers (affiliates who are neither partners nor employees). At the apex sit a relatively small number of firm owners (equity partners) who hold ownership stakes in the firm. The model fundamentally rests on two key pillars: leverage and the billable hour.

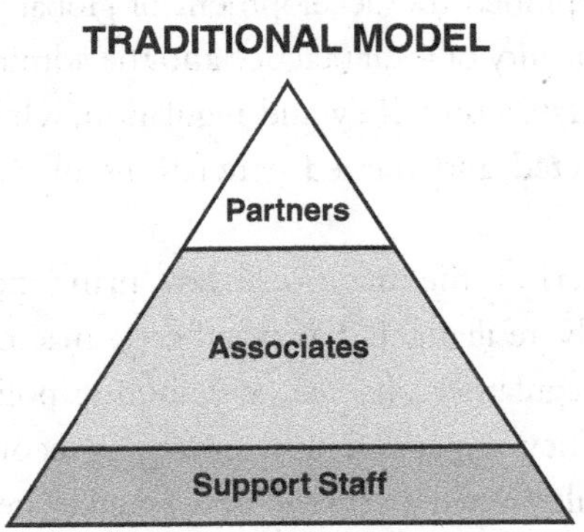

Figure 8.1   Simplified view of the traditional law firm model.
Source: Illustration by Logica Design.

Leverage

The firm's leverage equals the ratio of salaried professionals to owners. The higher the leverage of salaried professionals to owners (i.e., the more associates or other fee earners relative to equity partners), the more profitable the model is for equity partners.[2]

Firms generate leverage by hiring far more entry-level associates than they promote into the partnership.[3] Under a tenure policy sometimes referred to as 'up or out', associates have a certain number of years to prove themselves, at which point they are either promoted to the partnership or expected to leave the firm.[4]

The Billable Hour

Traditionally, the law firm model is based on charging clients for the time the firm's professionals spend on performing work for the client, rather than what the value of the output is to the client, or the complexity of the project or its scope.

Under this approach, firms charge clients for their professional time on an hourly rate basis. Lawyers track the amount of time spent on each matter, usually in increments of 1/10th of an hour, with rates varying based on seniority.[5] Every professional is given annual billable-hour targets, usually in the range of 1,800–2,200 hours, at rates high enough to generate a profit for the partnership after netting out the firm's overhead, including salaries.[6]

Equity partners are typically paid through regular profit distributions, with various models, including 'lockstep' models, in which compensation is based on years of service, with partners receiving regular pay increases as they gain seniority; formula-based (also known as 'eat-what-you-kill') models, in which payouts are tied to measurable results, such as billable hours, client revenue, or new business origination; and hybrid models, in which aspects of both are included, such as a lockstep component as well as a variable performance-based one.[7]

Criticisms of the Billable Hour   In recent decades, as the more-for-less challenge has grown, the billable-hour model has come under growing criticism.[8] Arguments have been made that it is sub-optimal for both clients and associates alike.[9]

Clients have long levelled criticisms at the hourly rate model, including that it misaligns law firm and client interests by rewarding time spent rather than efficiency; that hours billed often bear little relationship to the value delivered; that individual rates are often set based on seniority rather than demonstrable competence; and that all hours are priced equally regardless of the productivity or value of the output.[10] In addition, clients face variability and cost uncertainty where they increasingly require predictability and budgetary stability. These criticisms have become ever louder as the more-for-less challenge has intensified on the client side.

The billable-hour model can produce misaligned results. For example, a client might find strategically vital advice given during a short telephone call to be enormously valuable, yet the firm would only charge a small fee for it. By contrast, extensive work on a routine matter, conducted over several weeks, might result in a larger bill based on the hours spent by the firm, even if the output is less intrinsically valuable to the client than the telephone conversation.

At a deeper level, the model reveals a disconnect between how firms and clients define productivity. Productivity, as it is typically understood, measures how efficiently inputs, such as labour, generate outputs, such as services.[11] Clients certainly view productivity through an efficiency lens. In the law firm context, however, productivity is often equated with the number of billable hours lawyers record on matters.[12] As one observer has noted, 'total elapsed time without regard to the quality or usefulness of the result reveals nothing about a worker's value. More hours often mean the opposite of real productivity'.[13]

Hourly billing also takes a heavy toll on associates. As Yale Law School's pamphlet, *The Truth About the Billable Hour*, notes, if one factors in bathroom breaks, lunch, and a one-hour commute, 2,300 billable hours a year translates into associates working 14-hour days, five days per week, plus 9-hour days three Saturdays each month, excluding pro bono hours, internal administrative tasks, and any personal time spent during work hours.[14]

These long hours contribute to high levels of stress, burnout, and substance abuse across the profession. One broad study involving nearly 13,000 lawyers found that nearly 21% screened positive for hazardous and potentially alcohol-dependent drinking, while 28, 19, and 23% reported symptoms of depression, anxiety, and stress, respectively.[15] Long hours and chronic work–life imbalance are associated with these outcomes. As one commentator noted, 'It is not uncommon for lawyers to experience sleep deprivation, poor physical health, and career dissatisfaction/burnout as they push through a seemingly endless workload'.[16]

Alternative Fee Arrangements   Alternatives to the billable-hour model have gained traction as powerful e-billing and invoicing tools have enabled clients to scrutinise law firm charges with unprecedented precision. Corporate legal departments—far more sophisticated buyers than they were just a few years ago—now leverage professionalised procurement processes, maintain established panels of approved firms with pre-negotiated rates, and benchmark invoices across multiple providers. One result of this growing buyer sophistication has been the rise of alternative fee arrangements (AFAs)—non-traditional structures that price in ways other than the standard hourly rate.

AFAs come in many forms, including:

- **Blended hourly rates.** A single hourly rate applies to all lawyers on a matter.
- **Capped fees.** Total fees are capped at a maximum amount.
- **Collared fees.** Hourly rates fall within a defined range, with discounts if hours exceed the upper limit of that range.
- **Contingency fees.** Fees are paid only upon a successful outcome, typically as a percentage of the award or settlement.
- **Discounted rates.** Lower rates are offered for high-volume work or early payment.
- **Fixed fees.** The price for a specific matter is agreed in advance.
- **Flat fees.** A set amount applies for standard or routine work.
- **Hybrid fees.** A combination of billable hours for certain tasks and an AFA for the rest.
- **Retainers.** Upfront payments from which costs are drawn as work proceeds.[17]

Other AFAs include success or bonus fees linked to performance metrics, and subscription models, where a suite of services is provided for a flat recurring fee.[18]

Despite their apparent variety, however, most AFAs (including flat and fixed fees, which are the most common ones) are calculated based on the number of hours the matter is expected to take.[19] As such, they do not pose a meaningful threat to the billable-hour model. As of 2025, it remains the case that at least 80% of legal matters still use hourly billing.[20] One survey found that 80% of what were described as AFAs were in actuality simply hourly rate discounts.[21] Moreover, the fact that more than half of law firms admit to regularly producing 'shadow bills' (calculations showing what the matter would have cost under hourly billing), with 37% of in-house legal departments requesting them, suggests work still remains largely rooted in the hourly rate, despite much talk to the contrary.[22]

There are many potential reasons for the 'stickiness' of the billable hour, including that legal practice management software is configured to work off hourly rates, which remain embedded in both law firm culture and reward structures.[23] Things may change as AI embeds itself into legal department and law firm workflows and the number of hours it takes to complete large volumes of legal work compresses. As ever more work can be done by machines in minutes rather than by humans over days and weeks, the economic logic of hourly billing may become less tenable. The result could be the emergence of true AFAs, detached from time and input costs and based instead on the value of the outcomes.

A Good Model for Partners

Regardless of whether billable hours or AFAs are used, equity partners have greatly benefitted from the traditional law firm model. In fact, things have never been better.

In 2024, profits per equity partner reached $9.25 million at Kirkland & Ellis, $9.03 million at Wachtell, Lipton, and $8.64 million at Quinn Emanuel, the three highest-earning US firms. That same year, revenue across the top 100 firms grew at an average of 13.3%.[24] At the very top, some partners are now charging standard rates of as much as $3,000 per hour.[25]

Recent profitability has been partly driven by a historic surge in demand across a variety of practice areas and market segments. In the United States, midsize firms (regional or specialty firms outside the largest national rankings), Am Law 100 (the 100 highest-grossing US law firms) and Am Law Second 100 (ranked 101–200 by gross revenue) firms have all experienced demand spikes, with billing rates growing at their fastest pace since the GFC, even as inflation softened.[26] In the United Kingdom, the top 100 firms have similarly enjoyed strong results, with 97% reporting fee-income growth in 2024 and exceeding expectations.[27]

A Poor Model for Clients

Despite this record profitability and a century of resilience, however, clients are increasingly unhappy, as has been noted, with the traditional law firm model, both in terms of what it costs and what it delivers. Specifically, clients are facing growing financial strain. In a 2024 Axiom survey, 96% of GCs reported legal budget cuts averaging 11%, with the deepest reductions at companies exceeding $1 billion in revenue.[28] At the same time, 81% of GCs said they were critically understaffed, with 100% indicating that at least some of the work they outsourced could have been handled in-house if they had the right resources, signalling a desire to bring more of it in-house over time.[29]

These clients feel that they are paying increasingly more money yet receiving less value. A staggering 100% of GCs regret engaging law firms for cost, quality, or other reasons, while 89% state that law firms no longer offer a completely effective solution for their needs.[30] In addition to cost, GCs cite overly conceptual advice, limited commercial acumen, and a perceived lack of business prioritisation as major problems.[31]

Many firms are organised around narrowly defined and partner-led practice groups, with incentive structures that reinforce specialisation.[32] While this drives technical depth, it fragments knowledge across firm siloes and makes cross-disciplinary collaboration and the flow of data and knowledge across the firm difficult.

But collaborative and cross-disciplinary thinking is precisely what clients need in an increasingly volatile, uncertain, complex, and ambiguous world, where risks cut across geographies, disciplines, and regulatory regimes. To be actionable, advice must become more holistic and pragmatic.

As Harvard Law School professor, Heidi K. Gardner notes regarding the client experience:

> Most of their problems transcend traditional practice areas and disciplinary silos, and crisscross geographies and jurisdictions. Together these two trends—increased specialization and a growing complexity in client issues— create a demand for lawyers who are not only technical experts in their own particular domain but also lawyers who can collaborate with others throughout the firm, and often around the world, to solve multifaceted problems … Consequently, tackling client problems that transcend practice areas and disciplinary silos seriously challenges traditional models of law firm structure and ways of doing business.[33]

The result is a widening mismatch between hyper-specialised firms and clients increasingly demanding holistic and business-orientated solutions delivered at speed and scale. Firms need to find ways to better connect deep domain expertise with a broad-aperture lens that integrates knowledge, technology, and commercial insight.

Other professional services sectors are already making a similar shift. As Nick Studer, CEO of consulting firm Oliver Wyman has noted, clients 'don't want a suit with PowerPoint. They want someone who is willing to get in the trenches and help them align their team and co-create with their team'.[34] McKinsey & Company is moving in a similar direction. Managing Partner Bob Sternfels is reframing the firm from being an advisor to being an outcomes-focused partner that evolves alongside its clients, with its pay increasingly based on results rather than the work.[35]

As clients evolve around technology, consultants have come to realise that if they fail to evolve alongside them, they risk being left behind.

As Clayton M. Christensen, Dina Wang, and Derek van Bever have noted:

[T]he pace of change being managed by the traditional clients of consulting firms will continue to accelerate, with devastating effects on providers that don't keep up. If you are currently on the leadership team of a consultancy and you're inclined to be sanguine about disruption, ask yourself: Is your firm changing (at least) as rapidly as your most demanding clients?[36]

These are not surface issues for law firms either. With clients reporting such high levels of dissatisfaction with both the escalating cost and value of the core services provided, a flashing red light should be going off for law firm partners.

The challenge for partners is that the traditional model contains inherent structural deficits that prevent them from making radical changes to it. This problem is exacerbated by external dynamics that are making the need for radical change more urgent.

Inherent Structural Deficits

There are several structural features inherent to the traditional model that make it difficult for firms to evolve and adapt to client concerns.

Human-centric, Input-based Profit Engine

As noted above, the traditional law firm model rests on leverage and the billable hour, both of which incentivise firms to maintain large cohorts of lawyers who spend long hours generating work.

There are, however, signs that this model is beginning to fray. In certain transactional contexts, such as debt markets or corporate lending, where work has become highly standardised, firms are increasingly shifting towards fixed or market-based pricing. Standardisation brings predictability, allowing parties to agree on value in advance rather than measure it in hours.

Digital transformation is accelerating these shifts. As will be discussed further in Chapter 13, legal procurement and vendor management platforms such as PERSUIT are introducing market transparency by enabling clients to compare bids for similar matters across their preferred law firm panels. This transparency is exerting downward pressure on hourly rates for certain types of matters and is encouraging alternative fee structures that better align with price outcome.

Similarly, SaaS-based legal technologies, such as *Harvey Vault*, are allowing clients to store, process, and analyse documents at scale. These technologies are turning what was once bespoke human work, such as due diligence reviews, into digitised services. Routine tasks that were previously performed manually have become automated, while knowledge that was once proprietary is becoming ubiquitous.

Here again, developments in the legal industry mirror the evolution underway in consulting. Consultants long benefitted from information opacity, with clients paying high fees in order to tap into specialised knowledge that was otherwise hard to acquire. But increasingly, as Christensen, Wang, and van Bever note, 'as access to knowledge is democratized, opacity fades and clients no longer have to pay the fees of big consulting firms'.[37] Consequently, consulting firms have reinvented themselves around technology, partnering more deeply with clients and shifting towards outcomes-based pricing to deliver greater value. Under their evolved models, technology has become an integral part of the profit engine because it lowers input costs while amplifying the value of human expertise. This is changing how they work and hire, with McKinsey soon having one AI agent for every human in the firm.[38]

This model could be emulated by law firms. However, the still-prevalent logic of the billable-hour model makes it difficult to adopt technologies that materially reduce the number of hours worked. Doing so would threaten the very engine that sustains much of their profitability.

Consequently, many traditional firms continue to focus their innovation efforts on building faster horse-and-buggies rather than cars. But it is cars that clients are now building; and increasingly, they will expect their law firms to do the same.

The strain that technology is placing on the billable-hour model will be revisited in Chapter 9, where we review Richard Susskind's contention that legal work now spans a continuum from bespoke, to standardised, and ultimately commoditised. It is at this final stage that, he argues, the billable model breaks down because legal expertise can be accessed without directly consuming lawyers' time.[39]

Tasks that once sat squarely in the traditional billable-hour pricing structure are increasingly being unbundled and redistributed across a growing ecosystem of providers and solutions, with each capturing segments of the work they can most efficiently deliver, with digital solutions increasingly orchestrating this allocation.

Over time, as clients adopt new tools and approaches, the economic logic of the billable-hour model will likely fully erode. However, for now, the billable hour remains a central feature of most law firm profit models.

Partnership Dynamics

The traditional law firm partnership model rests on a narrow band of highly mobile senior equity partners to whom most of the firm's profits are distributed on a regular basis. This gives law firms a fragile organisational structure, a shallow capital base, and a short-term strategic horizon.

As equity stakes disappear when partners leave a firm, earnings are typically tied to productive years at the firm.[40] If senior partners, who are often the firm's key decision-makers, are nearing retirement, they may therefore prioritise the firm's short-term profitability over its long-term financial health. By contrast, junior partners, who wield less influence, may have longer-term interests in the firm.[41]

This dynamic can create misalignment on how much of earnings should be retained for capital expenditures and long-term investment versus being paid out in the near term.

As Jonathan T. Molot has noted:

It remains difficult for law firm partners to reach a consensus on a larger, more sustained investment program because partners have disparate time horizons and those with greater seniority tend to dominate firm management. If law firm managers are generally in their late-fifties or early-sixties, one can expect investments designed to generate returns over a period of several years, but not much longer.[42]

The result can lead to underinvestment in technology. At a time when many clients are investing heavily in AI systems, law firms may lack the leadership alignment needed to make correspondingly major investments in transformational change.

Even where strategic alignment exists, law firm partnerships typically lack access to substantial external capital because of their structural fragility. A firm's value largely rests on the future income its partners are expected to generate, rather than on hard assets or long-term capital reserves. Moreover, partners are effectively independent owners who can (and increasingly do) leave if they disagree with the firm's direction. This creates short-term horizons and discourages investments that might depress profits in the near term, even if they are essential for long-term health. As a result, major strategic investments, especially in technology or innovation, often struggle to gain the necessary financial backing.

The fragility of the partnership model means that slowing profitability can pose an existential risk. If profits decline, partners might leave, creating a self-reinforcing departure spiral.[43] And as fortunes dim, remaining partners may begin to worry about incurring personal liability for what remains, which can further intensify the downward spiral.

As John Morley, a Yale Law School observer who has studied law firm collapses over a 30-year period noted:

Law firms don't just go bankrupt—they collapse ... the force with which law firms shatter is amazing because it has no parallel in other kinds of businesses, Amazon lost money for more than 20 years. Chrysler filed for bankruptcy seven years ago. Yet both companies—like countless others that suffered financial problems before them—are still shipping goods and churning out cars. Law firms show no such resilience. No large law firm has ever managed to reorganise in bankruptcy and survive. And the pressures that bring law firms down are often surprisingly mild. Most collapsed firms crumpled when they were still current on their debts and earning a profit. Law firms die with extreme ease and astonishing speed.[44]

It should be noted that UK firms are somewhat less exposed to such sudden collapses because they typically impose lengthy notice periods (6–12 months for senior partners), 'garden leave' provisions, and other restrictive covenants.[45] Many of these are unavailable in the US context, where professional rules prohibit restrictions on post-departure practice.[46]

Siloed Practice Groups

Law firm practices are typically organised into semi-autonomous departments, with each operating like a mini-profit centre.[47] Financial incentives, including origination credits and billable-hour targets, discourage collaboration across practice groups.[48] In such an environment, investments in cross-practice technologies or knowledge-sharing platforms may struggle to gain support, as costs are collective, while benefits accrue unevenly.

In such environments, prestige and talent attraction often centre on star partners rather than institutional capabilities. The result is a structure optimised for individual maximising of immediate revenues, not for innovation, adaptability, or building the integrated systems clients increasingly expect.[49]

Risk-averse Culture

The cultural conservatism of many law firms reinforces their structural vulnerabilities. Historically, technology and new ways of working have been viewed with suspicion. As one study noted, the legal profession is 'attached to a culture that in some cases is severely outdated'.[50] When email and computers emerged in the mid-1990s, lawyers resisted them for fear they might compromise client confidentiality.[51] Indeed, Richard Susskind recounts that when, in the mid-1990s, he promoted greater use of email by lawyers and suggested the Web would become a powerful tool for legal research, the legal establishment indignantly called into question his grip on reality.[52]

For many lawyers, their instinctive caution reflects a deep commitment to client trust, confidentiality, and professional integrity, qualities that are rightly central to legal practice. However, this same caution can make lawyers hesitant to embrace new technologies that could benefit clients while still maintaining high ethical and security standards.

The occasional lack of technological fluency among senior lawyers can reinforce these instincts. One academic study found that experienced lawyers (those with 10 or more years in the profession) are particularly wary of the risks associated with technology adoption. They feel more comfortable avoiding new tools altogether, believing alternative methods might not be sufficiently secure and that new technology could expose firms to unfamiliar threats, such as data breaches or cyber-attacks.[53]

But lawyers also have a professional duty to zealously and competently represent their clients, which includes the appropriate use of technology. Comment 8 to Rule 1.1 of the US Model Rules (obligating lawyers to provide competent representation to clients) recognises this by explicitly referencing technology and requiring that lawyers 'keep abreast of changes in the law and its practice, including the benefits and risks associated with relevant technology'.[54]

The good news is that, over time, lawyers have managed to adapt to the use of emerging technologies, such as email and the Internet. The bad news is that the pace and scale of change in the AI era is of a different order of magnitude, requiring significant change at pace, rather than superficial change over longer time periods.

The Scale, Scope, and Learning Gap

As discussed in Chapter 7, AI is enabling corporate clients to scale, scope, and learn at near-zero marginal cost. Yet most law firms remain anchored in structures built for a pre-digital age. Their partnership models, labour-intensive workflows, and human-centric billing systems make it difficult to grow without adding cost and complexity. These attributes can constrain their ability to evolve in step with clients that operate as digital, data-driven enterprises.

Scale and Scope

GC 4.0 legal departments are developing intake and triage systems that deliver services more effectively and more quickly. As they roll these out, they will expect law firms to integrate into their workflows, sharing playbooks, clause libraries, and AI tools across organisational boundaries.

Clients will increasingly value smoother hand-offs between their own teams and external partners, and between automated systems and human experts. Firms that can integrate in this way will build deep and 'sticky' relationships that are also grounded in process and data, in addition to siloed personal knowledge. But firms whose intake systems remain bespoke, manual, and reactive will struggle to keep pace.

As legal department platforms tap into AI-enabled, enterprise-wide systems to deliver more integrated advice, they will increasingly seek external partners capable of matching that holistic approach. Client frustrations about 'overly conceptual' counsel reflect the limits of the traditional, siloed law firm model.

Adaptation will require firms to broaden their capabilities beyond pure legal expertise. The experience of the Big Four is instructive. As will be discussed further in Chapter 12, when elements of their core audit practices became increasingly commoditised, they expanded into adjacent areas such as technology and advisory, leveraging existing relationships to cross-sell these higher-value services. Since 2014, advisory revenues have surpassed audit revenues across the Big Four, providing greater profitability and portfolio stability.[55]

Continuous Learning and Humans in the Loop

GC 4.0 legal departments operate as systems: new information continuously updates playbooks, algorithms, and data repositories, allowing them to evolve and dynamically adapt. Most law firms lack comparable capabilities or, where they exist, they remain disconnected from client systems, slowing output and eroding value over time.

At the same time, the billable-hour model rewards keeping humans in the loop, even as clients automate routine work and redeploy people to higher-order tasks. AI systems scale, scope, and learn precisely because human bottlenecks are removed. Traditional law firm models, by contrast, are structurally designed to retain them, to maximise billing rather than optimise overall performance.

As clients continue their digital transformations, this divergence will create a widening structural mismatch between them and their law firms. Unless firms redesign their models to integrate expertise, technology, and human capital with client systems at scale and across disciplines, they risk falling behind.

As one industry survey on the innovation gap between clients and law firms observed:

Law firms that don't catch up, especially with regard to technology, will struggle to earn new business. Firms are going to have to do better … Law firms might see more success, and law departments might see them more as 'partners', if law firms invited their clients to work with them in the development of process and tools. By drawing the client into the innovation process early on, firms demonstrate their commitment to addressing and resolving actual pain points, and thereby start to bridge the increasingly wide innovation gap.[56]

Yet only 12% of clients report co-innovating together with their law firms, even though effective use of innovative technology is now a primary factor in selecting new counsel.[57]

This gap underscores the reality that, as clients become digital, their expectations will shift faster than most firms are evolving. GC 4.0 is therefore not just a competitive challenge but a structural one. Firms need to rethink how to create value in an era that is increasingly going to be defined by scale, scope, and learning.

9 | Nothing Changes—Until It Suddenly Does

'How did you go bankrupt?', Bill asked. 'Two ways', Mike said. 'Gradually and then suddenly'.

—Ernest Hemingway, *The Sun Also Rises*[1]

Change Is Coming

While the traditional law firm operating model has a long and, until now, successful pedigree, the structural dynamics outlined in Chapter 8 make it difficult for firms to pivot quickly in the face of change. This leaves firms exposed to the same risks that have trapped other successful incumbents (established players whose past success creates structural and cultural barriers to adaptation) when technological change has reshaped their markets. Inflection points, the signals that foreshadow such disruption, are notoriously hard for incumbents to detect until it is too late. Traditional law firms will be no exception. Moreover, with Moore's Law continuing to compound computational power at an exponential rate, alongside shifting client expectations and new competitors, disruption in the legal profession is likely to arrive faster and more forcefully than most firms anticipate.

The Innovator's Dilemma

Clayton Christensen's seminal book, *The Innovator's Dilemma*, explains why even the most successful incumbents in one generation of technology often struggle when the next wave of innovation arrives.[2] Initially, incumbents dominate the higher-margin segments of the market, producing products or services that are often too sophisticated, too expensive, or too complex for many customers.[3] New entrants typically emerge, offering 'disruptive' technologies that contain a very different value proposition, such as lower cost, simplicity, or ease of use. These new offerings appeal to customers in niche or lower-end parts of the market, even though they underperform mainstream offerings in the early stages of rollout.[4]

Because the new entrants seem to pose little threat, they are largely ignored by incumbents, who focus instead on high-margin work. Incumbents typically prefer to invest in 'sustaining' innovation that incrementally improves their existing offerings rather than in disruptive innovation that might cannibalise their core business. Over time, however, as disruptive technologies improve, they move upmarket and reset customer expectations, often catching incumbents off guard.

Christensen et al. summarise this dynamic as follows:

New competitors with new business models arrive; incumbents choose to ignore the new players or to flee to higher-margin activities; a disrupter whose product was once barely good enough achieves a level of quality acceptable to the broad middle of the market, undermining the position of longtime leaders and often causing the 'flip' to a new basis of competition.[5]

At the 'flip' point, the disruptive innovation has become 'good enough'—that is, its initial deficiencies are no longer determinative—and it moves into the mainstream market. Customers who previously didn't realise they wanted a new offering, suddenly decide that they prefer the new proposition to the established one.

As that shift occurs, the dominant incumbents, perfectly adapted as they are to the old paradigm, find themselves unable or unwilling to pivot.

They become victims of their own success, failing in the new era because they have perfectly evolved to serve the demands of a bygone era. They find themselves increasingly hampered by a business model anchored in legacy products, services, and structures that no longer fully meet evolving demands.

Nokia's Rise and Fall

The fortunes of Nokia in the face of Apple's disruption illustrate how the innovator's dilemma can play out.

In 2007, Nokia was the dominant incumbent in the global smartphone market, with a share of 48.7% and a market capitalisation of around $120 billion.[6] That November, *Forbes* featured Nokia on its cover, with the headline, 'Nokia: One Billion Customers—Can Anyone Catch the Cell Phone King?'[7]

By 2012, just five years later, Nokia's market capitalisation had collapsed to $8 billion, its global smartphone share had plummeted to just 3.5%, and in 2013, it sold its handset and services business to Microsoft for $7.2 billion, roughly equivalent to Apple's profit in the second quarter of that year.[8]

Nokia's downfall began in January 2007, when Apple entered the market with the launch of its first iPhone. At the time, Nokia's N95 model far outclassed the iPhone in traditional specifications, including GPS, a 5-megapixel camera, an LED flash, 3G and WiFi, and even a TV-out capability, all of which the iPhone lacked.[9]

But the iPhone offered a new and quite different value proposition. It had a sleek design and a revolutionary touchscreen interface that offered a vision for an emerging digital ecosystem. Nokia failed to appreciate these features. It dismissed the iPhone as 'not even a proper smartphone' and stuck to its 'QWERTY'-style keyboard, convinced consumers didn't want touchscreens.[10]

By 2008, Apple had launched the iPhone 3G with improved functionality, which moved it closer to being 'good enough' for users to consider it as a viable alternative to Nokia's handsets.

More importantly, in that same year, Apple also launched the App Store. Within the first week, users downloaded more than 10 million apps, attracting a flood of developers to the platform.[11] Google also entered the market, introducing the Android operating system, which Samsung and LG and other manufacturers soon adopted, as well as Google Play, a rival app marketplace.[12]

Apple's and Google's disruptive technologies shifted the competitive landscape from being centred on handset features to being centred on software ecosystems, apps, and services. In this new environment, Apple's touchscreen was more than just a fashionable design feature; it became a gateway to a new digital ecosystem.

Nokia's Failed Pivot—'The Focus Was on the Phone' Despite launching its own digital store (Ovi) and an operating system (Symbian), Nokia's strategic focus remained firmly on hardware, not software. As one Nokia engineer recalled, 'The focus was on the phone, because Nokia had this amazing factory that could crank out 100 million units a year if you got a hit'.[13]

Nokia failed to put the necessary marketing muscle behind Ovi, so developers mostly ignored it.[14] As for Symbian, in addition to being plagued by usability issues, it was incompatible with many apps, as well as the developer ecosystem, and Android and iOS.[15] As one former Nokia employee said, 'developing for Symbian could make you want to slice your wrists'.[16] Meanwhile, Apple and Google continued to nurture their thriving new ecosystems, creating network effects that Nokia could not match.

In the face of disruptive change, Nokia stuck to its old script, allocating a disproportionate amount of attention and resources to handsets at the expense of Ovi and Symbian.[17] Nokia's first touchscreen phone (the 5800) finally launched in 2008 and was a commercial success but came about 'one and a half years late'.[18] Gradually, the quality of Nokia's high-end phones began to decline relative to new entrants. The 5800's successor, the N97, launched in 2009, was, according to one top manager, 'a total fiasco in terms of the quality of the product'.[19]

The Flip The iPhone presented a radically different value proposition that was built around software, apps, and services. Customers didn't realise they wanted these features—until they suddenly realised that they did.

Nokia, perfectly adapted to the old handset-centric environment, found itself unable to pivot in time. It did not fail because it made poor handsets. Rather, it failed because it was *too good* at making handsets. So good, in fact, that it was unable to see the inflection points and disrupt its existing profit engine in favour of the disruptive new value proposition presented by the iPhone.

Law Firm Parallels

The dynamics described by Christensen are now beginning to play out across the legal industry. For decades, law firms have dominated the higher end of the market, offering complex, bespoke, and expensive services. However, their offerings are increasingly misaligned with evolving client expectations.

The turning point began in GC 3.0, when a shifting risk landscape and the more-for-less challenge began pushing clients towards alternative solutions. Beginning in the early to mid-2010s, new entrants, including ALSPs, began entering the market in growing numbers, offering automation, process improvement, and hybrid staffing solutions that streamlined costs and workflows, while introducing new pricing propositions. These providers initially targeted niche and lower-margin legal work, posing little threat to law firms, which remained focused on higher-margin matters.[20]

As is often the case in the early stages of disruption, these shifts attracted little attention from incumbents, who viewed them as peripheral to their core business. Those firms that did respond to shifting market dynamics, did so cautiously, concentrating on incremental innovations that would not threaten the billable-hour profit engine.

The Great Unbundling   Fast forward to the early 2020s and the disruptive entrants were no longer operating at the fringes. They were moving firmly into the mainstream and reshaping the architecture of legal service delivery. Automation, analytics, and platform solutions had begun to unbundle work once handled exclusively by traditional law firms.

This has intensified in GC 4.0. Today, disruptive innovation is beginning to fragment the market itself. The more that AI era legal departments digitise, the more they will seek providers that can integrate with their emerging technology-enabled operating models.

As Richard Susskind has observed, legal work now takes place across a continuum, ranging from the *bespoke* (handcrafted solutions honed specifically for individual matters), to the *standardised* (where standard processes are employed), to the *systematised* (the computerisation of checklists, procedure manuals, etc. into workflow systems), to the *commoditised* (where legal work is prepackaged and made available online, either for a fee or at no charge).[21] It is this final stage, Susskind argues, that poses a 'radical departure from the billable hour model because legal expertise is leveraged without directly consuming lawyers' time':

> There is no denying … rather ominously for lawyers, that some legal resources will become readily available online at no cost, perhaps even as a shared resource to which anyone can contribute and from which anyone can draw.[22]

An ever-growing volume of legal work now fits in this last category of becoming commoditised. Tasks that just a decade ago were bundled within the traditional 'one-stop-shop' law firm have now been unbundled and distributed across ALSPs, technology platforms, consulting firms, and in-house teams. Each of these players captures the segments of work they can most efficiently deliver, leaving traditional firms to compete over a shrinking pool of premium-priced bespoke work.[23]

These shifts have set the stage for an even deeper transformation. As AI reshapes corporate and legal department structures and workflows, the influence of new market entrants will continue to grow, while the position of the traditional law firm model will steadily erode.

GC 4.0 Acceleration and the Growing Client–law Firm Gap The arrival of GC 4.0 is accelerating the widening gap between corporate legal departments and their outside law firms. AI-enabled operating models now allow in-house teams to deliver fast, integrated, and data-driven solutions for a growing share of legal work, at lower cost and with greater consistency than many traditional firms have been able to match.

Law firms are struggling to adapt to this new dynamic. Most of their process improvement workflow initiatives have fallen short of client expectations.[24] Surveys confirm that clients view themselves as well ahead of law firms in deploying innovative people, process, and technology solutions.[25] A recent benchmark highlights this gap: 81% of in-house counsel report using AI for legal work, compared to only 55% of law firm attorneys.[26]

ALSPs Gaining Ground Meanwhile, the global ALSP market is expanding more rapidly than the traditional legal services market, growing at an 18% compound annual growth rate (CAGR) since 2021, to reach $28.5 billion in 2023.[27] It is projected to reach $50 billion by 2033, reflecting client demand for legal services that combine technology, efficiency, and price transparency in ways that traditional law firms have struggled to match.[28] Scale is only part of this story. ALSPs are also growing in sophistication, offering a broad suite of services that now range from consulting, advisory, training, and flexible resourcing, to e-discovery, regulatory compliance, and data-driven due diligence.[29]

And it is no longer just corporate law departments that are leveraging ALSPs. One-third of law firms (including over half of large firms) now report either establishing ALSP affiliates or partnering with independent providers to deliver services and technology solutions their legacy businesses cannot.[30]

Sluggish Incumbent Reaction As we have seen, despite these developments, most firms have been slow and fragmented in their response. Many lack coherent transformation strategies, hampered by siloed practice groups that make it structurally difficult to deliver the cross-disciplinary and technology-enabled solutions that GC 4.0 clients demand. As one industry survey concluded, the 'enormous gaps between what clients deem to be important and what their preferred law firms have implemented imply that most firms are either not listening or have not been able to implement the solutions their clients desire'.[31] Consequently, an increasingly complex legal services ecosystem has emerged, with ALSPs, law firms, and corporate legal departments competing and collaborating across various projects and matters.

For now, large firms remain very profitable by providing a core of complex, strategic legal work. Many of these law firms still operate as if their competitive advantage is permanent. Yet, as disrupters advance upmarket, equipped with leaner business models and powerful technology, the space reserved for high-end strategic legal advice will inevitably narrow.[32] ALSPs, AI-powered clients, and automation are eroding traditional billable-hour models, and as the pace of change inside legal departments accelerates, incumbents will need to keep up.

As Christensen et al. remind us:

The temptation for market leaders to view the advent of new competitors with a mixture of disdain, denial, and rationalization is nearly irresistible. U.S. Steel posted record profit margins in the years prior to its unseating by the minimills; in many ways it was blind to its disruption. As we and others have observed, there may be nothing as vulnerable as entrenched success.[33]

The parallel to today's law firms is hard to ignore. Those that fail to adapt to the emerging environment risk more than lost market share. They risk ceding the initiative to their clients and new entrants offering faster, cheaper, and more integrated solutions that are aligned with the emerging digital strategies of MNCs. It is this dynamic that will redefine the terms of competition in the GC 4.0 legal services market.

The Hardest Part Is Letting Go

Even when incumbents do embrace disruptive innovation, they can struggle to do more than just incorporate it into their existing business models. The corporate 'immune system'—the organisational reflex that resists threats to established structures, incentives, and ways of working—tends to deflect the innovation or blend it into the legacy model, avoiding the disruptive effects that a full embrace could pose.

A 'Kodak Moment'?

Eastman Kodak is a case in point. Famous for its 'Kodak Moment' commercials, the slogan has become a shorthand for failure to successfully navigate disruptive innovation.[34]

Founded in 1892, the company invented roll film and the first simple portable camera in 1888.[35] By pairing cheap cameras with consumable film, it dominated the global film market throughout the twentieth century, at one point controlling nearly 90% of it.[36] By the 1970s, Kodak was the very image of a 'blue-chip' MNC.

In 1975, Steven J. Sasson, a Kodak engineer, invented the first digital camera.[37] The first iteration hardly looked threatening. It was the size of a toaster, took 20 seconds to capture an image, was of low quality, and required a TV connection to view.[38] But it was filmless, and the potential for disruption was clear. Contrary to the popular narrative, Kodak did not miss this. It invested billions of dollars in digital technologies and even managed to carve out a strong market position, with technologies that simplified the transfer of digital images from cameras to computers.[39]

In 2001, before the emergence of Facebook, it acquired Ofoto, a photo-sharing site.[40] The acquisition could have positioned Kodak at the forefront of what would soon become the social media revolution, transforming image sharing into a much larger and connected digital ecosystem, much as Facebook and others would later do. But the company's corporate immune system kicked in. Rather than using these investments and expertise to reimagine photography for the digital age, Kodak repurposed Ofoto to promote photo printing, reinforcing its legacy business rather than disrupting it. When Sasson's digital camera patent expired in 2007, new entrants such as Apple seized the opportunity, embedding digital cameras into smartphones and building new ecosystems around them. By 2012, Kodak had filed for bankruptcy.[41]

As Scott Anthony has observed:

> The right lessons from Kodak are subtle. Companies often see the disruptive forces affecting their industry. They frequently divert sufficient resources to participate in emerging markets. Their failure is usually an inability to truly embrace the new business models the disruptive change opens up. Kodak created a digital camera, invested in the technology, and even understood that photos would be shared online. Where they failed was in realizing that online photo sharing was the new business, not just a way to expand the printing business.[42]

Law firms run the same risks with potentially disruptive legal technology. It can be tempting for them to leverage sustaining innovations that make their current model more efficient or profitable, rather than disruptive innovations that reimagine or reinvent the market altogether.

If they fail to heed the lessons of digital photography, however, they run the risk of having their own 'Kodak Moment'.

Snow Melts at the Edges ...

Another way of looking at this is to remember that disruption rarely happens all at once. It begins gradually, often at the edges of a market.[43] As former Intel CEO Andy Grove remarked, 'when spring comes, snow melts first at the periphery, because that is where it is most exposed'.[44] Early signals of change can be the precursor for powerful shifts in the competitive landscape.

Inflection Points

These shifts tend to develop gradually and in ways that do not draw the immediate attention of decision-makers. But once they crystallise, they can suddenly overturn the very assumptions upon which industries are built.

Columbia Business School professor, Rita McGrath, calls these 'inflection points'.[45] As she describes it, 'Changes in the environment in or around organizations can create new, entrepreneurial opportunities—and result in potentially devastating consequences for those still operating under the old model or assumptions. The effects are often compounded because institutional rules typically lag what is possible'.[46]

Inflection points arise when a mismatch develops between what once made an organisation successful and the present environment. Triggers can include technological, regulatory, political, or demographic changes in the environment that reconfigure realities before incumbents are able to fully adapt. However, the outcome the resulting gap creates is similar: performance drops sharply, and incumbents risk decline or demise.[47]

Inflection points don't just cause slow decline; once they crystallise, they can lead to sudden drops in performance.[48] However, as McGrath observes, they can be slow to arrive:

> Even when you see an inflection point on the horizon, it can take a lot longer than you think for it to actually arrive. Customers will only remain hostages for so long. Eventually the model that imprisons them is bound to collapse ... Deeply understanding the situations your customers are in, the jobs they are trying to get done in those situations, and the outcomes they are seeking is vital to anticipating how those situations might change.[49]

Why Incumbents Struggle

Incumbents often struggle to spot the signs of pending inflection points because they tend to rely too heavily on 'lagging indicators', such as profits, revenues, or returns on investment, all of which measure past performance rather than predict future threats. By the time those metrics signal trouble ahead, it can be too late to forestall organisational decline.

To detect shifts in time, organisations should focus on 'leading indicators', such as customer satisfaction, customer usage, employee engagement, or employee turnover, all of which hint at a future that has yet to fully crystallise. The problem is that most organisations tend to discount such signals because they feel uncertain and ambiguous.[50]

As McGrath notes, 'They are often qualitative rather than quantitative. They are often told as narratives rather than in meticulous PowerPoint charts. For that reason, executives are often wary about basing important decisions on them. This can be folly of the highest order in a world of strategic inflection points, because the leading indicators are where ideas about the future are to be found'.[51]

This blind spot is compounded by a corporate 'immune system' that typically resists change to the very model that has long underpinned success. Law firms are particularly vulnerable to this dynamic, given that the billable-hour model remains the primary mechanism through which firms assess lawyer productivity, quantify the financial value of matters and client relationships, and establish revenue targets.[52]

Early Warning Signs

McGrath identifies several signals of pending inflection points, including:

- Customers no longer being excited about what is offered.
- Customers finding cheaper, simpler solutions that are 'good enough', and competition emerging from unexpected places.
- Employees leaving and it being increasingly difficult to attract candidates.[53]

All these warning signs are visible in the legal services market today.

Client Dissatisfaction   Clients are increasingly dissatisfied with law firm offerings, viewing them as both overpriced and poorly aligned with their evolving needs. In a recent survey, 45% of in-house lawyers rated top 100 firms as offering 'poor' or 'terrible' value for money, while only 2% thought value was 'excellent'.[54]

Growing Competition   As McGrath notes, 'practices that displease or even enrage customers can create an opening for a disruptive player to come into your market and cause customers to defect'.[55] That warning is playing out in the legal sector. A 2024 survey found that 81% of law firms had reported a drop in demand over the preceding year.[56] By 2025, the picture had grown starker: nearly every firm surveyed (97%) acknowledged client attrition over the past 12 months, driven by tighter client budgets, consolidation of law firm panels, and the migration of work to lower-cost providers.[57]

These figures underscore a structural reallocation of legal work away from traditional firms. Clients are shifting to ALSPs and the Big Four for solutions that are 'good enough' for an expanding volume of legal work—so much so that most law firms are ironically sourcing services from the very same suppliers, sometimes 'white-labelling' it to clients.[58] Firms are also using other players at the edge of the new ecosystem, including consultants and technology companies.[59]

As Thomson Reuters has observed, 'Legal services providers of all varieties form an increasingly complex ecosystem in which providers may find themselves competing for work even as they serve as close collaborators—or in a vendor role—on another project or matter. A single independent ALSP may provide services not just to corporate law departments but also to law firms'.[60]

Growing Attrition Rates   Law firms are also struggling with increased attrition rates. Although lateral hiring has slowed, departures persist at all levels, from equity partners, to associates, to support staff.[61] Attrition among junior and senior associates is particularly pronounced, with rates nearly doubling between 2024 and 2025.[62] Many associates are leaving not just for in-house or corporate roles, but for good: in 2025, nearly twice as many departing associates reported that they no longer intend to practice law as compared to the prior year.[63]

As noted in Chapter 8, work–life balance challenges have long been a source of strain in law firms. Hybrid working tensions are a more recent addition to the mix; a lingering hangover from the COVID-19 era that has reshaped expectations around flexibility across many industries. Many firms continue to struggle to reconcile these expectations with the demands of client service and team cohesion. It is perhaps no surprise, then, that burnout remains widespread. One large-scale survey across leading law firms found that 17% of staff felt emotionally depleted by their work and lacked the energy to pursue what mattered to them.[64] More than half (52%) of respondents had taken at least one day off due to mental health difficulties in the past three months, while a quarter (26%) of stressed employees said they were considering quitting to safeguard their mental health.[65]

The cost of attrition is increasingly steep. Beyond disruption to client delivery, service quality, and workload for remaining teams, departures erode institutional knowledge and increase recruitment and training costs.[66] One recent study estimated that the cost of losing a third-year associate now exceeds $1 million.[67]

To stem the tide, firms have leaned on pay, with nearly one-third of firms reporting that they plan to raise compensation by approximately 10% to attract attorneys.[68] Between 2012 and 2024, first-year associate salaries grew by 48% and seventh-year associate compensation rose by 78%.[69] Profits per equity partner increased even more—up 141% in the same period.[70] However, given client concerns over rising legal costs, it is questionable whether ever-higher salaries will prove to be a sustainable solution to the attrition challenge firms are facing.

Recruitment Challenges Beyond attrition, law firms face a deeper challenge in attracting and retaining young talent for the long term. A global study of law students and young lawyers from the top 100 law schools ranked by *U.S. News & World Report* revealed a striking shift in career aspirations. While most respondents intended to begin their careers in law firms, only 23% were interested in the partnership track. Long-term goals veered away from firms, with 29% wanting to move in-house and 24% drawn to government or nonprofit positions. The main drivers were concerns over work–life balance (mirroring the motivators driving attrition), misalignment with personal interests and long-term goals, and a sense that law firm practice was inconsistent with their values. These findings suggest a generational shift in attitudes among Gen Z that threatens the traditional law firm partnership pipeline.

Jobs to Be Done

Another useful lens for understanding why traditional law firms are losing ground to ALSPs and in-house sourcing is Christensen's work on 'Jobs to be Done' (JTBD). More of a mindset than a rigid framework, JTBD argues that customers don't 'buy' products or services for their own sake; rather, they 'hire' them to perform a specific 'job' that will help them achieve outcomes.[71] Customers care about outcomes. Products or services have no intrinsic value; their worth lies in how well they can get the job done.[72] When a better solution emerges, customers 'fire' the old product or service and 'hire' the new one. For example, if the job is to get from point A to point B for a meeting, a customer might 'hire' a taxi. But if a ride-hailing app can do that job more reliably, with cleaner cars, transparent pricing, and a cash-free experience, the taxi might be 'fired' in favour of an Uber.[73]

Circumstances Are Important

Which solution gets hired by the customer to do a job depends on the underlying situation, which the JTBD approach refers to as 'circumstances'.[74] The overriding need might be to get to a meeting, but if it is raining, staying dry becomes part of the job. If traffic is heavy, speed becomes a circumstance. If the meeting is formal, peace and quiet to prepare may be important. Conversely, if it is casual and the weather nice, enjoying a pleasant outdoor experience along the way may come into play. In all of these cases, the overarching job (getting to the meeting) remains the same, but circumstances shape which solution—a taxi, an Uber, an electric scooter, or the subway—gets hired to do the job.

The Importance of Shifting Constraints

While circumstances influence which solution gets 'hired' to do a job, innovation can change what solutions are possible, or even create entirely new jobs. The smartphone, for example, replaced a large number of single-function devices, such as cameras, recorders, maps, and flashlights, by bundling them into one integrated solution. As McGrath notes, it 'has been brilliant in helping us get more and more jobs done, all without having to carry around specialised devices'.[75]

But the smartphone did more than improve existing jobs; it also created new ones, such as capturing and then instantly sharing experiences on social media. These were possibilities that older technologies couldn't do at all. As McGrath observes, smartphones exemplify how shifting constraints, such as 'the ability to take videos on a device that is probably in your pocket anyway—can help a company identify opportunities to change the customer journey and customer frustrations at not getting their jobs done'.[76]

Application to Legal Services

These dynamics also apply in the legal services context. Three observations are worth highlighting. First, technology is transforming *how* existing jobs get done. Second, it is creating entirely new kinds of legal work. Third, in a fast-changing landscape, firms need to be clear about *what* job clients are hiring them to do, and equally clear about the difference between the job and the means used to carry it out. We will explore these in turn.

Technology Is Transforming How Legal Jobs Are Done　Just as smartphones bundled multiple tools into a single device, legal technology platforms now allow clients to complete numerous legal tasks faster, cheaper, and at far greater scale than human lawyers could manage through manual processes. Automation, workflow systems, and contract analytics have not changed the purpose of these jobs, but they have radically altered the *means* of performing them.

Technology Is Creating Entirely New Legal Jobs　Legal innovation is no longer limited to improving how existing jobs get done; it is generating entirely new kinds of legal work, such as predictive analytics, automated compliance monitoring, and the integration of legal workflows into corporate platforms. These new jobs require data-driven systems and multidisciplinary expertise that most traditional law firm structures are not designed to deliver.

In the GC 4.0 era, this transformation is accelerating. Innovations in automation, analytics, and platform technology are creating new ways to deliver legal outcomes that were previously beyond reach.

Success Now Depends on Understanding the Real Job to Be Done　In a world where legal technology is expanding both the *ways* in which existing legal jobs get done and the *kinds* of jobs that clients now need to have done, law firms would be well advised to spend time clarifying what jobs clients are actually hiring them to do.

Corporate clients don't hire lawyers to provide legal analysis; they hire them to achieve specific outcomes, such as drafting a contract, managing discovery, negotiating a deal, or advising the board. The *circumstances* surrounding each job, including urgency, budget, risk appetite, or the desired impact on the intended audience, determine whether clients hire a premium law firm, an ALSP, a self-service solution, or in-house teams to do it.

This point has been well captured by Campbell, who notes:

> Some lawyers … misunderstand the nature of what lawyers offer clients. As with other services and product, consumers do not, at core, want a particular kind of product or service. Rather, they want a problem solved. As Harvard Business School professor Theodore Levitt used to tell his students, consumers don't want an electric drill,

they want a hole in the wall. Electric drills are one way to provide that result, but not the only way. There was a time when only lawyers could provide solutions to legal problems, but today those solutions can come from sources as diverse as smart phone apps and emerging 'professional' occupations.[77]

Levitt's observation is instructive. But circumstances and shifting constraints may mean that customers no longer want a hole at all; they may actually want a picture hung on the wall. If a new adhesive can get that job done without drilling holes, customers will 'hire' it instead. The same applies to law firms: unless they truly understand the client's job to be done, they risk offering the wrong solution, or solving a problem the client no longer has. Circumstances matter.

GC 4.0 Implications   The GC 4.0 era will amplify all three of these dynamics. Clients are redefining their jobs around speed, efficiency, and integration. Technologies are eliminating traditional constraints and enabling new forms of value creation and, by extension, new 'jobs'.

Undoubtedly, some traditional jobs will remain, such as solving highly complex legal challenges, where the credibility and judgement of a top-tier law firm are critical. But those represent the tip of a much larger legal services iceberg.

Success for firms will increasingly depend on understanding the jobs they are being hired to do and configuring themselves to deliver those jobs in the best way. The key questions they should ask are:

- What are the jobs to be done for clients in the AI era?
- Which ones are we most vulnerable to being 'fired' from?
- Which new jobs will clients be unlikely to hire us for at all?

Ultimately, success in GC 4.0 will depend on integrating changing circumstances and shifting constraints into firm strategy, moving beyond the delivery of legal inputs to becoming embedded partners in a client–centric ecosystem.

The Impact of Exponential Growth

All of these dynamics are magnified by the compounding effect of technological growth, which ensures that change will not simply continue but accelerate over the coming years. Moore's Law (which, as noted in

Chapter 4, is the observation that the number of transistors on a microchip doubles roughly every two years with minimal cost increases) has underpinned dramatic advances in computing since 1959. It has fuelled the rise of GC 3.0 and GC 4.0, and it continues to drive the accelerating capabilities in AI and automation today. For the legal industry, gains in computational efficiency have given rise to increasingly powerful legal technologies, including automation, contract analysis, knowledge systems, and workflow management tools.

As humans, we tend to think in linear terms, which can make it hard to comprehend the impact of compounding. Albert Einstein is said to have remarked that 'compound interest is the eighth wonder of the world. He who understands it, earns it; he who doesn't, pays it'.[78] The same applies to technology. Incremental improvements, compounded over decades, have created transformational change that can feel sudden and overwhelming in the real world.

The Indian Chessboard

One vivid metaphor for this impact is the legend of the Indian chessboard. A sage who invented the game of chess is said to have presented it to an Indian prince, who was impressed and offered the sage a reward. The sage asked for one grain of rice for the first square of the board, two for the second, four for the third, and so forth, doubling for each of the 64 squares. By the 32nd square (i.e., the halfway point), the single grain had multiplied into more than 4.2 billion grains. By the 64th and final square, the total exceeded 18 quintillion grains, roughly equivalent to the modern world's entire rice output for a decade.[79] What starts modestly grows astronomically through the impact of compounding.

Technology and the Second Half of the Board

The chessboard story has a parallel in the evolution of computing. In 1965, the year Gordon Moore made his prediction, a single chip had 64 transistors on it.[80] By 1971, Intel's 4004 contained 2,300.

By 2000, the Pentium 4 contained 42 million, still short of what smartphones would require.[81] By 2007, Intel's Quad Core Xeon had reached 820 million transistors, enabling the iPhone era to begin.[82]

By 2022, as Moore's Law entered the 'second half of the chessboard', Apple's M1 Ultra contained 114 billion transistors.[83] Nvidia's 2024 Blackwell

GPUs raised that figure to 208 billion transistors—more than 3 billion times the transistor count of 1965.[84]

In 2026, Nvidia announced the Vera Rubin platform, Blackwell's successor. It will contain 336 billion transistors—more than 5 billion times the count in 1965—while using about the same amount of power as the Blackwell, achieved through architectural improvements.[85]

A similar story can be told by looking at the evolution of floating-point operations per second (FLOPS), a performance benchmark for supercomputers (see Figure 9.1). In 1954, IBM's 704 managed 10,000 FLOPS.[86] By 2000, the ASCI White supercomputer performed 4.93 trillion FLOPS. By 2007, IBM's Blue Gene/L reached 478 trillion. In 2022, the HPE Cray surpassed 1 quintillion FLOPS (an exaFLOP). By 2025, El Capitan reached 1.809 exaFLOPS.[87] Put differently: if every person on Earth performed one calculation per second, it

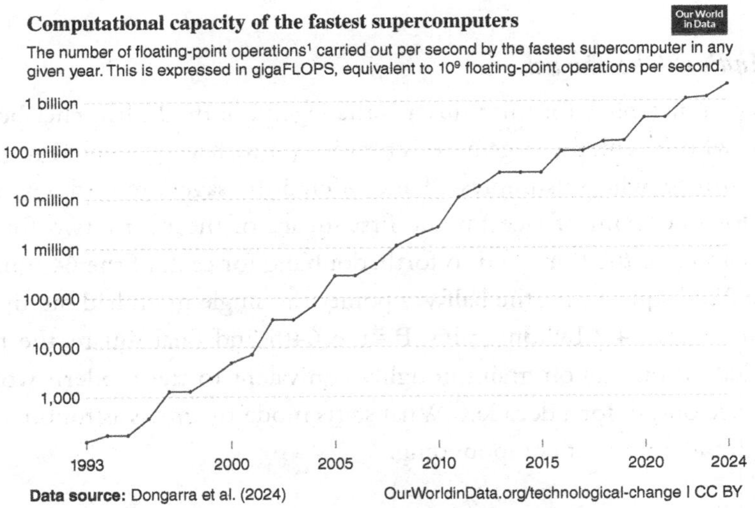

Figure 9.1   Computational capacity of supercomputers measured in gigaFLOPS.

Source: Dongarra et al. (2024)—with minor processing by Our World in Data. 'Computational capacity of the fastest supercomputers' [dataset]. Jack Dongarra, Martin Meuer, Horst Simon et al., 'TOP 500' [original data], https://archive. ourworldindata.org/20250909-093708/grapher/supercomputer-power-flops.html.

would take all 8 billion people over four years and four months to do the same calculation that today's supercomputers can complete in one second.[88]

At the same time, storage capacity has skyrocketed while costs have plummeted by orders of magnitude (see Figure 9.2). A standard laptop today typically contains 256 GB storage capacity. That would have cost around $20 billion in the 1950s in today's prices.[89] And the average smartphone today has millions of times more memory and hundreds of thousands of times more processing power than the Apollo 11 Guidance Computer that took humans to the Moon in 1969.[90]

Looking Ahead   There is an ongoing debate about how long Moore's Law can hold.[91] Some argue physical limits are close. Others, including ASML (the company that makes the machines producing the world's most advanced chips) see continued improvements in processing power by using exotic materials, advanced packaging technologies, and more complex 3D transistor designs.[92]

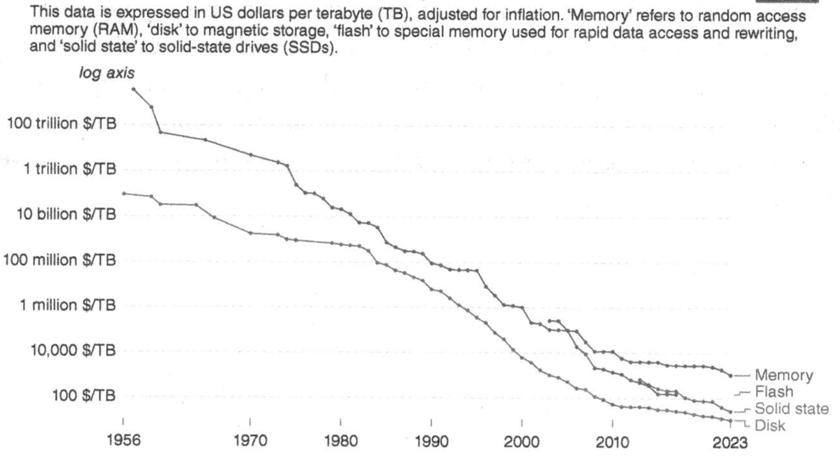

Figure 9.2   Declines in the cost of computer memory and storage.

Source: Our World in Data, 'Historical cost of computer memory and storage', using data from John C. McCallum (2023) and U.S. Bureau of Labor Statistics (2024), https://ourworldindata.org/grapher/historical-cost-of-computer-memory-and-storage.

Beyond chips, improvements in hardware, including increased optimisation of and improved synergies between CPUs, GPUs, and NPUs, as well as improvements in AI software, promise further significant gains.[93]

However this plays out, what seems safe to predict is that technology will continue to disrupt and profoundly reshape corporations and legal departments in the coming 5–10 years.

The Implications for Law Firms

For law firms, all of this is critical. Their structural and systemic challenges will collide with the compounding force of exponential technology and the disruptive innovations it is unleashing across companies and legal departments. ALSPs are also moving forward, while many incumbents remain slow to detect inflection points, and even slower to adapt their business models.

What makes this moment different is the speed and scale of technological change. In an exponential world, the costs of inaction compound rapidly, compressing the time available to respond. Each year of delay increases the gap between digitally enabled clients and firms still anchored in analogue operating models. The costs of inaction here rise geometrically, not linearly.

Unless firms can reimagine the jobs they are hired to do in the GC 4.0 era, their long-standing dominance will erode at an accelerating rate as technology advances and new competitors capture the ground ahead. The rise of ALSPs marks another frontier of disruption, and it is to them that we will now turn.

10 | Alternative Legal Service Providers

At the heart of capitalism is creative destruction.

—Joseph A. Schumpeter[1]

Alternative Legal Service Providers

There is no universally accepted definition of an ALSP. Much depends on how one defines 'legal services', since the term can include a broad and diverse set of providers. Legal market analyst Jordan Furlong, writing in 2014 and referring to ALSPs under the label *NewLaw*, offered perhaps the most useful characterisation: 'any model, process, or tool that represents a significantly different approach to the creation or provision of legal services than what the legal profession traditionally has employed'.[2]

The past two decades have seen the rise of ALSPs. Initially ignored by many incumbent law firms as peripheral and low-end providers, ALSPs have steadily expanded in their scope and sophistication, changing how legal services are delivered.

What started as a response to a growing demand by clients for alternative staffing and more cost-effective support for routine legal work has grown into a mature market that today covers virtually every link in the legal services value chain. Today, ALSPs provide services ranging from training and project management to contract lifecycle management, legal research and drafting, compliance, litigation, corporate secretarial, and intellectual property support, strategic consulting, hybrid staffing and substantive lawyering.

This growth has been fuelled by the twin forces discussed in Chapter 1: the demand for broader, more holistic support, and the more-for-less dynamic. On the supply side, globalisation during the GC 2.0 and 3.0 eras gave rise to cost-effective offshoring and hybrid staffing models, while technological advances allowed ever-increasing volumes of routine or repetitive work to be structured, automated, and migrated to the Cloud.[3]

ALSPs are now clearly established as part of the legal ecosystem. However, they too face the same forces of client-centric disruption that law firms are confronting. To stay competitive, they will need to continue to evolve and adapt at the pace of AI.

Origins

ALSPs first emerged in the early 2000s, driven by a widening gap in the market for affordable, routine corporate legal work.[4] During the consolidation wave of the 1990s, large law firms had increasingly moved upmarket, shifting their focus away from lower-margin, commoditised services and towards more complex, higher-value work. Meanwhile, demand for cost-effective routine legal support was quietly growing. Many of the technology start-ups that sprang up during the dot.com boom of the late 1990s needed flexible legal advice but could not afford premium rates. When the bubble burst in 2001, that demand intensified as margins tightened and cost pressures mounted.

On the supply side, a pool of capable legal talent was suddenly available. Many young in-house technology lawyers who had been laid off were looking for work and open to alternative career paths.[5] In the ensuing years—and into the GC 3.0 era—MNCs also came under pressure from the more-for-less dynamic, fuelling a broader search for scalable, lower-cost solutions. Together, these forces created fertile ground for the rise of ALSPs.

The first ALSPs specialised in offering fractionalised legal services, giving rise to what became known as the 'super temp' industry, that is, offshore, near-shore, or in-market lawyers who could be hired on a project or part-time basis to provide legal support during surge periods or for specific projects.[6]

As technology matured, ALSPs began to diversify into new areas, including document management, workflow optimisation, and process automation. With the advent of AI and the rise of increasingly sophisticated legal operations teams during the GC 3.0 era, corporate clients began to deconstruct the legal services value chain into ever smaller components. This unbundling created space for a wave of new entrants, including consultancies offering strategic advisory services, as well as more specialised operational or technology-driven providers.

Today, the market encompasses a wide range of services, from lower-tech and human-centric legal support to sophisticated, technology-enabled solutions, including:

- **Legal support** (46%). Ongoing, repeatable legal tasks and processes such as contract management and assistance with specific legal matters.
- **Flexible resourcing** (17%). Outsourcing, fractional staffing, and on-demand legal talent.
- **Consultancy and advisory** (17%). Strategic advice, legal operations consulting, training, and other advisory services.
- **Legal services** (10%). Legal services delivered by qualified legal professionals outside of the traditional law firm model.
- **Software** (10%). Legal technology products, including SaaS tools provided by ALSPs and, increasingly, law firms themselves.[7]

Driven by the increasingly sophisticated needs of clients, ALSPs have expanded their reach to cover nearly every slice of the legal services pie. Their offerings now span the full range of corporate legal needs, from routine, human-centric support to highly specialised, technology-enabled solutions.

As the ALSP industry evolves, the label 'alternative' is increasingly anachronistic. Over half (57%) of corporate legal departments now report using ALSPs, while 41% of law firms report doing so, either via third-party providers or through their own affiliated entities.[8] As David Wilkins and María J. Esteban have observed, the more corporate clients demand integrated, customised, and agile services, the more it becomes clear that what was once 'alternative' is now central to the practice of law. In effect, ALSPs have become mainstream providers for many core functions, while it is traditional law firms that risk appearing 'alternative', unless they can deliver such capabilities themselves or integrate closely within the broader array of services that clients now need. Indeed, this shift, Wilkins and Esteban note, is 'placing pressure on law firms to articulate how the services they provide contribute to delivering integrated client solutions'.[9]

Technology Providers—A Layered Ecosystem

As the ALSP market has matured, the notion of what constitutes an ALSP is broadening. What started as a people-centric outsourcing industry is now increasingly being shaped by legal technology providers. As AI assumes growing importance to both in-house and law firm practice in the GC 4.0 era, the relative bargaining power of leading technology companies is increasing.

However, the emerging landscape will not be monolithic. Instead, it will consist of a layered ecosystem of providers, each contributing to the whole with domain-specific capabilities (see Figure 10.1). Binding these layers together are application programming interfaces (APIs), the connective infrastructure that allows applications to connect with foundation models, retrieve external and proprietary content, and integrate with enterprise platforms.

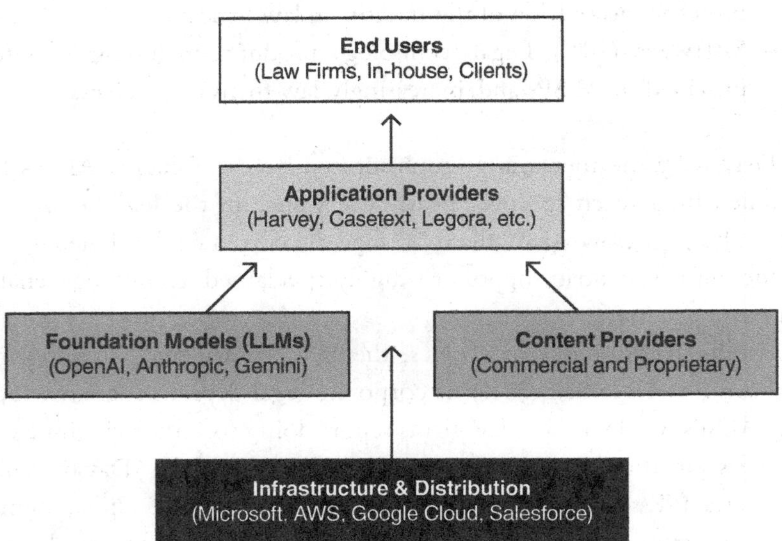

Figure 10.1   The layered legal AI ecosystem.

Source: Illustration by Logica Design.

Infrastructure and Distribution Platforms

The foundational layer of the emerging legal AI ecosystem consists of infrastructure and distribution platforms, such as Microsoft, AWS, Google Cloud, and Salesforce. These companies provide the computational power, enterprise integration, security, and productivity environments that enable users to operate legal AI at scale within corporate settings. Their offerings include familiar productivity suites, such as Microsoft 365 (Word, Excel, Outlook, OneDrive, and Teams) and Google Workspace (Docs, Sheets, Forms, Gmail, Drive, and Meet) that are deeply embedded into corporate and law firm workflows.[10]

Given the dominance these companies enjoy in enterprise software, they also act as distributors for other ecosystem players, including by embedding legal-specific AI capabilities directly into their tools and by offering access to distribution channels through corporate marketplaces. One example is *LexisNexis*, a global provider of legal, regulatory, and business information and analytics. The company has developed a suite of integrated solutions, including add-ins for Word (Lexis® Create), apps for Teams (Ask Legal and Lexis® Connect), and its own generative AI platform (Lexis+ AI), all of which are designed to connect directly with Microsoft's ecosystem. As Serena Wellen, Vice President of Product Management at LexisNexis has explained, the company made a strategic choice to become an early adopter of Microsoft's AI products so that its tools would meet customers where they already work, which is inside the Microsoft 365 environment.[11]

Another example from a different part of the ecosystem is *Harvey*, a leading application provider of generative AI solutions for the legal profession. Harvey has deployed its platform on Microsoft's Azure cloud and made it available through the Azure Marketplace (Microsoft's online store for enterprise applications and services). As Harvey announced, 'Microsoft and Harvey will collaborate closely to market and sell the Harvey on Azure solution to leading law firms, in-house teams, professional service providers, and private equity firms globally'.[12] Like LexisNexis, Harvey has integrated with SharePoint, Copilot, and Word, enabling customers to 'work more efficiently by leveraging Harvey's capabilities alongside the Microsoft ecosystem'.[13]

This is not to suggest that such symbiosis is always straightforward. Enterprise platforms impose constraints on the design paradigms that AI-native providers might otherwise prefer. As one group of Stanford researchers recently noted, 'founders are forced to build on top of Microsoft's relatively clunky feature suite, which enforces bottlenecks on the design paradigms they can use'.[14] Whether or not one accepts this critique, the ubiquity of large enterprise platforms in the corporate and law firm contexts means that, for practical purposes, other ecosystem players must build on top of them.

Foundation Models and Content Providers

Above this layer sit two parallel inputs. On the one side are foundation models, such as those developed by OpenAI, Anthropic, and Google, that provide the general-purpose reasoning capabilities of generative AI, powering products such as ChatGPT, Claude, and Gemini. These are large language models (LLMs) that have been trained on vast datasets to identify patterns and rules of language, allowing them to perform multiple tasks without requiring specific task training.[15] As many of such models are increasingly 'multimodal' (i.e., able to process not just text but also images, audio, and other media), they are often broadly referred to as 'foundation models'.[16] Although they are general in nature, foundation models can be adapted or 'fine-tuned' for domain-specific purposes, including legal tasks.[17]

On the other side are content providers with domain expertise, including LexisNexis, Thomson Reuters, and Wolters Kluwer, as well as proprietary providers, such as law firms or corporations themselves. These organisations maintain curated libraries of trusted legal knowledge, including case law, statutes, regulations, commentary, etc. that can reliably be used by the relevant portions of the technology stack.

Each of these players increasingly interacts with the others to deliver services. For example, Harvey leverages OpenAI's models alongside proprietary organisational data from law firms and other users (e.g., precedents and policies) to deliver services in partnership with Microsoft.[18]

Application Layer

These streams converge at the application layer, where providers such as Harvey, LexisNexis, and Thomson Reuters (*CoCounsel*) integrate infrastructure, foundation models, and content into practical tools and services for end users.[19] Their value lies in designing intuitive interfaces and embedding AI into enterprise platforms such as Microsoft 365, creating workflows that translate raw AI capability into user-friendly legal services. Common use cases include document review and extraction, document Q&A, summarisation, redlining, transcript analysis, chronology generation, and regulatory research.[20]

The market for legal AI applications is growing rapidly and is projected to grow from $1.53 billion in 2024 to $14.62 billion by 2035, representing a 22.77% CAGR, with the solutions segment dominating during this period. This growth is being fuelled by increasing adoption of AI by law firms and legal departments, a surging demand for automation of routine legal work, and a steady pipeline of new products and capabilities.[21] Benchmarking already shows striking efficiency gains. In one recent analysis, legal AI tools across seven legal tasks were found to be 'six times faster than the lawyers at the lowest end, and 80 times faster at the highest end'.[22]

End Users

At the top of the ecosystem are the end users, including law firms, in-house legal departments, and ultimate clients who consume the outputs. The quality of the end product is a function of close coordination across and interdependence between each of the elements.

Together, the legal technology ecosystem provides an increasingly dynamic and interdependent environment for new players and solutions to emerge in the coming years, among them the Big Four.

The Big Four

Among the more prominent adjacent entrants to the ALSP space have been the Big Four. They have a significant opportunity to disrupt the market and capture meaningful share by combining their multidisciplinary reach, technology capabilities, and global scale.

Over the past decade, the Big Four have steadily built out their legal services capabilities. They have done so by exploiting regulatory gaps that allow them to offer legal services in certain jurisdictions that traditionally have restricted multidisciplinary practices, and by operating in jurisdictions where regulatory restrictions on multidisciplinary practices are either weak, non-existent, or actively being reformed.[23]

Today, they have a significant presence in many major legal markets. In the United Kingdom, each now holds an 'Alternative Business Structure' (ABS) licence, enabling them to provide regulated legal services. They are even making inroads in the United States, despite long-standing prohibitions such as Rule 5.4 of the American Bar Association's *Model Rules of Professional Conduct*, which forbids fee-sharing or partnerships between lawyers and non-lawyers.[24] In February 2025, KPMG became the first of the Big Four to secure an ABS licence from the Arizona Supreme Court, entitling it to establish its own law firm, *KPMG Law US*.

As the Big Four's legal offerings have grown, they have expanded well beyond their traditional strength in tax and tax-related advisory work. They now operate across a wide spectrum of practice areas, ranging from employment, immigration, and restructuring, to technology, media, and telecommunications, and even into higher-margin areas, such as mergers and acquisitions, capital markets, and finance.[25]

Scholars note that this trajectory is unlikely to slow down any time soon. As one study concluded, 'there are good reasons to believe that the Big Four will be even more successful in penetrating the corporate legal services market in the decades to come'.[26]

Strategically, rather than copying the traditional law firm model, the Big Four are folding their legal services offerings into a broader suite of business solutions spanning legal, financial, risk, compliance, tax, technology, innovation, sustainability, and strategic management domains.[27] This allows them to provide multidisciplinary, end-to-end solutions to increasingly complex client problems.[28]

KPMG Law US, for example, explicitly positions itself as 'combining cutting-edge artificial intelligence and advanced technology solutions with legal services', aiming to become a 'first mover with this capability and to offer the most holistic range of tech-enabled services in the marketplace'.[29]

AI has the potential to accelerate this integrated model. The Big Four are already applying advanced data extraction and analytics to unstructured legal documents, giving them an edge in high-volume, efficiency-driven operations.[30]

Stuart Bedford, KPMG's Global Head of Legal Services, predicts that 'clients will increasingly turn to the Big Four for legal work because of their superior technology capabilities'.[31] Unlike traditional law firms constrained by thin capital structures, the Big Four not only possess the necessary technology stack but also the ability to reinvest profits to continually enhance it.[32]

Other Big Four firms have adopted a similar approach. Emily Foges, Lead Partner for Legal Managed Services at Deloitte, describes the firm's vision as combining 'high-quality legal advice with legal management consulting, legal managed services and legal technology', which allows Deloitte to provide outcomes-focused solutions rather than narrow advice.[33] Similarly, PwC highlights its ability to integrate structured data across business functions, offering insights that law firms cannot easily replicate.[34] As Bea Seravello notes, unlike law firms, 'the Big Four put a lot of investment around researching how they can take existing technologies that don't even relate to the practice of law, but can provide a client solution'.[35]

Scale and Global Reach

The Big Four possess significant resources globally, including capital, technology, and coverage. Their legal businesses, while small relative to their audit and advisory practices, are already substantial.

- KPMG: 3,800+ lawyers in 85 jurisdictions.
- PwC: 3,500 lawyers in 100 countries.
- EY: 3,400+ lawyers in 90 countries.
- Deloitte: 2,500+ lawyers in 75+ countries.[36]

Collectively, their legal revenues reached $1.5 billion in 2023, up from $900 million in 2015, and reflecting a 5% CAGR.[37] More broadly, all four can supplement their legal businesses with global workforces that number in the hundreds of thousands, and annual firm-wide revenues ranging from $38 billion (KPMG) to $67 billion (Deloitte).[38]

Equally important, the Big Four benefit from deep, long-standing relationships with virtually every major MNC. A remarkable 90% of all US public companies, including all of the Fortune 500 and the entire FTSE 100, are audited by the Big Four.[39] This client access provides a powerful platform from which to cross-sell their legal services.

Structural Constraints and Strategic Weaknesses

However, for all their strengths, the Big Four face structural impediments that have, until now, prevented them from fully capitalising on all their opportunities.

One of the most significant is siloed organisational design. Behind their global brands sit complex networks of independent, national, or regional partnerships, each with its own legal structure, balance sheet, and equity partners.[40]

These geographical and functional siloes can create complexity, breed internal turf battles, and reduce agility. As Mark Cohen has observed, their 'partner interests often diverge along economic, practice area, geographical, and generational lines'.[41] That divergence can create challenges for legal services partners competing for resources.

Another constraint is scale. Despite the size of the Big Four, their legal services businesses remain small relative to their core businesses. As Nick Woolf has noted, 'however big their legal practice, they are always going to pale into insignificance compared to other parts of the firm'.[42] In-house legal projects rarely match the size of those undertaken by larger enabling functions, such as HR or finance, where the Big Four are more accustomed to operating. That can leave legal services partners competing for internal resources in an environment where, echoing supermodel Linda Evangelista's famous line, other partners in the firm 'don't wake up for less than $10,000 a day'.[43]

Audit conflicts present further limitations. In order to protect auditor independence, audit services are highly regulated in many jurisdictions, with strict limits on the kinds of non-audit work that audit firms can offer their audit clients—including legal advice—and on the total fees they can charge audit clients for such work.[44] In practice, this means that when a company is an audit client, the audit firm's legal arm is often barred from advising it, even on unrelated matters. As Christopher Clark has noted, the conflicts created by their audit businesses prevent 'a large number of legal instructions from getting off the ground'.[45]

Finally, ethical and regulatory constraints remain hurdles in many markets. While jurisdictions such as the United Kingdom, Australia, Canada, and some US states have relaxed restrictions on multidisciplinary practices and non-lawyer ownership rules, many markets remain closed.[46] The Big Four's ability to scale their legal services businesses globally will depend in part on how rapidly these rules evolve.

Looking Ahead

Until now, the promise of the Big Four in the legal services market has been hampered by their inability to overcome the inherent structural and regulatory barriers they face. How they navigate these challenges will be paramount to their success going forward. That said, given how client-side demands are increasingly shifting towards multidisciplinary practice and technology-enabled solutions at scale, momentum may be on their side.

From Disruptors to Disrupted

Despite the disruptive impact ALSPs have had and continue to have on the legal market, they are no more immune from the same forces of client-centric disruption that law firms face. As legal departments digitally transform and evolve towards AI-centric models that will better support their corporations, they will expect more from their ALSPs beyond them offering low-cost and offshored or fractionalised human support or basic process optimisation tools. Solutions that were once cutting edge will increasingly become standardised, systematised, and commoditised as they get absorbed into fast-changing client delivery models.

To remain relevant, ALSPs will need to adapt rapidly and continue to innovate. They must take account not only of the moves of their clients but also those of law firms and competing ALSPs. No one will be standing still in the coming era.

Risk of Commoditisation

ALSPs initially emerged at the margins of the profession, offering cost-effective outsourcing for routine work. Over time, they expanded into technology-enabled solutions that are now ubiquitous across large corporations, including contract lifecycle management, document review, and compliance support. Many new entrants sought to eliminate inefficiencies across the legal services value chain, supplementing operational support with advisory services that helped legal departments improve their delivery models.

However, as client systems themselves become increasingly AI-enabled, ALSPs must continue to evolve. Human-centric offerings, such as alternative staffing, will need to be supplemented and, in some cases, replaced by even better enhancements than their clients are already deploying in-house. Technologies that were cutting-edge just a few years ago are already becoming commoditised in a crowded and AI-driven marketplace. As the *Financial Times* recently observed:

> New artificial intelligence tools are already disrupting the former disrupters, by enabling clients of so-called alternative legal service providers (ALSPs) to bring more of their work in-house. This, in turn, is starting to influence the nature of the work being outsourced to the service providers and their pricing models. There is a sense that generative AI could render unprepared providers obsolescent.[47]

Unilever provides a good example of this dynamic. As the company continues to digitise, its legal department is increasingly bringing legal work in-house, equipping teams of generalist lawyers around the world with generative AI tools. These tools now handle tasks that were once delegated to ALSPs, including contract drafting and negotiation, compliance audits, certain IP and privacy-related matters, as well as social media review. This has resulted in higher-quality, faster turnaround, streamlined workflows. Costs have reduced by as much as 60–80%, with some tasks completed 25% more quickly.[48]

Demand for Deeper Specialisation and Integration

As more work moves in-house, clients will increasingly become ALSPs' largest competitors. That is particularly true in relation to high-volume, commoditised work, where the 'job to be done' is centred on efficiency and cost. Varun Mehta, Chief Executive Officer of Factor Law, a global ALSP, has described how the Chief Investment Officer of a major private equity firm projected a fivefold increase in transaction volumes within a year, even as the cost per deal was set to reduce by 20–80% through the use of generative AI tools.[49]

However, disruption will also likely generate new opportunities for ALSPs that are able to occupy emerging competitive spaces. As Ed Sohn, former Global Head of Insights and Innovation at Factor Law, has observed, while some categories of work will disappear, AI may simultaneously generate more work, and greater volumes of it, as speed and data availability increase.[50]

The key to success for ALSPs in the AI era will be to integrate with client delivery models and technology platforms. As noted in Chapter 7, clients will increasingly view vendors as interoperable nodes that connect into their AI models. The value ALSPs bring will depend not only on the services they provide but also on how well they connect into client platforms. ALSPs, like law firms, must understand their clients' emerging operational environment and tailor their offerings accordingly.

At the same time, ALSPs will need to situate themselves strategically within the emerging technology ecosystem, as few ALSPs will survive this era without employing technology at scale. They also need to recognise that partnerships can shift in sudden ways and that their best customers may also be their greatest competitors. Above all, they must clearly understand where and how they bring value in the AI era, and how that should be priced. Those that remain narrowly focused on transactional support alone, using tools and technologies that are increasingly commoditised, will not survive. Those that evolve and adapt have the opportunity to capture new sources of value at scale and define the shape of the legal industry in the GC 4.0 era.

What Might Emerge?

Sooner or later everyone sits down to a banquet of consequences.
—Robert Louis Stevenson[1]

As we saw in Part III, traditional law firms face a series of structural impediments that make it difficult for them to evolve in the face of disruptive innovation. Many ALSPs will struggle for similar reasons. But with disruption come new opportunities. Part IV explores what might emerge in the wake of the changes that are now underway.

We begin by examining how law firms themselves might evolve in the AI era. A small number of firms may successfully transition into high-end 'boutiques', relying on a partner-heavy profit engine and leveraging technology, automation, and process optimisation to keep execution costs low. While this model may be lucrative for a very limited set of elite firms with truly scarce human expertise, it is not easily scalable, and most firms lack the niche skills needed to succeed. Even for those that do, the path will require them to fundamentally transform their operating and leverage models.

Another group of firms may pursue a very different approach: shifting towards corporate structures, characterised by external shareholders, boards, and CEO-led executive teams. Such models would unlock the

165

access to capital needed for major technology investments, acquisitions, and structural transformation. They would also enable firms to reimagine core profit and delivery models rather than simply defending their legacy structures in the face of disruptive change. Regulatory and ethical restraints have long limited these moves, but the rules are evolving. In several major markets, including the United Kingdom and Australia, as well as in parts of the United States, ABSs now permit non-lawyers to hold ownership or management interests in law firms under specific circumstances, creating new pathways and structures.

Alongside these shifts within law firms, entirely new models are emerging across the industry.

Hybrid organisations, which integrate legal services with a range of complementary capabilities, such as technology, consulting, and process engineering, are well positioned to scale efficiently and deliver multidisciplinary solutions. Several global law firms are already moving in this direction, while the Big Four continue to expand aggressively into the legal domain using hybrid models.

In parallel, platform models—technology-enabled infrastructures that connect clients, providers, data, and workflows—are also beginning to take shape. These platforms could become ecosystem orchestrators with significant influence as they embed themselves deeply into client systems, automating routing and triage, enabling real-time performance management and transforming how work is sourced, priced, and delivered. If they continue on this trajectory, platforms could profoundly reshape the competitive landscape for all legal industry players.

These dynamics raise a critical question: *how should law firms respond to all of this?*

Lessons from other industries suggest that firms can mitigate risk by investing in small, low-stakes ventures that sit outside the core business. These 'experiments' give firms a chance to explore new delivery models, technologies, and pricing mechanisms without triggering resistance from the legacy organisation. In the chapters that follow, we examine case studies, inside and outside the legal sector, where this approach has enabled successful adaptation.

Finally, law schools will also need to evolve to prepare future lawyers for the demands of GC 4.0. The traditional training pipeline, where schools delivered doctrinal foundations and firms developed professional competence through structured apprenticeships, is coming apart. Consequently, the gap between what schools teach and what the profession requires in the AI era is widening. Schools must clarify their purpose, focus on both analytical and practical skills, and rethink what they teach, how they teach it, and how the curriculum is structured across the full course of study.

11 | New Law Firm Models

The first step towards getting somewhere is to decide you're not going to stay where you are.

—John Pierpont, 'J.P.' Morgan[1]

Overview

For all the reasons discussed in Parts II and III, client-centric disruption is set to reshape the traditional law firm landscape. Given the scale and speed of change now underway, few firms will remain untouched. As these pressures intensify, the traditional law firm model will struggle to remain competitive without significant reform.

While the profession will undoubtedly see a contraction in the overall number of firms, it would be a mistake to assume that law firms will disappear. Those that adapt have the potential to thrive. But to thrive in the AI era will require an evolution in structure, strategy, and capability.

Not all firms that survive will evolve in the same direction. Instead, several distinct organisational archetypes are likely to emerge and co-exist. At one end of the spectrum are high-end boutiques, competing on deep expertise, judgement, and trust in narrow practice areas that remain difficult to automate or internalise. At the other end are corporate firms, characterised by scale, capital, professional management, and the ability to develop operational platforms that mirror those of their clients. Alongside these two anchor models are ABSs, investor-enabled or multidisciplinary vehicles that loosen the constraints of the traditional partnership and enable new combinations of legal, technological, and operational capability.

In all three models, the underlying operating models will evolve to incorporate technology at their core. A range of hybrid, ALSP, and platform-based models that blend legal, technological, and multidisciplinary capabilities will also likely rise to prominence in the AI era. These will be explored in detail in Chapters 12 and 13. This chapter focuses on the three models most immediately available to traditional firms: boutiques, corporate models, and ABSs.

Law Firms Can Adapt

The good news is that law firms have adapted to changes in the broader environment in the past. During GC 1.0 and 2.0, large law firms expanded internationally to service their MNC clients as they entered new markets during the wave of globalisation that began in the 1980s.[2] The ensuing expansion of law firms reshaped the profession, establishing large global players and new networks of firms. Firms shifted from traditional single-tier (equity-only) partnership models to multi-tier structures that included both equity plus non-equity partners, while experimenting with a variety of new models to keep pace with client demand.[3]

Later, as in-house teams grew and ALSPs entered the market, firms once again adapted. They began leveraging new technologies that replaced or enhanced tasks previously done manually, from document management and e-discovery to litigation support.[4] Many firms went further, creating their own ALSPs or partnering with external providers to augment service delivery.[5] As clients demanded changes in billing practices, firms have adapted. Today, most firms offer a range of alternative fee arrangements, including fixed fees, blended rates, and subscription models.

AI poses a different order of change from these prior adaptations and will require far deeper structural and operational shifts. However, history has shown that law firms can adapt when market forces compel them to. They may do so cautiously, but they are capable of adaptation.

The Boutique Law Firm

While the overwhelming direction of travel for most firms will involve deep structural change, not all firms face identical pressures or risk the same levels of disruption. A very small subset of highly elite law firms operate based on a different competitive logic. They rely less on scale and leverage and more on levels of expertise and trust that are extremely difficult to replicate, automate, or internalise.

These firms are rare. They possess truly compelling characteristics, or unique selling propositions (USPs), that clients continue to value at a premium and that neither AI nor insourcing can easily substitute. They offer concentrated pools of deep legal expertise in complex or highly specialised domains; institutional credibility when advising boards and C-suites on high-stakes matters; and enduring personal relationships with senior decision-makers that have been built on decades of trust.

Firms with these unique qualities are better positioned to sustain a human-centric profit model because, in a narrow set of situations, human judgement, strategic intuition, and accumulated experience remain irreplaceable. For these reasons, the high-end boutique firm represents one of the few law firm archetypes likely to remain resilient in the AI era. These boutiques deliver bespoke, partner-led, and nuanced legal counsel in complex or niche areas that are difficult to standardise or decompose (break into smaller, repeatable tasks that can be processed by technology).

That said, as we will see, even boutiques will not be immune from the need to evolve. Their organisational structures will also require rethinking as partners seek to maximise the value of senior human input while minimising overheads. These firms too will need to embrace AI and automation wherever possible, reshaping their internal leverage models in ways that differ from the traditional pyramid structure.

Limited Scalability

However, the very attributes that make boutiques indispensable also limit their scalability. As demand narrows at the top end of the market, there will only be room for a small number of boutique players.

The Savile Row of the Law   An analogy can be made to tailoring. In 1861, census figures show that London was home to approximately 24,000 tailors.[6] At that time, bespoke tailoring was not a luxury; it was the only way to obtain a suit. Today, by contrast, there are roughly 61 high-end bespoke tailors operating across London, including around 21 on Savile Row.[7] A high-end bespoke suit from one of these houses can still be had, sometimes for £10,000 or more, and there is still a thriving market among affluent consumers. But the market is now niche. What once was the norm for most consumers has become an exception for a small band of elites. This same dynamic will apply to boutique law firms in the AI era. The bespoke model will endure, but only for a relatively small number of firms.

The problem is that, while nearly every firm today considers the boutique route as its 'Plan B', many overestimate the extent to which their work is truly niche. And many more overestimate how competitive they would be in the boutique space. Much like law schools and rankings, there are at least 150 firms that believe they are among the top 10 in their field. For many, this won't be a viable path. Scalability will be limited and competition fierce.

Features of the Boutique Model

The boutique practice of GC 4.0 will likely have a smaller footprint, with a narrow focus on partner-led, high-margin work. Archetypal players will include firms with practices centred on strategic advisory for 'bet-the-company' litigation, regulatory crises, and complex corporate matters, as well as those with deep domain expertise in highly specialised areas that clients need too infrequently to justify maintaining comparable in-house resources.

The Profit Engine of the Boutique Model

Because the boutique model rests on the judgement and experience of its senior partners, most boutique firms will rely almost exclusively on price-inelastic, high-value work. GC 4.0 clients will continue to be willing to pay premium rates for 'artisanal' partner insight when it is called for. However, in the AI era, many will resist paying high rates for associate time, particularly for tasks that have become routine or standardised.

This dynamic may push boutiques away from the traditional pyramid structure, where profitability depends on leveraging a large base of associates. Instead, they may move towards billing models that maximise premium partner time. Some boutiques may alternatively abandon hourly billing altogether in favour of a value or outcomes-based pricing model, similar to those used today by some high-end strategic consultancies and financial advisors.

Either way, boutiques can remain profitable, and some may even increase their profitability, if they focus exclusively on high-value partner input while aligning with client demands for efficiency on the routine aspects of their work.

The Delivery Engine of the Boutique Model—The 'Rocket Ship'

While the profit engines of boutiques will continue to be driven by the value of partner input, their delivery engines will transform. In traditional boutique models, the profit and delivery engines have both been human-centric, relying on associate labour with partner oversight. But in the AI era, the logic will shift.

One way to conceptualise this shift is through what has been termed the 'rocket ship'.[8] The rocket ship is not a structural shape but a strategic architecture: a digitally native firm built around a technology core. Much like the AI factory at the heart of GC 4.0 legal departments, it is designed to amplify capability rather than headcount and is powered primarily by systems rather than people.

What distinguishes the rocket ship from the traditional boutique model is the separation of the firm's profit engine from its delivery engine. The profit engine remains human-centric, anchored in the premium that clients are willing to pay for senior partner judgement in complex or highly specialised matters. But the delivery engine—the part of the firm that executes work at scale—becomes technology-led. Rather than profitability being driven by associate leverage, a rocket ship model relies on AI, automation, and multidisciplinary teams to drive down delivery costs. The economic logic therefore shifts from 'more associates equal more profits' to 'more partner input plus scalable technology-enabled delivery equals more profit'. The rocket ship is, quite literally, built for operational speed and agility (hence the metaphor).

Structurally, the rocket-ship concept can underpin any number of specific operating models. In some configurations, such as the 'inverted pyramid', a broad base of partners is supported by a narrow base of associates. In others, such as the 'diamond model', partners are supported by a broad tier of experienced mid-level associates and a narrow base of juniors. In still others, such as the 'hourglass', a broad technology-enabled junior cohort remains and is supervised by a narrow mid-level tier. In all cases, technology drives the execution side of the model, with partner input as the core profit engine.

While compelling conceptually, the rocket ship comes with challenges. The underlying technology stack (data infrastructure, governance, workflow systems, and cybersecurity) requires significant upfront investment. Rapid scaling and agility also introduce new risks in oversight, accountability, and ethics. Career paths may flatten or become less predictable, creating difficulties in attracting and developing top legal talent. And for most traditional firms, the transformation required to adopt such architectures is profound.

Nevertheless, placing technology at the core of the firm's operating model, whatever its structural expression, offers a valuable strategic lens that invites firms to reimagine delivery around systems that enable scaling, accelerated learning, and new forms of value creation, rather than relying on incremental human capital leverage at the base and middle tiers.

With this conceptual foundation in mind, we now turn to three models that boutiques could employ to implement the rocket-ship concept for the AI era.

The Inverted Pyramid   One model that could help boutiques achieve this is the inverted pyramid. In this model, the traditional ratio of partners to associates is flipped (see Figure 11.1). Partners are supported by a lean team of senior associates or non-equity partners for complex work, with only a small contingent of junior associates at the base. The model leverages

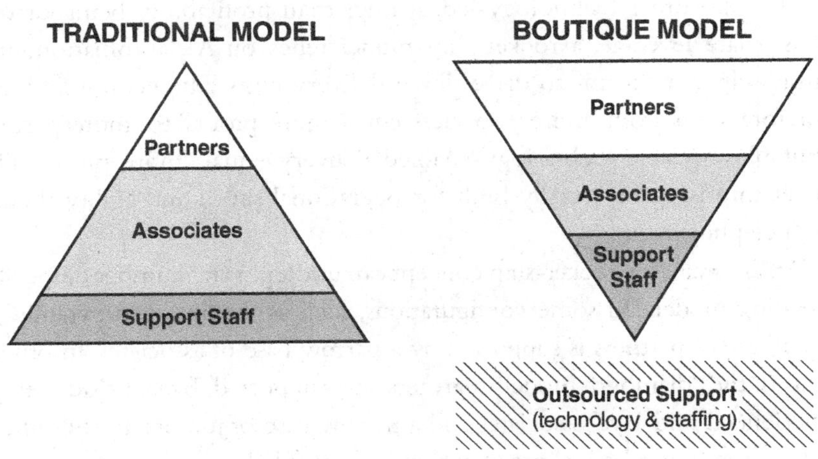

Figure 11.1 Traditional versus boutique model.

Source: Illustration by Logica Design.

automation and outsourcing to carry out routine tasks, either through captive or third-party ALSPs specialising in technology, process optimisation, and alternative staffing.

The strength of this approach lies in direct partner delivery: clients receive more hands-on involvement from senior lawyers, whose judgement they trust. The value of that advice is less diluted by time billed for associate input, making the premium price point more transparent and defensible.

However, the absence of a deep bench of associates could pose three issues. First, partner bottlenecks might arise if too much work gets concentrated at the top, stretching partners thin as they juggle delivering strategic advice and handling tasks traditionally delegated to juniors. Firms adopting an inverted pyramid model would need to maintain strict discipline to ensure that all associate-level work gets minimised and diverted to outsourced or technology layers. Doing this efficiently might require boutiques to maintain a multidisciplinary layer of technologists, project managers, and process experts to ensure a high-quality and effective delivery model. The success of this approach would also depend on the quality, cost, and availability of suitable outsourcing alternatives.

Second, a smaller associate pool would constrain the pipeline of future talent. Firms might need to adopt an apprenticeship model, carefully vetting new hires and investing in steady development and career progression, rather than relying on the large-intake, high-attrition 'tournament' approach more typically adopted in the traditional pyramid model.

Third, while boutiques with inverted pyramid models would remain well-placed to handle the strategic, judgement-heavy elements of major assignments, they would struggle to deliver the labour-intensive components of large-scale mergers and acquisitions, regulatory investigations, or complex litigation. Those aspects require substantial operational capacity, advanced technology, and deep experience with large project teams—capabilities more typically found in larger firms that are operationally configured to compete for such work. Boutiques will therefore need to either seamlessly integrate with such providers or persuade clients of the value of carving out space for their strategic contribution within a broader project ecosystem.

The Diamond Model Another possible organisational shape for the AI-era boutique model might be the diamond (see Figure 11.2). Here, the firm retains a broad mid-level of experienced lawyers, while triaging more

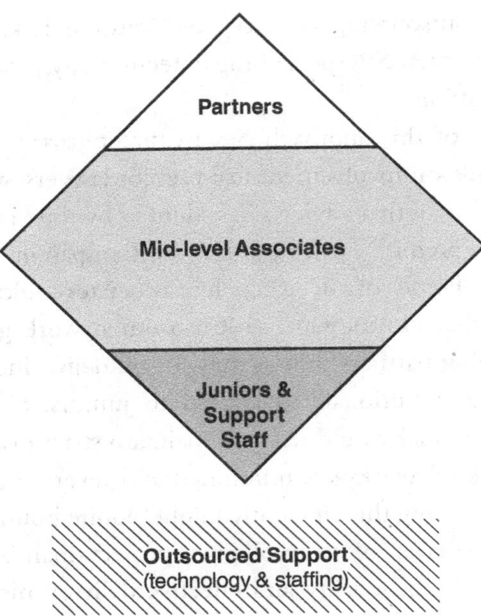

Figure 11.2   Diamond model.

Source: Illustration by Logica Design.

junior work to technology or outsourcing providers. This approach would retain some of the leverage of the pyramid, while reducing reliance on billing for partner input as the near-exclusive profit engine of the firm.

However, such an approach would not be without its challenges. Like the inverted pyramid, the diamond would suffer from a relatively shallow base of junior talent, which could impede both succession planning and knowledge transfer. Additionally, outsourcing would carry the same risks as in the inverted pyramid, including in relation to quality, cost, and availability. The model would also face similar challenges for firms when competing for large-scale, resource-intensive matters requiring deep levels of flexible capacity.

In addition, the diamond would also introduce additional complexities. A broad band of experienced mid-level associates would increase operating costs and place downward pressure on profit margins. At the same time, concentrating talent in a mission-critical middle tier would create upward mobility pressures. With more associates reaching seniority than there are partnership opportunities, firms might struggle with morale and attrition, with the consequent difficulties of handling the loss of hard-won expertise.

The Hourglass Model   A third structural approach is the hourglass model, in which a broad tier of equity partners at the top are supported by a narrow band of mid-level professionals and a wider base of junior associates (see Figure 11.3). This design addresses some of the challenges of the inverted pyramid and diamond models by reintroducing a larger internal team at the base to carry out routine work. This would ensure that high-volume tasks are kept within the firm, reducing reliance on external providers, while still maintaining a partner-led model at the top.

In this model, the wide base of junior lawyers would be supported by technology and automation, with the narrow tier of mid-level associates acting as a filtering, triaging, and quality control point for work flowing up to partners and back down to juniors. This structure enables partners to focus on high-value, complex matters, and on maintaining client relationships, relying on the junior base for much of the execution.

The hourglass would give firms the capacity to handle all aspects of sizeable matters while avoiding the higher costs associated with a large middle tier. It could be attractive for firms seeking to combine scalable delivery capability with deep senior expertise.

However, the hourglass has its risks. The narrow middle tier could come under significant pressure, responsible for supervising large volumes of work

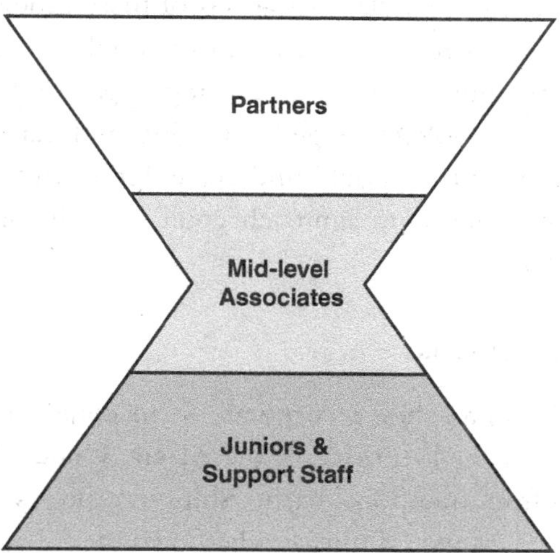

Figure 11.3   Hourglass model.
Source: Illustration by Logica Design.

from below while also meeting the demands of the partners above. Unless carefully managed, the middle tier could become a chokepoint, with a small number of overstretched professionals trying to juggle quality control, training, and project management. Without substantial investment in legal operations, workflow tools, staffing models, and automation to allow the base to be managed with minimal supervision, the result could be burnout and high turnover, undermining the stability of the delivery model.

To succeed, firms adopting this model would therefore need to carefully design the operating model to ensure the structure was balanced, scalable, and resilient.

Trade-offs and Consequences   Each of these structures might offer a credible path for boutique firms in the AI era. While they share some constraints, each has advantages as well as their own distinct trade-offs. The inverted pyramid risks the formation of bottlenecks at the top, the diamond suffers from higher costs and career-path tensions in the middle, and the hourglass runs the risk of resource constraints in the narrow centre.

In all cases, support staff, including project managers, data scientists, and technologists, are critical for success. For instance, a data scientist leveraging data to counteract alleged insider trading is capable of doing in days what would take months for a lawyer acting alone.

There are potentially endless variations of these models. Whatever the shape, boutique law firms would need to undertake a significant change journey to remain competitive, with resulting impacts on everything from firm culture and technology usage to pricing and career development. This is not a journey firms should undertake lightly. But for those able to successfully adapt, a boutique approach could be a highly profitable and competitive model.

Corporate Law Firms

Beyond boutique approaches, a corporate form could offer an additional alternative approach for law firms in the AI era. Under this model, firms would transform from traditional partnerships into professionally managed, CEO-led entities. This would mirror what investment banks and managed service providers have done in recent decades, as they evolved from partnerships into fully institutionalised corporate entities.

Unlike the traditional partnership model, where equity is held by individual partners and decisions are often made by consensus or majority vote, a corporate model would centralise decision-making authority in an executive leadership team. This team, headed by a fully empowered and professional CEO, would be able to drive strategy, manage operations, allocate capital, and set remuneration, with clear accountability to a board of directors, representing shareholders.

Ethical and regulatory constraints, most notably prohibitions on non-lawyer ownership of law firms and fee-sharing between lawyers and non-lawyers, have long impeded a broad adoption of this model.[9] However, rules have started to change. As we have seen, a growing number of jurisdictions, including England and Wales, Australia and parts of Canada and the United States, now permit ABSs, which allow non-lawyers to hold ownership interests in law firms under specific conditions.[10] These changes open the door to broader experimentation with the corporate model in the coming decade.

In some respects, a corporate structure takes the opposite approach of a boutique model. Boutique firms are small and concentrated, driving profit from the judgement, brand, and client relationships of a few high-value experts. Corporate firms, by contrast, are designed for scale, professionalised execution, and tighter structural integration with their corporate clients. They are better able to raise capital for strategic investments in technology and growth.

Corporate Governance Structure

A corporate model would be underpinned by Articles of Incorporation, vesting authority in a CEO, supported by a C-suite of professional executives overseeing newly empowered functions such as finance, technology, human resources, and operations. This executive team would report to a professional board of directors with fiduciary duties representing the interests of the shareholders. In the early stages, investors would likely include private equity or institutional capital, with a public listing as a future option once viability, scale, and leadership depth have been sufficiently demonstrated. This structure would enable firms to move with greater agility, pursue long-term strategies, and invest in capabilities that drive efficiency, margin, and client value.

Corporations Versus Swiss Vereins It is important to distinguish a corporate law firm model from the *Swiss Verein* approach adopted by some large firms today. While they share certain superficial similarities, including global branding, CEOs, and boards, they are fundamentally different constructs. The corporate model operates with a single, integrated business, aligned capital and governance structure, and a unified talent pool. This is fundamentally different from a 'Swiss Verein', which is a confederation of firms across markets, unified by brand but largely independent of each other in terms of their economics, ownership, and governance. Vereins, which will be discussed in greater detail in Chapter 12, are more akin to the models adopted by the Big Four.

Corporate models are centralised and strategic, while vereins are federated and flexible. Vereins are designed for fundamentally different purposes and do not possess the inherent adaptability and focus of a corporate model.

Compensation and Incentive Model

To succeed, a corporate model would need to offer a compensation structure that would rival or exceed that of the partnership model. The case for this, which would need to be made prior to any transition, would be to replace partner profit shares and variable draws with a mix of competitive base salaries, long-term incentives (LTIs), and annual incentive awards. Such an approach, while perhaps radical in the law firm context, would align closely with how leading corporations currently reward senior executives, often at levels that match or exceed partner draws.

Long-term Incentives LTIs could be issued on an annual basis. In the case of privately held firms, these would most likely take the form of 'phantom' or 'synthetic' shares (i.e., deferred compensation instruments that track the value of actual equity via various valuation mechanisms, without conferring ownership rights). Awards would typically vest over a multi-year period, often in three-year tranches, followed by an additional one-year holding period in the fourth year. Payouts would be based on the achievement of firm-wide and individual performance targets in each of the three years of the vesting period, with potential upside if stretch goals are achieved or exceeded.

LTIs would align the long-term personal incentives of the partners with those of the firm and would encourage retention, as partners would lose their unvested LTIs if they were to leave the firm prior to vesting or during the one-year additional holding period. By contrast, senior partners under a traditional partnership structure have little in the way of an aligned long-term interest in the health of the firm after they retire. This can potentially skew decision-making towards the short term in the years running up to their retirement.

Annual Bonuses　In addition to LTIs, partners would receive annual incentive payouts calibrated as a percentage of base salary and linked to a balanced set of firm-wide and individual performance objectives for the relevant year. This structure would ensure short-term alignment between partners and the firm around strategic and financial objectives for the relevant year.

Base Salary　Partners would also benefit from a competitive base salary, which would serve as the foundation for the calculation of LTIs and annual incentives.

Other Incentives　For senior partners, transition incentives and structured buyouts could also be added to support retention and reduce flight risk during a critical transition period. Mid-level partners, with longer time horizons, might find a structure that aligned compensation with long-term performance to be appealing.

Strategic Benefits

If successfully implemented, a corporate model could profoundly reshape the legal industry. Key advantages would include the following.

Access to Capital　Broad investor participation would unlock access to greater pools of capital, allowing investments in technology, client platforms, and scalable delivery models. Firms could also more effectively pursue strategic acquisitions of ALSPs, technology providers, and risk consultancies, improving their ability to offer the multi-faceted service that GC 4.0 clients seek.

Strategic, Long-term Thinking　Freed from the short-term pressures of handling annual profit distribution, the newly empowered executive team could more effectively pursue multi-year strategic planning and drive transformational initiatives. These might include reimagining how legal services are delivered, resourced, and priced. For example, value or outcome-based pricing models could replace the billable hour, which would better align fees with client-defined value, strengthening long-term relationships.

Attracting and Retaining Talent The corporate model would accommodate more attractive incentive structures for non-lawyer professionals, including technologists, process engineers, compliance professionals, and support staff, all of whom will be essential to legal service delivery in the GC 4.0 era. Performance-linked equity incentives would allow firms to attract and retain talent that is scarce and highly competitive in today's market.

Operational Efficiency Putting in place a centralised management team would enable firm structure and processes to be optimised, facilitating the integration of AI and other critical technologies as well as the integration of multidisciplinary teams.

The Goldman Sachs Analogy In 1999, Goldman Sachs, the last major private bank in the United States at the time, transitioned from a private partnership to a public corporation.[11] At the time, it cited three principal reasons for a stock exchange listing: 'to secure permanent capital to grow; to share ownership broadly among our employees now and through future compensation; and to permit us to use publicly traded securities to finance strategic acquisitions that we may elect to use in the future'.[12]

The transformation proved to be a resounding success. At the time of its initial public offering (IPO), the firm had 14,000 employees and $13 billion in net revenues. By 2024, the 25th anniversary of its listing, Goldman had more than 44,000 employees and revenues exceeding $46 billion.[13] Despite the structural shift, the firm has maintained cultural continuity and still calls its top leadership 'partners'.[14]

Law firms could follow a similar path. Much like Goldman, shedding outdated structural constraints and adopting the corporate form could enable them to access greater sources of capital, align employee incentives across all teams, and build greater scale and resilience.

Goldman's transition also illustrates that even elite professional firms can evolve structurally without sacrificing prestige, performance, and influence. In following the same trajectory, law firms would be acknowledging the reality that many of them are already corporate institutions in all but name. Embracing that identity could unlock the strategic and operational benefits of full incorporation, while retaining the best elements of their legacy cultures.

Challenges

Transitioning to a corporate model would not be without its challenges, however. Some of these include the following.

Partner Buy-in One major challenge would lie in persuading partners to relinquish control to a professional management team and accept new, performance-based compensation structures. Failure to placate such concerns would be fatal to any transition as it could potentially result in partner attrition and the eventual collapse of the firm.

If executed well, a corporate structure could attract rather than repel top talent. That said, success with existing partners would require early and ongoing conversations with the entire partnership to help frame both the upsides of the new model and the potential risks of doing nothing. A tailored approach would need to be applied, taking into account the unique situations of the different partner constituencies. As noted above, senior partners, who would have shorter time horizons, might need the reassurance of transitional payouts, while mid-level partners might be more interested in the long-term upsides of a corporate model.

Regulatory Hurdles It would be essential in any transition to consider the remaining regulatory and ethical restrictions on non-lawyer ownership models. In jurisdictions that permit ABSs, the regulatory frameworks have been loosened to allow experimentation with non-lawyer ownership or investment, fee-sharing, and multidisciplinary models. We will be exploring this in greater detail below as it pertains to the United States.

Exit and Liquidity Any corporate law firm model must also accommodate the expectations of external investors around revenue, capital allocation, and credible exit strategies. A public stock exchange listing could be one possible path. However, listing should be pursued only after careful preparation and once the firm had established strong internal corporate governance.

Early law firm IPOs have offered lessons in this regard. In some cases, listings were followed by ambitious acquisition strategies and rapid expansion plans that ultimately ended with restructurings or buyouts. Their experiences highlight how important timing, strategic clarity, and effective execution can be. The broader takeaway from the past is not that public ownership is inherently unsuitable for law firms. Rather, it is that listing introduces new dynamics, including elevated expectations around transparency, financial discipline, and strategy. Markets can be ruthless if companies fall short in these areas. With the right foundations in place, however, a public listing could be a compelling long-term option.

Alternative Business Structures

ABA Model Rule of Professional Conduct 5.4 has long prohibited both fee-sharing between lawyers and non-lawyers and non-lawyer ownership of law firms, effectively barring institutional investment in US law firms.[15] However, beginning in the 2010s and gaining momentum in the 2020s, several states began to reassess their legal regulatory frameworks, driven by concerns over access to justice, legal innovation, and consumer affordability of legal services.[16]

Reforms emerging from these reassessments have opened the door for US-based law firms to explore ABSs, which permit fee-sharing between lawyers and non-lawyers and non-lawyer ownership of law firms. Currently, only four US jurisdictions—Washington D.C., Puerto Rico, Utah, and Arizona—permit variations of such ABSs, with other jurisdictions retaining versions of Model Rule 5.4, including its core prohibitions on fee-sharing and non-lawyer ownership.[17]

In 2021, Arizona became the first of these four jurisdictions to fully eliminate Rule 5.4, which resulted in the establishment of a formal ABS licensing regime that permits non-lawyers to fully own law firms.

This reform has been met with a lot of excitement by law firms, legal service providers, and private equity and other investors. One 2025 report noted that 'much of the legal industry remains fragmented, underdigitized and operationally inefficient—particularly among small firms', creating 'opportunities to consolidate practices, introduce shared infrastructure and scale with technology'.[18]

These dynamics mirror early-stage consolidation trends in other professional services sectors, including healthcare, accounting, and financial services, where the gradual loosening of ownership restrictions gave rise to new investment vehicles, delivery models, and business structures.[19]

While ABSs in the United States are still in their early stages, several pathways to developing nationwide multidisciplinary practices have already been explored and, in some cases, are being developed. Two approaches, in particular, are at the forefront of current debate: the *two-company model* and the *staffing company model*.[20]

Two-company Model

In the two-company model, a non-lawyer-owned service company contracts with a law firm to provide the firm with operational support (e.g., technology, marketing, HR, and finance services). These services are provided to the law firm by the service company pursuant to a services agreement negotiated at arm's length. The service company is prohibited from controlling the firm's legal work or sharing in its profits. Instead, it charges reasonable, market-based fees for its services.[21]

According to experts, when carefully crafted, this model, which mirrors structures long used in the medical industry, is 'an acknowledged workaround designed to enable lawyers and law firms to access capital, as well as the expertise and assistance of those who are not lawyers'.[22]

As Lucian Pera, an expert in the area, observes:

> The two-company law firm allows law firms access to capital, and investors to participate in the economic success of law firms … Today, nonlawyer-owned service companies, operating perfectly lawfully under current rules in every U.S. jurisdiction, are increasingly the business and operational backbone of all sorts of law firms. They act as vendors to provide a law firm everything they need to operate, from marketing, to office space, to technology, to staff. We are starting to see these businesses begin to 'collect' law firms by buying the 'back offices' of law firms around the country that share practice niches or other similarities, even without then merging the law firms themselves.[23]

Although the model has not been expressly approved by any formal ethics opinion or court decision, Pera notes that sufficient authority exists to provide a roadmap for compliance with ethics rules and, despite its increasing use, no regulator has found against it.[24]

Staffing Company Model

A second model involves establishing a non-lawyer-owned, non-law firm, parent company that owns both a non-lawyer-owned legal staffing business (a structure that has been approved by ABA and other ethics opinions for many years) and an Arizona ABS law firm.[25] When operated separately, these entities can together 'create the functional equivalent of a law firm, that can operate nationally, under common ownership, with common marketing, and perhaps under a single brand family'.[26]

No ethics opinion or clear decisional authority has yet approved this combined ABS–staffing company structure. However, several major players are actively building businesses based on it, presumably operating on the view that Arizona's ABS authorisation, coupled with decades of authority approving non-lawyer-owned staffing companies, provides a foundation for expansion.[27]

Big Four Entry

In February 2025, KPMG Law US launched under an Arizona ABS licence, aiming 'to deliver a focused set of technology-enabled legal services powered by artificial intelligence … building upon the firm's established Legal Business Services practice'.[28] The new law firm announced plans to collaborate with the KPMG global network of law firms across more than 80 countries to 'provide legal managed services, legal operations consulting, and advanced legal technology innovation, to help clients gain efficiencies and empower their legal teams to concentrate on strategic priorities'.[29] This combination of capabilities could prove to be a powerful proposition in the GC 4.0 era.

Although KPMG's Arizona licence does not authorise it to practice law in states outside Arizona, the firm indicated that it plans to 'use staffing agencies and co-counseling relationships with other law firms to serve clients in other jurisdictions', suggesting that it is going to leverage a variant of the staffing company model for its expansion beyond Arizona.[30]

KPMG's entry into Arizona marked a major milestone in the US legal landscape, signalling that ABSs are beginning to gain traction. It also suggests a pathway by which institutional investors and diversified professional service organisations may increasingly play a role in consolidating and capitalising the US legal sector, potentially reshaping the competitive landscape for both traditional law firms and corporate legal departments in the country.

A Way Forward for Law Firms

While only a select number of traditional law firms are likely to survive and thrive in the AI era, there are clear paths to success for those able to adapt. There is no single future state model for all firms. Instead, a small number of distinct, but viable, future approaches are emerging, each suited to different competitive conditions.

Boutiques offer a compelling path for premier firms able to dominate narrow, high-margin segments. Their competitive strength lies in the deep pools of senior-partner expertise in highly specialised areas that remain difficult to automate, standardise, or internalise in-house. However, to remain competitive, boutiques must evolve, adopting a 'rocket-ship' architecture, in which profit engines move towards partner-led and value-based approaches, with technology, automation, and multidisciplinary teams lowering execution costs. As noted above, there are many ways this can be structured, including the inverted pyramid, the diamond, and the hourglass. Despite the potential profitability of these models, however, boutiques will struggle to scale. Moreover, few firms possess the truly niche expertise needed for boutiques; only a handful will succeed.

Corporate models offer an alternative approach, with firms moving beyond traditional partnership structures towards professionally managed, CEO-led organisations. This structure could unlock greater access to capital, strengthen strategic governance, enable scalable technology investment, and allow firms to operate more like their institutional clients. While corporate models could be highly successful, they must overcome cultural resistance and, in many jurisdictions, regulatory constraints.

ABSs provide a further alternative that allows firms to attract external capital and develop multidisciplinary delivery models without necessarily moving to a full corporate form. Where they are permitted, ABSs are creating new opportunities for firms to experiment with investment, technology integration, and multiple service offerings.

In all cases, transformation will require investments in technology and new pricing and delivery models. Success will also depend on careful, deliberate transformation, and a willingness to rethink assumptions about how firms are structured, managed, and generate profit. However, for firms willing and able to adapt and navigate the change impact, there is a viable, and even vibrant, road ahead.

As the GC 4.0 era matures, other structures will emerge alongside law firms, sometimes competing and sometimes collaborating with them. These will include hybrid and platform models that blend legal, technological, and multidisciplinary capabilities. It is to these that we now turn.

12 | The Hybrid

Innovation is the ability to see change as an opportunity—
not a threat.

—Steve Jobs[1]

As discussed in Chapter 11, law firms will very likely continue to exist in the years ahead. Many, however, will fade over time, finding themselves unable to adapt. Others will thrive by evolving, either adopting the boutique model to focus deeply on narrow, high-value verticals or transitioning towards a corporate or alternative business structure, backed by institutional capital that can create the conditions needed to reimagine their service delivery models.

However, reconfigured law firms will not be the only players in the AI-era landscape. Entirely new models are likely to emerge. These will be purpose-built for, and designed around the needs of, AI-enabled clients. While reconstituted law firms will continue to deliver deep verticals of legal expertise, new models that emerge alongside them may offer a broader and more integrated suite of capabilities that combine law with adjacent disciplines, including risk, technology, and strategy.

One model that is emerging in this respect is the 'hybrid' firm. Taking its cue from the Big Four, the hybrid is an integrated, multidisciplinary enterprise that offers clients a broader and more holistic offering under one organisational umbrella. It meets a growing demand for cross-functional problem-solving arising from the convergence of legal, commercial, technological, and ethical dimensions of risk, as discussed in Chapter 1.

Precision Instruments and Swiss Army Knives

Boutique law firms and the hybrid model provide different solutions for different needs. Whereas boutiques represent a continuation of the 'precision instrument' approach, offering deep expertise in one vertical, hybrids embody a more adaptable and multi-faceted 'Swiss Army knife' approach that seeks to solve for a broader spectrum of needs. Given their different positionings, both could easily evolve alongside each other in an unfolding landscape that will undoubtedly require a range of solutions.

Overview of the Hybrid Model

The hybrid model integrates a diverse range of capabilities within a single umbrella entity, including legal services, risk, technology, consulting, and other advisory activities. The strategic intent is to create a coherent, technology-enhanced, multidisciplinary structure capable of addressing the increasingly interconnected needs of AI-era legal departments.

The structure is somewhat analogous to that of the Big Four, which operate a form of hybrid model that combines technology, consulting, and other advisory services around a core of accounting. Similarly, legal hybrids could develop a portfolio of adjacent services, except they would be built around legal services rather than accounting. However, the vast scale of their businesses and the relatively modest scale of their legal practices have, at least so far, made it difficult for them to fully realise their potential in legal services.

A legal-centric hybrid, by contrast, would place legal at its core, with complementary services designed to enhance the legal offering, rather than dilute it. By operating in a more focused manner, legal hybrids can be more agile, responsive, and directly aligned to the needs of AI-era clients.

The most likely origin point for hybrid models is therefore today's large law firms. Indeed, a number of them are already moving in this direction. To achieve fully hybrid status, however, such firms will need to adopt a strategy that places integrated offerings at the core.

As some law firms evolve in the direction of a hybrid model, it is instructive to consider how adjacent professional service sectors have made that journey. No group illustrates this more than the Big Four, who have evolved from a deep vertical focus on accounting into broader multidisciplinary and technology-enabled service models. It is therefore useful to examine the Big Four model more closely, including how it emerged, how it is structured today, and what its limitations are.

The Contours of the Big Four Model

As discussed in Chapter 10, alongside their audit practices, the Big Four have developed broad advisory portfolios spanning legal, tax, compliance, risk, technology, innovation, sustainability, and strategic management services.[2]

Historical Evolution

This diversified model emerged over time. As MNCs expanded their global footprints during the GC 1.0 and GC 2.0 eras, the large accounting firms followed, broadening their own geographic reach and scale through a series of mergers and alliances. The Big Four globalised in step with their clients, adopting integrated, cross-jurisdictional operating structures that enabled them to deliver comprehensive and coordinated support in complex, cross-border engagements.[3]

As corporate needs grew more sophisticated, managers sought advisors who, as Cris Shore and Susan Wright note, could 'help them expand their enterprises and assets through mergers and acquisitions, new technologies, financial services and business strategies'.[4] Accounting firms responded by deepening their sector expertise, developing market-specific legal and regulatory capabilities, and leveraging advances in data processing and computer technology to expand well beyond audit services.[5]

By the 1980s, as Shore and Wright observe, 'the major accounting firms had aspirations of becoming "professional service firms" or multidisciplinary practices—global consulting firms, including legal services, with one-stop shopping'.[6]

Pricing Pressures The expansion of the Big Four into consulting was not driven by demand alone. It was also a response to declining profitability in audit. Despite their near monopoly over the audits of large publicly traded companies, 'the price companies were willing to pay for these services was declining rapidly'.[7] By the 1980s, clients were increasingly playing the major firms against one another, turning audit work into an unsustainable 'loss leader'.[8]

As Stephen Zeff observes:

Following their aggressive expansion overseas in the 1950s and 1960s … the major audit firms apparently concluded in the early 1970s that the audit market was becoming largely saturated. To compensate, the firms aggressively broadened the scale and scope of their consulting practices … The distribution of major firms' gross fees shifted markedly from accounting and auditing to tax and consulting services.[9]

Advisory as a Profit Engine This shift towards advisory services accelerated over the following several decades. Between 2000 and 2022, audit revenues across the Big Four declined while advisory service revenues increased by approximately 274%. This growth occurred despite the temporary constraints introduced by the Sarbanes–Oxley Act in the United States, which barred auditors from selling advisory services to their audit clients.[10] In response, all of the Big Four except Deloitte divested their consulting arms, only to rebuild them several years later after developing models that allowed them to serve non–audit clients without breaching independence requirements.[11]

Since then, advisory revenue has grown consistently. Between 2010 and 2015, it doubled, and it has continued to expand.[12] By 2014, advisory revenues exceeded audit revenues by 50% or more across the Big Four, a gap that has continued to widen steadily over the ensuing decade.[13]

Federated Model

During their global expansion, the leading auditing firms pioneered 'a new form of business entity that is neither a multinational corporation, a global partnership, nor a single firm'.[14] This model, now emblematic of the Big Four, operates as a federated network of affiliates 'unified around "brand", "risk", "quality", "values" and "ethics" by adhering to a common code of conduct'.[15]

Each network comprises independent firms operating under a global coordinating organisation funded by member contributions. Affiliates are typically owned by local partners, organised under domestic law, and serve defined geographic territories. Although globally aligned, they remain legally separate entities.[16]

As Hannah L. Buxbaum explains, 'There are no ownership ties between firms either vertically or horizontally … Each of the Big Four emphasizes that their member firms are separate and distinct legal entities, and that the networks do not constitute international partnerships'.[17]

Global governance is therefore coordinative, rather than managerial.[18] Operational integration is achieved contractually: each affiliate commits to the network's standards and requirements and, in return, accesses shared resources such as brand identity, technology platforms, training, insurance programmes, and global practice communities.[19]

Regulatory Compliance and Liability Limitation   This federated model enables the Big Four to operate globally while complying with jurisdiction-specific ownership and licensing rules, which made it impossible to structure cross-border accounting enterprises as single global partnerships.[20] The structure also limits liability across the network, which is critical in auditing, where litigation risk is material.

Importantly, this model has proven adaptable. As discussed in Chapter 11, KPMG has established a legal practice in Arizona and its development of ABS pathways illustrates how this architecture can evolve to accommodate regulated legal services delivery.

Shortcomings of the Big Four Model

Despite its advantages, several structural limitations of the Big Four model are particularly relevant for legal-centric hybrids.

Organisational Complexity   The network comprises numerous independent partnerships, linked by complex frameworks. Decision-making can therefore be slow, layered, and consensus-dependent, with accountability diffused across entities that have differing incentives and profit pools. The result is a system that can struggle to move at pace and with flexibility in fast-moving markets.

Governance Challenges   As Laura Empson has observed, the scale of these partnerships has eroded the traditional peer-based governance checks characteristic of law firms:

> *[In] … the partnership model … owners, managers, and major producers are one and the same. For smaller partnerships that can work very effectively. But, as partnerships grow, the leadership becomes more and more divorced from the partners.*

> *Publicly quoted firms benefit from the oversight of external shareholders and non-execs. By contrast, the largest partnerships (which are as large as many large global corporations) are stuck in an awkward in-between place.*
>
> *The leaders of these firms are no longer effectively subject to the traditional checks and balances of a well-run partnership—i.e. peer pressure and 'helpful' scrutiny from well-informed and highly involved partners. Instead, they rely increasingly on bureaucratic systems and structures, which serve to disenfranchise partners and disengage them from the governance of the firms that they own.[21]*

Similar concerns were raised by a 2023 Australian parliamentary inquiry into the Australian operations of the Big Four, which concluded that 'questions remain about whether the governance structures at Deloitte, EY, KPMG and PwC are suitable for … such economically significant partnerships' with structures 'spanning multiple professional services including accounting, audit, assurance, tax advice and a wide range of consulting services'.[22]

Siloed Model   Despite unified global branding, the practice and geographic siloes inside Big Four firms can lead to internal competition for work and resources. While some competition is healthy, too much can negatively impact cross-enterprise execution. This risk must be avoided. The central need of a GC 4.0 legal department is coordinated, data-connected, multidisciplinary service delivery. Legal hybrid models should therefore be careful to embed mechanisms that reinforce shared accountability, collaboration, and unified decision-making into their emerging models.

The Swiss Verein Versus the Big Four Model

A counterpart to the Big Four model in the legal industry is the *Swiss Verein*, a more loosely coupled organisational structure used by several global law firms, including Baker McKenzie, Dentons, and DLA Piper.[23] The Verein is a Swiss corporate holding structure that allows firms to operate under a unified global brand while maintaining full legal and financial independence at the local entity level. Each member firm retains its own profit pool, partner compensation system, and tax and accounting arrangements.[24]

The key distinction between the Verein and the Big Four model lies in the degree of integration. The Big Four networks are typically more centrally coordinated and contractually interwoven, with stronger global governance, common platforms, and standardised operating practices. By contrast, the Verein prioritises regulatory flexibility and liability protection, but results in weaker strategic and operational cohesion.

While the Verein can be an effective solution for traditional firms seeking global brand reach without shared financial risk, its looser integration makes it less suited to environments that require tightly coordinated multidisciplinary delivery, shared data platforms, and unified operating models. In the legal hybrid context, the Verein structure may therefore struggle to support the level of tight cross-functional integration and rapid execution that GC 4.0 legal departments increasingly expect from their external partners.

Designing the Legal Hybrid

Application to Legal Services

The Big Four model demonstrates how multiple regulated and non-regulated entities can operate under a shared brand and governance framework, without requiring common ownership, while benefitting from global scale, coordinated expertise, and shared platforms. As such, it offers a viable structural blueprint for legal-centric hybrids. In modified form, the model could enable legal hybrids to effectively deliver a broad range of complementary services while staying compliant with a diverse patchwork of regulatory regimes.

The Starfish Model   Organisationally, the legal hybrid might increasingly resemble a 'starfish', with semi-autonomous teams ('arms') focused on sectors, regions, or disciplines, connected by a shared central platform that provides culture, governance, administration, data, knowledge, and technology infrastructure. Commercial and operational decision-making would sit as close to the client as possible to maximise responsiveness and practical judgement, while the centre would focus on providing coherence, accountability, and a unified brand and client experience.

Debugging the Model   At the same time, legal hybrids will want to avoid the complex governance layers of the Big Four model, with its mix of partnership dynamics, corporate-style bureaucracy, and vast networks of legally separate member firms, all of which combine to create silo risks and oversight challenges.

While this poses a challenge, the scale and domain focus of a legal hybrid make success achievable. To mitigate the limitations of the Big Four model, legal hybrids will want to embed:

- *Key account leadership* to ensure clear client ownership and coordinated, cross-practice alignment.
- *Incentive structures* that reward collaboration and a calibrated mix of enterprise and team-level outcomes.
- *Streamlined but strong governance* providing effective, but not overly restrictive or complex, frameworks.

None of this is easy, particularly at a global scale, as the experience of the Big Four has shown. However, it is possible given the size and focus of the legal hybrid model.

Legal Hybrid Formations

While regulatory restrictions still limit non-lawyer ownership of legal practices in many jurisdictions, as discussed in Chapter 11, ABS reforms across several major legal markets, including the United States, United Kingdom, and Australia, are making legal hybrid models increasingly viable at global scale.

As the environment continues to become more favourable for such models, one can imagine them emerging along several pathways, including from within law firms, through continued Big Four expansion, via ALSPs moving into regulated legal services, or through investor-backed stand-alone models.

Law Firms

Much as the Big Four evolved from pure accounting firms into multidisciplinary consultancies, legal hybrids could evolve from the diversification already underway inside many law firms.

Big Law—Eversheds Sutherland   Global law firm Eversheds Sutherland provides a good example of what is happening inside cutting-edge firms today and how this might continue to unfold in the future. The firm's consultancy arm, *Konexo*, offers a broad range of consulting and alternative legal and compliance services, including:

- **Legal services.** Legal managed services, IP and brand management; litigation and investigative support; and regulatory research.
- **Technology and process optimisation.** Intake and matter management, contract lifecycle management, case management, and knowledge management.
- **Flexible staffing.** From GC and company secretaries to legal operations and technology experts, and from paralegals to project managers.
- **Consulting.** Strategic, operational, technology, and other advisory services.[25]

Konexo aims to provide a range of integrated, technology-enabled services supported by human expertise that free client teams to focus on higher-value strategic work.[26] Over time, these adjacent capabilities could expand and integrate more tightly with the firm's core legal practice, much like how advisory services grew alongside accounting within the Big Four.

Similar dynamics are taking place in a number of other firms, including A&O Shearman and Cleary Gottlieb, the operations of which are discussed in Chapter 14. In each case, the strategic challenge will be to integrate these offerings under a coherent identity and value proposition while continuing to maintain excellence and culture in the core legal services offering.

Private Equity as a Law Firm Catalyst   Private equity investment may accelerate hybrid formation. In the United Kingdom, where the regulatory environment permits non-lawyer ownership of legal service entities, private equity firms have invested nearly £1.2 billion in law firms since 2019, including £534 million in 2024 alone.[27]

Many investors employ a 'buy-to-build' strategy, in which 'a platform company is used to bolt on smaller businesses which enhance its potential—adding tech capabilities, or complementary practices'.[28] This approach could proliferate in the coming years, particularly if core legal services come under pressure.

The cultural challenge will be for outside investors to retain top legal talent through such a transition. While that challenge would also be present for evolutions that emanate organically from within a law firm, transformations would likely be easier if driven by the partnership itself as opposed to outside parties.

The Big Four and ALSPs

The formation of hybrid models could also come from the other direction via the Big Four and ALSPs moving further into the legal services space.

The Big Four, which already have substantial legal practices and employ thousands of legal professionals, are expanding selectively into law where they are able to do so from a regulatory perspective. For example, as discussed in Chapter 11, KPMG now operates a law firm in Arizona. In 2018, Deloitte acquired the non-US offices of immigration law firm Berry Appleman & Leiden, and PwC joined forces with US-based immigration firm, Fragomen, Del Rey, Bernsen & Lowey LLP.[29]

Likewise, advanced ALSPs are acquiring legal capabilities as regulatory constraints ease. In 2022, for instance, Elevate—a leading ALSP—acquired an ABS licence in Arizona, enabling it to merge with its affiliated law firm, ElevateNext to become the first non-lawyer-owned ALSP in the United States with its own integrated law firm.[30]

However, in both cases, cultural and operational integration remains a significant obstacle, as law firm partners may struggle within a larger organisation as their law firm identity erodes. Targeted alliances or joint ventures might therefore be more frequent in this context than full acquisitions.

Organic Stand-alone Entities

Stand-alone hybrid entrants might face the steepest barriers. Brand trust, regulatory complexity, legal talent recruitment, and the capital required to scale multidisciplinary services would all pose challenges to new entrants. A more likely scenario might be an investor-led hybrid assembled through phased acquisitions across the legal, ALSP, and technology domains rather than built from scratch.

The Way Forward

Given these dynamics, the legal hybrids most likely to gain traction will emerge from existing law firms that have the strategic vision, leadership alignment, and cultural readiness to evolve. As we have seen, some firms are already moving in this direction, even if they remain, for now, 'proto-hybrids'—organisations in which adjacent capabilities exist today but remain smaller and less central than core legal advisory. For these firms, the opportunity is significant. By continuing to expand across adjacent verticals and integrating those offerings around a strong legal core, they can deliver multidisciplinary value aligned with the needs of AI-era legal departments.

As in the Big Four, there is potential for adjacent capabilities to grow in relative importance as the traditional core becomes increasingly standardised and commoditised. A proto-hybrid model enables a firm to shape its trajectory over time, depending on how legal services trend. It can scale adjacencies aggressively if market shifts accelerate or maintain them in steady state if change unfolds more gradually. It also allows law firms to develop early intelligence on emerging trends, demand patterns, and delivery models, creating a strategic learning advantage over more static rivals.

The challenge for firms moving in this direction is both structural and strategic. As discussed in Chapter 9, it can be hard for successful incumbents to change today in anticipation of conditions that might emerge tomorrow. As many firms remain very profitable, the temptation to operate as if that will always be the case is strong. It can be hard to maintain the organisational discipline necessary to cultivate a mindset of being 'constructively discontent'; always asking what might change and exploring how the organisation can adapt in time.

We will explore practical approaches that firms can take in that regard in Chapter 14. For now, it is sufficient to note that the hybrid platform represents a credible and strategically coherent destination for some firms, despite the challenges it might take for them to fully get there.

13 | Platforms

Legal marketplaces are poised to evolve from static directories into dynamic service ecosystems.

—The Legal Tech Guide[1]

Unlike hybrid models, which integrate multiple capabilities within a single organisational structure, platforms connect clients with networks of external independent providers, technologies, and solutions.

Platforms do not perform the work themselves; rather, they optimise its flow. A platform, in this context, is a technology-enabled and data-driven infrastructure that connects participants across an ecosystem of buyers and sellers and intelligently orchestrates their interactions. Platforms often begin as buyer-centric marketplaces that efficiently and transparently match supply and demand. As they evolve, however, they can develop into adaptive operating layers that span both sides of the market, routing work, managing performance, and continuously optimising outcomes across a network of suppliers.

In the GC 4.0 environment, platforms will likely play a pivotal role, evolving from market connectors into intelligent orchestrators of value chain. As agentic AI matures, platforms could increasingly become strategic cogs in the GC 4.0 legal department wheel, embedding directly into both client and law firm workflows and transforming how work is sourced, priced, managed, and evaluated. As GC 4.0 legal departments build intake layers that automatically route matters to internal and external providers, platforms could become the connective tissue between them. It is therefore important to examine what they are, how they function, and how that could impact the legal industry in the AI era.

Technology Driven

Technology lies at the heart of the structured environments that platforms build.[2] They leverage data to drive transparency and matching, improving decision-making in what has historically been an opaque market. By introducing greater comparability and accountability into the process, platforms can reduce friction, expose hidden inefficiencies, and dynamically allocate work to the best-placed provider.

In addition to basic matchmaking, leading platforms today also offer vetting, rating, and pricing tools, as well as communication hubs, dashboards, and billing support. Increasingly, AI and agentic technologies are automating or enhancing these capabilities.[3]

In short, as they evolve, platforms are transforming legal procurement into an intelligent marketplace where real-time data drives both vendor selection and matter allocation. As Chambers and Partners observe, the rise of legal marketplaces and intelligent platforms is redefining how services are delivered, moving the market towards 'precision alignment'.[4]

While today's B2B platforms primarily link clients and law firms, the model is expanding to include a far broader ecosystem of providers, ranging from ALSPs to consultants, technology suppliers, and a growing range of other legal-adjacent vendors. As platforms mature, clients will likely also use them to bundle vendors for more complex projects, bringing multiple providers together into single, integrated teams of what might be termed 'coalitions of the willing'.

GC 4.0-era Precursors

Currently, no single platform matches the fully mature definition of a GC 4.0-era platform, acting as a deeply integrated orchestrator on both sides of the market. However, three provider archetypes offer discrete elements that could converge into large, open, and fully data-driven marketplaces: large law firm networks, legal integrators, and competitive sourcing platforms. Of these, the sourcing platforms most closely resemble mature-state GC 4.0 platforms. We will consider each in turn.

Large Law Firm Networks

Large networks of independent law firms, such as Lex Mundi, TerraLex, or Multilaw, possess the connective infrastructure and professional trust that a GC 4.0 platform needs to thrive. These networks operate as alliances and referral platforms, enabling member firms to collaborate with each other across jurisdictions without giving up their independence. For clients, they provide access to a curated global association of high-quality independent firms, coordinated via a central hub that ensures cross-border consistency, connectivity, and service integration.

Lex Mundi, the world's leading network, comprises 150 carefully selected member firms spanning more than 125 jurisdictions, each among the most established and longest-standing firms in its market.[5] TerraLex includes 139 firms across 209 jurisdictions, while Multilaw brings together 90 firms in 100 countries.[6]

Strong Relationships with Some Central Coordination

Much of the effectiveness of these networks stems from the deep, long-standing relationships forged among member firms, enabling smooth collaboration and mutual referrals. Their value is further enhanced by central coordination and shared services.

In the case of Lex Mundi, for instance, such services include professional development, innovation and technology advisory, leadership, and knowledge and insights.[7] Lex Mundi's Global Markets team also provides client-management support for complex multi-jurisdictional matters, ensuring tailored and consistent delivery across borders. Its *Equisphere* service adds a layer of advanced legal project management and technology-enabled oversight, giving clients a single point of contact, coordinated engagement terms and billing, and monthly reporting and dashboards that enhance transparency and control.[8]

Walled Gardens

Currently, however, these networks are 'walled gardens'; closed ecosystems that are limited to their member law firms and that exclude ALSPs, technology providers, or other adjacent service providers. While they possess high relationship capital and operational cohesion, they are not yet configured to deliver the digital-first, cross-industry connectivity outside their member firms of the kind required for a GC 4.0 platform.

To move towards that vision, these networks would need to reconfigure themselves around a data-driven strategy, install a sophisticated technology stack to allow direct client sourcing across providers, integrate shared dashboards and routing, and provide transparent performance analytics.

That said, many of the building blocks are in place. Lex Mundi, for instance, already has relational trust, governance frameworks, and coordination and infrastructure capabilities that could, over time, evolve into a legal services platform. If such a global network were to partner or merge with a competitive sourcing provider that possesses the necessary digital interface, for example, the resulting entity could become a formidable platform player.

Legal Talent and Delivery Integrators

Legal talent and delivery integrators combine human expertise with embedded technology to deliver legal and legal-adjacent services at scale. In so doing, they orchestrate the demand for and supply of legal talent, process, and technology across the legal market.

Prominent examples include Axiom Law and Elevate, both of which offer expertise, process excellence, and technology-enabled delivery to meet a variety of needs. Keystone Law, a publicly listed UK-based virtual law firm, occupies an adjacent niche. It operates an internal platform connecting independent lawyers, straddling the space between law firm networks and legal integrators, and offering a glimpse of how platform-like models can evolve within law firm structures themselves.

Axiom

Axiom offers a global network of more than 14,000 lawyers and legal professionals globally, each averaging more than 18 years of experience. Of these, more than 4,000 have served in Fortune 500 legal departments, and over 1,700 have worked at AmLaw 200 firms.[9] This deep talent pool enables Axiom to match client needs with precision, deploying the right expertise to the right matters at the right time. Engagements are coordinated through dedicated account management teams which oversee the process end-to-end, placing lawyers directly inside client legal departments, integrating them into hybrid project teams, or managing them through technology-enabled delivery models.[10]

To reduce the friction often associated with onboarding external providers, such as technology integration, familiarisation with company policies, and insurance coverage, Axiom equips its lawyers with appropriate technologies housed in secure environments, handles onboarding and training, and provides malpractice coverage.[11] The result is a model that is designed to seamlessly provide clients with access to scalable external legal resources as and when needed.

Elevate

Elevate offers a broad and integrated suite of legal, technology, and consulting services spanning strategic and operational advisory, enterprise legal management systems, and a wide range of law and law-adjacent offerings.[12] Its multidisciplinary delivery model combines an integrated law firm with deep process, data, and technology capabilities.[13] This allows it to pair seasoned lawyers with global teams to provide oversight and legal escalation for document review, contract management, and legal operations work. Functionally akin to a hybrid model but built around an ALSP core, Elevate's structure allows it to deliver holistic solutions that cut across a broad spectrum of needs.

Keystone Law—The Internally Integrated, Platformed Law Firm

Keystone Law operates an integrated, technology-enabled platform that brings together over 400 self-employed lawyers via a shared culture and a digital infrastructure that provides technology, compliance, billing, and marketing support.[14] This structure has allowed it to scale efficiently while avoiding the overhead or cultural and organisational challenges typical in a traditional law firm partnership. However, Keystone remains focused on providing core legal services and has yet to expand its platform beyond that to provide technology, advisory, or other legal-adjacent offerings.

Unlikely to Evolve Into True Platforms

By managing and coordinating the demand for and supply of legal talent, process, and technology solutions, legal integrators possess many of the attributes needed to evolve into multi-sided platforms. However, like hybrid models (and in contrast to law firm networks), they remain inward-facing, delivering all services from within their own organisational boundaries. Their existing platform-like capabilities are designed solely to serve their internal ecosystems.

To transition into open, multi-sided platforms, integrators would need to invite suppliers from third-party firms, not just contracted individuals, effectively shifting from proprietary delivery systems to 'infrastructure-as-a-service' models. This would require embedding AI-driven orchestration tools and other connective technologies to coordinate multiple providers across a shared platform.

The real barriers to such a shift, however, are likely to be more strategic and cultural than technical. Many integrators have built strong brand equity as providers rather than marketplaces. Opening their ecosystems to competitors would disrupt the very formula that has brought them such success to date and would require a fundamental repositioning.

While it is therefore unlikely that most integrators will evolve into true platform businesses, the category is diverse, leaving open the possibility that some might. Specifically, integrators with sophisticated technology stacks and broader third-party sourcing models could gradually expand in the direction of a platform or acquire the bolt-on capabilities to participate as such. For the majority, however, the more likely path will be as providers operating on the third-party platforms of the future rather than as platforms themselves.

Competitive Sourcing Models

Technology-driven competitive sourcing models, such as Priori Legal, Theorem, and PERSUIT, connect clients with lawyers and law firms based on specific client needs. Among today's emerging models, this archetype is best positioned to evolve into GC 4.0-era platforms because they already have all of the dimensions needed for the GC 4.0 platform equation: corporate clients seeking services, a population of independent suppliers, and a digital infrastructure that connects the two sides in various ways and that potentially can embed itself further into both client and provider systems as these evolve.

Priori Legal: Sourcing and Matching Across the Provider Spectrum

Priori operates a talent-matching and sourcing platform powered by simplified, data-driven requests for proposals (RFPs). Its *Talent Marketplace* connects a wide range of corporate legal departments (from Fortune 100 multinationals to high-growth technology start-ups) with a vetted global network of more than 8,000 lawyers, law firms, ALSPs, and legal operations professionals across 70 countries.[15]

The attorney network includes solo practitioners, boutique firms, and specialised practices, covering a broad spectrum of client needs, from flexible and interim staffing to full-time secondments, and project-based engagements requiring niche expertise.

Talent Marketplace's technology facilitates every stage of the sourcing process. Clients begin by completing a guided questionnaire that streamlines the RFP process through structured data and natural language inputs. The platform then searches and filters the talent network to produce a curated shortlist of qualified candidates, enabling clients to evaluate options via built-in application tools, video interviews, and reference checks.[16]

As co-founders Basha Rubin and Mirra Levitt explain, corporate clients use Talent Marketplace 'to fill the (vast) gaps left by their big firm partners, whether through flexible talent or more traditional outside counsel'.[17] As Priori has expanded, clients have also begun using the platform 'to "right-source", moving low-to-medium risk and complexity work away from costly firms and to boutique firms. Still others needed local counsel all over the company and the world'.[18]

In addition to Marketplace, Priori also offers *Scout*, an AI-enabled panel-management tool that helps corporate clients automate their management of and interaction with their panel of trusted outside counsel firms. Scout centralises client knowledge, structures data from disparate sources, and surfaces insights. By using Scout, legal teams can evaluate their outside counsel portfolios across key variables such as experience, rates, expertise, and engagement history. The platform combines internal and public data, leveraging AI to aggregate and organise it within a clear visual interface that preserves institutional knowledge and highlights actionable insights. The tool also enables clients to run live auctions for matters, creating competitive pressure among panel firms through the issuance of RFPs and reverse auctions.[19]

Together, Talent Marketplace and Scout allow clients to determine whether the most effective resource for a given matter is one of their existing panel firms or whether a broader external search is warranted, enabling true data-driven sourcing and smarter allocation of legal work.

Theorem LTS: Streamlining Legal Technology Adoption

Theorem Legal Tech Marketplace operates a platform that helps law firms and corporate legal departments identify, procure, and optimise their use of legal technology and digital solutions. In this sense, it complements the procurement model offered by Priori Legal.

Through its *Legal Tech Marketplace* platform, Theorem enables clients to catalogue and analyse their existing technology stack, assess utilisation, and explore other technologies available in the market, developed by law firms, ALSPs, and independent vendors. Advanced search and comparison tools allow users to access detailed information about legal technology offerings, including pricing, features, use cases, workflow compatibility, and interoperability. The feature also allows clients to connect directly with vendors, and request demos.

Theorem also assists clients in developing efficient procurement and supplier management processes, including helping them to track subscriptions, identify potential new use cases, and access technology reviews.

In 2025, the company launched an AI-powered RFP tool to help legal departments and firms connect more effectively with its marketplace of legal technology providers.

The tool leverages AI to match buyers with the most suitable providers based on defined client needs and existing stack configurations. In software procurement, for example, it draws on Theorem's technology-stack data to ensure that proposed solutions are compatible with the buyer's infrastructure and workflows. It also allows clients to issue requests anonymously to solicit competitive proposals or direct those requests to pre-approved panels of trusted firms and suppliers.[20]

Integration with Priori Legal Interestingly, Theorem has recently expanded its scope by adding Priori's Legal Marketplace to its partner network, extending its RFP coverage from legal technology procurement to include legal services, signalling a further step towards a more integrated, multi-sided legal platform.

PERSUIT: *Optimising Law Firm Selection and Performance Management*

PERSUIT is a competitive legal sourcing platform that enables corporate legal departments to compare, engage, and source outside counsel using structured, AI-enabled technology.[21] Founded in 2016 by Jim Delkousis, a former partner at King & Wood Mallesons and DLA Piper, PERSUIT says its mission is to bring transparency, competition, and accountability to the traditionally opaque process of law firm engagement. The company's platform is now used by some of the world's largest companies, including Citibank, Wells Fargo, Nestlé, and Walmart.

At its core, PERSUIT digitises and systematises the process of sourcing and managing law firm engagements. It supports every stage of the outside counsel management lifecycle, from matter intake to RFP creation and pricing negotiation, invoice review and payment through to performance tracking and benchmarking, transforming what was once a manual and relationship-driven process into one that is structured, transparent, and data-driven. The platform's analytics allow clients to rate law firm performance across a range of variables, including diversity, quality, cost, and predicted outcomes.

Clients initiate their sourcing process on the platform by creating an RFP, either directly or by using PERSUIT's structured templates. These help users to consistently scope matters, define deliverables, establish milestones, and request staffing and budget models across proposals.

Once an RFP is issued, a competitive bidding process is triggered among invited firms (often drawn from the client's existing panel). Participating firms submit detailed proposals that include fee structures, staffing models, and timelines. During the live bidding phase, firms have access to anonymised comparative data, enabling them to dynamically adjust their submissions in real time and compete on transparency and value.

After the bidding process ends, PERSUIT's analytics engine normalises all submitted data, allowing clients to compare submissions on a 'like-for-like' basis across the bidding firms. Interactive dashboards highlight differences in key variables such as fees, strategies, team composition, and diversity metrics. The platform's AI-driven scoring model highlights key variables to support more objective and value-based decisions, focusing on the best outcomes, not just the lowest price. Indeed, PERSUIT's data shows that in only 48% of matters is the lowest price chosen. The result is a transparent and data-grounded decision process that drives cost efficiency and deepens performance accountability.

Expansion to ALSPs and Legal-adjacent Providers The adaptable nature of its platform architecture allows clients to use it to procure ALSPs and other legal-adjacent providers in addition to law firms, illustrating PERSUIT's potential to evolve into a GC 4.0-era sourcing platform. As Delkousis explains, the platform's taxonomy and workflow were deliberately designed to 'expand in line with market needs', allowing the same structured model to be applied across numerous categories of work.

Workflow Integration and Billing Innovation   Once the client has engaged a provider, PERSUIT tracks law firm performance, aggregating data across matters to generate benchmarks, scorecards, and trend insights that help clients continuously optimise work allocation, fee negotiations, and panel composition.

In 2025, PERSUIT acquired Apperio, a legal billing and analytics company, to connect sourcing directly with value-based billing and outcomes. This integration allows clients to track performance against milestones, outcomes, and negotiated fee structures, linking procurement, performance, and pricing in one continuous system. As Delkousis explains, legacy billing models that focus on timekeeper recording and bill narratives are 'ill-suited to value-based engagements'. Instead, PERSUIT's approach enables in-house teams to manage external counsel through a single, data-grounded 'source of truth'.

AI Enablement: Persi   In 2025, PERSUIT launched *Persi*, the first agentic AI designed specifically for outside counsel management. Persi functions as an intelligent intake and orchestration layer that guides in-house teams through each stage of the sourcing lifecycle, from triaging where the work should be done (insource, outsource, law firm, ALSP, etc.), scoping work, to identifying and recommending providers (on-panel, off-panel, etc.), evaluating proposals, testing against benchmarks, selecting providers, and managing performance. Persi can draft and refine RFPs, summarise proposals, compare pricing and staffing models, and extract insights from historical data.

Perhaps most interestingly, Persi can act as an adaptive decision agent, incorporating client procurement rules to determine, at initiation, whether a matter should be routed to internal teams, an ALSP, or outside counsel. In this way, Persi is helping PERSUIT to evolve from a sourcing platform into a dynamic orchestration system that mirrors the intake layer in the GC 4.0 legal department platform.

Two-sided Market Development   Persi also enables PERSUIT to expand its capabilities on the law-firm side of the procurement space. Persi will enable law firms to leverage AI agents that can receive, interpret, and respond to incoming client RFPs. To ensure speed and agility, GC 4.0 legal departments increasingly demand such automated agentic connectivity between their intake and routing layers and the intake systems their firms use. Some firms may choose to build their own systems in response to such demand, but many others will lack the sophistication to do so, giving them the valuable option to adopt the agentic frameworks being developed by PERSUIT, which would also allow them to integrate more seamlessly with their client's processes.

This points towards a future where agentic automation exists on both sides of the procurement fence, with buyer and seller both leveraging agentic workflows provided by platforms such as PERSUIT to interact directly with each other within a digitally enabled procurement ecosystem.

Analytics and Market Intelligence   PERSUIT can aggregate large volumes of market data across its engagements, including rates, performance, staffing models, diversity metrics, and outcome patterns, giving both clients and firms powerful insights. As Delkousis explained, 'we can tell firms why they're losing, where they lack coverage, and where the opportunities lie'. These data-driven insights are becoming a magnet for supplier participation, accelerating network effects as more firms and providers join the platform.

Strategic Positioning   Historically focused on corporate panels, PERSUIT is now expanding into adjacent domains and positioning itself as the agentic connector in the GC 4.0 marketplace. Its evolution from sourcing platform to integrated decision infrastructure makes it one of the most interesting and credible examples of an AI-era legal platform, where technology, data, and human judgement intersect.

Implications

Competitive sourcing models are best positioned to evolve rapidly into full-spectrum GC 4.0-era platforms because they already possess all the elements needed: clients, suppliers, and integrating technologies. Some, such as PERSUIT, are nearly already there. They are evolving from marketplaces into end-to-end procurement ecosystems that cover routing, initiation, selection, and performance management and analytics. Increasingly, these providers are also pursuing bolt-on acquisitions or forming strategic alliances in ways that further extend their reach and capabilities, stitching together the building blocks of a fully integrated GC 4.0 legal marketplace.

AI Integrators and Value-chain Capture

Firms like PERSUIT are becoming intelligent orchestrators across the procurement value chain. Its agentic AI, Persi, illustrates how platforms have the potential to evolve from utilities to strategic infrastructure, embedding themselves directly into client and law firm workflows.

As GC 4.0 legal departments build intake layers that automatically route work to internal and external providers, such providers could supply that capability, integrating directly into the routing and bidding systems of both legal departments and law firms. This would create a seamless, technology-enabled value chain in which matters are automatically triaged intelligently between clients and providers. It is an ambitious vision, but one that is not out of reach as GC 4.0 evolves.

Integrators and Networks in the Emerging Ecosystem

While legal talent and delivery integrators are unlikely to evolve into open platforms themselves for the reasons already discussed, their technological sophistication and delivery capacity position well to operate on those platforms. Rather than hosting a marketplace themselves, they might become valuable participants within it, including as competitive bidders for services procured through them.

Law firm networks such as Lex Mundi, TerraLex, and Multilaw could, however, evolve in various directions. They will all certainly play important roles as participants within open platforms, but some could themselves evolve into curated or walled-garden platforms, leveraging their brand equity and deep trust capital to orchestrate closed-system platforms among vetted providers. Their future direction will depend on where they want to place their focus: as providers or as vetted marketplaces. Those that move in the latter direction could have a competitive advantage in that niche.

A Converging Landscape

Networks, integrators, and sourcing platforms will all play important roles in the emerging ecosystem. Networks possess client trust and collaborative experience; integrators bring delivery infrastructure and multidisciplinary expertise; and sourcing platforms possess data, technology, and client interface. As they interact, a multi-faceted marketplace of various kinds of platform might emerge; some open, some closed and curated, with all of them data and AI-enabled.

Implications for Hybrid Models

For emerging hybrid firms, platforms offer the potential to leverage their integrated capabilities and bid at scale for bundled, multidisciplinary mandates. Their challenge will be to integrate with evolving client technology stacks and emerging platform systems, while avoiding some of the coordination challenges the Big Four have experienced.

Implications for Clients

For GC 4.0 clients, there is only upside. Some large departments may build their own internal platforms as they develop intake and routing systems. Others will rely on external providers to help them. Either way, platforms will deliver unprecedented transparency, price predictability, and performance management capabilities.

The combination of platforms and agentic AI could change the strategic paradigm for clients, providing greater cost predictability and lower price variance across categories of work, with the ability to automate triage and routing in real time. This kind of automation is likely to emerge first in areas where pricing is becoming commoditised, such as for standard debt issuances. Performance management may also become more transparent, as agents filter and report operational metrics in real time. Finally, automated agentic triage could segment work allocation more consistently, both internally and externally, as well as across law firms, ALSPs, and other providers.

All of this will generate clearer strategic control over vendor management for in-house departments. Legal operations teams and the lawyers they support will become increasingly digitally native and metrics-driven as they leverage these new procurement capabilities, with platforms becoming a core part of the operational fabric of in-house workflows.

Implications for Law Firms

For law firms, the implications could be profound. As platforms evolve from simple procurement tools into intelligent and increasingly AI-enabled marketplaces, they will become important mediators of client–provider relationships, controlling and sorting the data and decision points that drive client loyalty. Firms that historically relied on relationships and reputation to secure client loyalty may find themselves competing more often based on hard data. Margins for a growing range of work could compress as pricing power erodes.

Vendor success in this new order will depend on platform readiness, including the ability to plug into digital client and platform workflows, respond dynamically to AI-generated RFPs, and collaborate effectively across internal and third-party networks. The firms that adapt could thrive, securing a competitive advantage based on demonstrated efficiency and measurable performance. Those that fail to do so, however, may find themselves victims of the shifting winds to come.

14 | What Can Law Firms Do?

Tomorrow's leaders have to be versed in both innovation and operational mindsets—ambidextrous leadership.

—Kyle Hermans[1]

As noted in Chapter 9, adapting in response to disruptive change is hard for traditional law firms. While some may successfully transition to boutique, corporate, or alternative business structures, many will struggle to compete as the market evolves.

The Innovation Trap

Established law firms, like incumbents in other markets, tend to focus on incrementally improving existing business models through 'sustaining' innovation rather than reinventing them through 'disruptive' innovation.

As Clayton Christensen observed in *The Innovator's Dilemma*, it is ironically the very practices that underpin the success of established firms, like being responsive to client needs and focusing on large, high-margin, and well-established markets, that make them resistant to disruptive innovation.[2] This is important because, as Christensen warned, it is disruptive technologies that ultimately redefine the value proposition in a market, even if they underperform when they first appear.[3]

Organisational Antibodies

Because disruptive technologies often appear inferior at first, legacy customers typically don't want them—until they suddenly do. That's why listening closely to what their biggest customers say they want can be a dangerous strategy for high-performing firms. Unfortunately, as Christensen notes, many of them 'have well-developed systems for killing ideas that their customers don't want' and by the time customers have changed their minds, it may be too late for them to pivot.[4]

That early-stage disruptive technologies are also often less profitable than legacy technologies further disincentivises established players. Why invest in technology your customers say they don't want, especially if that technology also underperforms your current model and is less profitable?

For these reasons, when established firms are confronted with disruptive opportunities, their 'organisational antibodies' (as Professor Rita McGrath terms it) often activate, causing them to reject or starve such initiatives.[5] As Christensen notes:

> Despite their endowments in technology, brand names, manufacturing prowess, management experience, distribution muscle, and just plain cash, successful companies populated by good managers have a genuinely hard time doing what does not fit their model for how to make money. Because disruptive technologies rarely make sense during the years when investing in them is most important, conventional managerial wisdom at established firms constitutes an entry and mobility barrier that entrepreneurs and investors can bank on. It is powerful and pervasive.[6]

The firm's immune system will inevitably attack disruptive ventures. When combined with negative customer feedback, leaders come to doubt the efficacy or wisdom of investing in such disruptive technologies, resulting in the withdrawal of the resources, talent, and leadership attention needed for them to succeed.

Structural Ambidexterity To escape this trap, firms must become structurally ambidextrous; able to invest in sustaining innovation that advances their core model while simultaneously exploring disruptive new innovations that may challenge it. There is an inherent tension in doing both of these things at once, especially within the same organisation.

Create an Independent Start-up

A better way to go, according to Christensen and subsequent scholars, is to acknowledge these dynamics and set up a separate organisational structure for the disruptive venture; one that is modelled on a start-up, operationally independent from the legacy firm and dedicated to disruptive innovation.[7]

The start-up should have its own leadership, organisation, budget, and mandate. It should be given full authority to invest in new models and chart its own strategy independent of the KPIs, cost structures, and culture of the legacy parent.

The ability to do this well is called 'organisational ambidexterity', which Michael L. Tushman and Charles O'Reilly (III) have defined as 'the ability to simultaneously pursue both incremental and discontinuous innovation … from hosting multiple contradictory structures, processes, and cultures within the same firm'.[8]

The Three Golden Rules of Forming a Legacy-backed Start-up

Theory and practice strongly suggest that incumbents who want to establish a start-up should make sure to follow three golden rules to ensure success.

Rule 1: Target New Markets and Customer Segments As we saw in Chapter 9, disruptive innovation often first emerges in overlooked or underserved edges of the market, among clients who find incumbent products and services too expensive or poorly configured for their needs. The start-up's focus should therefore be on seeking out and addressing the needs of customers and market segments that currently sit outside of the legacy firm's focus.

As Christensen observes, if the legacy organisation 'stretches or forces a disruptive technology to fit the needs of current, mainstream customers … it is almost sure to fail. Historically, the more successful approach has been to find a new market that values the current characteristics of the disruptive technology'.[9]

New and hitherto unexplored customers and markets are the perfect laboratories from which to gain real-world feedback and test revenue streams. Freed from legacy expectations, the start-up can experiment with pricing, delivery, and technology solutions that are most suitable for these contexts. Over time, as these solutions mature, some of them may also migrate upwards and get adopted by the core business.

Rule 2: Create Independent Objectives, Strategies, and Metrics   The start-up team must be free to establish its own distinct objectives and measures of success. It should also be able to independently create pricing and go-to-market strategies, unburdened by incumbent practices. Traditional metrics, such as profits-per-partner, are not well suited to the disruptive start-up context. Metrics involving growth, learning, market access, or new capability development would likely be more appropriate.

Compensation structures should also be aligned with an innovation objective. Collaboration, experimentation, or customer feedback should therefore be incentivised over billable hours or other parent-firm metrics.

Rule 3: Disrupt in a Non-disruptive Manner   Finally, the venture should be small enough not to pose a threat to the parent. By framing it as a 'small experiment', leadership can lower internal resistance and dampen the instinctive pushback of the firm's immune system. As McGrath and McManus have observed in the digital transformation context, 'starting big, spending a lot, and assuming you have all the information is likely to produce a full-on attack from corporate antibodies—everything from risk aversion and resentment of your project to simple resistance to change'.[10]

To avoid triggering such defensive reactions, it is better to start small and frame the effort as a learning experiment that gives the legacy firm an opportunity to explore and adapt at low cost.

Leaders should resist drumming up unrealistic expectations of immediate success. Instead, iterative learning and incremental improvements within the start-up should be allowed to unfold, with promising proofs of concept scaled progressively as they are validated. Granting the start-up this autonomy helps prevent the preferences, assumptions, and legacy instincts of the parent company from dominating the agenda and crowding out more innovative solutions. As McGrath and McManus note, by seeking 'to disrupt in a nondisruptive manner', firms can shift their focus from choosing a single predetermined model and towards learning their way to the model that best aligns their evolving strategy.[11]

When legacy firms experiment on a small scale, they also possess one significant advantage over start-ups: the capacity to fund a portfolio of small experiments in parallel, rather than going 'all-in' on a single bet, increasing the likelihood of discovering a successful new model.[12]

Like any start-up, the firm should expect many failures along the way. The start-up should be encouraged to experiment broadly and not concentrate all of its scarce resources on a single project or expect that its first attempt will be successful.

As Christensen puts it:

> Although the mortality rate for ideas about disruptive technologies is high, the overall business of creating new markets for disruptive technologies need not be inordinately risky. Managers who don't bet the farm on their first idea, who leave room to try, fail, learn quickly, and try again, can succeed at developing the understanding of customers, markets, and technology needed to commercialize disruptive innovations.[13]

For law firms, this means allowing the independent start-up to innovate, test, and iterate with new approaches. Successes and failures should, however, always be fed back to the parent so that they can capture insights and learning.

Over time, the parent might even find that some of the innovations developed by the start-up, whether successful or not in its own context, might be adaptable to the core business. In this way, sustaining innovations can be built off the back of disruptive ones.

Keeping it small will also energise the start-up team, giving it a licence to celebrate early progress and small wins in ways that don't get overshadowed by the size of huge objectives.

Klöckner and the Art of Disruptive Innovation

The case of German metals distributor Klöckner, as depicted by McGrath in her book, *Seeing Around Corners*, offers powerful lessons for how legacy organisations can successfully conduct ambidextrous and disruptive innovation.[14]

In 2009, when Gisbert Rühl assumed the role of CEO at Klöckner & Co., one of the world's largest independent distributors for steel and metal products, the steel industry faced numerous headwinds, including slowing demand, price pressure, and new entrants from China. Klöckner's traditional business model, which involved purchasing steel from large manufacturers, stocking it, and then selling it on to various users, was under strain. At the same time, the supply side of the market had consolidated while the producer/ distribution side was highly fragmented, leading to a highly inefficient market.

End customers lacked many of the basic capabilities common in modern purchasing, including the ability to compare prices, verify availability, place orders online, and access complementary products and services, such as plastic piping or insurance. In short, this legacy system was designed around the needs of suppliers rather than those of users.

Rühl sensed an opportunity to innovate away from Klöckner's core business by developing a digital trading platform that could more efficiently connect suppliers, customers, and third parties. As McGrath observed, 'Klöckner would be leading the charge in going from a linear process with lots of inefficiencies to an integrated ecosystem that could operate transparently'.[15]

Creating a Stand-alone Entity

Klöckner's initial attempt to drive disruptive innovation through an internal innovation group failed. The company's organisational antibodies kicked in and efforts to reimagine how to deliver products and services more effectively were essentially blocked. As McGrath recounts, 'the conversations about new possibilities were shot down by naysayers who couldn't get past the customary "we don't do it that way in the steel business" orthodoxies'.[16]

Recognising that a new approach was needed, Rühl tasked a couple of employees with creating a separate entity, which was named Klöckner.i to differentiate it from the parent company. A small headquarters was established in Berlin, allowing Klöckner.i to tap into the city's start-up ecosystem and recruit talent out of that environment rather than from the steel industry.

Allowed to technologically decouple from the parent company and establish its own platform, Klöckner.i developed a three-phase digital strategy. As McGrath notes:

> The first phase ... was to create more or less standalone tools that were customer-centric and dealt with specific pain points that existing systems did not touch. In the second phase, Klöckner planned to expose its own customers to the digital tools, allowing them to choose how they wanted to connect on the digital platform. The third phase ... was to open the platform to its competitors, allowing the experience of doing business on the platform to be as integrated for customers as possible.[17]

Building Linkages with the Legacy Business

Rühl understood that Klöckner.i's success ultimately depended on the engagement and buy-in of the legacy organisation. He therefore launched programmes to foster collaboration and understanding. These included digital training for parent company employees, rotational assignments within Klöckner.i, and the adoption of new ways of working and communicating that were borrowed from the start-up environment. Gradually, these bridge-building efforts paid off, and the culture of the parent company business began to shift.

Embracing Success

As digital capabilities matured, Klöckner employees increasingly came to understand and embrace the company's digitisation strategy. As Rühl noted, they began to 'adopt agile working methods from the start-up scene and act in a less persnickety manner than they did in the past. We as an organization have thereby become much faster and more agile overall'.[18]

By 2017, four years after it launched its digital strategy, Klöckner was generating 17% of its revenue through its digital channels, crediting its initiative with driving its return to profitability and growth. By the fourth quarter of 2021, that share had risen to 46%, as the company announced plans to digitalise and automate 80% of its sales processes.[19]

Application to Law Firms

Similar approaches can and have been adapted to fit the law firm context. Two global firms—Cleary Gottlieb Steen & Hamilton LLP and Allen Overy Shearman Sterling LLP (A&O Shearman)—exemplify how leading firms are applying structural ambidexterity to their innovation efforts. While each of them has launched innovation units, they have done so in different ways that reflect their unique circumstances and objectives.

Taking a closer look at how these two firms have approached this is instructive for law firms seeking to engage in disruptive innovation while also protecting the flanks of their legacy businesses.

ClearyX

ClearyX was launched by Cleary Gottlieb based on a simple but disruptive vision: 'Imagine the business that puts Cleary out of business—then let's build that business'.[20]

The initiative was conceived by Managing Partner Michael Gerstenzang, who recognised the relevance of the forces Clayton Christensen described in *The Innovator's Dilemma* and how they might apply to legal services. Gerstenzang believed that unless the firm took proactive steps, external players would increasingly erode client relationships and capture segments of work.

The resulting venture, which the firm named 'ClearyX' to distinguish it from the parent entity, was tasked with four strategic objectives (see Figure 14.1):

1. Focus on client pain points.
2. Leverage the firm's legacy culture without becoming hostage to it.
3. Foster a start-up ambition.
4. Apply a 'technology-first' approach.

Independent Business

The firm's leadership recognised Christensen's and McGrath's observations that disruptive innovation would be difficult to engineer from within the firm's existing structure. It concluded that a better approach would be to create an agile, independent entity, empowered to experiment with new service delivery models, free from the constraints of legacy structures.

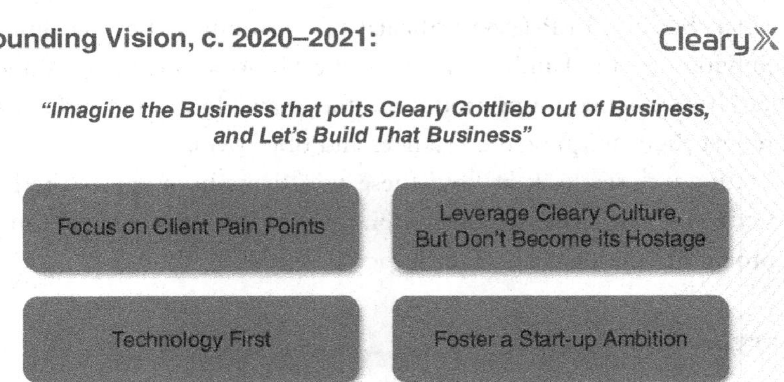

Figure 14.1 ClearyX's founding vision.

Source: Illustration by ClearyX. Provided for use with permission by ClearyX.

At the same time, the firm wanted to retain ownership of the unit in order to benefit from its successes and preserve work and client relationships that might otherwise migrate.

Founded in 2021 and publicly launched in 2022, ClearyX operates as an independent business, wholly owned by the firm but structurally separate from its partnership. Its CEO, Carla Swansburg, was recruited from outside the firm and given a clear brief: experiment boldly, fail fast, and design new service models without being constrained by the billable-hour logic or hierarchical decision-making of the parent firm.

Socialising the Venture Inside the Firm

The establishment of ClearyX met with little resistance from partners inside the firm, which is a testament to the leadership's success in socialising the idea across the partnership and championing its value. While some internal voices initially questioned whether ClearyX could match the firm's quality standards for due diligence, early results quickly proved that a dedicated tech-forward team could quickly meet and indeed exceed expectations.

Partners have since become strong advocates, serving as a source of referrals and distribution for ClearyX's products and services. Today, the venture often engages directly with clients who now proactively seek its support on diligence and technology-related matters.

Narrow Beginnings That Scaled with Success

With a small team of 15, ClearyX began with a narrow focus on transactional due diligence because it was a discrete, repeatable process where technology could deliver measurable gains. The early success ClearyX had in this area built credibility inside the firm while also demonstrating tangible value to clients. Within months, ClearyX showed that it could deliver faster, cheaper, and higher-quality outcomes through machine learning, automation, and process optimisation. Having completed more than 150 diligence exercises, it now operates as one of the most advanced technology-enabled diligence teams in the market.

Building on this foundation, the team has expanded horizontally into areas such as real estate, private funds, and capital markets, and vertically into custom software development. It now also opportunistically builds bespoke solutions for in-house teams and even other law firms, focusing on areas where technology can materially improve outcomes.

Targeting Client Pain Points

ClearyX has spent several years engaging directly with in-house teams, focusing its efforts entirely on what clients say they want and need, and what they believe is missing from the market. It deliberately set its sights on the 'middle' of the value chain, that is, work that was too complex for generic ALSPs yet too routine to justify partner-level rates. This segment, which is often overlooked by elite firms, provided an ideal testing ground for disruptive innovation, as it was in this space that clients often prioritised affordability, efficiency, and transparency over bespoke work.

Technology First

ClearyX has adopted a technology-first mindset. As Swansburg notes, 'technology is at the centre of everything we do, and we continue to have a mix of buying vs. building, focussed on building a better solution and integrating third party tools if they are the best option for the work'.

Recognising the limits of off-the-shelf tools, the unit pivoted to building proprietary software, including its own AI-powered diligence and project-management platform ('Cora'), complete with data-room integration, redaction engines, and client dashboards. This 'buy-versus-build' strategy reflects the venture's commitment to owning the client experience, controlling integration points, and ensuring scalability, all characteristic of its start-up mindset.

The team continues to explore new opportunities to leverage emerging AI capabilities through partnerships, joint ventures, and co-development, adopting whatever approach best accelerates innovation and client value.

Revenue Model

To date, ClearyX's revenue has almost exclusively come from due diligence work in connection with transactions the firm is working on. Increasingly, however, it is generating revenue from new sources, including:

- Expanding diligence partnerships with clients who may use other firms for some transactions but engage ClearyX for diligence, with plans to extend these partnerships to new geographies and clients.
- Developing technology solutions, such as contract management tools and a proprietary financial services regulation portal, licensed on a subscription basis for recurring revenue.

■ Building custom solutions for the firm, to which ClearyX assigns a market-based value for its internal accounting.

The team also has plans to launch its proprietary software as a service, generating SaaS-based subscription revenue.

Pricing flexibility is also a core principle. As Swansburg explains, 'We try to be a low-cost provider, but also work with clients to determine what best meets their needs. For example, we can do project fees, per-document fees, subscriptions of varying lengths—even hourly rates if required. As we don't currently have outside investors, we don't have the typical start-up revenue pressure which gives us more leeway'.

While ClearyX tracks all expenses, including firm resources allocated to it, profitability is not its sole objective. It also has a strategic mandate to strengthen client relationships and prospects and make those relationships more 'sticky' and less transactional.

Unlike many 'captive' ALSP models, ClearyX is truly empowered to build its own client base through independent marketing, business development, and branding, while benefitting from the firm's brand halo.

Redefining Success and Incentives

ClearyX operates as an independent business with its own compensation and evaluation frameworks. While time is tracked for internal purposes, hours billed are not used as a measure of value. Instead, success is measured based on learning velocity, client adoption, and capability development.

The team's bonus scheme is tied to both business and individual performance, rewarding outputs, behaviours, experimentation, and continuous improvement rather than utilisation. This also enables it to maintain more flexibility in how it conducts evaluations and provides incentives. The leadership team participates in a collective 'profit-sharing' model in which they all share in the firm's success, with a pool of funds set aside for allocation across the team where extra recognition is warranted. They have also established a 'spot bonus' pool where, throughout the year, awards can be made for above-and-beyond work or exemplary behaviour.

The firm also embraces failure by recognising the ways in which the team might try something even if it ultimately falls short. As Swansburg notes, 'We make sure to celebrate even the tiniest of wins—things like finding a great way to prompt AI to get a specific result, creating a really cool new way to visualize data, or finding a way to streamline a small aspect of our work'.

The unit, which became profitable by its second year, now draws revenue from SaaS subscriptions, custom builds, and diligence partnerships, including collaborations with clients and even other law firms not engaged by Cleary. The firm takes the view that it is better to disrupt one's own lower-margin work than to cede it to external players.

Feeding Learning Back to the Firm

While autonomous, ClearyX maintains tight feedback loops with Cleary's internal innovation team, sharing tools, pricing models, and lessons learned from agile experimentation. Some solutions are integrated back into the firm's workflows, while others remain stand-alone, client-facing products. This selective permeability ensures mutual benefit without compromising ClearyX's independence.

A Blueprint for Strategic Transformation

ClearyX exemplifies how elite law firms can create insulated innovation vehicles to explore disruptive markets, develop proprietary technology, and redefine success on their own terms. By freeing the venture from legacy metrics, empowering non-traditional talent, and focusing on client-centric problem-solving, Cleary has built an engine for both defensive adaptation and offensive growth.

Its evolution underscores a broader lesson for firms: innovation requires courage and a willingness to found a parallel organisation that is free to rethink how value could be created and delivered. ClearyX shows that, with the right autonomy, incentives, and client focus, disruption can be harnessed from within.

Key Learnings from ClearyX

- Create an autonomous unit, insulated from the parent firm's immune system.
- Follow the customer's 'jobs to be done', targeting underserved segments where affordability, efficiency, and transparency matter.

> - Redefine success metrics to include growth, learning, and capability development rather than profit per partner.
> - Embrace strategic cannibalisation: better to disrupt your own margins than let external players do it.
> - Use feedback loops to share learning with the core firm without compromising the independence of the innovation vehicle.

A&O Shearman's Markets Innovation Group: Engineering Moonshots

A&O Shearman has also learned the need for organisational ambidexterity. The firm's Markets Innovation Group (MIG) was launched with a bold proposition: to create a 'moonshot division' inside the firm that would explore the future of legal services free from the constraints of the traditional partnership.

Initially, the idea was to empower the unit to anticipate and respond to 'dislocation events' (market disruptions driven by regulatory, technological, macroeconomic, or other systemic shifts). The firm's leadership saw an opportunity to develop cross-practice, holistic, technology-driven solutions better suited to address such challenges than conventional law firm structures could. The vision was to assemble a multidisciplinary team able to re-engineer how complex and fast-moving issues could be addressed without being constrained by traditional KPIs, billable-hour logic, or annual financial cycles.

Market Shocks and Moonshots

MIG traces its origins to seismic crises such as Lehman's collapse, LIBOR reform, and Brexit. Responding effectively to such events requires cross-practice, cross-jurisdictional coordination. MIG was established to bridge traditional gaps, bringing together lawyers, technologists, engineers, and data scientists to develop and deploy holistic, scalable solutions for such complex challenges.

At the same time, emerging technologies were beginning to reshape the legal industry. The firm's leadership recognised that developing an effective response could not be achieved through fragmented initiatives; it required a multidisciplinary approach. They viewed the effective harnessing of technological innovation as a 'moonshot' opportunity. With no other firm having stepped forward to fill the void, A&O Shearman set about creating MIG to do just that.

A Commercial, Future-centric Mindset

From the outset, MIG's objective was commercially grounded: to explore emerging market trends, not as an abstract innovation lab, but as a profit-seeking business unit, with a clear mandate to identify and test new approaches and develop effective and scalable business models that could transform how the firm and the industry operated.

Its remit was to anticipate disruptive change and translate it into commercial opportunity. Rather than merely reacting to current challenges, the objective was to identify what might be coming and then develop business models to meet the evolving needs of clients.

MIG was fully backed from the outset by the firm's senior leadership. David Wakeling, a senior partner, who was appointed Global Head of MIG, collaborated closely with the senior leadership to design the unit's structure and purpose. As Wakeling explained, 'the strategy was to start exploring how to make money, build a profitable business, train people, and create a sustainable enterprise'.

Over time, MIG has evolved from an informal group into a formal unit within the firm. Today, MIG has approximately 50 professionals worldwide, roughly half of whom are lawyers and half technologists, data scientists, and engineers.

Future-literate, Client-centric Approach

From the outset, MIG adopted a big-picture, client-centric perspective. As Wakeling explains, the team 'would read the *Financial Times*, *The Wall Street Journal* and *The Economist* and ask ourselves, "What's big? What are the top three things that boards are going to worry about?"'

They focused on big-cycle issues, such as what a post-recessionary environment might mean, how geographical fragmentation and Brexit could reshape markets, and what major regulatory shifts might entail for the financial and other sectors. These insights were then applied back to the firm, helping assess how well positioned it was to support clients in navigating such shifts.

By taking this approach, MIG was able to sidestep the firm's operational focus on the current financial cycle, shifting its lens from what the firm needed today to what clients would need tomorrow.

This future-literate approach enabled A&O Shearman to focus on AI well before it became mainstream, recognising the scale of change ahead even before ChatGPT's launch. As a result, the team was able to position itself ambitiously around AI and develop a forward-looking vision, anticipating where the technology was likely to be 6–12 months out, not merely where it stood at the time.

MIG was also able to draw on the insights of its multidisciplinary team, including internal technologists who were embedded in different ecosystems from the lawyers, giving it an early, informed view of where things were heading and what the implications would be for the legal industry.

A Start-up Mentality

The firm's leadership recognised that an exploratory innovation unit could not thrive within the constraints of billable hours, annual budget cycles, and operational KPIs. MIG was therefore created as a 'start-up within the firm'; a semi-autonomous entity with the freedom to operate differently from the rest of the partnership and independent of its legacy model.

To ensure that independence, a dedicated Innovation Fund was established, giving MIG financial autonomy and insulating it from utilisation pressures. This enables the team to focus on learning and experimentation with a view towards creating long-term value. The objective is to create a space where innovation can be pursued as a commercial venture in its own right, measured by outcomes and insights, rather than hours billed.

Although the size of the fund is modest by venture standards, it was significant enough to underwrite prototyping, product design, and strategic partnerships, notably with OpenAI, Microsoft, and Harvey.

Despite its big-picture lens and moonshot mentality, MIG has remained disciplined in its execution, scaling only gradually as evidence supports the likelihood of success. By keeping initiatives small at first, it has avoided triggering unnecessary challenges around investment thresholds and profit margins. As Wakeling says, 'it's a bad idea to attract attention until you've delivered the goods'.

Strategic Partnerships

Partnerships have become key to MIG's model. As the potential scale and impact that AI could have on the legal sector became evident, strategic partnerships became the preferred way forward because they allow MIG to develop proprietary tools grounded in curated datasets ('benches'), while leveraging external partners for Cloud scale and specialist AI capabilities.

This hybrid 'buy-and-build' strategy avoids the capital intensity of pure development while retaining control over legal logic, data curation, and IP. It also enables MIG to build a SaaS model with clients and other customers including, in some cases, other law firms.

From Projects to Products and Services

Increasingly, MIG has evolved from delivering bespoke client projects to developing scalable, technology-enabled products and services. Two flagship offerings exemplify this direction: ContractMatrix and Harvey.

ContractMatrix Developed in collaboration with Microsoft and Harvey, ContractMatrix is a SaaS platform that automates contract analysis, classification, and remediation. It codifies complex regulations into digital playbooks and can ingest thousands of contracts, color-coding compliance ('green', 'amber', 'red') and generating targeted fixes.

A dedicated module, *ContractMatrix Vantage*, powers large-scale diligence and remediation exercises. For example, it can help clients comply with the European Union's Digital Operational Resilience Act (DORA) by reviewing thousands of supplier contracts and producing bespoke side-letter amendments. This results in faster, cheaper, and more consistent results for clients that are delivered under fixed-fee arrangements, which preserve margins and allow MIG to compete effectively with ALSPs.

Harvey Collaboration MIG is currently collaborating with Harvey, an AI platform built on LLMs such as Open AI's ChatGPT and trained on extensive legal datasets to serve the legal and professional services industries. As part of this collaboration, MIG and Harvey are working on an advanced reinforcement learning initiative, in which the Harvey platform has access to Shearman's extensive knowledge repositories across 60 jurisdictions, which enables it to fine-tune its outputs. These are then deployed via Microsoft and integrated directly into client enterprise systems, where they are further enhanced by the client's own organisational knowledge.

The result is a flow of insight from firm to client. In-house teams can, for example, use the software to analyse their own contract databases against evolving regulatory requirements to ensure compliance without external intervention. As Wakeling explains, 'in the day-to-day work of the in-house lawyer, if they want to check on regulatory compliance, we can push that knowledge through our SaaS product, so they don't need to phone us. Instead, they pay a license fee for that'.

Once exportable, these tools can be embedded within the client's own operating systems, extending their efficacy from legal and into other functions, such as treasury, finance, and so on.

Other modules, such as the new merger control one, allow users to upload deal data, trigger cross-jurisdictional analysis across 50+ regimes, and generate regulatory checklists and filings, all while keeping 'humans in the loop' to manage risk. MIG's long-term vision is one of safe automation: embedding agentic intelligence into client workflows without compromising professional standards.

Marketing and Communications

In keeping with its autonomous start-up mindset, MIG's marketing and communications strategy blends traditional and digital approaches in ways that set it apart from the conventions of most law firms. When it launched ContractMatrix as a SaaS product, for instance, MIG orchestrated a hybrid rollout that paired an exclusive feature in the *Financial Times* in print, online, and via LinkedIn, with techniques more typical of the software industry. These included a dedicated product landing page featuring a demonstration video and a lead generation form directing potential clients to a dedicated email channel.

The results were immediate: as soon as the *Financial Times* article and the LinkedIn post went live, inquiries began flooding in, with interest accelerating further in the weeks that followed. MIG adopted a similar media-first approach when announcing its collaboration with Harvey to develop its merger control tool, again leveraging an exclusive *Financial Times* feature to build visibility and momentum.

Positioning for the AI Era

Through MIG, A&O Shearman is expanding its value proposition, blending elite legal expertise with client-integrated solutions delivered via cutting-edge digital tools and strategic partnerships. These tools plug directly into client operating models, facilitating the exchange of insights across the enterprise, allowing the firm to create stickier, more collaborative relationships.

By embedding itself into clients' digital ecosystems, the firm positions itself not just as a legal advisor, but as a data and technology partner, a powerful evolution of its business model at a time when clients are transforming.

Key Takeaways for Law Firms

- Start small and scale from success to minimise resistance and build credibility.
- Ring-fence funding to insulate innovation from short-term pressures.
- Build multidisciplinary teams that blend legal, technical, and data science expertise.
- Adopt a 'buy-and-build' strategy, partnering for scale and expertise the law firm doesn't have.
- Target ALSP territory by offering efficient, tech-enabled solutions at competitive prices.
- Integrate with client systems to enhance stickiness and co-create value.

The Art of the Possible

As the above case studies illustrate, incumbent firms can move beyond the innovation trap, pursuing disruptive innovation while continuing to strengthen their legacy businesses.

The key is to avoid triggering the organisational antibodies by starting small and in an unthreatening manner. A proven way to do this is to establish an autonomous unit, infused with a start-up mindset and its own leadership, organisation, budget, incentives, and mandate.

The entity should be free to invest in new models, chart its own strategy, and target emerging customer segments with distinct pricing and go-to-market approaches. As the ClearyX and MIG case studies show, firms should ring-fence funding to shield innovation from short-term pressures, follow the customer's 'jobs to be done', and integrate where possible with client systems.

Success metrics must also evolve to encompass growth, learning, and capability development, supported by feedback loops that channel insights back to the parent firm. Finally, assembling multidisciplinary teams will ensure that innovation is both creative and commercially grounded.

15 | The Future of Legal Education

The goal of law school should be to train people to think like a lawyer, behave like a business professional, and be an innovator.

—Professor Michele DeStefano[1]

AI and the Changing Demands on Legal Education

AI is reshaping not only how legal work is done but also what it means to be a lawyer. As legal departments, law firms, and ALSPs re-engineer their service delivery models, they increasingly need digitally fluent, multidisciplinary, and adaptable professionals. However, the skills needed by GC 4.0 lawyers are evolving faster than the law schools that train them.

As noted in Chapter 2, the training pipeline historically rested on a division of labour. Law schools provided doctrinal grounding and analytical discipline while firms developed professional competence through structured apprenticeships embedded in the Cravath model. That pipeline is now breaking down. Large firms are no longer reliably training junior lawyers, yet many law schools continue to operate based on the Cravath model. The result is a widening gap between what schools teach and what the profession requires.

This does not absolve firms or corporations of responsibility. As David Wilkins and Scott Westfahl argue, the system must involve all participants in the ecosystem, and 'the narrow debates about who bears responsibility for what aspect of lawyer development need to turn to broader discussions around how law schools, law firms, and clients can collaborate and leverage each other's strengths'.[2] But schools cannot wait for this to become a reality. To remain effective incubators of future legal talent, they must preserve the intellectual rigour of the traditional model, while preparing students for a GC 4.0 reality shaped by technology and new organisational forms.

Though this chapter uses the US three-year postgraduate model as its reference point, its conclusions apply globally. The US model is increasingly influential elsewhere, including in large markets like China and India. As a report for the Legal Services Board notes, the UK pathway (an undergraduate degree combined with apprenticeship) is attracting less international traction; even jurisdictions such as Australia and Canada, which have historically followed the UK model, are moving towards the US approach.[3]

The Rise and Fall of the Langdell–Cravath Model

Langdell and the Reinvention of Legal Education

The modern US law school began with the reforms introduced by Harvard Law School Dean Christopher Columbus Langdell in the late nineteenth century.[4] Before Langdell, legal education resembled the unstructured legal environment of the Gilded Age. Many aspiring lawyers trained through apprenticeships, as law schools were embryonic. Practitioners (rather than academics) delivered lectures that were transcribed and memorised by students.[5] There was little class discussion, no coherent curriculum or required courses, and often no fixed period of study.[6] Methodology took various forms, from 'text plus lecture' formats to Columbia's 'Dwight method', which relied on student recitations and lectures.[7]

As Laura Webb observes, Langdell transformed this system by changing 'who could attend Harvard Law School, who taught there, and how they taught'.[8] Admission standards were raised to require an undergraduate degree; the programme was extended to three years; and five core subjects—Property, Contracts, Torts, Civil Procedure, and Criminal Law— became mandatory in the first year. Practitioners were replaced by full-time academics. Assessment became more rigorous, with complex hypotheticals requiring students to apply doctrine to real-world problems, while grading became based on both class and test performance. This structure still defines the US law school curriculum.[9]

Most importantly, Langdell replaced passive learning with active reasoning. The 'casebook method' required students to analyse appellate opinions while the 'Socratic method' used dialogue to uncover legal principles and test reasoning. This reflected Langdell's view of the law as a science governed by discoverable rules.[10] Students engaged directly with 'original sources' (printed judicial opinions) to extract underlying principles.[11] Langdell's method became widely adopted throughout the United States. Although innovations have emerged since, his case method, in various forms, remains the dominant paradigm.[12]

The Cravath System and the Rise of Professional Development

As discussed in Chapter 2, while elite schools were adopting Langdell's model, large law firms were developing the Cravath System, which gave young lawyers practical training. Associates underwent a multi-year probationary period involving rotational assignments and mentorship, enabling them to develop judgement, client interaction, ethics, and business understanding.[13] Work was structured analytically, with cases broken into components, assigned to associates, and reassembled under partner supervision.[14] Associates who mastered the required skills advanced; those who did not left.

If law schools tested analytical reasoning, the Cravath System tested professional competence. This symbiosis created a development pipeline that endured for decades.[15]

Some have questioned, however, whether this pipeline was ever optimal. As Dean Martin Brinkley notes, 'law school has never purported to provide more than a fraction of the training a lawyer needs', with the profession leaving 'critical parts of the lawyer's apprenticeship … to an unstructured, chance-ridden set of arrangements that only take purchase after a law degree is earned'.[16] Nonetheless, the division of labour between schools and firms trained countless generations of US lawyers.

The Erosion of the Langdell–Cravath Pipeline

As noted above, this pipeline is now coming apart due to shifts in talent and client markets.[17] Wilkins and Westfahl identify four key mutually reinforcing trends driving this. First, associate attrition has increased, driven by inter-firm poaching, work–life pressures, expanding career options, and declining prospects and job security at the partnership level. These factors, they note, have 'produced a world in which law firms pay significantly more for talent but have significantly less incentive to invest in the kind of apprenticeship training … on which the Cravath model … depends'.[18]

Second, expanding partner–associate ratios, combined with increased demands on partners to devote more time to business generation, is leaving senior lawyers with less capacity for training and mentoring.[19]

Third, clients now resist paying for associate training. As they seek 'to reduce the price law firms charge for their services, particularly for work that does not directly benefit the client … the training and development of associates has been one of the primary targets of this budgetary axe'.[20]

Finally, firms are pushing associates to specialise earlier to maximise their short-term profitability, undermining the generalist, rotational development model at the heart of the Cravath approach.[21] This, in turn, is prompting associates to leave earlier to avoid becoming overly specialised and thus unemployable except in large law firms, 'and to find other jobs where they believe they will have broader and more satisfying experiences'.[22]

While many firms are increasingly unwilling or unable to maintain their side of the pipeline, law schools continue to prioritise intellectual enrichment over professional training. This approach needs a fundamental reassessment.

The Growing Insufficiency of the Langdell Model As it turns out, relying exclusively on a model designed for a nineteenth-century professional environment has proved to be unwise. As Webb observes, 'There are 150 years separating today's law students from the law students—and society— for whom the [Langdell] method was first imagined. This … should give us pause'.[23] Graduates entering the AI era need professional competencies as well as fluency in new skills, including technology, systems thinking, and multidisciplinary collaboration. Meanwhile, the traditional approach does not prioritise any of these.

There is a long-standing debate over the virtues and shortcomings of the Langdell model.[24] That debate lies beyond the scope of this book. The question here is narrower and more practical: How should legal education evolve in order to prepare students for the AI-enabled GC 4.0 legal environment?

A useful way to explore this is to examine four interlocking dimensions of legal education: its purpose, its methods, the subjects it teaches, and the time available to teach them.

The Legal Education Triangle

These four dimensions of legal education can be visualised as a triangle (see Figure 15.1). At its centre lies *purpose*. Legal education for the AI era must begin with a clear understanding of what it is meant to achieve. The three sides of the triangle represent the key design choices that flow from purpose: *content* (what subjects should students learn); *time* (how should the curriculum be sequenced and allocated); and *method* (how should those subjects be taught). We consider each below.

Purpose

As American baseball legend Yogi Berra once quipped, 'If you don't know where you are going, you'll end up someplace else'.[25] A clear understanding of purpose is the essential starting point.

Langdell's Original Purpose: Uncovering Universal Principles   A good place to begin exploring purpose is Langdell. As Edward Rubin notes, Langdell saw the law as 'a form of natural science … a system whose specific rules could be derived from a relatively small number of general principles'.[26] Just as a natural scientist discerns gravitation by observing falling objects, he believed legal scholars could only discern universal legal principles by studying decided cases and, in doing so, they could improve the law.[27]

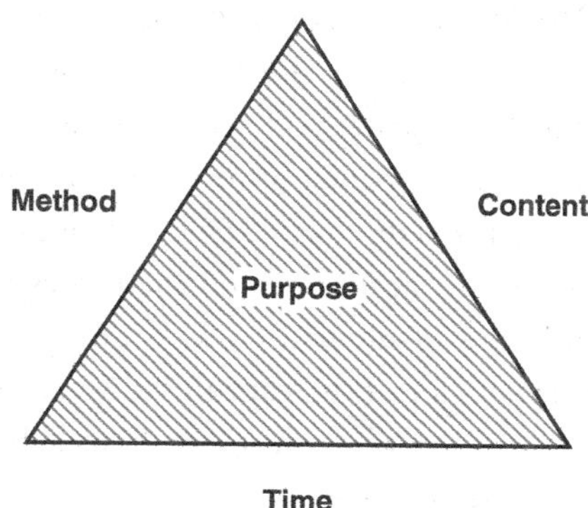

Figure 15.1 The legal education triangle.

Source: Illustration by Logica Design.

Rubin explains the logic:

> For [Langdell and his contemporaries], the law consisted of a set of definitive statements that could be found in authoritative sources ... To determine the law meant to consult these sources. To study the law ... meant to discern the principles that determined good decisions and gave those decisions coherence. To improve the law meant to alter or overrule judicial decisions that conflicted with those principles so that the totality ... formed a conceptually coherent unit. This framework permitted the analogy between the study of law and the study of natural science.[28]

Langdell's pedagogy was built around this scientific endeavour. Students needed analytical skills to extract principles from cases, and his casebook and Socratic methods were tools designed to cultivate them.

As the social sciences emerged, Langdell's conception of the law as a natural science was abandoned, but his methods remained because they were effective. As Langdell's successor, James Barr Ames, observed, studying cases teaches students 'to discriminate between the relevant and irrelevant facts ... to draw just distinctions ... and to discover true analogies', thereby producing 'sound legal thinkers, competent to grapple with new problems because of their experience in mastering old ones'.[29] Russell Weaver adds that the case method develops effective argumentation; an appreciation of precedent; an understanding of lawyering and the legal process; mental toughness; and the ability to think on one's feet.[30]

The Academic—Professional Tension   Langdell's vision challenged long-held views that the purpose of legal education was to produce practitioners. He justified placing legal training in universities by distinguishing legal *study* from *practice*, arguing that if law was not a science, it was just 'a species of handicraft', best learned through apprenticeship.[31]

This tension between the academic and the professional continues; it is, as Brinkley notes, 'an old, well-plowed field'.[32] The Carnegie Foundation's landmark report on legal education captures this tension, describing law schools as hybrid institutions that must instil 'well-honed skills of legal analysis' as well as 'strong skill in serving clients'.[33]

The tension is also not uniquely American. In his famous 1967 Inaugural Lecture at Queen's University Belfast, 'Pericles and the Plumber', William Twining captured it through the figures of Pericles (lawyer as statesman, lawgiver, judge, and leader) and the plumber (lawyer as technician).[34] In Australia, David Barker outlines a divide 'between those who regard legal education in instrumental terms, namely training individuals as future legal practitioners, and those who regard it as an academic discipline with its own intrinsic value'.[35]

But with firms no longer reliably providing practical training, schools can no longer focus on academics at the expense of professional skills. There must be a rebalancing; but where should the equilibrium lie? There is no universal answer because it depends on the institution's mission: elite schools preparing students to be academics, judges, and leaders may lean towards the academic and conceptual. Schools serving local communities may tilt towards the practical and vocational. However, in all cases, the goal should be to produce outstanding and well-rounded legal professionals.

Towards a Modern Unified Purpose In the AI era, legal graduates will pursue many different careers, some of which do not yet exist. Given such uncertainty, law schools must instil enduring academic and technical foundations that allow graduates to thrive regardless of what comes next. To do that, they must iron out the tension noted above and seamlessly weave together a structured, balanced curriculum. As Anthea Roberts notes, 'our lodestar should be what students will be doing in the workforce'.[36] Perhaps the best articulation of a unified purpose centred around this need is therefore a paraphrased version of DeStefano's formulation, cited at the start of this chapter:

> Legal education should teach students to think like lawyers and equip them with the professional competencies, adaptability, and innovative capacity required to thrive in a wide range of roles in the GC 4.0 landscape.

Three points emerge from this.

First, schools must not discard core cognitive training. Whatever criticisms of the Langdellian model may be valid, cultivating analytical discipline remains foundational.

Second, with the pipeline eroding, schools must calibrate between the academic and the professional in ways that reflect their missions.

Third, the professional end of the spectrum must expand to encompass the skills lawyers need in the GC 4.0 era.

With purpose in mind, we can consider content.

Content

If the purpose is to train students to think like lawyers, excel as professionals, and be adaptive and innovative, what content should schools teach?

The Core Courses—Learning to 'Think Like a Lawyer' The first-year core courses remain highly effective at providing students with a rigorous analytical foundation. They include Langdell's original five foundational subjects plus several new ones, including Constitutional Law and Legal Research and Writing.

These courses have endured because they fulfil two needs. First, they represent the basic architecture of the legal system. It is hard to imagine lawyers without any grounding in these domains. Even with increasingly capable AI, humans must know what questions to ask; that requires baseline knowledge. Second, they provide conceptual density, which helps develop analytical competence. The core should remain intact—but with professional and technical competencies built around it.

New Domains: Excel as Professionals To excel in the GC 4.0 era, students must cultivate additional competencies that most firms and schools are still not systematically developing. These include:

- business literacy, strategy, and leadership;
- technological and digital fluency; and
- creativity, design thinking, and interdisciplinary problem-solving.

These competencies are critical in the GC 4.0 environment. We consider them below.

Business Literacy, Strategy, and Leadership GC 4.0 legal professionals need business fluency, strategic thinking, and leadership skills. A basic understanding of financial statements, capital structures, and commercial transactions is essential in every legal domain and in navigating risk. Lawyers also need business fluency to participate in organisational decision-making. As *U.S. News and World Report* notes, 'Over the last few decades, trends in law and business have led to significant overlap between these two fields. Lawyers are increasingly called upon to think in terms of business strategy, and business leaders spend more time than ever grappling with legal regulations, compliance and risks'.[37] Not surprisingly, law schools are integrating these domains, with dual JD/MBA degrees increasingly prevalent.

While the extent to which these competencies are needed will vary by institution and student, domains that need to be covered include:

- **Financial literacy** (accounting, financial analysis, valuation, budgeting).
- **Strategy** (creating organisational value, planning, maintaining competitive advantage).
- **Negotiation** (theoretical frameworks and applied practice).
- **Communication** (conveying complex ideas clearly and compellingly; active listening).
- **Leadership** (influencing and motivating teams, collaborating, setting objectives, shaping culture).

The objective is not to turn lawyers into MBAs, but to ensure that GC 4.0 lawyers can operate effectively.

Technological and Digital Fluency   GC 4.0 lawyers must also have training in legal data systems, digital platforms, and AI-enabled workflows; a grounding in data ethics, governance, and privacy; and a working knowledge of cybersecurity. These competencies are essential to collaborating with technologists, product engineers, cybersecurity specialists, data scientists, and other colleagues in multidisciplinary teams.

Here again, the objective is not to train technologists, but to ensure that lawyers can use, supervise, and integrate technology responsibly and intelligently. As Anthea Roberts explains, GC 4.0 lawyers must 'know how to orchestrate and optimise human–AI collaboration, recognise when something appears suspicious, identify when deeper inquiry is required, and know what to ask, how to test, and how to validate'. They must develop an instinct for when they can delegate tasks to technology, and how and when to verify output.[38]

Creativity, Design Thinking, and Interdisciplinary Problem-solving   GC 4.0 challenges are ambiguous, cross-functional, and fast-moving. They often lack clear precedents or obvious solutions, and they arise within a legal ecosystem that is itself transforming. To operate effectively in this environment, lawyers must be able to generate novel insights, reframe complex problems, and integrate knowledge across disciplines. That requires creativity. As Elizabeth Beesley notes, creativity is 'a powerful tool for lawyers to tackle multifaceted challenges and adapt to changing legal landscapes'. It strengthens problem-solving by enabling lawyers to explore new approaches and challenge conventional wisdom.[39]

Design thinking fosters this creative capability. Centred on user empathy, rapid prototyping, and iterative learning, it encourages the brainstorming, ideation, and experimentation needed to question assumptions and test alternatives.[40] Its mindset is indispensable in the AI era, where multidisciplinary analysis and adaptable methods are central.[41]

Since many schools and firms still underinvest in these competencies, outside organisations such as *Law Without Walls* (LWOW) fill the gap. Developed by Professor Michele DeStefano, LWOW brings together professionals and students across law, business, and technology to build creative, collaborative, and interdisciplinary skills for the GC 4.0 environment.[42] Some law schools are following. Stanford's Legal Design Lab, for example, integrates design, technology, and law to improve access to justice and reimagine legal service delivery.[43]

These competencies can be taught in various ways. What matters is that they become central to legal education, rather than optional. If the core curriculum remains essential for developing analytical skills, these new domains are critical to developing the professional, technical, and cognitive skills lawyers need in the AI era.

Time

If these additional competencies must be added, how should they be allocated across the time available?

Is Three Years Too Much?   The *Juris Doctor* (JD) degree is a three-year programme. Year one is traditionally devoted to the foundational subjects, and the next two to upper-level doctrinal courses and electives ranging from the deeply academic to the highly specialised. Interspersed throughout are reinforcing activities, including work on journals and in clinics (supervised programmes where students work with clients).

Critics argue that the most meaningful coursework occurs in the first two years and that the third year is of limited professional value relative to cost because it is unstructured and filled with electives that don't meaningfully add to the professional competence of graduates. One well-known saying captures this: 'In the first year, they scare you to death; in the second year, they work you to death; in the third year, they bore you to death'.[44]

Towards a More Structured Format This criticism has merit, but only if the third year is left unstructured. The full three-year journey should be holistically structured, including the third year, to ensure that every student graduates with the essential foundational and professional competencies needed in GC 4.0. It is unrealistic to expect all students to choose wisely across electives without guardrails.

Two points support this proposal. First, law schools cannot shoulder the burden of providing additional professional competencies without better use of the third year. Second, as DeStefano notes, cultivating intellectual and professional depth in students takes time. Learning to 'think like a lawyer' isn't just a matter of accumulating information; it is a developmental process.[45] The third year provides space to consolidate, apply, and deepen ideas and skills cultivated in the first two years.

The Carnegie Report argues for precisely this. It urges law schools to unite 'formal knowledge and experience of practice' more deliberately in the second and third years, treating year three as a capstone for specialised knowledge, advanced clinical work, and reflective development.[46]

The first year should remain anchored in the core curriculum, with selective exposure to other subjects to help bridge the academic–professional divide that students will navigate later. The second and third years are a natural place to deepen familiarity with the new professional competencies outlined above.

Method

As schools add new competencies to their curricula through a more intentionally structured three-year programme, they must also diversify their methodologies, as many of these new competencies are best taught using methods other than the Socratic and casebook methods. That does not mean traditional methods should be discarded, but there should be clear thinking about how and when they are methodologically suitable.

Retain and Evolve Traditional Methods The Socratic and casebook methods endure because they are very effective at what they do. However, they are not universal tools.

The Socratic Method   The Socratic method has faced sustained criticism, which falls into three categories: psychological harm; ideological bias; and pedagogical insufficiency.[47]

The first (and most common) criticism is the potential for psychological harm, including anxiety and humiliation. Critics describe the method as demeaning and unnecessarily combative.[48] As Orin S. Kerr summarises it, Socratic professors can be 'quick to criticize imperfect student answers, subjecting students to public degradation, humiliation, ridicule, and dehumanization. This torture often scars students for life'. Women and minorities have also reported feeling singled out or stereotyped. Beyond anxiety, 'the method's natural tendency to deconstruct preconceived beliefs leaves students feeling vulnerable and disoriented'.[49]

These experiences should not be dismissed. They reflect genuine shortcomings in how the method has sometimes been applied. However, these are failures of implementation, not of the method itself. Modern practice shows that Socratic teaching can be delivered without harm, particularly when combined with 'softened' questioning and blended teaching styles that create a more supportive classroom environment.[50]

A second critique is that the method reinforces hierarchical dynamics by allowing professors to project power and dominance. Again, this is a function of poor teaching, not inherent methodological flaws. In capable hands, the method remains a powerful way to cultivate analytical discipline.

A third criticism is that the Socratic method cannot teach the full range of skills required in a GC 4.0 environment. This is correct. It excels at instilling analytical depth, but it may be less suited to developing some of the new professional competencies outlined earlier. These often require collaboration, experimentation, and practical application, which are best taught using different methodologies.

The Casebook Method   The casebook method, in which students study appellate decisions and analyse them through Socratic dialogue, has long been a defining feature of US legal education. It develops doctrinal understanding, deep reading skills, and critical reasoning. By working through complex fact patterns, identifying what matters, and extracting rules, students also cultivate mental discipline. The method also exposes them to how rules evolve, how social and political forces shape doctrine, and how inconsistencies arise across jurisdictions and over time. When combined with Socratic dialogue, it teaches students to prepare rigorously, engage actively, and apply principles, rather than memorising them.

As with the Socratic method, however, critics rightly note that the casebook method is incomplete. It develops doctrinal and analytical reasoning but does little to cultivate broader GC 4.0 competencies such as teamwork, communication, leadership, and technological fluency. The method is not a comprehensive pedagogical tool. Like the Socratic method, it remains indispensable but must be used alongside other methodologies.

With all this said, the casebook is due an upgrade. Three shortcomings stand out.

First, casebooks often prioritise historically significant cases for their doctrinal clarity, even when the material feels detached from contemporary practice.

Second, edited appellate opinions often strip away important sociological, empirical, or economic contexts that would help students appreciate the operational environment in which the law functions.

Third, an emphasis on appellate decisions creates a narrow view of legal authority that underplays statutes, regulations, administrative materials, policies, and other modern sources of law.

True, casebooks have adapted to address some of these shortcomings. By the mid-twentieth century, they began incorporating statutes, notes, questions, and explanatory text. But there are limits to what paper or e-reader formats can do.

Stephen Johnson proposes to transform the casebook into a 'course source': a dynamic platform incorporating simulations, drafting exercises, research problems, negotiation scenarios, hypotheticals, and assessments.[51] This would significantly expand the toolkit. His idea, first proposed in 2016, holds even more potential in the AI era.

AI could indeed transform casebooks into living simulators; interactive environments that dynamically teach doctrine, context, and professional skills holistically. An AI-enabled platform could personalise learning; provide real-time feedback; surface alternative statutes or cases; provide richer context; and embed multiple pedagogical approaches alongside traditional ones. This 'flipped classroom' model would preserve foundational analytical training while allowing students to engage in drafting, negotiation, advising, and problem-solving in simulated environments. In short, casebooks could become integrated, technology-enabled learning platforms.

Such platforms could also support new pedagogical methods, including 'reverse Socratic' techniques in which students generate questions to frame doctrinal ambiguities, test logical limits, and probe assumptions. As Anthea Roberts notes, using AI, students could develop the skills to ask increasingly sophisticated questions, thereby improving their ability as AI orchestrators.[52]

The Cloister and the Starship   Niall Ferguson of Stanford's Hoover Institute has expressed caution about the rapid integration of AI into education. He worries that LLMs encourage students 'to shirk the acquisition of skills such as sustained reading, critical thinking, and analytical writing', and warns that excessive reliance on AI could 'lead to arrested cognitive decline'.[53] To forestall this, he proposes 'cloisters': AI-free zones where students would spend about seven hours per day pursuing traditional learning methods, with AI-enabled work confined to outside the cloister (i.e., the 'starship').

Ferguson's argument is provocative and thought-provoking. He is right to highlight the continued importance of traditional cognitive training. But the dichotomy he proposes is excessive. Segregating traditional and AI-enabled methodologies risks weakening both. True power lies in adapting and intelligently integrating them.

Rather than quarantining technology, law schools should safeguard traditional methods and experiment with new ones. This may require embedding certain traditional practices to ensure they are maintained, including long-form writing assignments, in-class Socratic dialogue, oral examinations, and banning the use of AI for certain assignments.

Foster Additional Methodologies   In order to avoid such quarantining and more effectively teach new competencies, law schools should ensure that other methodologies are applied alongside evolved versions of the Socratic and casebook methods, including business-school-style cases, problem-based approaches, and experiential learning.

The Business School Case Methods   Adapted from Langdell's approach and introduced at Harvard Business School in 1920, the business school case method now dominates graduate management education.[54] Unlike law school cases, which are built around edited appellate opinions, business school cases are faculty-written narratives that are centred on real managerial problems.[55] As George J. Siedel notes, they 'are action-oriented', making students decision-makers whose choices shape outcomes.[56] Students work on cases in teams before class, with collaborative work and participation forming a significant part of their grades.

Benjamin H. Barton highlights several advantages of the business case method over the law school model. First, it teaches students to make real-world decisions under uncertainty by placing them in executive, not judicial, roles. Second, teamwork mirrors modern practice and develops competencies that law schools often underweight, such as collaboration, communication, and leadership. Third, it routinely integrates multidisciplinary perspectives that are absent from most appellate opinions.

For these reasons, the business school approach is well suited to domains beyond litigation, including transactional practice, regulatory work, corporate governance, compliance, legal operations, and risk management.[57] Used alongside traditional methods, it can cultivate contextual judgement and new competencies essential for GC 4.0 students.

Problem-based Methodologies Many law schools now use problem-based approaches modelled partly on the business school case method. These materials, ranging from simulations and hypothetical client files to adapted business cases, require students to diagnose and solve the legal challenges in context.[58]

Harvard Law School's Case Study Method exemplifies this approach. Faculty write cases based on interviews or public sources, often using disguised or composite versions of real events.[59] Unlike business schools, law faculties sometimes employ invented fact patterns to tailor learning to specific themes.[60]

When well designed, these approaches also foster contextual reasoning, practical decision-making, teamwork, and the integration of legal analysis with strategy and ethics and provide a valuable complement to traditional methodologies.

Clinical and Practical Learning Clinics, externships, and labs play an important and growing role. Historically, however, clinics were marginalised. As Stephen Wizner and Jane Aiken note, clinics long faced 'resistance and internal conflict', with clinicians often excluded from faculty governance and lacking job security.[61] That has improved in recent years. As J. Damian Ortiz notes, the American Bar Association (ABA) now requires US law schools 'to offer students experiential programs in their curricula', though it does not yet (but should) mandate clinical participation.[62]

In a GC 4.0 environment, clinics must play a larger role. They foster professional skills and can also be a valuable source of training for technology and business domains. Yale's Entrepreneurship and Innovation Clinic is a good example of the latter. Students gain exposure to business, financial, and human capital skills by representing entrepreneurs.[63]

Adjuncts and practitioners must also feature more prominently. They teach over 40% of elective courses at most schools. However, they often occupy the lowest rungs of academic hierarchies, despite teaching subjects that full-time academics cannot.[64] As T. Markus Funk, Andrew S. Boutros, and Eugene Volokh observe, many adjuncts 'effectively pay for the privilege of teaching', with law schools realising extraordinary returns relative to their compensation.

This imbalance must be corrected. Other professional schools, such as medicine and business, routinely rely on leading practitioners who are respected for the real-world experience they bring. As the Carnegie Report notes, most law schools pay 'only casual attention' to helping students apply legal thinking to real-world settings, reinforcing the habits of the student rather than instilling those of the practitioner.[65] Greater integration of clinics and practitioner-teachers is essential to closing this gap.

The Way Forward

As law schools assume greater responsibility for preparing lawyers for the GC 4.0 environment, they must clarify their purpose and commit to developing graduates with both analytical depth and practical skills competence. Doing so will require rethinking what is taught, how it is taught, and how the three years of study are structured. For it is only by doing this that graduates will enter a rapidly transforming workplace with the skills they will need to succeed.

Conclusion

As AI becomes more capable, the legal profession must confront a fundamental question: *What does it mean to be a lawyer in the AI era?* This requires rethinking the purpose, value, and structure of legal work, including what clients need, what lawyers do, and how legal services are delivered, priced, and consumed.

This reorientation begins with the client as, in the AI era, clients will be the central drivers of disruption in the legal sector and their evolving expectations will set the pace and direction of change across the entire ecosystem. AI is reshaping how companies and legal departments operate. Digital processes scale in ways that reward early movers: the more an organisation can harness data, automation, and systems-led delivery, the more value it creates and captures. This dynamic is placing existential pressure on companies to transform their operating models.

For in-house teams, the historical pattern holds. As companies transform in response to a shifting operating environment, so too will legal departments. And as legal departments reconfigure around AI, automation, and data-driven workflows, the competitive dynamics of the entire legal ecosystem will shift. Changes will cascade across the value chain, impacting everything from workforce skills and composition to service delivery models.

The needs of the GC 4.0 legal department, which will operate off the back of a stable, AI-enabled platform, will steadily diverge from the offerings of traditional law firms. As agentic AI becomes embedded in client workflows, it will redefine how clients perceive and use firms. As their capabilities expand, in-house teams will gain access to specialist capabilities that rival those of external partners, prompting GCs to rethink how and when they source legal services.

The implications for law firms are profound. Yet record profitability and deep structural inflexibility may make it hard for them to evolve from their human-centric, input-cost-driven pyramid models. Digitally transformed clients, however, will expect their external partners to tightly integrate with their increasingly AI-enabled structures. Many firms will struggle to adapt.

This is a classic case of Christensen's 'innovator's dilemma'. Traditional firms are not failing because they are bad at what they do, but because they are too good at what they do, making it exceptionally difficult to disrupt their existing lucrative models.

That being said, not all traditional law firms will falter. A small number of highly sophisticated firms will evolve into boutiques that continue to deliver niche, judgement-based expertise required for complex and high-stakes matters that remain difficult to automate. But only a handful possess this expertise, and even they will need to reconfigure their operating models, shifting from traditional pyramids to various 'rocket-ship' architectures where partner-led profit engines are supported by technology, automation, and multidisciplinary teams to reduce delivery costs.

Other firms will follow the path taken by investment banks and adopt corporate or alternative business structures. These models will give them access to external capital, stronger governance, and the strategic discipline needed to develop innovative, value-based pricing models and undertake major transformation. As efficiency pressures intensify and client expectations grow, regulatory frameworks will adjust. Over time, as ethical and regulatory restrictions in major jurisdictions soften, structures of this kind will become increasingly viable and common.

ALSPs will also face challenges. Those that succeed in the GC 4.0 landscape will be the ones that can position themselves effectively within the emerging digital ecosystem, deploy technology at scale, and understand precisely where they create value and how it should be priced. ALSPs that remain narrowly focused on transactional support, however, using tools that are rapidly becoming commoditised, will not endure.

New models will also emerge. Integrated, multidisciplinary hybrid firms, combining an array of legal adjacent offerings centred around a legal services core, will gain traction. In parallel, technology-enabled and data-driven platforms will continue to evolve. These platforms will connect clients with a range of providers and may ultimately serve as ecosystem orchestrators, embedding themselves within legal department workflows to triage demand and transform how legal work is sourced, priced, managed, and evaluated.

Traditional firms do not need to be passive observers to all of this. Case studies show that they can take meaningful steps now by launching small, low-risk 'experiments' at the periphery of their core businesses. These ventures neither threaten nor undermine existing models but allow firms to learn, iterate, and position themselves for the future.

Legal education is also at a crossroads. The shifts described in this book, from AI-enabled clients to transformed law firms and ALSPs, cannot be sustained without a talent pipeline equipped for the GC 4.0 environment. As the Cravath pipeline fractures, law schools must clarify the purpose of legal education in the AI era and prepare graduates for a profession that will increasingly be defined by data and technology. This will require embedding professional and technical competencies more rigorously alongside doctrinal and analytical training, and restructuring curricula, time allocation, and teaching methods accordingly. Without this realignment, the profession's capacity to adapt will be constrained at its foundation.

While variations in regulatory structures, technological maturity, and market dynamics mean the shifts explored in this book will not happen uniformly across jurisdictions, the overall direction is clear: the AI era represents a profound, disruptive, and client-centric shift for the legal profession.

The first move belongs to the client. How law firms, ALSPs, law schools, and other ecosystem participants respond will determine who succeeds and who fails.

Chapter Notes

Introduction

1. For a definition of AI and a discussion of it and related concepts, see Chapter 5.

2. ALSPs, which will be discussed and defined in greater detail in Chapter 10, are organisations that provide legal and legal-adjacent services outside the traditional law firm model by leveraging models, processes, or tools that represent a significantly different approach to creating or providing legal services than what the legal profession traditionally has employed. See Jordan Furlong, 'An Incomplete Inventory of NewLaw', *Law21 blog*, 13 May 2014, https://www.law21.ca/2014/05/incomplete-inventory-newlaw/. ALSPs often provide these services more effectively, and at lower cost, than law firms or in-house teams can. Services offered by ALSPs typically include flexible staffing, contract management, document review, e-discovery, regulatory compliance, and legal operations support, as well as a growing range of consultancy and advisory, software, and even legal advisory services.

3. We will consider the contours of a GPT in greater detail in Chapter 5, but it can be defined as 'a single generic technology, recognizable as such over its whole lifetime, that initially has much scope for improvement and eventually comes to be widely used, to have many uses, and to have many spillover effects'. Richard G. Lipsey, Clifford T. Bekar, and Kenneth I. Carlaw, 'The Consequences of Changes in GPTs', in *General Purpose Technologies and Economic Growth*, ed. Elhanan Helpman

(Cambridge, MA: MIT Press, 1998), 193–218, cited in Nicholas Crafts, 'Artificial Intelligence as a General-Purpose Technology: An Historical Perspective', *Oxford Review of Economic Policy* 37, no. 3 (2021): 521, https://doi.org/10.1093/oxrep/grab018.

For a discussion of how AI is transforming how companies are structured, how they operate, and how they create value, see Marco Iansiti and Karim R. Lakhani, *Competing in the Age of AI: Strategy and Leadership When Algorithms and Networks Run the World* (Boston, MA: Harvard Business Review Press, 2020). See also McKinsey & Company, 'The State of AI: How Organizations are Rewiring to Capture Value', 12 March 2025, https://www.mckinsey.com/capabilities/quantumblack/our-insights/the-state-of-ai and Sumeet Gupta and Carl Jones, 'Rethinking Business Models with AI', *FTI Consulting*, 8 January 2025, https://www.fticonsulting.com/insights/articles/rethinking-business-models-with-ai.

4. See LexisNexis, 'Majority of Corporate Legal Departments Anticipate Gen AI to Slash Expenses', *LexisNexis Insights*, 11 March 2024, https://www.lexisnexis.com/community/insights/legal/b/thought-leadership/posts/majority-of-corporate-legal-departments-anticipate-gen-ai-to-slash-expenses-76-in-house-counsel-agree. (The vast majority of corporate executives at Fortune 1000 companies expect their investment in Gen AI to increase over the course of the next five years, and they have high hopes for how this investment will ultimately reduce their operational costs.) See also Thomson Reuters, 'Pricing AI-Driven Legal Services: Lead or Follow?', 30 January 2024, https://www.thomsonreuters.com/en-us/posts/legal/pricing-ai-driven-legal-services-lead-or-follow/. (2025 is likely to be a year in which lawyers need to start making decisions around AI and define the changes they want to see—or those changes will be defined for them.)

5. For a discussion of this, see Rita Gunther McGrath, *Seeing Around Corners: How to Spot Inflection Points in Business Before They Happen* (Boston, MA: Houghton Mifflin Harcourt, 2019).

6. Nisum, 'Top 10 Thought-Provoking Quotes from Experts That Redefine the Future of AI Technology', 25 July 2023, https://www.nisum.com/nisum-knows/top-10-thought-provoking-quotes-from-experts-that-redefine-the-future-of-ai-technology.

7. Iansiti and Lakhani, *Competing in the Age of AI*.

8. Ibid., 41.

9. For a discussion of AI-related risks, see National Institute of Standards and Technology (NIST), *Artificial Intelligence Risk Management Framework (AI RMF 1.0)*, NIST AI 100-1, January 2023, https://nvlpubs.nist.gov/nistpubs/ai/nist.ai.100-1.pdf and 'Artificial Intelligence and Compliance: Preparing for the Future of AI Governance, Risk, and Compliance', *NAVEX blog*, 13 February 2025, https://www.navex.com/en-us/blog/article/artificial-intelligence-and-compliance-preparing-for-the-future-of-ai-governance-risk-and-compliance/. For an exploration of how and why corporate lifespans are shortening, see Gerti Tashko, 'The Rise and Fall of Corporations: Why Lifespans are Shrinking', *LinkedIn*, 8 February 2025, https://www.linkedin.com/pulse/rise-fall-corporations-why-lifespans-shrinking-gerti-tashko-md-2tuye.

10. See Deloitte, 'The Future of Legal Work? The Use of Generative AI by Legal Departments: Our Perspectives and the Results from Our Generative AI Survey for Corporate Legal Departments', June 2024, https://www.deloitte.com/content/dam/assets-shared/docs/services/legal/2024/dttl-genai-legal-work-full-report.pdf and Thomson Reuters, 'Artificial Intelligence and Corporate Legal Departments', January 2025, https://legal.thomsonreuters.com/en/insights/articles/artificial-intelligence-ai-report for good overviews of where models and usage are heading.

11. Thomson Reuters, 'The Future of the Law Firm – No Time for Bystanders Amid AI's Increasing Influence', 2025, https://legal.thomsonreuters.com/en/insights/white-papers/future-of-law-firm-amid-ai-increasing-influence/form?gatedContent=%252Fcontent%252Fewp-marketing-websites%252Flegal%252Fgl%252Fen%252Finsights%252Fwhite-papers%252Ffuture-of-law-firm-amid-ai-increasing-influence.

12. David B. Wilkins, 'The Impact of Artificial Intelligence on Law Firms' Business Models', *Center on the Legal Profession, Harvard Law School*, 24 February 2025, https://clp.law.harvard.edu/knowledge-hub/insights/the-impact-of-artificial-intelligence-on-law-law-firms-business-models/.

13. The billable hour refers to a time-based approach to billing that charges for inputs rather than value or outcomes.

14. See Debra Cassens Weiss, 'Law Firm Profitability is at Near-Record High, New Report Says', *ABA Journal*, 11 November 2024,

https://www.abajournal.com/news/article/law-firm-profitability-is-at-near-record-high-report-says; Karen Sloan, 'Law Firm Profits Climbed as 2024 Ended, but Boom Times May Not Last', *Reuters*, 10 February 2025, https://www.reuters.com/legal/legalindustry/law-firm-profits-climbed-2024-ended-boom-times-may-not-last-2025-02-10/; and Suzi Ring, 'Latham & Watkins Hits $7bn Revenue Mark for First Time on Resurgent Dealmaking', *Financial Times*, 11 March 2025, https://www.ft.com/content/bb27302d-f684-4b8c-89c8-01182e49acd7.

15. Axiom, 'GCs' 2024 Outlook on Legal Budgets, Talent, and Innovation', *Axiom Law*, 2024, https://www.axiomlaw.com/resources/articles/gc-survey-report.

16. Ibid.

17. Law firms are currently facing the 'innovator's dilemma'. Clayton M. Christensen, in his eponymous book, noted that companies that are dominant in one generation of technology are vulnerable to disruptive technologies, which initially underperform in mainstream markets but over time improve and cause the decline of incumbents that fail to recognise and adapt in time. Clayton M. Christensen, *The Innovator's Dilemma: When New Technologies Cause Great Firms to Fail* (Boston, MA: Harvard Business School Press, 1997). We will explore the implications of the innovator's dilemma to law firms in Chapter 9.

18. Christensen, *The Innovator's Dilemma*.

19. In 2020, Arizona became the first US state to amend rules barring non-lawyers from having an economic interest in law firms, allowing them to establish so-called ABSs in which non-lawyers can have co-ownership in law firms with court approval. In 2025, KPMG won approval from Arizona's Supreme Court to launch a law firm in Arizona, making it the first of the Big Four accounting firms to be able to practice law in the United States. Most states still allow only lawyers to practice law, own law firms, and share legal fees. Utah introduced limited reforms similar to those in Arizona, in 2020. But efforts to do so in other states, including California, have stalled, in part over fears of ethical abuses if providers are not fully bound by professional rules. Sara Merken, 'Arizona Hits New Milestone under Loosened Law Firm Ownership Rules', *Reuters*, 25 September 2024, https://www.reuters.com/legal/government/arizona-hits-new-milestone-under-loosened-

law-firm-ownership-rules-2024-09-25/. For a discussion of ABSs, see Chapter 11.

20. Firms are advised to consider pricing these value services at rates that are 25–40% higher than classic advice and to increase fees ahead of inflation. By doing this and reducing overhead, it is believed that a new economic model might emerge that could generate higher profit per equity partner than current models. Of course, the ability to do this will depend on the value of the 'upskilled' advice. Thomson Reuters, 'The Future of the Law Firm'.

21. See, for example, 'How Goldman Sachs Grew Up: 25 Years Since Wall Street's Elite Firm Went Public', *Financial Times*, 5 May 2024, https://www.ft.com/content/b3b060dd-2680-4a11-b086-e429dcbab6d4.

22. Stephen Foley, 'Grant Thornton US Goes Global in Private Equity-Backed Buying Spree', *Financial Times*, 23 April 2025, https://www.ft.com/content/0b544478-f063-416d-bcea-a9fb0ac610da.

Part I   How Corporations and Their Legal Departments Co-evolve

1. Jane McConnell, 'Leadership Everywhere Means Reversed Leadership', *Global Peter Drucker Forum blog*, 30 September 2020, https://www.druckerforum.org/blog/leadership-everywhere-means-reversed-leadership-by-jane-mcconnell/.

2. Unity Technologies, 'Fourth Industrial Revolution (4IR)', *Unity Glossary*, 2025, https://unity.com/glossary/fourth-industrial-revolution.

3. Iberdrola, S.A., 'What is the Fourth Industrial Revolution', in *Industry 4.0: Which Technologies Will Mark the Fourth Industrial Revolution*, https://www.iberdrola.com/about-us/our-innovation-model/fourth-industrial-revolution#:~:text=The%20concept%20of%20the%20Fourth,fundamentally%20different%20from%20previous%20revolutions.

4. Generative AI, a branch of deep learning that uses exceptionally large neural networks called large language models (with hundreds of billions of neurons) that can learn especially abstract patterns, will be discussed in Chapter 5.

Chapter 1   The General Counsel's Evolving Needs

1. Steve Jobs, quoted in QuoteFancy, https://quotefancy.com/quote/911620/Steve-Jobs-Get-closer-than-ever-to-your-customers-So-close-that-you-tell-them-what-they.
2. Richard Susskind, *Tomorrow's Lawyers: An Introduction to Your Future*, 3rd ed. (Oxford: Oxford University Press, 2022), Kindle edition, 11–12.
3. For further discussion of risk convergence in the GC context, see Bjarne P. Tellmann, *Building an Outstanding Legal Team: Battle-Tested Strategies from a General Counsel* (London: Globe Law and Business, 2017), 38.
4. See Tellmann, *Building an Outstanding Legal Team*, 46–48.
5. Ibid. See also OpenText, 'The Evolving Role of General Counsel: Securing a Seat at the Table', *OpenText blog*, 4 August 2021, https://blogs.opentext.com/the-evolving-role-of-general-counsel-securing-a-seat-at-the-table/ (citing a recent survey of 289 GCs in which 87% agreed or strongly agreed that the role of the GC is shifting from the traditional legal advisor to a strategic and influential partner to other senior executives).
6. Tellmann, *Building an Outstanding Legal Team*, 46–49.
7. Russell Reynolds Associates, 'The Expanding Remit of the Fortune 500 General Counsel', 1 March 2024, https://www.russellreynolds.com/en/insights/reports-surveys/the-expanding-remit-of-the-fortune-500-general-counsel.
8. Tellmann, *Building an Outstanding Legal Team*, 49.
9. Ibid.
10. Mitchell Nazarov, 'Enterprise Risk Management (ERM) Fundamentals', *AuditBoard*, 8 August 2023, https://auditboard.com/blog/enterprise-risk-management/.
11. Adam Hayes, 'Enterprise Risk Management (ERM): What It Is and How It Works', *Investopedia*, 10 April 2025, https://www.investopedia.com/terms/e/enterprise-risk-management.asp.
12. Ibid.
13. Ibid.
14. Committee of Sponsoring Organizations of the Treadway Commission (COSO), 'Enterprise Risk Management Guidance', https://www.coso.org/guidance-erm and ACCA Global, 'COSO's Enterprise Risk

Management Framework', https://www.accaglobal.com/gb/en/student/exam-support-resources/professional-exams-study-resources/strategic-business-leader/technical-articles/coso-enterprise-risk-management-framework.html.

15. Cornell University Division of Financial Services, 'About the COSO Framework', https://finance.cornell.edu/controller/internalcontrols/cosoframework.

16. 'A Black Swan is an event with the following three attributes: First, it is an outlier, as it lies outside the realm of regular expectations, because nothing in the past can convincingly point to its possibility. Second, it carries an extreme impact. Third, in spite of its outlier status, human nature makes us concoct explanations for its occurrence after the fact, making it explainable and predictable'. Nassim Nicholas Taleb, *The Black Swan: The Impact of the Highly Improbable* (New York: Random House, 2007), xvii.

17. John Fraser, Rob Quail, and Betty Simkins, 'What's Wrong with Enterprise Risk Management?', *Journal of Risk and Financial Management* 17, no. 7 (2024): 4, https://doi.org/10.3390/jrfm17070274.

18. Risk Management Studio, 'Black Swans: Cost and Prediction', https://www.riskmanagementstudio.com/black-swans-cost-and-prediction/.

19. Alfonso Natale, Thomas Poppensieker, and Michael Thun, 'From Risk Management to Strategic Resilience', *McKinsey & Company*, 9 March 2022, https://www.mckinsey.com/capabilities/risk-and-resilience/our-insights/from-risk-management-to-strategic-resilience. See also Kerstin Dornberger, Oberlehner Simone, Zadrazil Nicole et al., 'Challenges in Implementing Enterprise Risk Management', *ACRN Journal of Finance and Risk Perspectives* 3, no. 3 (November 2014): 1–14.

20. David Denyer, *Organizational Resilience: A Summary of Academic Evidence, Business Insights and New Thinking* (London: BSI and Cranfield School of Management, 2017), 5.

21. Dana Maor, Michael Park, and Brooke Weddle, 'Raising the Resilience of Your Organization', *McKinsey & Company*, 12 October 2022, https://www.mckinsey.com/capabilities/people-and-organizational-performance/our-insights/raising-the-resilience-of-your-organization.

22. Nassim Nicholas Taleb, *Antifragile: Things That Gain from Disorder* (London: Allen Lane, 2012), Kindle edition.

23. Ibid., 5.

24. Alexander Puutio, 'Resilience and Antifragility are the Best Strategies for 2024', *Forbes*, 8 April 2024, https://www.forbes.com/sites/alexanderpuutio/2024/04/08/resilience-and-antifragility-are-the-best-strategies-for-2024/.

25. Ibid.

26. Anthea Roberts, 'Dragonfly Thinking', https://www.anthearoberts.com/dragonfly-thinking. DT encourages a wide-angle, multi-faceted view of risk. Roberts's broader scholarship spans a diverse range of disciplines and applies a 'Risk, Reward and Resilience' framework to develop integrated solutions for complex problems. For an example of how Roberts has applied her holistic approach to risk analysis in the geopolitical context, see, for example, Anthea Roberts, 'From Risk to Resilience: How Economies Can Thrive in a World of Threats', *Foreign Affairs*, 24 October 2023, https://www.foreignaffairs.com/world/risk-resilience-economics.

27. Emily Osterloff, 'Dragonflies: The Ultimate Hunters', *The Natural History Museum, London*, https://www.nhm.ac.uk/discover/dragonflies-the-ultimate-hunters.html.

28. Roberts, 'Dragonfly Thinking'.

29. Ibid.

30. For a discussion of the 'more-for-less' challenge, see Susskind, *Tomorrow's Lawyers: An Introduction to Your Future*.

31. Axiom, 'GCs' 2024 Outlook'.

32. 45% of GCs in departments of 10 employees or less report they have been forced to prioritise budgets over core department values (vs. 27% of GCs in larger departments). Ibid., 7.

33. A 2025 survey of 200 US GCs at companies with a minimum of $250 million in annual revenue found that 55% reported an average budget increase of 4% in 2024. See Axiom, 'The 2025 In-House Legal Budgeting Report – How In-House Legal Teams are Evolving Budgeting Strategies for the Future', *Axiom Global*, 2025, https://www.axiomlaw.com/resources/articles/2025-legal-budgeting-survey-report. However, this increase was below the rate of inflation as the PPI for legal services rose from 284.352 in January 2024 to a preliminary figure of 296.175 in December 2024, suggesting an approximate increase of 4.2% over the year. See U.S. Bureau of Labor Statistics, *Producer Price*

Index for Legal Services, https://www.bls.gov/regions/mid-atlantic/ data/producerpriceindexlegal_us_table.htm.

34. Ernst & Young, 'Amid Disruption, How Can Legal Departments Innovate with Confidence?', 9 April 2025, https://www.ey.com/ en_gl/insights/law/amid-disruption-how-can-legal-departments- innovate-with-confidence.

35. Axiom, 2025, 10, 13 and Ernst & Young, 2025.

36. This is sometimes referred to as the 'partner–guardian tension'. For a good discussion of it, see Chapter 3 of Ben W. Heineman, Jr, *The Inside Counsel Revolution: Resolving the Partner–Guardian Tension* (Chicago, IL: American Bar Association, 2016), Kindle edition.

37. Compliance & Risks, 'What is Product Compliance?', https://www. complianceandrisks.com/blog/what-is-product-compliance/.

38. Yin Yin Lu, 'AI Can Help Explain the Boring World of Regulation', *WIRED*, 4 February 2022, https://www.wired.com/story/understanding- regulation-ai-regtech/.

39. For example, the European General Data Protection Regulation (GDPR) and the US Cloud Act mandate fundamentally different approaches to data protection, which can result in conflicts, uncertainties, and the risk of criminal charges for companies stuck in the middle. Conceptboard, 'The US Cloud Act: Threatening European Data Protection', *Conceptboard blog*, 22 September 2023, https:// conceptboard.com/blog/us-cloud-act-european-data-protection/. See also Georgia Wood and James Andrew Lewis, 'The CLOUD Act and Transatlantic Trust', *Center for Strategic and International Studies*, 29 March 2023, https://www.csis.org/analysis/cloud-act-and-transatlantic-trust.

40. Ibid.

41. For a discussion of black swan events, see Nassim Nicholas Taleb, *The Black Swan: The Impact of the Highly Improbable*, 2nd ed. (New York: Random House, 2010).

42. West describes the confluence of these risks as cutting across three dimensions: (i) geolegal risks (as political cooperation erodes, so do rules and laws); (ii) artificial politics (AI is transforming and reorganising economies, creating national security tensions); and (iii) legal AI (involving the impact of automation and social control, as well as the rising influence of personalised law). Sean West, *Unruly: Fighting*

Back when Politics, AI, and Law Upend the Rules of Business (New York: Wiley, 2025).

43. Ibid., 139.

44. See Lauren Landry, 'What Are Network Effects?', *Harvard Business School Online*, 12 November 2020, https://online.hbs.edu/blog/post/what-are-network-effects. For a discussion of platform economies and network effects, see Marco Iansiti and Karim R. Lakhani, *Competing in the Age of AI: Strategy and Leadership When Algorithms and Networks Run the World* (Boston, MA: Harvard Business Review Press, 2020), Chapter 7 and John Soroushian, 'Digital Platforms Primer: Digital Platforms and Competition (Part 3)', *Bipartisan Policy Center*, 19 November 2021, https://bipartisanpolicy.org/explainer/digital-platforms-primer-digital-platforms-and-competition-part-3/.

45. See Stéphane Garelli, 'Why You Will Probably Live Longer Than Most Big Companies', *IMD Business School*, December 2016, https://www.imd.org/research-knowledge/disruption/articles/why-you-will-probably-live-longer-than-most-big-companies/ (discussing the average lifespan of S&P companies) and U.S. Bureau of Labor Statistics, *Number of Jobs, Labor Market Experience, Marital Status, and Health for Those Born 1957–1964*, news release USDL-23-1854, 26 August 2025, https://www.bls.gov/news.release/pdf/nlsoy.pdf (discussing the average length of lifetime employment of Americans).

Chapter 2   GC 1.0: Early Modern Globalisation (1945–1989)

1. Carl D. Liggio, Sr, 'A Look at the Role of Corporate Counsel: Back to the Future—Or Is It the Past?', *Arizona Law Review* 44, no. 3 (2002): 621 and Eli Wald, 'Getting In and Out of the House', 622–623.

2. The term 'Gilded Age' refers to the period of rapid growth and industrial expansion that took place in the United States between 1870 and 1900. The term was popularised by historians who referred to Mark Twain's 1873 novel *The Gilded Age: A Tale of Today*. 'Gilded Age', *Wikipedia*, last modified 9 June 2025, https://en.wikipedia.org/wiki/Gilded_Age.

3. Wald, 'Getting In and Out of the House: The Worlds of In-House Counsel, Big Law, and Emerging Career Trajectories of In-House Lawyers', *Fordham Law Review* 88, no. 5 (2020), 1768.

4. Liggio, 'A Look at the Role of Corporate Counsel', 622 and Wald, 'Getting In and Out of the House', 1768.

5. Wald, 'Getting In and Out of the House', 1768.

6. Ibid. Legal Evolution, 'The Original Gilded-Age Lawyers', 26 June 2022, https://www.legalevolution.org/2022/06/the-original-gilded-age-lawyers-312/.

7. However, the popular perception of the Cold War as a period of absolute isolation between these blocs is incorrect, as trade policies between the two varied considerably across periods of time. Rodolfo Campos, Benedikt Heid, and Jacopo Timini, 'The Economic Consequences of Geopolitical Fragmentation: Evidence from the Cold War', *VoxEU.org*, Centre for Economic Policy Research, 1 July 2024, https://cepr.org/voxeu/columns/economic-consequences-geopolitical-fragmentation-evidence-cold-war. Also, while trade between the two blocs declined significantly as compared to pre-war levels, trade within each bloc grew strongly. UN Department of Economic and Social Affairs, 'Chapter II – Post-war Reconstruction and Development in the Golden Age of Capitalism', in *World Economic and Social Survey 2017* (New York: United Nations, 2017), 30, https://www.un.org/development/desa/dpad/wp-content/uploads/sites/45/WESS_2017_ch2.pdf.

8. Andrew G. Terborgh, 'The Post-War Rise of World Trade: Does the Bretton Woods System Deserve Credit?', Working Paper No. 78/03 (Department of Economic History, London School of Economics, September 2003), 1, https://eprints.lse.ac.uk/22351/1/wp78.pdf.

9. U.S. Department of State, 'The Bretton Woods Conference, 1944', *Office of the Historian*, https://2001-2009.state.gov/r/pa/ho/time/wwii/98681.htm.

10. It is estimated that, all else being equal, Bretton Woods participation increased trade between countries by about 20%. Terborgh, 'The Post-War Rise of World Trade', 2.

11. Sandra Kollen Ghizoni, 'Creation of the Bretton Woods System', *Federal Reserve History*, 22 November 2013, https://www.federalreservehistory. org/essays/bretton-woods-created.

12. U.S. Department of State, 'The Bretton Woods Conference, 1944'.

13. BeyondVerse, 'The Birth of Modern Forex: How the Bretton Woods System Shaped the Market', *Medium*, 10 July 2023, https://medium. com/@beyond_verse/the-birth-of-modern-forex-how-the-bretton-woods-system-shaped-the-market-7d9815f990a and Sarah Lee, 'The Evolution of Bretton Woods', *Number Analytics*, 25 May 2025, https:// www.numberanalytics.com/blog/evolution-of-bretton-woods-system.

14. The IMF exists to promote global economic growth, financial stability, and international monetary cooperation by monitoring economic developments and providing member countries with policy advice, financial assistance, technical assistance and training. International Monetary Fund, 'IMF at a Glance', last updated April 2025, https:// www.imf.org/en/About/Factsheets/IMF-at-a-Glance.

15. The IBRD today provides loans, guarantees, risk management products, and advisory services to middle-income and creditworthy low-income countries, as well as by coordinating responses to regional and global challenges. It forms part of the World Bank Group, together with four other specialised organisations that were formed during the period of early modern globalisation to help facilitate international development: the International Development Association (formed in 1960), the International Finance Corporation (founded in 1956), the International Centre for Settlement of Investment Disputes (founded in 1965), and the Multilateral Investment Guarantee Agency (founded in 1988). See World Bank, 'Getting to Know the World Bank', 26 July 2012, https://www.worldbank.org/en/news/feature/2012/07/26/ getting_to_know_theworldbank. See also 'World Bank Group', *Wikipedia*, last modified 2 June 2025, https://en.wikipedia.org/wiki/ World_Bank_Group.

16. Ghizoni, 'Creation of the Bretton Woods System'.

17. Ibid.

18. Lee, 'The Evolution of Bretton Woods'.

19. '[T]he post-war environment of free trade was achieved not instantaneously, but gradually, through continual negotiations.' Terborgh, 'The Post-War Rise of World Trade', 4.

20. From its creation in 1947 to its evolution into the World Trade Organization (WTO) in 1995, GATT reduced average tariffs among member countries from over 20% to around 5% or less. Legal Information Institute, Cornell Law School, 'GATT', last modified 2022, https://www.law.cornell.edu/wex/gatt#:~:text=From%20its%20creation%20to%20its,over%2040%25%20during%20the%201930s. GATT and/or WTO has been found to have increased trade between members by 171% and trade between member and non-member countries by about 88%. Mario Larch, José-Antonio Monteiro, Roberta Piermartini, and Yoto V. Yotov, 'On the Effects of GATT/WTO Membership on Trade: They Are Positive and Large after All', Working Paper No. 7721 (CESifo, 2019), https://www.cesifo.org/DocDL/cesifo1_wp7721.pdf.

21. Created by the signing of the Treaty of Rome in 1957, the EEC 'established the foundations for free trade in most goods among member states and created a full-fledged customs union with a common external tariff against the outside world and a free flow of labor, services, and capital within'. EBSCO Research Starters, 'European Common Market Established', https://www.ebsco.com/research-starters/history/european-common-market-established#:~:text=Of%20these%2C%20the%20EEC%20was,%2C%20services%2C%20and%20capital%20within.

22. These include the Organization for Economic Co-operation and Development (OECD, 1961); the United Nations Conference on Trade and Development (UNCTAD, 1964); the Association of Southeast Asian Nations (ASEAN, 1967); and the Latin American Free Trade Association (LAFTA, 1960), which later transformed into the Latin American Integration Association (ALADI, 1980).

23. Howard Cox, 'The Evolution of International Business Enterprise', in *Global Business Strategy*, ed. R. John (London: International Thomson Press, 1997), 9–46, 25, https://eprints.worc.ac.uk/250/1/Evolution_of_International_Business.pdf.

24. Terborgh, 'The Post-War Rise of World Trade', 3.

25. The term 'foreign direct investment' is somewhat of a misnomer in the sense that it is not, in either an accounting sense or an economic sense, an 'investment'. FDI occurs when the book value of the net worth of an investment controlled by investors in a country other than the country in which the investment is legally domiciled increases, which mostly happens where the 'investment' is a MNC subsidiary.

The net worth of the subsidiary on its balance sheet is the value of its assets minus liabilities owed to entities other than its owners. From a balance of payments perspective, FDI from one nation to another is therefore mostly net increases in the paid-in capital of investors in the first nation to their subsidiaries in the second plus any increase in the retained earnings of those subsidiaries. Edward M. Graham and Paul R. Krugman, 'Foreign Direct Investment in the World Economy', Working Paper No. 95/59 (International Monetary Fund, 1995), https://www.elibrary.imf.org/view/journals/001/1995/059/article-A001-en.xml.

26. Edward M. Bernstein, 'The Fund and the Postwar World: The Anglo-American Monetary Negotiations, 1941–1946', *Finance & Development* 10, no. 2 (1973): 22–27, https://www.elibrary.imf.org/view/journals/024/1973/002/article-A005-en.xml.

27. Cox, 'The Evolution of International Business Enterprise', 24–25.

28. Ibid.

29. Ibid., 24–25.

30. Mark Pendergrast, *For God, Country and Coca-Cola: The Definitive History of the Great American Soft Drink and the Company That Makes It* (New York: Basic Books, 2000), 163.

31. Ibid., 135; Michael E. Porter and Rebecca Wayland, 'Coca-Cola vs. Pepsi-Cola and the Soft Drink Industry', Harvard Business School Case 391-179 (Boston, MA: Harvard Business School Publishing, 1991; rev. 1994), 6.

32. Pendergrast, *For God, Country and Coca-Cola*, 135.

33. Ibid., 136.

34. Ibid.

35. Ibid.; Robometrics Machines, 'Coca-Cola's Long-Term Vision During World War II', *Robometrics Machines blog*, https://www.robometricsagi.com/blog/design-innovation/coca-colas-long-term-vision-during-world-war-ii; Porter and Wayland, 'Coca-Cola vs. Pepsi-Cola and the Soft Drink Industry', 6.

36. Ibid.

37. Graham and Krugman, 'Foreign Direct Investment in the World Economy'.

38. Ibid., 26.

39. Jonathan Zeitlin, 'Flexibility and Mass Production at War: Aircraft Manufacture in the United States during World War II', *Enterprise & Society* 18, no. 4 (December 2017): 885–923, https://www.jstor.org/stable/26568010, 266.

40. Ibid., 267.

41. N. Crafts, 'Western Europe's Growth Prospects: an Historical Perspective', European Commission, PDF, 'Fast European growth in the 1950s and 1960s was based on policies and institutions which facilitated high rates of investment and the diffusion of American technology in the era of Fordist manufacturing', 1.

42. *Britannica*, 'Economy of Japan: Post-World War II Growth, Industrialization, Modernization', https://www.britannica.com/money/economy-of-Japan.

43. Ibid.

44. Crafts, 'Western Europe's Growth Prospects', 3.

45. Ibid.; Robert E. Hoskisson, Charles W. L. Hill, and Myung-Ki Kim, 'Corporate Restructuring and Strategy in Diversified Firms: A Reassessment', *Journal of Management* 19, no. 3 (1993): 563–588, 269–270.

46. Wald, 'Getting In and Out of the House', 1769.

47. Deborah A. DeMott, 'The Discrete Roles of General Counsel', *Fordham Law Review* 74, no. 3 (2005): 959–960, https://ir.lawnet.fordham.edu/flr/vol74/iss3/2.

48. Wald, 'Getting In and Out of the House', 1769.

49. David B. Wilkins and G. Mitu Gulati, 'Reconceiving the Tournament of Lawyers: Tracking, Seeding, and Information Control in the Internal Labor Markets of Elite Law Firms', *Virginia Law Review* 84, no. 8 (1998): 1581–1583.

50. Wald, 'Getting In and Out of the House', 1770. See also Tyler J. Replogle, 'The Business of Law: Evolution of the Legal Services Market', *Michigan Business & Entrepreneurial Law Review* 6, no. 2 (2017): 287–323, 288. https://repository.law.umich.edu/mbelr/vol6/iss2/5.

51. David B. Wilkins and Scott A. Westfahl, 'The Missing Institutional Link: The Legal Profession's Role in the Development of Professional Education', *Stanford Law Review* 69, no. 6 (June 2017): 1670.

52. Wald, 'Getting In and Out of the House', 1770. See also Replogle, 'The Business of Law', 288.
53. Wilkins and Westfahl, 'The Missing Institutional Link', 1671.
54. Wald, 'Getting In and Out of the House', 1770.
55. Ibid.
56. Liggio, 'A Look at the Role of Corporate Counsel', 622 and Wald, 'Getting In and Out of the House', 622–623.
57. Ibid., 623.
58. Ibid., 622 and Wald, 'Getting In and Out of the House', 623.
59. Liggio, 'A Look at the Role of Corporate Counsel', 623–624.
60. Ibid.
61. DeMott, 'The Discrete Roles of General Counsel'.
62. Liggio, 'A Look at the Role of Corporate Counsel', 625.

Chapter 3   GC 2.0: Classic Globalisation (1989–2007)

1. Tony Hsieh, 'Profitability without values is like fuel without an engine', in '30 Business Ethics Quotes to Inspire Integrity in the Workplace', *Enterprise League blog*, 20 November 2024, https://enterpriseleague. com/blog/business-ethics-quotes/.
2. Paul A. Laudicina and Erik Peterson, 'From Globalization to Islandization', *Kearney Global Business Policy Council*, 5 January 2016, https://www.kearney.com/service/global-business-policy-council/ article/-/insights/from-globalization-to-islandization.
3. Raufhon Salahodjaev, Oybek Yuldashev, and Bekhzod Omanbayev, 'What Drives Foreign Direct Investment into Post-Communist Economies?', MPRA Paper No. 73277 (Munich Personal RePEc Archive, 22 August 2016), https://mpra.ub.uni-muenchen.de/73277/.
4. See Francis Fukuyama, *The End of History and the Last Man* (New York: Free Press, 1992).
5. Francis Fukuyama, 'The End of History?', *The National Interest*, no. 16 (Summer 1989): 3–18, https://www.jstor.org/stable/24027184.
6. The Conversation, 'Trump: How We Got Here', *The Conversation*, 22 January 2017, https://theconversation.com/trump-how-we-got- here-71675.
7. Laudicina and Peterson, *From Globalization to Islandization*.
8. By 1984 and 1990, global FDI flows soared from \$49.5 billion to \$222 billion. Edward M. Graham, 'Foreign Direct Investment in the World

Economy', IMF Working Paper (International Monetary Fund, 1995), https://www.elibrary.imf.org/view/journals/001/1995/059/article-A001-en.xml.

9. Ibid.

10. World Trade Organization, 'The WTO in Brief: Principles of the Trading System', https://www.wto.org/english/thewto_e/whatis_e/tif_e/fact2_e.htm.

11. Alessandro Nicita and Carlos Razo, 'China: The Rise of a Trade Titan', UNCTAD, 27 April 2021, https://unctad.org/news/china-rise-trade-titan.

12. Ibid.

13. Graham Boden, 'China's Accession to the WTO: Economic Benefits', *The Park Place Economist* 20 (2012), https://digitalcommons.iwu.edu/parkplace/vol20/iss1/8.

14. Ibid., 14.

15. Ibid. FIEs are enterprises that are registered and established in China but are wholly or partly invested in by foreign investors (including foreign natural persons, corporations, and other organisations). See 'Foreign-Invested Enterprise (FIE) (外商投资企业)', *Practical Law*, Thomson Reuters, published 2 August 2024, https://uk.practicallaw.thomsonreuters.com/6-521-9509.

16. Ibid.

17. For a brief discussion, see Haradhan Kumar Mohajan, 'Third Industrial Revolution Brings Global Development', *Journal of Social Sciences and Humanities* 7, no. 4 (2021): 240, https://mpra.ub.uni-muenchen.de/110972/1/MPRA_paper_110972.pdf. Beyond technology, the Second Industrial Revolution catalysed a shift in the structure of capitalism itself: ownership of the means of production expanded as common stock became more widely held by individuals and institutions, laying the foundation for today's capital markets. Robert Angus Buchanan, 'History of Technology', *Encyclopaedia Britannica*, https://www.britannica.com/technology/history-of-technology.

18. Mohajan, 'Third Industrial Revolution Brings Global Development', 240.

19. 'Rise of the Internet and the World Wide Web: EBSCO', *EBSCO Information Services, Inc.*, https://www.ebsco.com/research-starters/history/rise-internet-and-world-wide-web.

20. Ibid.

21. 'A Short History of the Web', *CERN*, https://home.cern/science/computing/birth-web/short-history-web.

22. Yodai Takeuchi, 'History of E-Commerce: The World Wide Web and e-Commerce Boom', *Medium*, 21 December 2023, https://yodai.medium.com/history-of-e-commerce-the-world-wide-web-and-e-commerce-boom-9aa14ec31666.

23. Ibid.

24. Ibid. eBay's 'user-driven marketplace' model refers to the structure of its platform, which enables business-to-consumer (B2C) and consumer-to-consumer (C2C) transactions to take place. With eBay acting as the middleman, individuals and businesses buy and sell items with each other on the platform, with sellers responsible for shipping. eBay maintains no inventory and generates revenue through the fees it charges to its sellers, which is mostly based on a percentage of the final sale price, as well as, in some cases, a listing fee. See 'How Does eBay Make Money? Business & Revenue Model Explained', *Yo!Kart blog*, https://www.yo-kart.com/blog/how-does-ebay-make-money/.

25. Steve Wasserman, 'The Amazon Effect', *The Nation*, 10 February 2016, https://www.thenation.com/article/archive/amazon-effect/.

26. Takeuchi (2023). David Kiriakidis, 'History of E-Commerce', *Fleximize*, 6 June 2025, https://fleximize.com/articles/006970/history-of-ecommerce#:~:text=With%20the%201997%20public%20launch,%2C%20you%20guessed%20it%20%E2%80%93%20eBay.

27. Ibid.

28. Ibid.

29. Adam Hayes, 'Understanding the Dotcom Bubble: Causes, Impact, and Lessons', *Investopedia*, updated 10 August 2025, https://www.investopedia.com/terms/d/dotcom-bubble.asp.

30. See Zhu Wang, 'The Evolution of E-Commerce', *Federal Reserve Bank of Richmond Economic Quarterly* 100, no. 2 (Second Quarter 2014): 77–104, https://www.richmondfed.org/publications/research/economic_quarterly/2014/q2/wang and 'The Evolution of E-commerce: A Comprehensive Retrospective Analysis', *HulkApps Ecommerce Hub*, https://www.hulkapps.com/blogs/ecommerce-hub/the-evolution-of-e-commerce-a-comprehensive-retrospective-analysis.

31. For more on the growth of e-commerce during this period, see 'E-Commerce 2000', *US Department of Commerce E-Stats*, 18 March 2002, https://www.census.gov/content/dam/Census/library/publications/2002/econ/2000estatstext.pdf. For a discussion of consumer adoption, see John B. Horrigan, 'Part 1. Trends in Online Shopping', *Pew Research Center*, 13 February 2008, https://www.pewresearch.org/internet/2008/02/13/part-1-trends-in-online-shopping/#:~:text=Today%2C%20e%2Dcommerce%20accounts%20for,rates%20in%202001%20and%202002.

32. Citigroup Global Markets, 'Future of the Global Supply Chain' (Citi Research, March 2021), https://www.citiwarrants.com/home/upload/citi_research/rsch_pdf_30191955.pdf.

33. Mohammed Bin Rashid Al Maktoum Digital School, 'The Impact of the Internet and Technology on Supply Chains: Innovation and Digital Transformation', *MDD*, https://en.mdd.sa/post/the-impact-of-the-internet-and-technology-on-supply-chains-innovation-and-digital-transformation.

34. Ibid.

35. For example, the outreach of container gantry cranes became longer (up to 22 containers wide), gained greater lifting capacity (e.g., ZPMC developed cranes with up to 120 tons of lifting capacity), and spreaders became more sophisticated (e.g., double lift, twin lift, and tests by ZPMC for triple lifts). Theo Notteboom and Jean-Paul Rodrigue, 'Containerisation, Box Logistics and Global Supply Chains: The Integration of Ports and Liner Shipping Networks', *Maritime Economics & Logistics* 10, no. 1 (March 2008): 156, https://doi.org/10.1057/palgrave.mel.9100196.

36. Daniel M. Bernhofen, Zouheir El-Sahli, and Richard Kneller, 'Estimating the Effects of the Container Revolution on World Trade', *Journal of International Economics* 98 (January 2016): 36–50. See also James Hennessy, 'The Past & Future of the Supply Chain', *Contrary*, 31 October 2023, https://www.contrary.com/blog/the-past-and-future-of-the-supply-chain/.

37. Notteboom and Rodrigue, 'Containerisation, Box Logistics and Global Supply Chains', 152–174, 153.

38. Ibid. A TEU is a measure of volume in units of 20-foot-long containers. One 20-foot container equals one TEU. Flexport, 'Twenty-Foot

Equivalent Unit (TEU)', *Flexport Glossary*, https://www.flexport.com/glossary/twenty-foot-equivalent-unit/.

39. Ibid., 158. See also Supply Chain Game Changer, 'How Shipping Containers Revolutionized the Supply Chain Industry', https://supplychaingamechanger.com/how-shipping-containers-revolutionized-the-supply-chain-industry/ and Mark Slipp, 'Rapid Global Improvement: Container + Internet', *LinkedIn*, https://www.linkedin.com/pulse/rapid-global-improvement-container-internet-mark-slipp/.

40. Hennessy, 'The Past & Future of the Supply Chain'.

41. Ibid.

42. Notteboom and Rodrigue, 'Containerisation, Box Logistics and Global Supply Chains', 158.

43. Ben W. Heineman Jr, *The Inside Counsel Revolution: Resolving the Partner–Guardian Tension* (Charlottesville, VA: Ankerwycke/American Bar Association, 2016).

44. Ibid., 18.

45. Erik Ramanathan and John Coates, *Corporate Purchasing Project: How S&P 500 Companies Evaluate Outside Counsel*, Harvard Law School Case Study, Program on the Legal Profession (Cambridge, MA: Harvard Law School, 2011), 36.

46. Heineman, *The Inside Counsel Revolution*, 24. See also Liggio, 'A Look at the Role of Corporate Counsel', 624.

47. 'The In-House Counsel Movement', *The Changing Role of the Global General Counsel, Harvard Law School Center on the Legal Profession*, https://clp.law.harvard.edu/knowledge-hub/magazine/issues/the-changing-role-of-the-global-general-counsel/the-in-house-counsel-movement/.

48. Ramanathan and Coates, *Corporate Purchasing Project*, 33–34.

49. Ibid., 34.

50. Grant R.M. Visconti and Massimo Visconti, 'The Strategic Background to Corporate Accounting Scandals', *Long Range Planning* 39, no. 4 (August 2006): 361–383.

51. Benford Brown & Associates, 'The History of Sarbanes-Oxley (SOX) and its Importance to Businesses Today', https://benfordbrown.

com/the-history-of-sarbanes-oxley-sox-and-its-importance-to-businesses-today/.

52. For IBM, see MBI Deep Dives, 'The Great Decoupling of Labor and Capital', 2 November 2025, https://www.mbi-deepdives.com/the-great-decoupling-of-labor-and-capital/. For Walmart, see Walmart, Inc., *2007 Annual Report for Walmart Stores, Inc.* (Bentonville, AR: Walmart, Inc., 2007), https://stock.walmart.com/_assets/_9892d162c46e32522aec622a96529b9b/walmart/db/950/9634/annual_report/2007-annual-report-for-walmart-stores-inc_130221018733842956.pdf. For South Africa, see 'South Africa GDP Growth Rate | Historical Chart & Data', *MacroTrends*, https://www.macrotrends.net/global-metrics/countries/zaf/south-africa/gdp-growth-rate.

53. Wald, 'Getting In and Out of the House', 1771.

54. Ibid.

55. Heinemann, *The Inside Counsel Revolution*, 33 and 439.

56. Wald, 'Getting In and Out of the House', 1778.

Chapter 4 GC 3.0: The Fourth Industrial Revolution (2007–2022)

1. Klaus Schwab, *The Fourth Industrial Revolution*, quoted in Goodreads, https://www.goodreads.com/work/quotes/48730776-the-fourth-industrial-revolution.

2. World Economic Forum, 'Fourth Industrial Revolution', https://www.weforum.org/focus/fourth-industrial-revolution/.

3. Gordon E. Moore, 'Cramming More Components onto Integrated Circuits', *Electronics*, 19 April 1965, 114–117, https://www.cs.utexas.edu/~fussell/courses/cs352h/papers/moore.pdf.

4. Mind Lattice, 'Winner-Take-Most Markets—Mental Model Explained', https://mindlattice.app/mental-models/winner-take-most-markets.

5. Klaus Schwab, 'The Fourth Industrial Revolution: What It Means and How to Respond', *Foreign Affairs*, 12 December 2015, https://www.foreignaffairs.com/world/fourth-industrial-revolution.

6. 'The Basics of Microchips', *ASML*, https://www.asml.com/en/technology/all-about-microchips/microchip-basics.

7. An integrated circuit (IC), also known as a microchip or simply chip, is a set of electronic circuits on a small, flat piece of silicon. On the chip, transistors act as miniature electrical switches that can turn a current on or off. The pattern of tiny switches is created on the silicon wafer by adding and removing materials to form a multilayered latticework of interconnected shapes. 'The Basics of Microchips', https://www.asml.com/en/technology/all-about-microchips/microchip-basics.

   Computers in 2007 packed roughly 400 million times more switching elements onto a single chip than the very first IC in 1958. The first IC, developed by Jack Kilby at Texas Instruments in 1958, contained a single transistor. Intel's Core Duo 'Wolfdale', launched in 2007, contained 411 million transistors. See 'Integrated Circuit Celebrates 40th Birthday', *HPCwire*, 18 September 1998, https://www.hpcwire.com/1998/09/18/integrated-circuit-celebrates-40th-birthday/ and 'Transistor Count', *Wikipedia*, last modified July 2025, https://en.wikipedia.org/wiki/Transistor_count.

8. 'The Basics of Microchips', https://www.asml.com/en/technology/all-about-microchips/microchip-basics. RAM (Random Access Memory) is a type of volatile memory that temporarily stores data and instructions that a computer is actively using. In contrast, ROM (Read-Only Memory) is non-volatile memory that permanently stores essential instructions required for the computer's start-up and basic functions. See 'What's the Difference Between RAM and ROM?', *Corsair Explorer*, https://www.corsair.com/us/en/explorer/diy-builder/memory/whats-the-difference-between-ram-and-rom.

9. The below figures are all taken from Thomas L. Friedman, *Thank You for Being Late: An Optimist's Guide to Thriving in the Age of Accelerations* (New York: Farrar, Straus & Giroux, 2016), Kindle edition, 269–325.

10. 'Airbnb vs. The Global Hotel Industry', *Craft.co blog*, published approximately July 2023, https://global.craft.co/blog/airbnb-vs-global-hotel-industry/.

11. Friedman, *Thank You for Being Late*, 325.

12. Feyzi Kaysi, Mehmet Yavuz, and Emrah Aydemir, 'Investigation of University Students' Smartphone Usage Levels and Effects', *International Journal of Technology in Education and Science* 5, no. 3 (2021): 412, Figure 1.

13. Oberlo, 'Mobile Commerce Trends', https://www.oberlo.com/statistics/mobile-commerce-trends.

14. Esteban Ortiz-Ospina, 'The Rise of Social Media', *Our World in Data*, 18 September 2019, https://ourworldindata.org/rise-of-social-media.

15. 'What Is Cloud Computing', *Microsoft Azure Cloud Computing Dictionary*, https://azure.microsoft.com/en-us/resources/cloud-computing-dictionary/what-is-cloud-computing.

16. 'What Is Cloud Computing?', *McKinsey Explainers*, 31 July 2024, https://www.mckinsey.com/featured-insights/mckinsey-explainers/what-is-cloud-computing.

17. 'A Decade in the Cloud: 2010–2020', *Hyve Managed Hosting*, https://www.hyve.com/insights/a-decade-in-the-cloud-2010-2020/.

18. Ibid.

19. Wenjie Chen, Mico Mrkaic, and Malhar S. Nabar, 'The Global Economic Recovery 10 Years After the 2008 Financial Crisis', Working Paper No. 2019/083 (International Monetary Fund, 26 April 2019), https://www.elibrary.imf.org/view/journals/001/2019/083/article-A001-en.xml.

20. Mary E. Daly, Neil Bhutta, and Randal Verbrugge, 'Federal Reserve Unconventional Policies: The Tools, Transmission, and Impacts', Federal Reserve Bank of San Francisco Economic Letter (November 2012), https://www.frbsf.org/research-and-insights/publications/economic-letter/2012/11/federal-reserve-unconventional-policies/ and 'Unpacking the US Federal Reserve Balance Sheet Expansion', *QNB Global*, 12 January 2020, https://www.qnb.com/sites/qnb/qnbglobal/en/areconomics12jan20news.

21. 'Unpacking the US Federal Reserve Balance Sheet Expansion', https://www.qnb.com/sites/qnb/qnbglobal/en/areconomics12jan20news.

22. 'Goldilocks Economy', *Investopedia*, updated 10 March 2025, https://www.investopedia.com/terms/g/goldilockseconomy.asp.

23. 'End of the 'Goldilocks' Era—Enter the Bear', *Davy MarketWatch*, July 2022, https://www.davy.ie/market-and-insights/insights/marketwatch/2022/july-2022/end-of-the-goldilocks-era-enter-the-bear.html.

24. Lawrence H. Summers, 'The Age of Secular Stagnation: What Is It and What Do About It', *Foreign Affairs* 95, no. 2 (2016): 2–3, https://www.jstor.org/stable/43948172.

25. Summers (2016), 2–9.

26. Ian Bremmer and Nouriel Roubini, 'A G-Zero World: The New Economic Club Will Produce Conflict, Not Cooperation', *Foreign*

Affairs 90, no. 2 (March/April 2011): 2–7, https://www.jstor.org/stable/25800451. See also Ian Bremmer, *Every Nation for Itself: Winners and Losers in a G-Zero World* (New York: Portfolio/Penguin, 2012).

27. James Manyika, Susan Lund, Jacques Bughin et al., *Digital Globalization: The New Era of Global Flows*, McKinsey Global Institute, March 2016, 2, https://www.mckinsey.com/~/media/mckinsey/business%20functions/mckinsey%20digital/our%20insights/digital%20globalization%20the%20new%20era%20of%20global%20flows/mgi-digital-globalization-full-report.pdf.

28. Manyika et al., *Digital Globalization*.

29. Ibid., 8.

30. Ibid., 6.

31. The term 'network effect' refers to a situation in which the value of a product, service, or platform depends on the number of buyers, sellers, or users who leverage it (Lauren Landry, 'What Are Network Effects?', *Harvard Business School Online*, 24 March 2020, https://online.hbs.edu/blog/post/what-are-network-effects). For a discussion of platform economies and network effects, see Iansiti and Lakhani (2020), Chapter 7 and John Soroushian, 'Digital Platforms Primer: Digital Platforms and Competition (Part 3)', *Bipartisan Policy Center*, 19 November 2021, https://bipartisanpolicy.org/explainer/digital-platforms-primer-digital-platforms-and-competition-part-3/.

32. Ocean Tomo, 'Intangible Asset Market Value Study', 2020. https://oceantomo.com/intangible-asset-market-value-study/.

33. Gita Gopinath, 'The Great Lockdown: Worst Economic Downturn Since the Great Depression', *International Monetary Fund blog*, 14 April 2020, https://www.imf.org/en/blogs/articles/2020/04/14/blog-weo-the-great-lockdown-worst-economic-downturn-since-the-great-depression.

34. Laura LaBerge, Clayton O'Toole, Jeremy Schneider, and Kate Smaje, 'How COVID-19 Has Pushed Companies over the Technology Tipping Point—and Transformed Business Forever', *McKinsey & Company*, 5 October 2020, https://www.mckinsey.com/capabilities/strategy-and-corporate-finance/our-insights/how-covid-19-has-pushed-companies-over-the-technology-tipping-point-and-transformed-business-forever.

35. Catherine Thorbecke, 'The Winners in a Pandemic Economy: Big Tech and Lockdown Essentials Soar', *ABC News*, 26 August 2020, https://abcnews.go.com/Business/winners-pandemic-economy-big-tech-lockdown-essentials-soar/story?id=72495436.

36. See RainmakerThinking, *Hiring Challenges in 2021: Short-Term and Long-Term Factors*, https://rainmakerthinking.com/hiring-challenges-in-2021short-term-and-long-term-factors/, noting that employers in 2021 were facing more severe talent shortages than any time since they began their workplace research in 1993.

37. *Global Risks Report 2023* (Geneva: World Economic Forum, 2023), PDF file, https://www3.weforum.org/docs/WEF_Global_Risks_Report_2023.pdf.

38. World Intellectual Property Organization, 'Global Innovation Index 2024: R&D Spenders', *WIPO Global Innovation Index blog*, 30 April 2025, https://www.wipo.int/en/web/global-innovation-index/w/blogs/2024/r-and-d-spenders#:~:text=a%20competitive%20edge.-,Amidst%20rapid%20technological%20advancements%20and%20evolving%20innovation%20trends%2C%20companies%20are,more%20than%20%E2%82%AC75%20billion.

39. Liz Koehler, Ankur Kumar, and Matt Stone, 'Memo to the CFO: A New Approach to 2021 Budgeting Starts Now', *McKinsey & Company*, 10 September 2020, https://www.mckinsey.com/capabilities/strategy-and-corporate-finance/our-insights/memo-to-the-cfo-a-new-approach-to-2021-budgeting-starts-now.

40. David B. Wilkins and Maria J. Esteban Ferrer, 'The Global Age of More for Less', *Harvard Law School Center on the Legal Profession*, April 2017, https://clp.law.harvard.edu/knowledge-hub/magazine/issues/the-global-age-of-more for less/the-global-age-of-more for less/.

41. *ACC Chief Legal Officers Survey Report*, Association of Corporate Counsel, PDF file, January 2015, https://d2f5upgbvkx8pz.cloudfront.net/sites/default/files/inline-files/ACC%20chief%20legal%20officers.pdf.files/ACC%20chief%20legal%20officers.pdf.

42. *2008 Law Department Operations Survey Report*, Blickstein Group, PDF file, November 2008, 8, https://cdn.prod.website-files.com/66b0dd4f1f3a4829e0fc796c/66d7a191ca5c3c0fe3a96031_LDOSurvey-2008.pdf.

43. Mark Liggio, 'The Law Department of the Future: More Than a Cost Center', *Arizona Law Review* 49, no. 4 (2007): 7771–7805, PDF file, 631.

44. Ibid.

45. Tellmann, *Building an Outstanding Legal Team*, 39.

46. Ibid.

47. Corporate Legal Operations Consortium, 'What Is Legal Ops?', https://cloc.org/what-is-legal-ops/.

48. Sterling Miller, 'The Evolution of Legal Operations: How Corporate Legal Departments Can Stay Ahead of the Curve', *Thomson Reuters Law blog*, 25 November 2024, https://legal.thomsonreuters.com/blog/the-evolution-of-legal-operations-how-corporate-legal-departments-can-stay-ahead-of-the-curve/.

49. Ibid.

50. 'The State of the Legal Operations Role in Legal Departments', *Association of Corporate Counsel*, 10 January 2022, PDF file, https://www.acc.com/sites/default/files/2022-06/The%20State%20of%20the%20Legal%20Oprations%20Role%20in%20Legal%20Departments.pdf.

51. '2021 Global Legal Department Benchmarking Survey', *KPMG International*, March 2021, PDF file, https://assets.kpmg.com/content/dam/kpmg/xx/pdf/2021/03/global-legal-department-benchmarking-survey.pdf.

52. Casey Flaherty, 'CLOC Las Vegas – Why Are We Here?', *Artificial Lawyer*, 9 May 2022, https://www.artificiallawyer.com/2022/05/09/cloc-las-vegas-why-are-we-here/.

53. Ibid.

54. Axiom, 'Alternative Legal Service Providers: Why the Future Looks Strong', *Axiom Law blog*, March 2024, https://www.axiomlaw.com/blog/alternative-legal-service-providers-strong-future.

55. Bob Ambrogi, 'Alternative-Legal-Services Market Grows to $28.5B as Industry Faces 'Critical Juncture,' Thomson Reuters Report Finds', *LawNext*, 28 January 2025, https://www.lawnext.com/2025/01/alternative-legal-services-market-grows-to-28-5b-as-industry-faces-critical-juncture-thomson-reuters-report-finds.html.

56. 'ALSP Now More Than a $10 bn Market, According to TR Study', *Legaltech News*, 29 January 2019, https://legaltechnology.com/2019/01/29/alsp-now-more-than-a-10bn-market-according-to-tr-study/.

57. Law firm and Big Four investments in their own ALSP capacities grew from $0.2 and 0.9 billion respectively in 2015 to $1.8 and

1.6 billion respectively in 2023. Ambrogi, 'Alternative-Legal-Services Market Grows'.

58. Thomson Reuters, 'The 2021 Alternative Legal Service Provider (ALSP) Report', July 2021, PDF file, 2, https://www.thomsonreuters. com/en-us/posts/wp-content/uploads/sites/20/2021/07/ALSP_2021-Report_FINAL-1.pdf.

59. Ibid.

60. For a discussion of these developments, see Tellmann, *Building an Outstanding Legal Team*, 51–53.

61. Irving Wladawsky-Berger, 'The Rise of the T-Shaped Organization', *The Wall Street Journal CIO Journal*, 18 December 2015, http://blogs. wsj.com/cio/2015/12/18/the-rise-of-the-t-shaped-organisation/, quoted in Tellmann, *Building an Outstanding Legal Team*, 385.

62. Tellmann, *Building an Outstanding Legal Team*, 50.

63. Gillian Tett, *The Silo Effect: The Peril of Expertise and the Promise of Breaking Down Barriers* (New York: Simon & Schuster, 2015), cited in Tellmann, *Building an Outstanding Legal Team*, 385.

64. For a discussion of this dilemma, see Tellmann, *Building an Outstanding Legal Team*, 46–49.

Part II   The AI Era

1. Allison Dunn, '75 Quotes about AI: Business, Ethics, and the Future', *DeliberateDirections.com*, 16 April 2025, https://deliberatedirections. com/quotes-about-artificial-intelligence/.

2. Iansiti and Lakhani, *Competing in the Age of AI*, 17.

3. Ibid., 4. Weak AI can be contrasted with 'strong AI'. According to Kira Schreiberling, 'Weak AI, also known as "Narrow AI", refers to AI systems specialized in a specific task or problem and operate within this defined scope … Weak AI is used in numerous applications, including virtual assistants, speech recognition systems, recommendation systems in e-commerce platforms'. By contrast, strong AI (also referred to as artificial general intelligence, or AGI) 'describes the ability of a system to perform any intellectual task that a human brain can handle … strong AI strives to gain a comprehensive understanding of complex concepts and to react flexibly to new situations. For example, a strong AI could independently learn to understand human language, learn

from experiences, and make complex decisions'. Kira Schreiberling, 'Strong AI vs. Weak AI: Definition, Differences & Examples', *OMR Reviews – Content Hub*, 7 February 2024, https://omr.com/en/reviews/contenthub/starke-ki-schwache-ki.

4. Agentic AI will be defined and discussed more closely in Chapter 5.

Chapter 5   GC 4.0—The AI Impact

1. Andrew McAfee, 'Competing in the AI Economy: An Interview with MIT's Andrew McAfee', *McKinsey Analytics*, 30 March 2018, https://www.mckinsey.com/capabilities/quantumblack/our-insights/competing-in-the-ai-economy-an-interview-with-mits-andrew-mcafee.

2. Dominique A. Harroch and Richard D. Harroch, '15 Quotes on the Future of AI', *Time*, https://time.com/partner-article/7279245/15-quotes-on-the-future-of-ai/.

3. Marco Iansiti and Karim R. Lakhani, 'Competing in the Age of AI', *Harvard Business Review*, January–February 2020, https://hbr.org/2020/01/competing-in-the-age-of-ai.

4. See Iansiti and Lakhani, *Competing in the Age of AI*, Chapters 1 and 2.

5. See Charles Gildehaus, David Allred, Euvin Naidoo, and Anil Podduturi, 'Powering the Innovation Flywheel in the Digital Era', *Boston Consulting Group*, 12 March 2021, https://www.bcg.com/publications/2021/driving-business-impact-with-the-innovation-flywheel-approach.

6. Jacobellis v. Ohio, 378 U.S. 184 (1964).

7. Paul D. Weitzel, 'Defining Artificial Intelligence' (SSRN Scholarly Paper No. 5154389, 25 April 2025), Social Science Research Network, 3, https://papers.ssrn.com/sol3/papers.cfm?abstract_id=5154389.

8. See Richard Susskind, *How to Think About AI* (Oxford: Oxford University Press, 2025), Kindle edition, 10.

9. Dagmar Monett and Colin Lewis, 'Getting Clarity by Defining Artificial Intelligence—A Survey', in *Philosophy and Computing: Essays in Epistemology, Philosophy of Mind, Logic, and Ethics*, ed. Paola C. Rodriguez (Cham: Springer, 2018), https://doi.org/10.1007/978-3-319-96448-5_21.

10. Weitzel, 'Defining Artificial Intelligence', 53.

11. Susskind, *How to Think About AI*, 10.

12. 'What Is AI (Artificial Intelligence)?', *McKinsey & Company*, 3 April 2024, https://www.mckinsey.com/featured-insights/mckinsey-explainers/what-is-ai.

13. Ajay Bandi, Bhavani Kongari, Roshini Naguru et al., 'The Rise of Agentic AI: A Review of Definitions, Frameworks, Architectures, Applications, Evaluation Metrics, and Challenges,' *Future Internet* 17, no. 9 (2025): 404, https://doi.org/10.3390/fi17090404.

14. Anirban Mukherjee and Hannah Hanwen Chang, 'Agentic AI: Autonomy, Accountability, and the Algorithmic Society', *arXiv*, February 2025, https://arxiv.org/abs/2502.00289, 3.

15. Vicent Botti, 'Agentic AI and Multiagentic: Are We Reinventing the Wheel?', *arXiv*, June 2025, https://arxiv.org/abs/2506.01463, 10 and Bandi et al., 'The Rise of Agentic AI'.

16. Botti, 'Agentic AI and Multiagentic', 10.

17. 'What is Agentic AI?', *IBM Think*, https://www.ibm.com/think/topics/agentic-ai.

18. Mukherjee and Chang, 'Agentic AI', 4.

19. 'Agentic AI Use Cases in the Legal Industry', *Thomson Reuters Legal*, 18 August 2025, https://legal.thomsonreuters.com/blog/agentic-ai-use-cases-in-the-legal-industry/.

20. Danny Tobey, Ashley Carr, Karley Buckley, and Kyle Kloeppel, 'The Rise of "Agentic" AI: Potential New Legal and Organizational Risks', *DLA Piper*, 9 June 2025, https://www.dlapiper.com/en-gb/insights/publications/ai-outlook/2025/the-rise-of-agentic-ai--potential-new-legal-and-organizational-risks.

21. Tobey et al., 'The Rise of "Agentic" AI'.

22. Erik Brynjolfsson and Andrew McAfee, 'The Business of Artificial Intelligence: What It Can—and Cannot—Do for Your Organization', *Harvard Business Review*, 18 July 2017, https://hbr.org/2017/07/the-business-of-artificial-intelligence.

23. Ben McMann, 'AI as a General Purpose Technology: Transforming Business in the 21st Century', *Lantern Studios*, 20 March 2025, https://lanternstudios.com/insights/blog/ai-as-a-general-purpose-technology-transforming-business-in-the-21st-century/. See also Andrew McAfee, *Generally Faster: The Economic Impact of Generative AI*, Technology & Society Visiting Fellow Report (Google, 25 April 2024),

https://ide.mit.edu/wp-content/uploads/2024/04/Davos-Report-Draft-XFN-Copy-01112024-Print-Version.pdf?x76181.

24. For a discussion of applications and implementations of AI across different sectors, see Tanvir Rashid and Abhishek Kausik, 'AI Revolutionizing Industries Worldwide: A Comprehensive Overview of Its Diverse Applications', *Hybrid Advances* 7 (December 2024): 100277, 2, https://www.sciencedirect.com/science/article/pii/S2773207X24001386.

25. Rashid and Kausik, 'AI Revolutionizing Industries Worldwide', 100246, 2.

26. Bond Capital, 'Trends in Artificial Intelligence', PDF, 2025, 19–20, https://www.bondcap.com/report/pdf/Trends_Artificial_Intelligence.pdf.

27. Rashid and Kausik, 'AI Revolutionizing Industries Worldwide', 100277, 10.

28. Ibid., 9.

29. McAfee, *Generally Faster*, 7.

30. Ibid., 16.

31. Ritu Jyoti and Dave Schubmehl, '2024 Business Opportunity of AI: Generative AI Delivering New Business Value and Increasing ROI', *InfoBrief*, sponsored by Microsoft (Needham, MA: IDC, November 2024), 5, https://143485449.fs1.hubspotusercontent-eu1.net/hubfs/143485449/2024%20Business%20Opportunity%20of%20AI_Generative%20AI%20Delivering%20New%20Business%20Value%20and%20Increasing%20ROI.pdf.

32. Myk Eff, 'The AI Cambrian Explosion: When Machines Learned to Think', *Medium*, 14 June 2025, https://medium.com/higher-neurons/the-ai-cambrian-explosion-when-machines-learned-to-think-56b7de31d364.

33. 'In recent years, generative AI models have also shown an accelerated pace of growth in training compute as compared to past AI models. Between 2010 and May 2024, the training compute of AI models, measured in number of mathematical operations (i.e. floating-point operations per second, or FLOPS), has grown about 4.4-fold per year, as compared to a yearly 1.5-fold growth pre-2010.' OECD, 'Is Generative AI a General-Purpose Technology?', No. 40 (Paris: OECD Publishing, 2025), 26, https://doi.org/10.1787/704e2d12-en.

34. Brynjolfsson and McAfee, 'The Business of Artificial Intelligence'.

35. Ibid.

36. Rashid and Kausik, 'AI Revolutionizing Industries Worldwide', 100277, 27.

37. Brynjolfsson and McAfee, 'The Business of Artificial Intelligence'.

38. Timothy F. Bresnahan and Manuel Trajtenberg, 'General Purpose Technologies "Engines of Growth?"', *Journal of Econometrics* 65, no. 1 (January 1995): 84, https://doi.org/10.1016/0304-4076(94)01598-T.

39. Rashid and Kausik, 'AI Revolutionizing Industries Worldwide', 100277, 9. For a more comprehensive explanation of natural language processing, see Cole Stryker and Jim Holdsworth, 'What is NLP (natural language processing)?', IBM, 11 January 2026, https://www.ibm.com/think/topics/natural-language-processing.

40. Nicholas Bloom, Charles I. Jones, John Van Reenen, and Michael Webb, 'Are Ideas Getting Harder to Find?', *American Economic Review* 110, no. 4 (April 2020): 1105–1144, https://doi.org/10.1257/aer.20180338.

41. Bloom et al., 'Are Ideas Getting Harder to Find?'.

42. McKinsey, 'The Next Innovation Revolution—Powered by AI', *QuantumBlack AI*, 20 June 2025, https://www.mckinsey.com/capabilities/quantumblack/our-insights/the-next-innovation-revolution-powered-by-ai.

43. McKinsey, 'The Next Innovation Revolution'.

44. McAfee, *Generally Faster*, 6. For an interesting exploration of recent trends in synthetic protein and materials development, see Alok Jha (host), 'Synth Wave: Designing Proteins and Genomes from Scratch', *Economist Podcasts*, 9 July 2025, https://podcasts.apple.com/gb/podcast/synth-wave-designing-proteins-and-genomes-from-scratch/id508376907?i=1000716506312.

45. See Iansiti and Lakhani, *Competing in the Age of AI*, Chapter 2, 24–25.

46. See David J. Teece, 'Business Models and Dynamic Capabilities', *Long Range Planning* 51, no. 1 (2018): 40–49, https://doi.org/10.1016/j.lrp.2017.06.007. See also Iansiti and Lakhani, *Competing in the Age of AI*, 28.

47. See Teece, 'Business Models and Dynamic Capabilities'.

48. See Iansiti and Lakhani, *Competing in the Age of AI*, 28.

49. Accelare, 'Business Model vs. Operating Model: What are the Differences?', *Accelare*, 1 August 2024, https://www.accelare.com/blog/business-model-vs-operating-model-what-are-the-

differences#:~:text=What%20is%20an%20Operating%20 Model,Operating%20Model:%20Key%20Differences.

50. Iansiti and Lakhani, *Competing in the Age of AI*, 29.

51. Espen Andersen, 'Chandler: Scale and Scope', *Applied Abstractions blog*, 17 January 2010, https://appliedabstractions.com/2010/01/17/ chandlerscaleandscope/.

52. For more on Kaizen, see Kaizen Institute, 'What is KAIZEN™', https://www.kaizen.com/what-is-kaizen/.

53. Andersen, 'Chandler'.

54. Iansiti and Lakhani, *Competing in the Age of AI*, 9. Interestingly, the emergence of IT in the 1960s and 1970s did not disrupt or transform the multidivisional administrative structure. Indeed, in some ways IT teams reinforced it by developing systems and applications inside existing silos. This in turn created huge disincentives to transform as any integration across silos would be extremely challenging, disruptive, and complex. Ibid., 87.

55. Iansiti and Lakhani, *Competing in the Age of AI*, ix, 88.

56. Iansiti and Lakhani, *Competing in the Age of AI*, 9.

57. A debate is underway about how best to delineate roles between humans and machines in the AI context. Growing out of a narrower 'humans-in-the-loop' debate about defining the role of humans in the machine learning and AI system design, it has since expanded into a broader debate about where the touchpoints should be placed across the enterprise. While there is no 'one-size-fits-all' consensus, much of the discussion coalesces around shifting humans from execution to oversight roles, such as architecting, objective setting, and setting governance and ethical guardrails. For a few good sources on this debate, see Cosimo Spera and Garima Agrawal, 'Reversing the Paradigm: Building AI-First Systems with Human Guidance', *arXiv*, 2025, https://arxiv.org/abs/2506.12245; Sriraam Natarajan, Saurabh Mathur, Sahil Sidheekh et al., 'Human-in-the-Loop or AI-in-the-Loop? Automate or Collaborate?', *arXiv*, 2024, https://arxiv.org/ abs/2412.14232; Mohsin et al., 'A Unified Framework for Human–AI Collaboration in Security Operations Centers', *arXiv*, 2025, https:// arxiv.org/abs/2505.23397; and Trinh Nguyen and Amany Elbanna, 'Understanding Human–AI Augmentation in the Workplace: A Review', *Information Systems Frontiers*, 2025, https://link.springer.com/ article/10.1007/s10796-025-10591-5.

58. The small incremental cost that remains is the negligible expense for additional computing capacity, which, as discussed in Chapter 4, is readily available from Cloud providers.

59. Tim Stobierski, 'What Are Network Effects?', *Harvard Business School Online*, 12 November 2020, https://online.hbs.edu/blog/post/what-are-network-effects.

60. Ibid.

61. Juan Jesus Velasco, 'Zero Marginal Cost: The Key to Scalability in Digital Businesses', *Medium*, 28 February 2025, https://medium.com/@jjv/zero-marginal-cost-the-key-to-scalability-in-digital-businesses-a265d6ec1a98.

62. Pete Bigelow and Grayson Brulte, 'Tesla's Data Advantage in the Race to Develop Autonomous Driving', *The Road to Autonomy Podcast*, 8 March 2024, https://www.roadtoautonomy.com/tesla-data-advantage/.

63. Fred Pope, 'Tesla's Neural Network Revolution: How Full Self-Driving Replaced 300,000 Lines of Code with AI', *fredpope.com*, 24 June 2025, https://www.fredpope.com/blog/machine-learning/tesla-fsd-12.

64. Ibid.

65. See ByteSimplified, 'Tesla's Over-the-Air Updates: Revolutionizing Future', 25 October 2023, https://bytesimplified.com/newsletter/f/teslas-over-the-air-updates-revolutionizing-future.

66. Tina Bellon, Hyunjoo Jin, and David Shepardson, 'Tesla Software Updates Allow Quick Fixes—And Taking Risks', *Reuters*, 18 February 2022, https://www.reuters.com/business/autos-transportation/tesla-software-updates-allow-quick-fixes-taking-risks-2022-02-18/.

67. For Netflix statistics, see BullFincher, 'Netflix—Revenue, Employees & Other Key Stats', https://bullfincher.io/companies/netflix/number-of-employees; DemandSage, 'Netflix Subscriber Count', https://www.demandsage.com/netflix-subscribers/; and Bytebridge, 'Netflix: Industry Leader in Streaming Entertainment', *Medium*, 19 January 2025, https://bytebridge.medium.com/netflix-industry-leader-in-streaming-entertainment-3fddb2c7f15d. For Comcast statistics, see Macrotrends, 'Comcast Total Number of Employees 2006–2025', https://macrotrends.net/stocks/charts/CMCSA/comcast/number-of-employees; The Desk, 'Comcast Q4 2024 Earnings Results', January 2025, https://thedesk.net/2025/01/comcast-q4-2024-earnings-results/; and Peter Lauria, 'Two Maps That Explain Why Comcast Wants to Buy Time Warner Cable', *BuzzFeed News*, https://www.buzzfeednews.com/article/peterlauria/two-maps-that-explain-why-comcast-wants-to-buy-time-warner-c.

68. Bryce Hall, Eric Lamarre, Rob Levin et al., 'Rewired and Running Ahead: Digital and AI Leaders Are Leaving the Rest Behind', *McKinsey & Company*, 12 January 2024, https://www.mckinsey.com/capabilities/mckinsey-digital/our-insights/rewired-and-running-ahead-digital-and-ai-leaders-are-leaving-the-rest-behind.

69. Ibid.

70. Ibid.

71. Jim Tyson, 'Only 4% of Companies Reap Full Value from AI: BCG', *CFO Dive*, 24 October 2024, https://www.cfodive.com/news/only-4-companies-reap-full-value-ai-bcg-artificial-intelligence/730982/.

Chapter 6   GC 4.0—The AI Factory

1. Jon Taylor, '16 Inspiring Quotes About AI', *Peak.ai Hub blog*, 16 February 2024, https://www.peak.ai/hub/blog/16-inspiring-quotes-about-ai/.

2. Iansiti and Lakhani, *Competing in the Age of AI*, 53–54.

3. Ibid., 54.

4. Ibid., 53.

5. Ibid., 53.

6. Ibid., 57.

7. Kate Gibson, 'The AI Factory: What It Is & Its Key Components', *Harvard Business School Online*, 4 November 2025, https://online.hbs.edu/blog/post/ai-factory.

8. Gibson, 'The AI Factory'. The term 'garbage in, garbage out' (GIGO) is a principle used in computer programming and mathematics that refers to the notion that the quality of the output is directly linked to the quality of the input. The phrase traces its origins to early computing and references made by Charles Babbage in the 1800s. 'Garbage In, Garbage Out (GIGO)', EBSCO Research Starters: Computer Science, https://www.ebsco.com/research-starters/computer-science/garbage-garbage-out-gigo#:~:text=%22Garbage%20in%2C%20garbage%20out%22,meaningful%20results%20across%20various%20applications.

9. Iansiti and Lakhani, *Competing in the Age of AI*, 57 of 267.

10. Gibson, 'The AI Factory'.

11. Ibid.

12. Iansiti and Lakhani, *Competing in the Age of AI*, 57.

13. Gibson, 'The AI Factory'.

14. Optimizely, 'A/B Testing', *Optimizely*, https://www.optimizely.com/optimization-glossary/ab-testing/#:~:text=A/B%20testing%20(also%20known,results%20for%20your%20conversion%20goals.

15. Iansiti and Lakhani, 'Competing in the Age of AI', *Harvard Business Review* 98, no. 1 (January–February 2020): 60–67, https://hbr.org/2020/01/competing-in-the-age-of-ai; Gibson, 'The AI Factory'.

16. Gibson, 'The AI Factory'.

17. Iansiti and Lakhani, *Competing in the Age of AI*, 87.

18. Marco Iansiti and Karim R. Lakhani, 'Competing in the Age of AI', *Harvard Business Review.*

19. Iansiti and Lakhani, *Competing in the Age of AI*, 117.

20. Ibid., 118.

21. Ibid., 118.

22. Ibid., 96.

23. Ibid., 120.

24. Adnan Masood, 'The AI Operating Model: A Five-Year Review of the New Competitive Mandate', *Medium*, 23 July 2025, https://medium.com/@adnanmasood/the-ai-operating-model-a-five-year-review-of-the-new-competitive-mandate-7b0bc3c67577.

25. See Supermarket News Staff, 'Target's Drive Up is Red-Hot', in *6 Grocers Leading in Curbside Pickup* (Supermarket News), https://www.supermarketnews.com/6-grocers-leading-in-curbside-pickup/target-s-drive-up-is-red-hot; Pattern, 'Target and Target Plus Growth', *Pattern*, https://pattern.com/blog/target-and-target-plus-growth; Hyperight, 'Deep Brew: Transforming Starbucks into a Data-Driven Company', *Hyperight*, https://hyperight.com/deep-brew-transforming-starbucks-into-a-data-driven-company; Stuart Lauchlan, 'COVID's digital DIY boom - how Home Depot and Lowe's omni-channel retail prep rode out the pandemic crisis', *diginomica*, 18 June 2020, https://diginomica.com/covids-digital-diy-boom-how-home-depot-and-lowes-omni-channel-retail-prep-rode-out-pandemic-crisis; and Analytics Institute, 'IKEA Case Study', *Analytics Institute of Australia*, https://analyticsinstitute.edu.au/ikea-casestudy/#:~:text=Over%20the%20past%20three%20years,adapt%20at%20an%20unprecedented%20pace.

26. The Economist, 'How Walmart Became a Tech Giant—and Took Over the World', *The Economist*, 15 May 2025, https://www.economist.

com/business/2025/05/15/how-walmart-became-a-tech-giant-and-took-over-the-world.

27. Iansiti and Lakhani, *Competing in the Age of AI*, 5.

28. The Economist, 'How Walmart Became a Tech Giant'.

29. AInvest Research, 'Walmart's AI Super Agents and the Future of Commerce: A Strategic Analysis of Competitive Advantage and Shareholder Value Creation', *AInvest*, 25 July 2024, https://www.ainvest.com/news/walmart-ai-super-agents-future-commerce-strategic-analysis-competitive-advantage-shareholder-creation-2507/ and Walmart, Inc., *Location Facts*, last modified 2025, https://corporate.walmart.com/about/location-facts.

30. The Economist, 'How Walmart Became a Tech Giant'.

31. Ibid.

32. AInvest Research, 'Walmart's AI Super Agents'.

33. Endeavour Marketing LLP, 'Walmart's Omni-Channel Retail Strategy'.

34. AInvest Research, 'Walmart's AI Super Agents'.

35. Ibid.

36. The Economist, 'How Walmart Became a Tech Giant'.

37. Kailyn Rhone, '*Walmart Joins Tech Giants With $1 Trillion Market Valuation*', *The New York Times*, 3 February 2026, https://www.nytimes.com/2026/02/03/business/walmart-trillion-market-value.html.

38. Ibid.

39. McKinsey & Company, *The Economic Potential of Generative AI: The Next Productivity Frontier*, June 2023, 3, https://www.mckinsey.com/~/media/mckinsey/business%20functions/mckinsey%20digital/our%20insights/the%20economic%20potential%20of%20generative%20ai%20the%20next%20productivity%20frontier/the-economic-potential-of-generative-ai-the-next-productivity-frontier.pdf.

40. Indeed, McKinsey estimates AI could eventually replace up to 60–70% of employee time in the workplace, generating productivity gains of between $2.6 trillion and $4.4 trillion each year across 63 use cases alone. And this number could double if one looks beyond those limited number of use cases. McKinsey & Company, *Economic Potential of Generative AI*, 2023, 3.

41. Aisera, 'Agentic AI: The Future of Autonomous Enterprise Operations', *Aisera blog*, 22 May 2024, https://aisera.com/blog/agentic-ai/; Lucy

Colback, 'AI Agents: From Co-Pilot to Autopilot', *Financial Times*, 7 May 2025, https://www.ft.com/content/3e862e23-6e2c-4670-a68c-e204379fe01f.

42. Xoriant, 'Agentic AI and Continuous Learning: Creating Ever-Evolving Systems', *Xoriant*, https://www.xoriant.com/thought-leadership/article/agentic-ai-and-continuous-learning-creating-ever-evolving-systems.

43. AInvest Research, 'Walmart's AI Super Agents'.

44. Colback, 'AI Agents: From Co-Pilot to Autopilot'.

45. For a few good sources on this debate, see Spera and Agrawal, 'Reversing the Paradigm'; Natarajan et al., 'Human-in-the-Loop or AI-in-the-Loop? Automate or Collaborate?'; and Nguyen and Elbanna, 'Understanding Human–AI Augmentation in the Workplace'.

46. Sacha Alanoca, Shira Gur-Arieh, Tom Zick et al., 'Taxonomizing AI Regulation: Towards a Conceptual Framework for Global AI Governance', *arXiv*, May 2025, https://arxiv.org/pdf/2505.13673.

47. Regulatory regimes range, for example, from permissive and non-binding measures in the UK framework to the extensive regulation contained in the EU's AI Act. While the emerging regimes in China and the United States seem to focus on technology-based coverage, the European Union, Canada, and Brazil have adopted a hybrid approach targeting applications and technology. See Alanoca et al., 'Taxonomizing AI Regulation', 2025.

48. Scale is a particular concern in this regard, since one biased person might impact a small number of people but an AI system that is biased can discriminate on a systemic level. See, for instance, Cathy O'Neil, *Weapons of Math Destruction: How Big Data Increases Inequality and Threatens Democracy* (New York: Crown Publishing Group, 2016).

49. See Project Management Institute, 'Top 10 Ethical Considerations for AI Projects', *PMI blog*, https://www.pmi.org/blog/top-10-ethical-considerations-for-ai-projects. See also Christina Pazzanese, 'Great Promise But Potential For Peril: Ethical Concerns Mount as AI Takes Bigger Decision-Making Role', *Harvard Gazette*, 26 October 2020, https://news.harvard.edu/gazette/story/2020/10/ethical-concerns-mount-as-ai-takes-bigger-decision-making-role/.

50. Technical University of Munich, 'Inclusivity and Responsible AI', *TUM News*, 23 August 2023, https://www.tum.de/en/news-and-events/all-news/press-releases/details/inclusivity-and-responsible-ai.

51. McKinsey & Company, *What is Digital Transformation?*, https://www.mckinsey.com/featured-insights/mckinsey-explainers/what-is-digital-transformation.

52. Ibid.

53. Stephanie L. Woerner, Ina M. Sebastian, Peter Weill et al., 'Grow Enterprise AI Maturity for Bottom-Line Impact', *MIT CISR Research Briefing*, 21 August 2025, https://cisr.mit.edu/publication/2025_0801_EnterpriseAIMaturityUpdate_WoernerSebastianWeillKaganer?.

54. Woerner et al., 'Grow Enterprise AI Maturity for Bottom-Line Impact'.

55. Dana Daher, Saurabh Gupta, and Phil Fersht, 'Only 12% of Enterprises Have Cracked the AI Maturity Code—It's Catch-Up Time for the Rest', *HFS Research*, 4 February 2025, https://www.hfsresearch.com/research/enterprises-cracked-ai-maturity/.

56. Woerner et al., 'Grow Enterprise AI Maturity for Bottom-Line Impact'.

57. Ibid.

58. Will Damron, 'Gains from Factory Electrification: Evidence from North Carolina, 1905–1926', *Explorations in Economic History* 96 (April 2025): 101654, https://www.sciencedirect.com/science/article/abs/pii/S0014498325000014.

59. Paul Hlivko, 'The AI Revolution Won't Happen Overnight', *Harvard Business Review*, 24 June 2025, https://hbr.org/2025/06/the-ai-revolution-wont-happen-overnight.

60. Benjamin Todd, 'AI is the Most Rapidly Adopted Technology in History', *Benjamin Todd Substack*, 11 July 2025, https://benjamintodd.substack.com/p/when-people-say-ai-isnt-finding-real.

61. Hlivko, 'The AI Revolution Won't Happen Overnight'.

62. In 2019, the company adopted its 'Agile Operating Model', selecting a standard platform to accelerate the new model. See TBM Council, 'How TBM & Product Costing Helped John Deere Accelerate Their Agile Transformation', *TBM Council Case Studies*, https://www.tbmcouncil.org/case-studies/how-tbm-product-costing-helped-john-deere-accelerate-their-agile-transformation/.

63. Lucintel, 'The Future of Farming: John Deere Unveils Autonomous Tractor Fleet', *Lucintel Brief*, https://www.lucintel.com/lucintel-brief/Chemical/the-future-of-farming-John-Deere-unveils-autonomous-tractor-fleet.aspx.

64. Rachel Jewett, 'John Deere Tasks Satellite to Connect New Frontiers in Agriculture', *Via Satellite*, 24 July 2023, https://interactive.satellitetoday.com/via/articles/john-deere-tasks-satellite-to-connect-new-frontiers-in-agriculture.

65. Danny Kitishian, 'John Deere's AI Strategy: Analysis of Dominance in Agriculture', *Klover.ai*, 22 July 2025, https://www.klover.ai/john-deere-ai-strategy-analysis-of-dominance-in-agriculture/; Martha DeGrasse, 'John Deere Cultivates a Data Business', *Fierce Wireless*, 6 April 2023, https://www.fierce-network.com/wireless/john-deere-cultivates-data-business; and Dominika Sarnecka, 'John Deere: Using AI to Reimagine Farming', *Harvard Business School Digital Initiative*, 3 December 2019, https://d3.harvard.edu/platform-digit/submission/john-deere-using-ai-to-reimagine-farming/.

66. John Deere, *Generation 4 Displays: Software Update 19-2 Release Notes, OS Version 10.14.978-88* (Moline, IL: Deere & Company, 2019), https://www.deere.com/assets/pdfs/common/stellarsupport/19-2-Gen-4-CommandCenter-New-Features_English.pdf.

67. DeGrasse, 'John Deere Cultivates a Data Business'.

68. DeGrasse, 'John Deere Cultivates a Data Business'.

69. Carl Surran, 'Deere Gains as Melius Upgrades, Seen Near Recurring Revenue Upside from Data Offerings', *Seeking Alpha*, 6 June 2025, https://seekingalpha.com/news/4456300-deere-gains-as-melius-upgrades-seen-near-recurring-revenue-upside-from-data-offerings.

Chapter 7   GC 4.0—The AI Era Legal Department

1. Quote made by Áine Lyons to the author in correspondence, 12 October 2025.

2. Nearly 75% of CEOs have already taken significant action to change how their companies create, deliver, and capture value, and close to half of them view AI integration into corporate technology platforms, business processes, and workflows to be one of their biggest priorities. IBM Institute for Business Value, 'The CEO's Guide to Generative AI', 6 January 2025, 27, https://www.ibm.com/thought-leadership/institute-business-value/en-us/report/ceo-generative-ai-book and PwC, '28th Annual Global CEO Survey: Reinvention on the Edge of Tomorrow',

6, 12, https://www.pwc.com/gx/en/ceo-survey/2025/28th-ceo-survey.pdf.

3. NACD Staff, '2025 Public Company Board Practices and Oversight Survey—Survey Analysis: AI', *National Association of Corporate Directors*, 28 July 2025, https://www.nacdonline.org/all-governance/governance-resources/governance-surveys/surveys-benchmarking/2025-public-company-board-practices--oversight-survey/2025-board-practices-oversight-ai/.

4. According to a cross-industry McKinsey survey, over 75% of organisations were using AI in at least one business function in 2025, up from 72% in 2024 and 55% in 2023. McKinsey & Company, 'The State of AI: How Organizations Are Rewiring to Capture Value', 5 November 2025, 1, 15, https://www.mckinsey.com/capabilities/quantumblack/our-insights/the-state-of-ai.

5. This echoes what Susskind refers to as his 'shareholder test' challenge to GCs: When a costed proposal for a transaction or dispute is under consideration, would a commercially astute shareholder familiar with the many alternative ways of sourcing legal work consider the way it is being contemplated as representing value for money? Richard Susskind, *Tomorrow's Lawyers: An Introduction to Your Future*, 3rd ed. (Oxford: Oxford University Press, 2023), 119.

6. GoBeyond.ai Team, 'How JP Morgan Uses COIN AI to Automate Contract Analysis and Revolutionize Legal Document Processing', *GoBeyond.ai*, 27 July 2025, https://www.gobeyond.ai/ai-resources/case-studies/jpmorgan-coin-ai-contract-analysis-legal-docs.

7. K. Tulsi, Arpan Dutta, Navneet Singh, and Deepansh Jain, 'Transforming Financial Services: The Impact of AI on JP Morgan Chase's Operational Efficiency and Decision-Making, 211', *International Journal of Scientific Research and Engineering Trends* 10, no. 1 (January–February 2024), https://ijsret.com/wp-content/uploads/2024/01/IJSRET_V10_issue1_138.pdf.

8. Tulsi et al., 'Transforming Financial Services'.

9. GoBeyond.ai Team, 'How JP Morgan Uses COIN AI'.

10. Tulsi et al., 'Transforming Financial Services', 210.

11. GoBeyond.ai Team, 'How JP Morgan Uses COIN AI'.

12. Digital Defynd, '10 Ways JP Morgan is Using AI [In Depth Case Study]', https://www.digitaldefynd.com/IQ/jp-morgan-using-ai-case-study/

and 5D Vision, 'Case Studies: How JPMorgan Chase Cracked the AI Code While Others Waited', *5D Vision*, published July 2025, https://www.5dvision.com/post/case-studies-how-jpmorgan-chase-cracked-the-ai-code-while-others-waited/.

13. Tulsi et al., 'Transforming Financial Services', 211.

14. See Sievo, 'Spend Analysis 101: Complete Guide for Procurement', updated 11 August 2025, https://sievo.com/en/resources/spend-analysis-101; and GEP, '3 Reasons AI-Powered ESG Analysis is the Key to Sustainable Procurement', *GEP blog*, 13 February 2025, https://www.gep.com/blog/technology/ai-powered-esg-analysis-tool-importance-benefits-in-procurement.

15. See Sievo, 'Spend Analysis 101' and GEP, '3 Reasons AI-Powered ESG Analysis is the Key to Sustainable Procurement'.

16. Financial Times, 'Meet the Specialists Digitising Companies' Legal Teams', *Financial Times*, 12 November 2024.

17. Sydney Scott, 'Continuous Learning: Adapting AI Agents to Evolving Business Needs', *Workday blog*, 18 July 2025, https://blog.workday.com/en-us/continuous-learning-adapting-ai-agents-evolving-business-needs.html.

18. Ibid.

19. Sievo, 'Spend Analysis', 101

20. Tulsi et al., 'Transforming Financial Services', 210.

21. Thomas H. Davenport, Abhijit Guha, and Dhruv Grewal, 'How to Design an AI Marketing Strategy', *Harvard Business Review*, July–August 2021, https://hbr.org/2021/07/how-to-design-an-ai-marketing-strategy.

22. Nick Whitehouse, Nicole Lincoln, Stephanie Yiu et al., 'Better Bill GPT: Comparing Large Language Models Against Legal Invoice Reviewers', *Onit, Inc.*, April 2025, https://arxiv.org/pdf/2504.02881.

23. Financial Times, 'Meet the Specialists Digitising Companies' Legal Teams'.

24. Ibid.

25. See Tellmann, *Building an Outstanding Legal Team*, 90–127.

26. Blickstein Group, 'Law Department Operations Survey: 10 Year Anniversary Report, 2017', https://cdn2.hubspot.net/hubfs/470182/LDO%2010%20Year%20Anniversary%20Packet.pdf.

27. Deloitte Legal, 'How Generative AI is Changing Legal Department Functions', Deloitte, 6 September 2024, https://www.deloitte.com/

global/en/services/legal/perspectives/how-generative-ai-is-changing-legal-department-functions.html.

28. Blickstein Group, '17th Annual Law Department Operations (LDO) Survey Report', presented in collaboration with FTI Consulting, 2024, 5, https://www.blicksteingroup.com/law-department-operations-survey.

29. Kelsey Provow, 'Legal Operations: Navigating Growth, Challenges, and AI in Corporate Legal Departments', *Axiom*, June 2024, https://www.axiomlaw.com/blog/legal-operations-growth-challenges-ai-adoption.

30. Kevin Cohn, 'What is Legal Operations in 2025?', *Brightflag*, 17 July 2025, https://brightflag.com/resources/what-is-legal-operations/.

31. Gartner, 'Gartner Predicts Global Legal Technology Market Will Reach $50 Billion by 2027 as a Result of GenAI', 25 April 2024, https://www.gartner.com/en/newsroom/press-releases/2024-04-25-gartner-predicts-global-legal-technology-market-will-reach-50-billion-by-2027-as-a-result-of-genai.

32. Lauren Burnside, '5 Legal Operations Trends to Have on Your Radar in 2025', Mitratech, 11 January 2026, https://mitratech.com/resource-hub/blog/5-legal-operations-trends-to-have-on-your-radar-in-2025/.

33. Ibid.

34. PwC Canada, '5 Reasons Your People Will Make or Break Your Digital Transformation', *PwC Canada blog*, https://www.pwc.com/ca/en/services/consulting/transformation/front-office-transformation/five-reasons-your-people-will-make-or-break-your-digital-transformation.html.

35. See, for example, Streamline AI, 'Streamline AI: Your Legal Front Door & Intake Automation', https://www.streamline.ai/?utm_source.com; Aubrey Owens, Jr, 'Technologies Shaping Legal Operations'; Knovos, 'How AI is Revolutionizing Legal Operations in 2025', *Knovos*, 9 July 2025, https://www.knovos.com/blog/how-ai-is-revolutionizing-legal-operations-in-2025/; Tonkean, 'The Ultimate Legal Ops Technology Handbook', https://www.tonkean.com/resources/legal-ops-handbook; and Streamline AI, '5 Best AI Tools for Law in 2025', *Streamline AI blog*, 2025, https://www.streamline.ai/tips/best-ai-tools-law.

36. Metadata is data that provides information about other data. It summarises or describes the data in ways that make it easier to find and work with. For example, in documents, metadata may include

information about the author, creation date, and keywords associated with the content. Metadata facilitates the organising, discovering, and managing of data by providing context and relevant details needed to efficiently use the data. File Republic, 'How Does Metadata Help in Legal Cases? Find Out More with File Republic', *Legal Support Network*, 23 October 2024, https://www.legalsupportnetwork.co.uk/resource/how-does-metadata-help-in-legal-cases-find-out-more-with-file-republic/.

37. Legal playbooks are documents that outline strategies, best practices, and procedures for handling specific matters or scenarios that the legal department routinely encounters. Playbooks act as reference guides that provide structured approaches for how to act in and make decisions in those situations. They are frequently used in connection with contract management, regulatory affairs, data privacy and security management, litigation management, crisis management, record-keeping, risk management, and communication protocol management, to name a few. See Krishnapriya Agarwal, 'Prepping for Progress – Why Do You Need a Legal Playbook?', *SpotDraft blog*, 7 December 2023, https://www.spotdraft.com/blog/need-for-legal-playbook.

38. SpotDraft, 'Leveraging AI Agents for Scalable Support in Legal Ops', *SpotDraft blog*, 14 April 2025, https://www.spotdraft.com/blog/leveraging-ai-agents-for-scalable-support-in-legal-ops.

39. QuoteFancy, 'It's Tough to Make Predictions, Especially About the Future', attributed to Yogi Berra, https://quotefancy.com/quote/941544/Yogi-Berra-It-s-tough-to-make-predictions-especially-about-the-future.

40. Susskind, *Tomorrow's Lawyers*, 256.

41. William Gibson, quote on Goodreads, 'The Future is Already Here—It's Just Not Evenly Distributed', *Goodreads*, https://www.goodreads.com/quotes/681-the-future-is-already-here-it-s-just-not-evenly.

42. Unilever, 'Legal Leadership: Harnessing GenAI to Revolutionise our Legal Teams', https://www.unilever.com/news/news-search/2024/legal-leadership-harnessing-genai-to-revolutionise-our-legal-teams/.

43. Yasmin Lambert, 'In-house Legal Teams Start to See AI Gains', *Financial Times*, 13 September 2024, https://www.ft.com/content/285f1c78-6deb-47ac-b5d3-1b59b78e15c1.

44. Unilever, 'Legal Leadership'.

45. Lambert, 'In-house Legal Teams Start to See AI Gains'.

46. For a discussion of T-shaped professionals, see Tellmann, *Building an Outstanding Legal Team*, 50–51.

47. The following section draws on information provided by Workday, including written materials and conversations with Rich Sauer (Chief Legal Officer and Head of Corporate Affairs), Áine Lyons (Senior Vice President & Deputy General Counsel, Global Legal Services & Strategy), and Greg Bennett (Director of Legal Operations). The author would like to thank them and Workday for their generous time and valuable insights.

Part III   The Impact

1. Robert Wiblin and Keiran Harris, '#162 – Mustafa Suleyman on getting Washington and Silicon Valley to tame AI', *80000 Hours Podcast*, 1 September 2023, https://80000hours.org/podcast/episodes/mustafa-suleyman-getting-washington-and-silicon-valley-to-tame-ai/.

2. Valtech, 'Digital Transformation: Leading Through Tech Anxiety', 6, 13, and 14, https://go.valtech.com/rs/353-SAE-487/images/Valtech%20-%20Digital%20Transformation-Leading%20through%20tech%20anxiety.pdf.

3. Tim Bradshaw, 'Big Tech groups race to fund unprecedented $660bn AI spending spree', *Financial Times*, 9 February 2026, https://www.ft.com/content/d503afd5-1012-40f0-8f9d-620dcb39a9a2.

4. Rolfe Winkler, Nate Rattner, and Sebastian Herrera, 'Big Tech's $400 Billion AI Spending Spree Just Got Wall Street's Blessing', *The Wall Street Journal*, 31 July 2025, https://www.wsj.com/tech/ai/tech-ai-spending-company-valuations-7b92104b.

5. See Winkler, Rattner, and Herrera, 'Big Tech's $400 Billion AI Spending Spree' and Jesse Noffsinger, Maria Goodpaster, Mark Patel et al., 'The Cost of Compute: A $7 Trillion Race to Scale Data Centers', *McKinsey Quarterly*, 28 April 2025, https://www.mckinsey.com/industries/technology-media-and-telecommunications/our-insights/the-cost-of-compute-a-7-trillion-dollar-race-to-scale-data-centers.

6. Reuters, 'Nvidia Poised for Record $5 Trillion Market Valuation', 29 October 2025, https://www.reuters.com/business/nvidia-poised-

record-5-trillion-market-valuation-2025-10-29/; 'Microsoft (MSFT) – Market capitalization', *CompaniesMarketCap.com*, reporting a market cap of \$3.789 trillion as of August 2025, https://companiesmarketcap.com/microsoft/marketcap/; 'Apple Inc. (AAPL)—Market Capitalization: \$3.421 Trillion USD', *CompaniesMarketCap.com*, https://companiesmarketcap.com/apple/marketcap/; 'Amazon.com, Inc. (AMZN)—Market Cap \$2.431 Trillion USD as of August 2025', *CompaniesMarketCap.com*, https://companiesmarketcap.com/amazon/marketcap/; 'Alphabet (Google) (GOOG)—Market Cap \$2.442 Trillion USD', *CompaniesMarketCap.com*, reporting Alphabet's estimated market cap as of August 2025, https://companiesmarketcap.com/alphabet-google/marketcap/; and 'Meta Platforms (Facebook) (META)—Market Cap \$1.887 Trillion USD', *CompaniesMarketCap.com*, reporting a market cap of \$1.887 trillion as of August 2025, https://companiesmarketcap.com/meta-platforms/marketcap/.

7. 'Goldman Sachs Chief David Solomon Questions Start-Ups' AI Valuations', *Financial Times*, 16 January 2025, https://www.ft.com/content/4f20fbb9-a10f-4a08-9a13-efa1b55dd38a.

8. Christensen, *The Innovator's Dilemma*.

Chapter 8   The Traditional Law Firm Model

1. Clayton M. Christensen, Dina Wang, and Derek van Bever, 'Consulting on the Cusp of Disruption', *Harvard Business Review*, October 2013, https://hbr.org/2013/10/consulting-on-the-cusp-of-disruption.

2. Steven J. Harper, *The Lawyer Bubble: A Profession in Crisis* (New York: Basic Books, 2013), 77.

3. Ibid., 77.

4. John Oller, *White Shoe: How a New Breed of Wall Street Lawyers Changed Big Law* (New York: Penguin Press, 2019), 31.

5. Nancy B. Rapoport and Joseph R. Tiano, Jr, 'Fighting the Hypothetical: Why Law Firms Should Rethink the Billable Hour in the Generative AI Era', *Washington Journal of Law, Technology & Arts* 20, no. 2 (2025): 49, https://scholars.law.unlv.edu/facpub/1475.

6. Ibid., 49.

7. Velocity Work, 'Law Firm Compensation Models: A Strategic Guide to Partner Pay Structures', *Velocity Work blog*, 28 February 2025, https://

www.velocitywork.com/post/law-firm-compensation-models-partner-pay-structures.

8. See Joshua Yan, 'Out with the Old, in with the Alternative: A Critical Examination of How Lawyers Can Use Alternative Fee Arrangements to Satisfy Increasingly Powerful Clients', *Bond Law Review* 32, no. 1 (October 2020), https://www.researchgate.net/publication/352689133_Out_with_the_Old_in_with_the_Alternative_A_Critical_Examination_of_How_Lawyers_Can_Use_Alternative_Fee_Arrangements_to_Satisfy_Increasingly_Powerful_Clients.

9. Susan S. Fortney, 'The Billable Hours Derby: Empirical Data on the Problems and Pressure Points', *Fordham Urban Law Journal* 33, no. 1 (2005): 171, available via Hofstra or Texas A&M digital repositories.

10. Bruce MacEwen and Janet Stanton, 'Pricing AI-driven Legal Services: The Billable Hour is Dead, Long Live the Billable Hour', *Thomson Reuters Institute*, 10 September 2024, https://www.thomsonreuters.com/en-us/posts/legal/pricing-ai-driven-legal-services-billable-hour/.

11. 'What is Productivity?', Productivity Commission (Australia), explaining that productivity measures the efficiency of output produced per unit of input, such as labour, capital, or raw materials, https://www.pc.gov.au/what-is-productivity.

12. Harper, *Lawyer Bubble*, 78.

13. Ibid., 78.

14. Yale Law School Career Development Office, 'The Truth About the Billable Hour' (New Haven, CT: Yale Law School, July 2002), 3, https://law.yale.edu/sites/default/files/area/department/cdo/document/billable_hour.pdf.

15. Patrick R. Krill, Ryan Johnson, and Linda Albert, 'The Prevalence of Substance Use and Other Mental Health Concerns Among American Attorneys', *Journal of Addiction Medicine* 10, no. 1 (2016): 46–54, https://www.ncbi.nlm.nih.gov/pmc/articles/PMC4736291/.

16. Charles Herd, 'Attorney Wellness and Mental Health: A Seldom-Discussed Crisis of the Legal Profession', *Herd Law Firm blog*, 24 September 2024, https://herdlawfirm.com/firm-update/attorney-wellness-and-mental-health-a-seldom-discussed-crisis-of-the-legal-profession/.

17. David Brown, 'Billable Hours Endure as Law Firms Expand Offerings', *Best Law Firms Insights*, 4 November 2024, https://www.bestlawfirms.com/articles/billable-hours-endure-law-firms-expand-offerings/6208.

18. Ibid.

19. Bloomberg Law, 'Legal 2021 Operations: Topline Results from Legal Operations and Tech Survey', *Bloomberg Law*, March 2021, https://aboutblaw.com/XmZ?utm_source=ANT&utm_medium=ANP.

20. Robert J. Couture, 'The Impact of Artificial Intelligence on Law Firms' Business Models', *Harvard Law School Center on the Legal Profession*, 24 February 2025, https://clp.law.harvard.edu/knowledge-hub/insights/the-impact-of-artificial-intelligence-on-law-law-firms-business-models/.

21. Harper, *Lawyer Bubble*, 171.

22. Bloomberg Law, 'Legal 2021 Operations'.

23. Onit, 'The Death of the Billable Hour—Long Forecast, But Refusing to Go Away', *Onit blog*, 30 July 2023, https://www.onit.com/blog/billable-hour-and-alternatives/.

24. Debra Cassens Weiss, 'This Law Firm is Ranked No. 1 After Posting $8.8 B in Gross Revenue; Which Other Firms are Category Leaders?', *ABA Journal*, 16 April 2025, https://www.abajournal.com/news/article/this-law-firm-is-ranked-no-1-after-posting-88b-in-gross-revenue-which-other-firms-are-category-leaders and Marcus Belanger, 'Law Firm Rates in 2024: The Bull, Bear & Base Case for Rates and What It Means for Realization', *Thomson Reuters*, 17 October 2024, https://www.thomsonreuters.com/en-us/posts/legal/law-firm-rates-bull-bear-base-case.

25. David Thomas and Mike Scarcella, 'More Lawyers Join the $3,000-an-Hour Club, as Other Firms Close In', *Reuters*, 27 February 2025, https://www.reuters.com/legal/legalindustry/3000-an-hour-lawyer-isnt-unicorn-anymore-2025-02-27/.

26. Joy A. Long, 'The State of the Legal Industry: Law Firms See Record-Breaking Performance and Changing Models', *ORBA*, 21 February 2025, https://www.orba.com/the-state-of-the-legal-industry-law-firms-see-record-breaking-performance-and-changing-models/.

27. PwC UK, 'Law Firm Performance Surpasses Expectations with Continued Growth Amidst Global Market Volatility', *PwC Law Firms' Survey 2024*, 21 October 2024, https://www.pwc.co.uk/press-room/press-releases/research-commentary/2024/law-firm-performance-surpasses-expectations-with-continued-growt.html.

28. Axiom Law, 'View from the Top: GCs' 2024 Outlook on Legal Budgets, Talent, and Innovation', 29 March 2024.

29. Ibid., 6, 9.
30. Ibid., 9, 11.
31. Ibid., 9.
32. Heidi K. Gardner, 'Collaboration in Law Firms', *Harvard Law School Center on the Legal Profession*, published in the *Knowledge Hub* section on 'Teamwork and Collaboration', https://clp.law.harvard.edu/knowledge-hub/magazine/issues/teamwork-and-collaboration/collaboration-in-law-firms/.
33. Ibid.
34. Chip Cutter, 'AI is Coming for the Consultants. Inside McKinsey, "This is Existential"', *The Wall Street Journal*, 2 August 2025, citing the *Future of Everything* newsletter version, https://www.wsj.com/tech/ai/mckinsey-consulting-firms-ai-strategy-89bf1be.
35. Ibid.
36. Clayton M. Christensen et al., 'Consulting on the Cusp of Disruption'.
37. Ibid.
38. Cutter, 'AI is Coming for the Consultants'.
39. Susskind, *Tomorrow's Lawyers*, 177.
40. Jonathan T. Molot, 'What's Wrong with Law Firms? A Corporate Finance Solution to Law Firm Short-Termism', *Southern California Law Review* 88, no. 1 (2014): 1–43, 4, https://southerncalifornialawreview.com/wp-content/uploads/2018/01/88_1.pdf.
41. Ibid., 6.
42. Ibid., 6.
43. John Morley, 'Why Law Firms Collapse', *The Practice Magazine*, March/April 2017, Harvard Law School Center on the Legal Profession, https://clp.law.harvard.edu/knowledge-hub/magazine/issues/why-law-firms-collapse/why-law-firms-collapse/.
44. Ibid.
45. Zulon Begum and Holly Buick, 'The Legal and Cultural Challenges of Lateral Hiring by US Firms in London', *Law.com (International Edition)*, 17 February 2020, https://www.law.com/international-edition/2020/02/17/the-legal-and-cultural-challenges-of-lateral-hiring-by-us-firms-in-london/.
46. Ibid.
47. Leann Pickard, 'Building Bridges: Fostering Collaboration Between Law Firm Departments', *JurisDigital Research*, last updated 22 July 2024,

https://jurisdigital.com/research/collaboration-between-law-firm-departments/#:~:text=Despite%20the%20best%20intentions%2C%20 fostering,operations%2C%20further%20impeding%20smooth%20 collaboration.

48. Stephen Embry, 'Law Firm Leadership: How to Knock Down Silos', *TechLaw Crossroads*, 3 November 2020, https://www.techlawcrossroads. com/2020/11/law-firm-leadership-how-to-knock-down-silos/.

49. Sarah Lee, 'Mastering Change in Law Firms', *Number Analytics blog*, 22 June 2025, https://www.numberanalytics.com/blog/mastering-change-in-law-firms#:~:text=Conservative%20culture:%20Law%20 firms%20often,of%20the%20new%20technology.%22%201.

50. Kalliopi Michalakopoulou, David Bamford, Iain Reid et al., 'Barriers and Opportunities to Innovation for Legal Service Firms: A Thematic Analysis-Based Contextualization', *Production Planning & Control* 34, no. 7 (2023): 604–22, 610, https://doi.org/10.1080/09537287.2 021.1946329.

51. Abraham C. Reich and Hala Zawil, 'The Metaverse for the Risk-Averse: Legal Ethics in the Virtual World, Part I', *Fox Rothschild LLP*, 20 October 2022, https://www.foxrothschild.com/publications/the-metaverse-for-the-risk-averse-legal-ethics-in-the-virtual-world-part-i.

52. Susskind, *Tomorrow's Lawyers*, 177.

53. Michalakopoulou et al., 'Barriers and Opportunities to Innovation', 611.

54. American Bar Association, *Model Rules of Professional Conduct*, Rule 1.1, cmt. 8, https://www.americanbar.org/groups/professional_ responsibility/publications/model_rules_of_professional_conduct/ rule_1_1_competence/comment_on_rule_1_1/. While a similar direct mandate does not exist in England and Wales, there are implicit references to the need to stay ahead of technology in the service of clients. Principle 7 of the SRA Standards and Regulations requires solicitors to act in the best interests of their clients. Solicitors Regulation Authority, *Principles*, SRA Standards and Regulations, last updated 11 April 2025, https://www.sra. org.uk/solicitors/standards-regulations/principles/. SRA guidance on technology and legal services notes that 'Technology can help firms complete work more quickly and accurately. This is particularly the case with AI applications that can automate routine process work. Clients value quick and predictable conclusions, and the most common cause for complaints to the Legal Ombudsman is delays. The combination of

rapid processing of routine tasks with greater engagement is therefore likely to make clients more satisfied'. The guidance goes on to discuss the need to maintain cyber security and safe practices in the use of technology. Solicitors Regulation Authority, *Technology and Legal Services*, SRA Research and Publications, 11 December 2018, https://www.sra.org.uk/sra/research-publications/technology-legal-services/.

55. R. Mithu Dey and Lesia Quamina, 'Surveying a Shifting Landscape', *The CPA Journal*, 24 July 2024, https://www.cpajournal.com/2024/07/24/surveying-a-shifting-landscape/ and Nicola Stewart, 'The Big 4's Revenue: Advisory is the New Audit', *Projectworks*, https://www.projectworks.com/blog/2024-the-big-4s-revenue#:~:text=the%20Big%204,Advisory%20over%20audit:%20Combined%20revenue%20of%20the,4%20by%20audit%20and%20advisory&text=In%202023%2C%20Deloitte%2C%20PwC%2C,and%20acquisitions%2C%20and%20HR%20consulting.

56. Thompson Hine LLP, 'Minding the Gaps: Are You Getting What You Need from Outside Counsel? Third Innovation Report' (Cincinnati, OH: Thompson Hine, 2023), 14, https://admin.thompsonhine.com/wp-content/uploads/2023/06/MindingTheGaps_2023.pdf.

57. Ibid., 14.

Chapter 9   Nothing Changes—Until It Suddenly Does

1. Ernest Hemingway, *The Sun Also Rises* (London: Tech Tok Ltd, 2023), Kindle edition, 130.

2. Christensen, *The Innovator's Dilemma*.

3. Anurag Bana, '"Times are a-Changin"': Disruptive Innovation and the Legal Profession', *Manupatra Intellectual Property Reports* (MIPR), July 2017, 145, https://docs.manupatra.in/newsline/articles/Upload/4DAAB6C8-7259-4BF0-9A18-84965B12AFB0.pdf.

4. Ibid., 145.

5. Christensen et al., 'Consulting on the Cusp of Disruption'.

6. Nick Bilton, 'The End of an Era in Mobile', *Bits (New York Times blog)*, 3 September 2013, https://archive.nytimes.com/bits.blogs.nytimes.com/2013/09/03/the-end-of-an-era-in-mobile.

7. Barry Ritholtz, 'Can Anyone Catch Nokia?', *The Big Picture blog*, 26 October 2022, https://ritholtz.com/2022/10/can-anyone-catch-nokia/.

8. Bilton, 'The End of an Era in Mobile'.

9. Lisa Duke and Julian Birkinshaw, 'The Rise and Fall of Nokia', *London Business School Case Study*, 1 September 2011, 6.

10. Ibid., 6 and SlideUpLift, 'The Tragic Downfall of Nokia: From a Giant to a Shadow [Case Study]', *Medium*, 28 May 2024, https://slideuplifts.medium.com/the-tragic-downfall-of-nokia-from-a-giant-to-a-shadow-case-study-98c83e8875bf.

11. Duke and Birkinshaw, 'The Rise and Fall of Nokia', 6.

12. Ibid., 6 and Haydn Shaughnessy, 'Apple's Rise and Nokia's Fall Highlight Platform Strategy Essentials', *Forbes*, 8 March 2013, https://www.forbes.com/sites/haydnshaughnessy/2013/03/08/apples-rise-and-nokias-fall-highlight-platform-strategy-essentials/.

13. Duke and Birkinshaw, 'The Rise and Fall of Nokia', 7.

14. Ibid., 7.

15. SlideUpLift, 'The Tragic Downfall of Nokia'.

16. Duke and Birkinshaw, 'The Rise and Fall of Nokia', 7.

17. Quy Huy and Timo Vuori, 'Who Killed Nokia? Nokia Did', *INSEAD Knowledge*, 22 September 2015, https://knowledge.insead.edu/strategy/who-killed-nokia-nokia-did.

18. Ibid.

19. Ibid.

20. Bana, 'Times are a-Changin', 143; David G. Billings, 'Disruptive Innovation Within the Legal Services Ecosystem', *International Journal of Applied Management & Technology* 19, no. 1 (Winter 2020): 27, https://scholarworks.waldenu.edu/cgi/viewcontent.cgi?article=1356&context=ijamt.

21. Susskind, *Tomorrow's Lawyers*, 43–49.

22. Ibid., 43–49.

23. Tellmann, *Building an Outstanding Legal Team*, 43.

24. Billings, 'Disruptive Innovation', 31.

25. Thompson Hine, 'Minding the Gaps', 14. Nearly half of clients said they were superior in that respect, while only 12% believed their firms were.

26. Legal.io, 'Law Firms Trail Legal Departments in AI Adoption, Raising Business Risk', *Legal.io*, 10 June 2025, https://www.legal.io/articles/5686548/Law-Firms-Trail-Legal-Departments-in-AI-Adoption-Raising-Business-Risk?utm.

27. Thomson Reuters Institute, 'Alternative Legal Services Providers 2025', January 2025, https://www.thomsonreuters.com/en-us/posts/wp-content/uploads/sites/20/2025/01/ALSP-Report-2025.pdf.

28. Grand View Research, 'Alternative Legal Service Providers Market Size, Share & Trends Analysis Report, 2025–2033', June 2025, https://www.grandviewresearch.com/industry-analysis/alternative-legal-services-providers-market-report.

29. Thomson Reuters Institute, 'Alternative Legal Services Providers 2025'.

30. Ibid.

31. Thompson Hine, 'Minding the Gaps', 10.

32. Christensen et al., 'Consulting on the Cusp of Disruption'.

33. Ibid.

34. Scott D. Anthony, 'Kodak's Downfall Wasn't About Technology', *Harvard Business Review*, 15 July 2016, https://hbr.org/2016/07/kodaks-downfall-wasnt-about-technology.

35. Britannica, 'Eastman Kodak Company', *Britannica*, 15 December 2025, https://www.britannica.com/money/Eastman-Kodak-Company.

36. Brenda Holben, 'Brand Management: The Last Kodak Moment?', *Branding Strategy Insider*, 6 December 2011, https://brandingstrategyinsider.com/brand-management-the-last-kodak-moment/.

37. Helen Gebremeskel Tesfaye and Thi Hong Nhung Nguyen, *Incumbent Firms and Response to Disruptive Innovation through Value Network Management: Lessons from Eastman Kodak's Failure in the Digital Era* (MSc thesis, Linköping University, 2012), 35, https://www.diva-portal.org/smash/get/diva2%3A556607/fulltext01.pdf.

38. Anthony, 'Kodak's Downfall'.

39. Ibid.

40. Ibid.

41. David Gann, 'Kodak Invented the Digital Camera—Then Killed It. Why Innovation Often Fails', *World Economic Forum*, 23 June 2016, https://www.weforum.org/stories/2016/06/leading-innovation-through-the-chicanes.

42. Anthony, 'Kodak's Downfall'.

43. McGrath, *Seeing Around Corners*, 20.

44. Ibid., 26.

45. Elisabet Lagerstedt, 'Inflection Points: A Strategic Imperative for Future-Fit Organizations', *Future Navigators blog*, 11 February 2025, https://www.future-navigators.com/blog/104141-inflection-points-a-strategic-imperative.

46. Rita McGrath, *Seeing Around Corners*, 92, 19.

47. Ibid., 18–19.

48. Ibid., 92.

49. Ibid., 134.

50. Ibid., 63.

51. Ibid., 67.

52. Thomson Reuters, 'How Law Firms Ended Up with the Billable Hour Model', *Thomson Reuters*, 11 February 2025, https://www.thomsonreuters.com/en-us/posts/legal/billable-hour-history/.

53. McGrath, *Seeing Around Corners*, 92.

54. Katherine Bryant, 'State of In-House 2025: Are Law Firms Delivering?', *Juro blog*, 31 March 2025, juro.com/general-counsel/state-of-in-house-2025.

55. McGrath, *Seeing Around Corners*, 134.

56. BigHand, 'Emerging Trends in Law Firm Talent Management', *BigHand*, October 2024, https://www.bighand.com/en-us/resources/whitepapers/emerging-trends-in-law-firm-talent-mgmt/.

57. BigHand, 'Navigating the Million Dollar Problem: Resource Management for Profitability, Client and Talent Retention', *Resource Management Report, BigHand*, 2025, 6, https://www.issuu.com/bighandmedia/docs/fy_26_bighand_rm_report_-_navigating_the_million_d/3.

58. Thomson Reuters Institute, 'Alternative Legal Services Providers 2025', 10.

59. Ibid., 10.

60. Ibid.

61. BigHand, 'Navigating the Million Dollar Problem', 12.

62. Ibid., 6.

63. Ibid., 14.

64. Debra Cassens Weiss, 'BigLaw Associates at Higher Risk of Burnout Than Colleagues, Survey Says', *ABA Journal*, 2 November 2023, https://www.abajournal.com/news/article/biglaw-associates-at-higher-risk-of-burnout-than-colleagues-survey-says.

65. Ibid.

66. BigHand, 'Navigating the Million Dollar Problem', 12.

67. Ibid., 15.

68. Robert Freedman, 'By Looking Elsewhere, Companies Send Big Law a Message', *Legal Dive*, 7 October 2024, https://www.legaldive.com/news/BigHand-survey-law-firm-attrition-corporate-clients-lower-spend-DEI/729111/.

69. BigHand, 'Navigating the Million Dollar Problem', 15.

70. Roy Strom, 'How Big Law Partner Pay Outran Associate Salaries in a Flash', *Bloomberg Law*, 24 April 2025, https://news.bloomberglaw.com/business-and-practice/how-big-law-partner-pay-outran-associate-salaries-in-a-flash.

71. Clayton Christensen Institute, 'Jobs to be Done Theory', https://www.christenseninstitute.org/theory/jobs-to-be-done/.

72. Hubble, 'An Overview of Jobs-to-be-Done', *Hubble blog (UX Research Foundations)*, UseHubble, https://www.usehubble.io/blog/jobs-to-be-done-framework#:~:text=At%20its%20core%2C%20the%20Jobs,and%2C%20more%20importantly%2C%20why.

73. For a good discussion of transportation as an example of this, see McGrath, *Seeing Around Corners*, 122–127.

74. SIVO, 'What Are "Circumstances" in JTBD? | SIVO Insights', https://mrx.sivoinsights.com/blog/understanding-circumstances-in-jobs-to-be-done-jtbd. See also Christensen Institute, 'Jobs to be Done Theory'.

75. McGrath, *Seeing Around Corners*, 121.

76. Ibid., 122.

77. Ray Worthy Campbell, 'The End of Law Schools: Legal Education in the Era of Legal Service Businesses', *Mississippi Law Journal*, forthcoming; Peking University School of Transnational Law Research Paper No. 15-7 (26 November 2014), 45, https://papers.ssrn.com/sol3/papers.cfm?abstract_id=2530051.

78. Goodreads, 'Compound Interest is the Eighth Wonder of the World', *Goodreads*, https://www.goodreads.com/quotes/76863-compound-interest-is-the-eighth-wonder-of-the-world-he.

79. Thomas M., 'Five Financial Lessons That Can Backfire #2: A Mountain of Rice', *Richland Library blog*, 9 April 2022, https://

www.richlandlibrary.com/blog/2022-04-09/five-financial-lessons-can-backfire-2-mountain-rice.

80. David Patterson, 'Moore's Law B. 1965, D. 2015', *ASPIRE Lab, UC Berkeley*, 10 May 2015, https://aspire.eecs.berkeley.edu/2015/05/moores-law-b-1965-d-2015/.

81. Intel, '60 Years of the Transistor: Timeline of Moore's Law / Intel', *Intel Timeline: Moore's Law*, PDF, https://leria-info.univ-angers.fr/~jeanmichel.richer/ens/l3info/ao/img/timeline_moorelaw.pdf.

82. Ibid.

83. Apple, 'Apple Unveils M1 Ultra, the World's Most Powerful Chip for a Personal Computer', *Apple Newsroom*, 8 March 2022, https://www.apple.com/newsroom/2022/03/apple-unveils-m1-ultra-the-worlds-most-powerful-chip-for-a-personal-computer/.

84. Damanpreet Kaur Vohra, 'NVIDIA Blackwell GPUs: Architecture, Features, Specs', NexGen Cloud, 1 October 2024, https://www.nexgencloud.com/blog/performance-benchmarks/nvidia-blackwell-gpus-architecture-features-specs#:~:text=The%20Blackwell%20GPU%20is%20the,and%20a%20seamless%20GPU%20experience.

85. Blake Crosley, 'NVIDIA Rubin Enters Full Production: The 336 Billion Transistor GPU Reshaping AI Infrastructure', Introl, 8 January 2026, https://introl.com/blog/nvidia-rubin-full-production-ces-2026-ai-infrastructure#:~:text=NVIDIA%20executed%20an%20aggressive%2018,represents%20Rubin's%20most%20significant%20advancement.

86. Visual Capitalist, 'Visualizing the Trillion-Fold Increase in Computing Power', https://www.visualcapitalist.com/visualizing-trillion-fold-increase-computing-power/.

87. Jeremy Thomas, 'El Capitan Retains Title as World's Fastest Supercomputer in Latest Top 500', *Lawrence Livermore National Laboratory*, 17 November 2025, https://www.llnl.gov/article/53596/el-capitan-retains-title-worlds-fastest-supercomputer-latest-top500-list.

88. ECMWF, 'Supercomputers: Decoding the Science', https://stories.ecmwf.int/supercomputers/index.html#:~:text=Flop,ExaFlops%20%E2%80%93%20a%20billion%20billion%20flops.

89. Edouard Mathieu, 'The Price of Computer Storage Has Fallen Exponentially Since the 1950s', *Our World in Data*, 21 May 2024, https://ourworldindata.org/data-insights/the-price-of-computer-storage-has-fallen-exponentially-since-the-1950s#:~:text=The%20price%20of%20computer%20storage,(That's%20in%20today's%20prices.

90. Graham Kendall, 'Your Mobile Phone vs. Apollo 11's Guidance Computer', *RealClearScience*, 2 July 2019, https://www.realclearscience.com/articles/2019/07/02/your_mobile_phone_vs_apollo_11s_guidance_computer_111026.html.

91. See Madeline Ricchiuto, 'Is Moore's Law Dead? We Spoke to Intel, AMD, Nvidia, and Qualcomm, and Both Sides of the Debate Agree: The Only Constant is Progress', *Laptop Mag*, 5 February 2025, https://www.laptopmag.com/laptops/cpu-gpu-interview-highlights-from-intel-amd-qualcomm.

92. ASML, 'Moore's Law', *All About Microchips*, https://www.asml.com/technology/all-about-microchips/moores-law.

93. Rishika Patel, 'GPU – CPU – NPU: Understanding the Differences and Their Strategic Importance', *CIO Influence*, 18 September 2024, https://cioinfluence.com/hardware/gpu-cpu-npu-understanding-the-differences-and-their-strategic-importance/. See also Ricchiuto, 'CPU, GPU Interview Highlights'.

- *CPUs (Central Processing Units)* are components of a computer system that control the interpretation and execution of instructions. CPUs are designed for general-purpose computing, with a few powerful cores optimised for sequential task execution.

- *GPUs (Graphics Processing Units)* are designed to accelerate the rendering of images and videos on a device. Initially developed for video games and computer-aided design applications, they have evolved to manage a variety of parallel processing tasks and are now a critical component of modern computing.

- *NPUs (Neural Processing Units)* are specialised hardware components designed to accelerate the execution of AI and machine learning algorithm tasks.

Patel, 'GPU – CPU – NPU'.

Chapter 10 Alternative Legal Service Providers

1. Joseph A. Schumpeter, 'Creative Destruction is the Essential Fact About Capitalism', *AZQuotes*, https://www.azquotes.com/quote/928596.

2. Jordan Furlong, 'An Incomplete Inventory of NewLaw', *Law21 blog*, 13 May 2014, https://www.law21.ca/2014/05/incomplete-inventory-newlaw/.

3. Tellmann, *Building an Outstanding Legal Team*, 166.

4. Ibid., 162–166.

5. Ibid., 165.

6. Ibid., 165.

7. Thomson Reuters, 'Alternative Legal Services Providers 2025', 5.

8. Ibid., 10, 13.

9. David B. Wilkins and María J. Esteban Ferrer, 'Taking the "Alternative" Out of Alternative Legal Service Providers: Remapping the Corporate Legal Ecosystem in the Age of Integrated Solutions', in *New Suits: Appetite for Disruption in the Legal World*, ed. Michele DeStefano and Guenther Dobrauz-Saldapenna, Harvard Law School Center on the Legal Profession Research Paper No. 2019-1 (2019), 3, https://ssrn.com/abstract=3379056.

10. Virginia State Bar, 'The Future of Law: Report 2025' (Richmond, VA: Virginia State Bar, 2025), 28, https://vsb.org/common/Uploaded%20files/docs/pub-future-law-report-2025.pdf.

11. Srini Raghavan, 'Transforming Legal Workflows with AI Using Copilot for Microsoft 365', *LexisNexis Thought Leadership*, 13 September 2024, https://www.lexisnexis.com/community/insights/legal/b/thought-leadership/posts/transforming-legal-workflows-with-ai-using-copilot-for-microsoft-365.

12. Winston Weinberg and Gabe Pereyra, 'Harvey Launches AI-Powered Professional Services Platform on Microsoft Azure', *Harvey blog*, 19 March 2024, https://www.harvey.ai/blog/harvey-launches-ai-powered-professional-services-platform-on-microsoft-azure?utm_.

13. Winston Weinberg and Gabe Pereyra, 'Announcing Harvey Integrations with Microsoft', *Harvey blog*, 5 December 2024, https://www.harvey.ai/blog/announcing-harvey-integrations-with-microsoft?utm_=.

14. Aksh Garg and Megan Ma, 'Opportunities and Challenges in Legal AI' (Stanford Law School, January 2025), 5, https://law.stanford.edu/wp-content/uploads/2025/01/Legal-AI-Opportunities-and-Challenges-Whitepaper.pdf.

15. See, for example, 'An Antimonopoly Approach to Governing Artificial Intelligence', *Yale Law & Policy Review*, https://yalelawandpolicy.org/antimonopoly-approach-governing-artificial-intelligence and University of Arizona Library, 'What is a Large Language Model (LLM)?', https://ask.library.arizona.edu/faq/407985.

16. While sometimes used interchangeably, LLMs are, in fact, a subset of foundation models, which also include multimodal models and, increasingly, vision-based foundation models, as well as domain-specific models for specialised applications in fields such as healthcare, finance, or legal services. For a discussion of the similarities and differences between foundation models more broadly, and LLMs in particular, see, for example, Sean Kalaycioglu, Bob Liu, Colin Hong, and Haipeng Xie, 'AI-Powered Legal Intelligence System Architecture: A Comprehensive Framework for Automated Legal Consultation and Analysis', August 2025, https://arxiv.org/abs/2508.17499; Shenghao Xie, Wenqiang Zu, Mingyang Zhao et al., 'A Survey from the Autoregression Perspective: Towards Unifying Understanding and Generation in the Era of Vision Foundation Models', October 2024, https://arxiv.org/html/2410.22217v1; 'Foundation Models—Definition, Use Cases, and Examples', *Iguazio Glossary*, https://www.iguazio.com/glossary/foundation-models/; and 'Foundational Model vs LLM: Understanding the Differences', *Medium*, Novita.ai, https://medium.com/@marketing_novita.ai/foundational-model-vs-llm-understanding-the-differences-820a4428dbc3.

17. See, for example, 'An Antimonopoly Approach to Governing Artificial Intelligence', *Yale Law & Policy Review*; University of Arizona Library, 'What is a Large Language Model (LLM)?'; and IMD, 'Large Language Models (LLMs)', *Digital Transformation blog*, https://www.imd.org/blog/digital-transformation/large-language-models-llms/.

18. David Wakeling, 'A&O Shearman: Transforming Legal Services Through AI Innovation', *Harvey*, https://www.harvey.ai/customers/a-and-o-shearman.

19. Vals AI, 'Vals Legal AI Report (VLAIR)', *Vals AI & Legaltech Hub*, February 2025, https://www.vals.ai/vlair.

20. Ibid.

21. RootsAnalysis, 'Legal AI Software Market Overview', https://www.rootsanalysis.com/legal-ai-software-market.

22. Robert Ambrogi, 'Legal AI Tools Show Promise in First-of-its-Kind Benchmark Study, with Harvey and CoCounsel Leading the Pack', *LawNext*, 28 February 2025, https://www.lawnext.com/2025/02/legal-ai-tools-show-promise-in-first-of-its-kind-benchmark-study-with-harvey-and-cocounsel-leading-the-pack.html.

23. Wilkins and Esteban Ferrer, 'Taking the "Alternative" Out', 13.

24. American Bar Association, 'Model Rules of Professional Conduct, Rule 5.4: Professional Independence of a Lawyer', https://www.americanbar.org/groups/professional_responsibility/publications/model_rules_of_professional_conduct/rule_5_4_professional_independence_of_a_lawyer/. See also Daniel R. Fischel, 'Lawyers and Confidentiality', *University of Chicago Law Review* 65, no. 1 (1998): 1–33.

25. David B. Wilkins and María José Esteban, 'The Integration of Law into Global Business Solutions: The Rise, Transformation, and Potential Future of the Big Four Accountancy Networks in the Global Legal Services Market', *Law & Social Inquiry* 43, no. 3 (Summer 2018): 982, https://papers.ssrn.com/sol3/papers.cfm?abstract_id=3013154.

26. Ibid., 982.

27. Bryce Welker, 'Exploring the Big Four Accounting Firms: What You Need to Know', *Miami Herald*, https://www.miamiherald.com/careers-education/big-four-accounting-firms/.

28. Wilkins and Esteban Ferrer, 'Taking the "Alternative" Out', 13, 15–16.

29. 'KPMG LLP Launches KPMG Law US, The First Big Four Law Firm Serving the US Market', *KPMG*, 27 February 2025, https://kpmg.com/us/en/media/news/kpmg-llp-launches-kpmg-law-us.html. See also Samantha Whitsel, 'Accounting for Change: KPMG Law and the Global Rise of ABS Models', *International & Comparative Law Review*, 29 March 2025, https://international-and-comparative-law-review.law.miami.edu/accounting-for-change-kpmg-law-and-the-global-rise-of-abs-models/.

30. 'How The Big Four Are Using Technology in Legal Services to Reshape the Industry', *Today's Managing Partner*, 19 February 2025,

https://todaysmanagingpartner.com/how-the-big-four-are-using-technology-in-legal-services-to-reshape-the-industry/.

31. 'Big Four Accounting Firms Looking to Grab a Bigger Slice of the Legal Services Pie', *Consulting.us*, 26 February 2025, https://www.consulting.us/news/11457/big-four-accounting-firms-looking-to-grab-a-bigger-slice-of-the-legal-services-pie.

32. Consulting.us, 'Big Four Accounting Firms'.

33. LexisNexis, 'Are the Big Four Reshaping the Future of Legal Services?', 2025, quoting Emily Foges, Lead Partner for Legal Managed Services at Deloitte, 'the vision for Deloitte Legal has always been that you bring together high-quality legal advice with legal management consulting, legal managed services and legal technology. This way you can provide a complete end-to-end service to the client and achieve the outcomes they are looking for, not just give them advice on those outcomes', https://www.lexisnexis.co.uk/research-and-reports/big-4-report.html#read-full-report.

34. LexisNexis, 'Are the Big Four Reshaping the Future of Legal Services?'.

35. LexisNexis, 'Are the Big Four Reshaping the Future of Legal Services?', quoting Bea Seravello, 'the Big Four put a lot of investment around researching how they can take existing technologies that don't even relate to the practice of law, but can provide a client solution'.

36. See PwC Legal Germany, 'About Us', *PwC Legal*, https://legal.pwc.de/en/about-us; Deloitte Legal, 'Careers', *Deloitte Legal Germany*, https://www.deloittelegal.de/en/careers.html; 'New Player: EY Law Debuts in Portugal', *Iberian Lawyer*, 18 November 2024, https://iberianlawyer.com/new-player-ey-law-debuts-in-portugal; and 'International Business', *KPMG Law Germany*, https://kpmg-law.de/en/international-business.

37. Charlie Moloney, 'Big Four Increasing Share of Legal Market', *Law Gazette*, 16 February 2023, https://www.lawgazette.co.uk/practice/big-four-increasing-share-of-legal-market/5115164.article.

38. Will Kenton, 'The Big 4 Accounting Firms: An Overview', *Investopedia*, updated 26 August 2025, https://www.investopedia.com/terms/b/bigfour.asp.

39. See 'Big 4 Audit Clients | Deloitte, PwC, EY, & KPMG', *Management Consulted*, updated 15 July 2025, https://managementconsulted.com/big-4-audit-clients/ (noting that the Big Four audit 100% of the Fortune 500 and FTSE 100, and nearly 90% of US Large Accelerated

Filers) and Financial Reporting Council, 'Big Four Increase Their Market Share of UK Audit', *FRC News and Events*, 28 October 2019, https://www.frc.org.uk/news-and-events/news/2019/10/big-four-increase-their-market-share-of-uk-audit/.

40. Mark A. Cohen, 'Why the Big Four Should Adopt a Corporate Structure', *Forbes*, 5 July 2022, https://www.forbes.com/sites/markcohen1/2022/07/05/why-the-big-four-should-adopt-a-corporate-structure/.

41. Ibid.

42. Maria Ward-Brennan, 'Big Four: The Slow Death of KPMG, EY, PwC and Deloitte's Legal Dream', *City A.M.*, 25 March 2025, quoting Nick Woolf, 'however big their legal practice, they are always going to pale into insignificance compared to other parts of the firm', https://www.cityam.com/big-four-the-slow-death-of-their-legal-dream/.

43. 'Linda Evangelista', *Oxford Reference* (Oxford: Oxford University Press), https://www.oxfordreference.com/display/10.1093/acref/9780191826719.001.0001/q-oro-ed4-00016802, citing *Vogue*, October 1990.

44. See, for example, Regulation (EU) No. 537/2014 of the European Parliament and of the Council of 16 April 2014 on specific requirements regarding statutory audit of public-interest entities, 2014 O.J. (L 158) 77 and Sarbanes-Oxley Act of 2002, Pub. L. No. 107-204, 116 Stat. 745 (2002).

45. Christopher Clark, director at Definitum Search, as quoted in Ward-Brennan, 'Big Four'.

46. See, for example, American Bar Association, *Model Rules of Professional Conduct* r. 5.4 (Am. Bar Ass'n 2020). On relaxation of rules, see, for example, Louise L. Hill, 'Alternative Business Structures for Lawyers and Law Firms: A View from the Global Legal Services Market', *Oregon Review of International Law* 18 (2020): 135–84, https://scholarsbank.uoregon.edu/server/api/core/bitstreams/3769ff28-e8a9-439d-88aa-cb46ee33e29f/content; 'Enter the Sandbox', *The Practice Magazine*, Harvard Law School Center on the Legal Profession, January/February 2021, https://clp.law.harvard.edu/knowledge-hub/magazine/issues/perspectives-on-legal-regulation/enter-the-sandbox/; and *WP-11: Alternative Business Structures and Multi-Disciplinary Practices*, Legal Framework Review,

New Zealand, 2023, https://legalframeworkreview.org.nz/wp-content/uploads/2023/03/WP-11-Alternative-Business-Structures-and-Multi-Disciplinary-Practices-final.pdf.

47. *Financial Times*, 'Generative AI's Challenge to Legal Sector's Alternative Providers', 6 June 2024, https://www.ft.com/content/dca849c0-09c5-4f73-9950-2c8bbd9d5759.

48. Ibid.

49. Ibid.

50. Ibid.

Part IV   What Might Emerge?

1. Robert Louis Stevenson, 'Quotes – Page 4', *Goodreads*, https://www.goodreads.com/author/quotes/854076.Robert_Louis_Stevenson?page=4.

Chapter 11   New Law Firm Models

1. John Pierpont Morgan (attributed), 'The first step towards getting somewhere is to decide you're not going to stay where you are', quotation commonly attributed to Morgan, *Goodreads*, https://www.goodreads.com/quotes/8868097-the-first-step-towards-getting-somewhere-is-to-decide-you-re.

2. D. Daniel Sokol, 'Globalization of Law Firms: A Survey of the Literature and a Research Agenda for Further Study', *Indiana Journal of Global Legal Studies* 14, no. 1 (2007): 5.

3. Ibid., 5.

4. Tyler J. Replogle, 'The Business of Law: Evolution of the Legal Services Market', *Michigan Business & Entrepreneurial Law Review* 6, no. 2 (2017): 295, https://repository.law.umich.edu/mbelr/vol6/iss2/5.

5. See Thomson Reuters, 'Alternative Legal Services Providers 2025', 10–14.

6. 'Victorian London – Populations – Census 1861', *Victorian London*, https://www.victorianlondon.org/population/census1861.htm.

7. Simon Crompton, 'The (61) Bespoke Tailors I Have Known (Part 1: London)', *Permanent Style*, 30 October 2024, https://www.permanentstyle.com/2024/10/the-tailors-i-have-known-part-1-london.html; Charlie Thomas, 'The Ultimate Guide to Savile Row',

Gentleman's Journal, https://www.thegentlemansjournal.com/article/ultimate-guide-savile-row/.

8. See, for example, The Tech Lawyered, 'The Law Firm Pyramid Model' and Charlotte Cocker, 'Deconstructing the Pyramid', *SCL Student Bytes*, 30 June 2020.

9. See 'Rule 5.4: Professional Independence of a Lawyer', American Bar Association, https://www.americanbar.org/groups/professional_responsibility/publications/model_rules_of_professional_conduct/rule_5_4_professional_independence_of_a_lawyer/.

10. See Samantha Whitsel, 'Accounting for Change: KPMG Law and the Global Rise of ABS Models', *International & Comparative Law Review*, https://international-and-comparative-law-review.law.miami.edu/accounting-for-change-kpmg-law-and-the-global-rise-of-abs-models/.

11. Reed Alexander and Emmalyse Brownstein, 'How 9 New Goldman Sachs Partners Celebrated Their Big Day', *Entrepreneur*, 13 November 2024, https://www.entrepreneur.com/business-news/how-9-new-goldman-sachs-partners-celebrated-their-big-day/482798.

12. 'Goldman Sachs: Moments—1999 IPO', Goldman Sachs, https://www.goldmansachs.com/our-firm/history/moments/1999-ipo.

13. 'Goldman Sachs Rings in 25 Years of Public Life with Stock at Record', *The Business Times*, 7 May 2024, https://www.businesstimes.com.sg/companies-markets/banking-finance/goldman-sachs-rings-25-years-public-life-stock-record.

14. Alexander and Brownstein, 'How 9 New Goldman Sachs Partners Celebrated Their Big Day'.

15. *ABA, Model Rule 5.4*, 'Professional Independence of a Lawyer'.

16. L.E.K., 'Private Capital in Law Firms: Strategic Entry via ABSs', *L.E.K. Consulting*, 2024, 5, https://www.lek.com/sites/default/files/insights/pdf-attachments/law-abs-v2.pdf.

17. Lucian T. Pera, *ABS Playbook Outside Arizona* (Memphis, TN: Adams and Reese LLP, 2025), https://www.adamsandreese.com/people/lucian-pera, 1. See also Benjamin Joyner, 'Puerto Rico Allows ABS Law Firms, but Program is Still Work in Progress', *Legaltech News*, 23 June 2025, https://www.law.com/legaltechnews/2025/06/23/puerto-rico-opens-the-door-to-abs-law-firms-but-program-is-still-work-in-progress/.

18. L.E.K. Consulting, 'Private Capital in Law Firms', 3.

19. Ibid., 9.

20. See Pera, *ABS Playbook Outside Arizona*.

21. Ibid., 27.

22. Ibid., 20.

23. Ibid., 20

24. Ibid., 25–27.

25. Ibid., 28–35.

26. Ibid., 31.

27. Ibid., 33.

28. 'KPMG LLP Launches KPMG Law US, The First Big Four Law Firm Serving the US Market', KPMG, 27 February 2025, https://kpmg.com/us/en/media/news/kpmg-llp-launches-kpmg-law-us.html.

29. Ibid.

30. Justin Henry and Roy Strom, 'KPMG Wins Approval to Launch First US Law Firm for Big Four', *Bloomberg Law*, 27 February 2025, https://news.bloomberglaw.com/business-and-practice/kpmg-becomes-first-accounting-firm-allowed-to-practice-law-in-us.

Chapter 12   The Hybrid

1. Steve Jobs, 'Innovation is the Ability to See Change as an Opportunity – Not a Threat', *Goodreads*, https://www.goodreads.com/quotes/12333908-innovation-is-the-ability-to-see-change-as-an-opportunity.

2. Bryce Welker, 'Big Four Accounting Firms', *Miami Herald*, https://www.miamiherald.com/careers-education/big-four-accounting-firms/.

3. Hannah L. Buxbaum, 'A Case Study of the Big Four Accounting Firms', *UC Davis Law Review* 48, no. 5 (2015): 1499–1572, 1794, https://lawreview.law.ucdavis.edu/sites/g/files/dgvnsk15026/files/media/documents/48-5_Buxbaum.pdf.

4. Cris Shore and Susan Wright, 'How the Big 4 Got Big: Audit Culture and the Metamorphosis of International Accountancy Firms', *Critique of Anthropology* 38, no. 4 (May 2018): 6.

5. Ibid., 5, 7–8.

6. Bernard Ascher, *The Audit Industry: World's Weakest Oligopoly?* AAI Working Paper No. 08-03 (Washington, DC: American Antitrust Institute, August 2008), 12.

7. Wilkins and Esteban, 'The Integration of Law into Global Business Solutions', 4–5.

8. Ascher, 'The Audit Industry', 20.

9. Stephen A. Zeff, 'How the U.S. Accounting Profession Got Where It Is Today: Part II', *Accounting Horizons* 17, no. 4 (December 2003): 270–271.

10. Mithu Dey and Quamina, 'Surveying a Shifting Landscape'.

11. Ibid.

12. Ibid.

13. Ibid.

14. Shore and Wright, 'How the Big 4 Got Big', 8.

15. Ibid.

16. Buxbaum, 'A Case Study of the Big Four Accounting Firms', 1791–1807.

17. Ibid., 1798.

18. Ibid., 1791–1807.

19. Ibid., 1791–1807.

20. Ibid., 1801–1802.

21. Laura Empson, 'Big Four Firms Rethink Governance After Year of Scandal', LinkedIn, 31 October 2023, https://www.linkedin.com/posts/professor-laura-empson-69820773_big-four-firms-rethink-governance-after-year-activity-7147904539168239616-PEMm/.

22. Parliament of Australia, Joint Committee on Corporations and Financial Services, 'Structural and Governance Challenges in the Big Four Firms', Chapter 3.4, *Consultancy Firms Report*, https://www.aph.gov.au/Parliamentary_Business/Committees/Joint/Corporations_and_Financial_Services/ConsultancyFirms/Report/Chapter_3_-_Structural_and_governance_challenges_in_the_Big_Four_firms.

23. D. R. Richmond, 'Professional Responsibility and Liability Aspects of Vereins' (University of Missouri School of Law Legal Studies Research Paper No. 2015-18, 14 July 2015), 917, https://ssrn.com/abstract=2630559.

24. Ibid., 918.

25. See Eversheds Sutherland, 'Konexo – Alternative Legal and Consulting Services', https://www.eversheds-sutherland.com/en/united-states/capabilities/services/konexo.

26. Ibid.

27. See Neil Rose, 'Private Equity Invests £1.2bn in the Law in Just Five Years', *Legal Futures*, 27 February 2025, https://www.legalfutures.

co.uk/latest-news/private-equity-invests-1-2bn-in-the-law-in-just-five-years and Acquira Professional Services, *Private Equity's Next Frontier: Transforming UK Law Firms* (London: Acquira Professional Services), February 2025.

28. Acquira Professional Services, *Private Equity's Next Frontier*, 7.

29. Heather Suttie, 'Big Four's Next Big Bite', *HeatherSuttie Insights*, July 2019, https://heathersuttie.ca/insights/big-fours-next-big-bite/.

30. Elevate, 'Elevate Becomes First-Ever Law Company to Receive an Alternative Business Structure (ABS) License in the U.S.', *Elevate News & Events*, 13 January 2022, https://elevate.law/news/elevate-becomes-first-ever-law-company-to-receive-an-alternative-business-structure-abs-license-in-the-u-s/#:~:text=Back%20to%20News-,Elevate%20Becomes%20First-Ever%20Law%20Company%20to%20Receive%20an%20Alternative,Supreme%20Court%20in%20late%202021.

Chapter 13   Platforms

1. 'What are Legal Marketplaces?', *The Legal Tech Guide*, 15 September 2025, https://thelegaltechguide.com/legal-marketplaces.

2. Ibid.

3. Ibid.

4. 'Rewriting Legal Delivery: The Global Rise of Platform-Based Legal Services', *Chambers and Partners*, 29 May 2025, https://www.chambers.com/articles/rewriting-legal-delivery-the-global-rise-of-platform-based-legal-services.

5. Lex Mundi, https://www.lexmundi.com/. The author is a member of Lex Mundi's Client Advisory Council.

6. See TerraLex, https://www.terralex.org/ and MultiLaw, https://www.multilaw.com/.

7. See Lex Mundi, https://www.lexmundi.com/. For the sake of full disclosure, the author is a member of Lex Mundi's Client Advisory Council.

8. Lex Mundi, 'Lex Mundi Equisphere – Global Reach', https://www.lexmundi.com/global-reach/lex-mundi-equisphere/.

9. *Axiom Law*, 28 October 2025, https://www.axiomlaw.com/.

10. Ibid.

11. Ibid.

12. Elevate, https://elevate.law/.

13. Ibid.

14. Keystone Law, 'About Us', https://www.keystonelaw.com/about-us. Also based on conversations between the author and James Knight, Chief Executive Officer, Keystone Law, 29 May 2025.

15. Priori Legal, 'Talent Marketplace', https://www.priorilegal.com/talent-marketplace/ and Priori Legal, 'Introducing RFP: The Next Step in Priori's Journey', *Priori blog*, 12 November 2024, https://www.priorilegal.com/blog/introducing-rfp-the-next-step-in-prioris-journey/.

16. Priori Legal, 'Priori Marketplace: A Legal Platform for Finding Outside Counsel', *Priori blog*, 12 April 2023, https://www.priorilegal.com/blog/priori-marketplace-a-legal-platform-for-finding-outside-counsel/.

17. Priori Legal, 'Introducing RFP'.

18. Ibid.

19. Priori Legal, 'Priori Announces Artificial Intelligence Powered Scout Platform', *Priori blog*, 20 December 2023, https://www.priorilegal.com/blog/priori-announces-artificial-intelligence-powered-scout-platform/.

20. Robert Ambrogi, 'Theorem Launches Private Offer RFP Tool for Legal Tech and Legal Services Providers', *LawNext*, 24 March 2025, https://www.lawnext.com/2025/03/theorem-launches-private-offer-rfp-tool-for-legal-tech-and-legal-services-providers.html.

21. The information provided in this section is based on information gathered on PERSUIT's website (https://www.persuit.com/platform), as well as via conversations and communications between the author and PERSUIT's CEO, Jim Delkousis, in October 2025.

Chapter 14   What Can Law Firms Do?

1. Kyle Hermans, 'Ambidextrous Leadership', *BCRGS*, 20 September 2023, https://bcrgs.com/insights/ambidextrous-leadership#:~:text=Tomorrow's%20leaders%20have%20to%20be,%2C%20antifragile%2C%20and%20courageous%20leader.

2. Christensen, *The Innovator's Dilemma*, 269–270.

3. Ibid., 13.

4. Ibid.

5. McGrath, *Seeing Around Corners*, 191.

6. Christensen, *The Innovator's Dilemma*, 266–267.

7. For a discussion of this approach, see Christensen, *The Innovator's Dilemma*, 271–272.

8. Charles A. O'Reilly III and Michael L. Tushman, 'Organizational Ambidexterity: Past, Present and Future', *Academy of Management Perspectives* (in press, working paper dated 11 May 2013), 3. This paper contains a helpful review of the state of research on this topic. See also McGrath, *Seeing Around Corners*, Chapter 7.

9. Christensen, *The Innovator's Dilemma*, 264–265.

10. Rita McGrath and Ryan McManus, 'Discovery-Driven Digital Transformation', *Harvard Business Review*, May–June 2020, https://hbr.org/2020/05/discovery-driven-digital-transformation.

11. McGrath and McManus, 'Discovery-Driven Digital Transformation'.

12. Ibid.

13. Christensen, *The Innovator's Dilemma*, 266.

14. The following summary of the case is based on the case study presented in McGrath, *Seeing Around Corners*, 191–205.

15. Ibid., 195.

16. Ibid., 197.

17. Ibid., 198.

18. Ibid., 200.

19. Klöckner & Co. Annual Report 2021, *Klöckner & Co. SE*, 2021, 15, https://www.annualreports.com/HostedData/AnnualReportArchive/K/Klockner-co-se_2021.pdf.

20. This case study is based on a series of conversations and written exchanges between the author and Carla Swansburg, CEO of ClearyX, and Michael Gerstenzang, Managing Partner of Cleary Gottlieb Steen & Hamilton LLP, conducted in March, September, and October 2025.

Chapter 15   The Future of Legal Education

1. Remark made by Michele DeStefano, Professor of Law, University of Miami, Visiting Professor, Harvard Law, Founder of Law Without Walls to the author in an interview on 7 November 2025.

2. Wilkins and Westfahl, 'The Missing Institutional Link', 1671–1672.

3. John Flood, 'Legal Education in the Global Context: Challenges from Globalization, Technology and Changes in Government Regulation' (London: University of Westminster School of Law, report for the Legal Services Board, 2011), 32, https://www.legalservicesboard.org.uk/wp-content/media/International-legal-education.pdf.

4. Ibid., 18.

5. Laura A. Webb, 'Reimagining Langdell's Legacy: Puncturing the Equilibrium in Law School Pedagogy' (University of Richmond Law Faculty Publications, 2023), 126, https://scholarship.richmond.edu/cgi/viewcontent.cgi?article=2699&context=law-faculty-publications.

6. Ibid., 126.

7. Russell L. Weaver, 'Langdell's Legacy: Living with the Case Method', *Villanova Law Review* 36, no. 2 (1991): 524–525, https://digitalcommons.law.villanova.edu/vlr/vol36/iss2/3.

8. Webb, 'Reimagining Langdell's Legacy', 126.

9. Ibid., 128–129.

10. Flood, 'Legal Education in the Global Context', 17–18 and Webb, 'Reimagining Langdell's Legacy', 129–131.

11. Weaver, 'Langdell's Legacy', 527–528.

12. Flood, 'Legal Education in the Global Context', 18.

13. Wilkins and Westfahl, 'The Missing Institutional Link', 1676–1678.

14. Flood, 'Legal Education in the Global Context', 17–18 and Wilkins and Westfahl, 'The Missing Institutional Link', 1677.

15. David B. Wilkins and G. Mitu Gulati, 'Reconceiving the Tournament of Lawyers: Tracking, Seeding, and Information Control in the Internal Labor Markets of Elite Law Firms', *Virginia Law Review* 84, no. 8 (1998): 1581–1583.

16. Martin H. Brinkley, 'Teaching Leadership in American Law Schools: Why the Pushback?', *Baylor Law Review* 73 (2021): 202, https://scholarship.richmond.edu/cgi/viewcontent.cgi?article=2699&context=law-faculty-publications.

17. Wilkins and Westfahl, 'The Missing Institutional Link', 1681.

18. Ibid., 1682.

19. Ibid., 1683.

20. Ibid., 1684.

21. Ibid., 1681–1687.

22. Ibid., 1685.

23. Webb, 'Reimagining Langdell's Legacy', 133.

24. Ibid., 132 n. 67–68.

25. Yogi Berra, 'Yogi Berra Quotes (Author of The Yogi Book)', *Goodreads* (n.d.), https://www.goodreads.com/author/quotes/79014.Yogi_Berra.

26. Edward Rubin, 'What's Wrong with Langdell's Method, and What to Do About It', *Vanderbilt Law Review* 60, no. 2 (2007): 632.

27. Ibid., 632.

28. Ibid., 640.

29. Weaver, 'Langdell's Legacy', 551, citing James Barr Ames, *Lectures on Legal History* (Cambridge, MA: Harvard University Press, 1913), 354–362.

30. Weaver, 'Langdell's Legacy', 545–561.

31. Ibid., 529 and 535, citing Charles Warren, *History of the Harvard Law School and of Early Legal Conditions in America*, vol. 2 (New York: Lewis Publishing Company, 1908), 374.

32. Brinkley, 'Teaching Leadership in American Law Schools', 201.

33. William M. Sullivan, Anne Colby, Judith Welch Wegner, Lloyd Bond, and Lee S. Shulman, *Educating Lawyers: Preparation for the Profession of Law* (San Francisco, CA: Jossey-Bass, 2007), 4.

34. Craig Collins, 'Pericles was a Plumber: Towards Resolving the Liberal and Vocational Dichotomy in Legal Education', in *Knowledge as Value*, 189–208 (Leiden: Brill, 2012), 190, https://doi.org/10.1163/9789401206143_013.

35. Daniel Goldsworthy, 'The Future of Legal Education in the 21st Century', *Adelaide Law Review* 41, no. 1 (2020): 245–46, quoting David Barker, *A History of Australian Legal Education* (Alexandria, NSW: Federation Press, 2017), 239.

36. Based on a conversation between Anthea Roberts and the author on 4 November 2025.

37. U.S. News & World Report, 'How (and Why) to Apply for J.D./M.B.A. Programs', *U.S. News & World Report*, https://www.usnews.com/education/blogs/law-admissions-lowdown/articles/how-why-to-apply-for-j-d-mba-programs.

38. Based on a conversation between Anthea Roberts and the author on 4 November 2025.

39. Elizabeth Beesley, 'The Role of Creativity in Legal Problem-Solving', *AllAboutLaw*, 12 April 2024, https://www.allaboutlaw.co.uk/

school-leaver-law-careers/becoming-a-lawyer/the-role-of-creativity-in-legal-problem-solving.

40. IDEO U, 'Design Thinking Framework, Innovation & Methodology', https://www.ideou.com/en-gb/pages/design-thinking#:~:text=Design%20thinking%20is%20a%20human,does%20it%20avoid%20unintended%20harm?; London School of Business Administration, 'The Importance of Design Thinking in Business Innovation', https://londonsba.org.uk/blog/the-importance-of-design-thinking-in-business-innovation/.

41. Blount, 'DLA Design Thinking in Context of the Law'.

42. LawWithoutWalls, 'Why LWOW?', https://lawwithoutwalls.org.

43. Stanford Legal Design Lab, 'Legal Design Lab – New Generation of Legal Services', https://www.legaltechdesign.com/.

44. Travis Whitsitt, 'Does Law School Need to be Three Years Long?', *Vault*, 4 August 2025, https://vault.com/blogs/vaults-law-blog-legal-careers-and-industry-news/does-law-school-need-to-be-three-years-long?utm_source=chatgpt.com.

45. Remark made by Michele DeStefano, Professor of Law, University of Miami, Visiting Professor, Harvard Law, Founder of LawWithoutWalls to the author in an interview on 7 November 2025.

46. Sullivan et al., *Educating Lawyers*, 4.

47. Orin S. Kerr, 'The Decline of the Socratic Method at Harvard', *Nebraska Law Review* 78, no. 1 (1999): 113–134, 116, file:///mnt/data/33139319.pdf.

48. Lowell Bautista, 'The Socratic Method as a Pedagogical Method in Legal Education', *Faculty of Law, Humanities and the Arts – Papers (Archive)* (University of Wollongong, 2014), 4, file:///mnt/data/33139319.pdf, citing Christie A. Linskens, 'The Socratic Method in Legal Education: Uses, Abuses and Beyond', *European Journal of Law Reform* 12 (2010): 340–61, at 342.

49. Kerr, 'Decline of the Socratic Method', 119.

50. Ibid., 131–132.

51. Stephen M. Johnson, 'The Course Source: The Casebook Evolved', *Capital University Law Review* 44 (2016): 591–654.

52. Based on conversations with Anthea Roberts and the author in April 2025.

53. Niall Ferguson, 'The Cloister and the Starship', *UATX Substack*, 20 June 2025, https://uatx.substack.com/p/the-cloister-and-the-starship.

54. Gregory J. Marsden & Soledad Atienza, 'Doing Law School Wrong: Case Teaching and an Integrated Legal Practice Method', 546–547, 66 St. Louis U. L.J. (2022), https://scholarship.law.slu.edu/lj/vol66/iss3/7.

55. Ibid., 547.

56. Ibid., 547, quoting George J. Siedel, 'Legal Complexity in Cross-Border Subsidiary Management', *Texas International Law Journal* 36 (2001): 611, 614.

57. Benjamin H. Barton, *A Tale of Two Case Methods* (essay), file:///mnt/data/bartonarticle.pdf.

58. Marsden and Atienza, 'Doing Law School Wrong', 556.

59. Ibid., 556.

60. Ibid., 556.

61. Stephen Wizner and Jane Aiken, 'Teaching and Doing: The Role of Law School Clinics in Enhancing Access to Justice', *Fordham Law Review* 73, no. 3 (2004): 999, file:///mnt/data/144223744.pdf.

62. J. Damian Ortiz, 'The Need to Make Clinical Teaching Mandatory as Part of the Experiential Methodology to Prepare Students for the Practice of Law in the Twenty-First Century', *UIC Law Review* 57, no. 4 (2024): 698, https://repository.law.uic.edu/cgi/viewcontent.cgi?article=2930&context=lawreview.

63. Yale Law School, 'Entrepreneurship and Innovation Clinic', https://law.yale.edu/studying-law-yale/clinical-and-experiential-learning/our-clinics/entrepreneurship-and-innovation-clinic.

64. Deborah J. Merritt, 'Caste Revisited', *Law School Café*, 13 August 2021, https://www.lawschoolcafe.org/2021/08/13/caste-revisited/.

65. Sullivan et al., *Educating Lawyers*, 6.

Index

Note: Page numbers in *italics*
indicate figures.

A
agentic AI
    application in legal practice, 66–7
    defining, 65–6
    rise of, 65–7
    risks and governance challenges, 67
AI era legal department, 91–112
    changing legal department landscape,
        95–6
    GC 4.0 organisational architecture,
        96–102, *96*
    human professionals, 106–7
    humans in the loop, 94–5
    law firms, ALSPs, and external pro-
        viders, 112
    scale, scope, and learning, 92–4
    Unilever, 103–6
    Workday, 107–12
AI factory, 79–90
    COVID-19 pandemic, 84–6
    generative and agentic AI applications,
        86
    humans in the loop, 87
    journey, 81–4, *82*

regulatory, geopolitical, and ethical
        dimensions, 87–8
    setting up, 80–1
    traditional MNCs transformation,
        88–90
    Walmart, 85–6
AI models
    benefits of, 74–7
    economies of scale, 75
    economies of scope, 75–6
    learning, 76–7
alternative business structures (ABSs), 6,
        184–7, 215, 252
alternative legal service providers
        (ALSPs), 151–63
    Big Four firms, 157–61
    deeper specialisation and integration,
        162–3
    disruptive impact, 161–3
    expansion, 209
    origins, 152–4
    risk of commoditisation, 161–2
    technology providers, 154–7
Amazon, 38
antifragility, 17
A&O Shearman, 197, 221, 227–32
Apple, 75–6

artificial intelligence (AI), 64–71
  complementary innovation, 70–1
  integrators, 212
  pervasiveness, 68
  rapid improvement, 68–70, *69*
Axiom, 204–5

B
Big Four firms, 157–61
Big Four model
  advisory services, 192
  and ALSPs, 198
  contours of, 191–4
  debugging, 195–6
  federated model, 192–3
  governance challenges, 193–4
  historical evolution, 191–2
  organisational complexity, 193
  pricing pressures, 191–2
  regulatory compliance and liability
     limitation, 193
  shortcomings of, 193–4
  siloed model, 194
  vs. Swiss Verein, 194–5
boutique law firm, 171–8
  delivery engine of, 173–8
  diamond model, 175–6, *176*
  features of, 172
  hourglass model, 177–8, *177*
  inverted pyramid model, 174–5, *174*
  limited scalability, 171
  profit engine of, 172–3
  rocket-ship concept, 173–8
  trade-offs and consequences, 178
business models, 72
business school case methods, 248–9

C
casebook method, 237, 246–8
ClearyX, 221–7
  client pain points, targeting, 224
  feeding learning back to the
     firm, 226
  independent business, 222–3

  redefining success and incentives,
     225–6
  revenue model, 224–5
  socialising venture inside firm, 223
  strategic transformation, 226–7
  technology-first mindset, 224
cloister and starship, 248
compensation and incentive model
  annual bonuses, 181
  base salary, 181
  long-term incentives (LTIs), 180–1
  other incentives, 181
competitive sourcing models, 206–11
ContractMatrix, 230, 231
corporate governance structure, 179–80
corporate law firms, 178–84
  access to capital, 181
  challenges, 183–4
  compensation and incentive model,
     180–1
  corporate governance structure,
     179–80
  exit and liquidity, 183
  operational efficiency, 182
  partner buy-in, 183
  regulatory hurdles, 183
  strategic, long-term thinking, 181–2
  strategic benefits, 181–3
  talent, attracting and retaining, 182
corporate thinking, 15–18
corporations
  vs. Swiss Verein, 180
  and their legal departments, 9–11
Cravath System, 29, 116, 237

D
demand drivers, 19–21
  geopolitical instability and disruptive
     technologies, 20
  regulatory growth, 19–20
  technology and 'unruly triangle',
     20–1
diamond model, 175–6, *176*
disruptive innovation, 219–21

E

early warning signs
  client dissatisfaction, 141
  growing attrition rates, 142–3
  growing competition, 141–2
  recruitment challenges, 143
eBay, 38
e-commerce, 38–40
Elevate, 205
enterprise risk management (ERM),
  15–16
Eversheds Sutherland, 196–7
exponential growth, impact of, 146–50

F

foreign direct investment (FDI), 26, 35
foundation models, 156
  Fourth Industrial Revolution. *see* GC
  3.0 (2007–2022)

G

GC 1.0 (1945–1989)
  Bretton Woods System, 25–6
  Coca-Cola Company, 26–9
  early modern globalisation, 23–32
  Gilded Age as forerunner of, 23–4
  legal department, 30–2
  new international system, 24–5
  professionalisation wave, 29–30
  and United States, 26
GC 2.0 (1989–2007)
  acceleration of globalisation, 33–4
  classic globalisation, 33–45
  economic liberalisation, 34–5
  governance in complex environment,
    42
  legal department, 42–5
  supply chain revolution, 40–2
  Third Industrial Revolution (3IR),
    36–40
  World Trade Organization in 1995 and
    China's accession, 35–6
GC 3.0 (2007–2022)
  alternative legal service provider, 58–9

  broader context of, 48–55
  cloud computing, 51
  convergence and disruption, 47–8
  Fourth Industrial Revolution, 47–60
  from global flows to digital domi-
    nance, 53
  legal departments in, 55–60
  legal operations, rise of, 56–8
  macroeconomic turbulence and goldi-
    locks, 52–3
  more-for-less challenge, 55–6
  platform models and winner-takes-
    most dynamics, 53–4
  polycrises, rise of, 54–5
  role proliferation, risk convergence and
    rise of T-shaped GC, 59–60
  technology—microchips and expo-
    nential growth, 48–50
  world transformed by smartphones,
    50–1
GC 4.0 (2000–present)
  AI era legal department, 91–112
  AI factory, 79–90
  AI impact, 63–77
  benefits of AI models, 74–7
  hybrid delivery teams, 102
  legal operations as 'engine room',
    97–8
  operating models in AI era, 71–3
  organisational architecture,
    96–102, *96*
  specialists and generalists, 102
  technology adoption, 98
  technology integration, 98
  technology platform, 98–102, *99*
  technology selection, 97
General Counsel, 10–11
  demand drivers, 19–21
  evolution of corporate thinking on
    risk, 15–18
  evolving approaches to risk, 14–18
  evolving needs, 13–22
  expectations from, 14–15
  implication for, 21

General Counsel (*Cont.*)
   legal advice, 18
   more for less dynamic, 18–22
   supply constraints, 21–2
Goldman Sachs, 182–3

H
Harvard Business School, 248–9
Harvey, 230–1
hourglass model, 177–8, *177*
hybrid model, 189–99
   Big Four model, contours of, 191–4
   designing, 195–6
   legal hybrid formations, 196–8
   organic stand-alone entities, 198
   precision instruments, 190
   private equity, 197–8
   and Swiss Army knives, 190
   Swiss Verein *vs.* Big Four model, 194–5

I
incumbents, 140–1
inflection points, 139–40
in-house lawyers, 44–5
The Innovator's Dilemma (Christensen),
   132–8
inverted pyramid model, 174–5, *174*

J
'Jobs to be Done' (JTBD), 143–6
   GC 4.0 implications, 146
   legal jobs creating, 145
   legal jobs expanding, 145–6
   legal jobs transforming, 145
   legal services, 144
   shifting constraints, 144
John Deere, 89–90
JP Morgan Chase, 92–3

K
Keystone Law, 204, 205
Klöckner & Co., 219–21
'Kodak Moment' commercials, 138–9
KPMG Law US, 158, 186–7

L
Langdell–Cravath Model, 236–8
   academic-professional tension, 240–1
   Cravath System and professional
      development, 237
   erosion of, 237–8
   growing insufficiency of, 238
   original purpose, 239–40
   reinvention of legal education, 236–7
large law firm networks, 203–4
law firm parallels, 135
   ALSPs, 136–7
   disruptive innovation, 135–6
   GC 4.0 acceleration, 136
   growing client-law firm gap, 136
   sluggish incumbent reaction, 137–8
law firms, 29–30, 170, 187–8, 196–8,
   215–33
   A&O Shearman, 227–32
   application, 221
   ClearyX, 221–7
   disruptive innovation, 219–21
   implications, 150, 213–14
   independent start-up, 217–19
   innovation trap, 215–16
   Klöckner & Co., 219–21
   as knowledge gatekeepers, 32
   Markets Innovation Group (MIG),
      227–32
   organisational antibodies, 216
   structural ambidexterity, 216
layered legal AI ecosystem, *154*
   application layer, 156–7
   end users. 157
   foundation models and content pro-
      viders, 156
   infrastructure and distribution plat-
      forms, 155–6
legal education, 235–50
   and AI, 235–6
   business literacy, strategy, and leader-
      ship, 242–3
   changing demands on, 235–6
   content, 242–4

creativity, design thinking, and
  interdisciplinary problem-solving,
  243–4
methodologies, 245–50
purpose, 239–41
reinvention of, 236–7
rise/fall of Langdell–Cravath model,
  236–8
structured format, 245
technological and digital fluency, 243
three-year programme, 244–5
time, 244
triangle, 239–50
Lex Mundi, 203, 204, 212

M
Markets Innovation Group (MIG), 227–32
  commercial, future-centric mindset,
    228
  future-literate, client-centric approach,
    228–9
  marketing and communications, 231
  market shocks and moonshots, 227–8
  positioning for AI era, 232
  from projects to products/services,
    230–1
  start-up mentality, 229
  strategic partnerships, 230
Multilaw, 203, 212
multinational companies (MNCs)
  European and Japanese competitors,
    28–9
  expanding internationally, 26
  FDI and continued rise of, 35
  law-firm lawyers, 30
  local and flexible, 27–8
  traditional, 88–90

N
Netflix, 75
new law firm models, 169–88
  alternative business structures, 184–7
  boutique law firm, 171–8
  corporate law firms, 178–84

law firms, 187–8
  overview, 169–70
Nokia, 133–4
non-binary/integrated risk decisions,
  17–18

O
operating models, 71–3
  analogue operating model, limits of, 73
  business models, 72
  disrupting traditional models, 71–2
  scale, scope, and learning, 72–3, 74
organisational resilience, 16–17

P
Persi, 210–11
PERSUIT (legal sourcing platform)
  AI enablement, 210
  ALSPs and legal-adjacent providers, 209
  analytics and market intelligence, 211
  law firm selection, optimising, 208–11
  performance management, 208–11
  strategic positioning, 211
  two-sided market development, 210–211
  workflow integration and billing
    innovation, 210
platforms, 201–14
  competitive sourcing models, 206–11
  GC 4.0-era precursors, 202
  implications, 211–14
  large law firm networks, 203–4
  legal talent and delivery integrators,
    204–6
  technology driven, 202
Priori Legal, 206–7
private equity, 197–8

R
resilience, 16–17
risk
  evolution of corporate thinking on,
    15–18
  evolving approaches to, 14–18
rocket-ship concept, 173–8

S

Socratic method, 246
staffing company model, 185, 186
starfish model, 195
supply chain revolution, 40–2
'Swiss Army knife' approach, 190
Swiss Verein *vs.* Big Four Model, 194–5

T

technology platform, 98–102, *99*
 AI agents, 102
 application layer, 100–101
 governance and control layer, 101
 intake and workflow, 99–100
 integration layer, 101
 knowledge and data layer, 100
TerraLex, 203, 212
Tesla, 76–7
Theorem Legal Tech Marketplace,
 207–8
Third Industrial Revolution (3IR),
 36–40
traditional law firm model, 115–29, *116*
 alternative fee arrangements, 119–20
 billable hour, 117–19
 for clients, 121–2
 continuous learning and humans in
 the loop, 128–9
 human-centric, input-based profit
 engine, 123–4
 inherent structural deficits, 122–7
 leverage, 117
 for partners, 120
 partnership dynamics, 124–6
 risk-averse culture, 126–7
 scale and scope, 127–8
 siloed practice groups, 126
T-shaped GCs, 59–60
two-company model, 185–6

U

Unilever, 103–6
 Business Group, 104
 Corporate Centre, 103
 Legal Operations, 104
 Powerhouses, 104
 technology platform, 105–6

W

walled gardens, 203–4
Walmart, 85–6
Workday, 107–12